IN THE WAKE OF FREEDOM INDIA'S TRYST WITH COOPERATIVES

About the authors

L.C. Jain – *Born 13 December 1925.* Joined the Quit India movement during the freedom struggle, was invited by the Central Relief Committee of All-India Congress Committee to look after the post-partition refugee camps; later joined Kamaladevi Chattopadhyaya in founding the Indian Cooperative Union (ICU) to build rural cooperatives and revive the traditional handicrafts and handlooms of India. Starting as a village cooperative organiser in 1948, was later elected General Secretary of ICU. Apart from rural cooperatives he was actively involved with major endeavours of ICU: building of the Faridabad industrial township by refugees on self-help basis, development of the Central Cottage Industries Emporium and the setting up of the first Super Bazaar, as a cooperative store, and research studies. He was also non-official Chairman of the All India Handicrafts Board. Over the past 5 decades he has been active in advocacy of democratic decentralisation and just and equitable economic policies whether as a member of the State Planning Boards of Uttar Pradesh, Karnataka and Assam or as a member of the National Planning Commission, or as a writer in newspapers and journals. He received the Magsaysay award for Public Service in 1989. Currently, he is Chairman of Industrial Development Services – a techno-economic consultancy organisation, and of the Institute of Social Change and Development an ICSSR sponsored institute for the north east region. He is co-author of *Grass Without Roots, Rural Development Under Government Auspices.*

Karen Coelho – *Born 3 June 1963.* Who currently holds a faculty position at the Bureau of Applied Research in Anthropology (BARA) at the University of Arizona, has an M.Phil in Development Studies from the University of Sussex, U.K. She earlier worked for several years with Asian Community Health Action Network (ACHAN) in Madras, and has extensive experience in networking and training in various Asian countries and in different parts of India. In 1994 she worked as a Consultant on Women and Panchayat Raj with Mahila Samakhya, Karnataka (MSK), where she helped to document the experiences of the newly elected Panchayat members from the MSK women's sanghas, and to devise training curricula for them. Her current work at BARA includes food security analyses of various African, Latin American and Carribean countries for CARE, and a project on integrating gender concerns into agricultural policy for the FAO.

IN THE WAKE OF FREEDOM
INDIA'S TRYST
WITH
COOPERATIVES

L. C. Jain

Karen Coelho

Acknowledgement
INDIAN COOPERATIVE UNION
&
FRIEDRICH NAUMANN STIFTUNG

Published by
CONCEPT PUBLISHING COMPANY, NEW DELHI-110059

ISBN 81-7022-647-3

First Published 1996

Published and Printed by
Ashok Kumar Mittal
Concept Publishing Company
A/15-16, Commercial Block. Mohan Garden
NEW DELHI-110059
Phones: 5554042, 5504042

PREFACE

WHEN the country attained its freedom in 1947, the cooperative idea representing economic democracy was seen to provide a ray of hope and an appropriate institutional vehicle for the economic and social advancement of millions of small farmers and artisans dispersed over lakhs of villages. Ever since then, the cooperatives have been struggling for liberation, albeit unsuccessfully, from draconian cooperative law and administration which have, in fact, been worsening. This in spite of the fact that the State has regularly proclaimed its support for cooperatives. But what the State actually did in practice was destructive of the very first cooperative principle, namely, inner democratic control of members over their affairs. Though statistically, the number of cooperatives has gone up, the promise of the cooperative idea has remained stillborn.

There is, however, a change in the objective situation today. The focus of the economic policy on creating a competitive environment offers, in theory at least, unexpected opportunities, not only for the corporate sector, but also for the cooperatives. It provides a hope for the revival of the cooperative idea and instrument. In practice, however, it may be long before the potential of cooperatives is realized, given the fact that the slate is unclean, with the bureaucracy deeply entrenched in the cooperative sector. It is not surprising, therefore, that the State which is otherwise spearheading liberalization is continuing to impede the independence of the cooperatives from the bureaucratic stranglehold. In contrast, it has acted swiftly to provide a full dose of liberalization to the corporate sector. The only notable exception is the State of Andhra Pradesh which enacted a liberal democratic cooperative law in 1995.

Comprehensive and sustainable economic reforms require that the organizational investment and productivity needs of millions of our small farmers, artisans and small enterprises in the unorganized sector, who constitute the bulk of our workforce, must also be met. The corporate sector, private or public, has throughout been indifferent to the organizational and productivity needs of these millions of small, rural and urban producers. It is not likely to have any unique interest in them in the future as well. Thus, the cooperative form of institution still remains the only option for the poor and unorganized rural and urban producers. There is no other institutional form which can help them to survive in the emerging, market-dominated economic milieu.

There is a popular misconception that the market comprises of only private corporate enterprises. It needs to be understood that cooperatives too are a part of the same market from which they also draw their strength and sustenance – or at least want to in preference to dependence on the State.

Besides the push provided by economic reforms, there is also likely to be a pull for developing cooperatives from panchayats.

The recent 73rd Amendment to the Constitution relating to panchayats has opened up unprecedented and challenging opportunities for cooperative endeavour and cooperative enterprises in the rural areas. As a result of this Amendment, panchayats will come into existence in every village and every district of the country by the year 1996. The Amendment has mandated that the primary function of the panchayats will be to undertake " area planning for economic development and social justice".

In the nature of things, agricultural development implying efficient management of land, water and labour will necessarily constitute the core of the village area plans. These area plans have also to be implemented. But panchayats are essentially political institutions, which have to play an enabling role. They will themselves not be able to undertake economic activities.

As has been pointed out earlier there is little prospect of the corporate sector or public sector coming down to the village level to assist the village panchayats and the village economy in meeting this challenge. In the circumstances, cooperatives are the only institutional vehicle available to assist the panchayats in the implementation of the various components of the local area plans.

If cooperatives are the principal ally of the poor and the panchayats then we must combat the challenges they face. First, the process of liberation from the bureaucratic spider's web will have to embrace not only the big business, but all forms and scales of economic enterprises including cooperatives. Second, the cooperatives, too, must be set free and enabled to compete in the market place without any officially imposed hurdles as exist today. Third, for these hurdles to go and in good time, public opinion has to exert informed and sustained pressure on the State. In this endeavour, the cooperatives and other voluntary organizations have to take the lead.

This book recalls the history and struggles of a voluntary organization: the Indian Cooperative Union (ICU) born in 1948, in the flush of freedom to participate in the exciting venture of rebuilding India principally through self-help cooperative endeavours. The ICU's history provides testimony to the unending struggles against the mindset and system built during the colonial rule which, alas, have continued unabated and unamended till today, frustrating many fruitful field ventures.

The book is based on the belief that the story of the ICU, its achievements and frustrations, will be a source of inspiration to those who recognize the social significance of cooperatives and the need for their liberation from State control. And, that it will also provide some constructive leads to grassroot organizations engaged in fostering community-led social and economic endeavours through voluntary action.

L. C. JAIN
KAREN COELHO

ACKNOWLEDGEMENTS

THE acknowledgements here run into two streams. First, gratitude towards some of those who made the ICU possible and what it was able to do. Second, thanks to those who made this book possible and helped in many ways to nurture its birth.

The ICU's list of acknowledgements has to begin with Gandhiji for his blessings to the blueprint for founding the ICU and to the people affected by partition in whose service the ICU devoted itself from day one and exclusively thereafter for about five years before extending its spheres of service to communities other than refugees. Particular gratitude is due to Sardar Bhag Singh who led the refugee landless agricultural workers to start the Such Khand Multipurpose Cooperative Society at village Chattarpur in Mehrauli, Delhi. This cooperative venture was the ICU's very first step in the field. It turned out to be a pioneering force which drew hundreds of other landless workers to form similar cooperatives in different villages in and around Delhi.

Sardar Bhag Singh, who served as an elected Vice-President of the ICU for over a decade, was the moving spirit behind all of the ICU's work in the rural areas besides with refugee farmers. He was joined by Master Ramjee Lal from village Sultanpur – a non-refugee farmer with amazing leadership qualities – who guided the ICU's entry and work among farmers other than refugees. The ICU's work among the NWFP refugees at Faridabad was guided by refugee leaders Salar Sukhram and Sardar Kalyan Singh both with extraordinary qualities of leadership and practical wisdom. They too were for long years elected Vice Presidents of the ICU.

Several refugee leaders. Sardar Takhat Singh, Mrs. Vasanti Devi, Shri Inder Prakash, to name some, led the ICU's endeavour to organize refugee urban industrial workers' and weavers' cooperatives and women's industrial cooperatives. Shri Vishwa Nath helped with consumer cooperatives which had a mix of refugee and non-refugee members.

Some of the ICU's outstanding organizers for rural and urban cooperatives and marketing services such as the Central Cottage Industries Emporium, Export Division and Super Bazaar, who deserve special mention, were Mulkraj Sethi, Ratan Singh, Moti Ram, Gurbachan Singh,

Amar Nath, Swaran Datta, N.N. Datta, S.V. Bedi, Gopikrishna, B.L. Dhar, Kamala Rana, Charan Singh, Teji Vir Singh, Prem Bery, Krishan Lal, and Krishna Kapur. Much is owed to Prof. Raj Krishna, who directed the ICU's research division and invested its studies with rare insights, practical wisdom and professional competence. Som Benegal aided by Sina Kaul did the same with creative writing and editing of the ICU's publications and their production.

In its formative years the ICU was strengthened by many supporters and sympathisers from within the country and abroad. A glimpse of them is provided by the ICU's Tenth Anniversary Report in 1958:

> We are beholden to the Prime Minister of India, Jawaharlal Nehru, who gave inspiration and encouragement and to his National Relief Fund which gave valuable aid in the formative years of the Union.
>
> The ICU is indebted to the Ministries of Rehabilitation, Commerce and Industry, Food and Agriculture, to the All-India Handicrafts Board, to the Central Social Welfare Board, with all of whom the Union has collaborated in many significant projects and received generous cooperation and assistance.
>
> Among our friends from abroad who have helped the ICU over the years, we are grateful to Lady Edwina Mountbatten and Mr. Nelson A. Rockefeller, Mr. Jerry Vorhis of the Cooperative League of USA and the League's representatives in India, Mr. Thomas B. Keehn and Dr. A.C. Felder for their very active contribution to many programmes of the ICU. In particular, Mrs. Martha Keehn acted as a volunteer in the ICU's Social Welfare Programme. Dr. Lotta Hitschmanova of the Unitarian Service Committee of Canada, CORSO of New Zealand, the Indian Relief Committee, London; CARE and the Associated Country Women of the World among others also deserve our gratitude.
>
> Finally we express our deepest appreciation of all our member cooperatives, sympathisers, workers and organizers who have given the best of their idealism, talent and time during these ten years.
>
> We also ask for forgiveness of those whom over these years we may have failed.

For this book, we are grateful to the ICU for allowing the reprint of its various studies, reports and other information. In gratitude all royalties from this book are committed to the ICU. We also gratefully acknowledge the permission granted by the copyright holders of selected works of Jawaharlal Nehru for some of the extract reproduced here, as also the Times of India for reproducing some of L.C. Jain's articles here.

From the ICU family, we received continuous help and encouragement from Gopikrishna, B.L. Dhar, Devaki Jain and Rama Chattopadhyaya. We are also indebted to the Cooperative Development Foundation (CDF), Hyderabad, and the support of Friedric Naumann Stiftung for meeting some of the expenditure relating to the preparation of this book. Thanks are also due to the leading lights of CDF, Rama Reddy and Shashi Rajagopal, for constant encouragement and friendly pressure to complete the exercise. Several research assistants, particularly Josyula Lakshmi, and Radhika Kurapati extended a good helping hand. Most generous and dedicated help was provided by Claude Bart in constructive editing of most chapters and many valuable suggestions. Besides, at the work table gratitude is due to S. Thanukuttan, Uma Naidu, Veena Kapur and S. Prakash Babu for their untiring work with the typing and revisions of the script.

Thanks to other publications quoted here.

CONTENTS

INTRODUCTION

THE historical circumstance was the partition of India. Millions were uprooted. They crossed the borders and made for the first refugee camp. There were hundreds of such camps and thousands of volunteers to serve them. There were 10,000 refugees in Hudson Lines in the Kingsway Camp close to Delhi University where I was enrolled for a Master's degree. Before I knew, I had abandoned classes and volunteered to look after this camp. Yes, we had tents, kitchens, dispensaries and schools all improvised overnight. Just as I began to feel that life in the camp was settling down after many a storm, a visitor came and unsettled it all for me. That visitor was Kamaladevi Chattopadhyaya a veteran freedom fighter and socialist leader. And it took just a couple of questions from her to unsettle the settled: "What is their future? How long are they to live in the camps?"

As busloads of refugees poured in day after day, and all day long, with food to be cooked and distributed for 10,000, thrice a day and uncontrollable emotional traumas and upheavals to be contended with and soothed, we lived by the hour. None of us, the volunteers in the camp, had a moment to entertain any question about the day after, let alone the future.

Kamaladevi's question transfixed me. We arranged to meet the following day. The "we" included a group of those who were called socialists in the Congress Party. After hours of deliberation we arrived at the conclusion that the refugees had to build their own future and that self-help, or self-initiative was fundamental to this. Given the enormity of the problem and the meagre resources of the individual households, which had lost most of what they had in the migration from Pakistan to India, mutual aid was indispensable. The only known instrument fitting this description was a "co-operative". The next step was to share the idea with the refugees for their response. But cooperation was only an idea. What content each cooperative would have, what tasks it would undertake and how it would accomplish them, had to be determined by each cooperative itself. Nevertheless, to carry the idea to them, to receive their response, to offer them counsel, and to facilitate their journey in case they chose the path, necessitated a platform. We needed something like a mother-cooperative which would foster new cooperatives and create an environment to protect them from unfriendly external forces.

We started with inspiration of cooperative principles: one person, one vote and democratic control of members over management, i.e. both equity and accountability. We took to the road with cheerful assumptions of setting in motion a process for building a new India, through mutual effort largely outside the State, though alongwith it.

It was thus that almost overnight, the Indian Cooperative Union (ICU) was born to act as a mother-cooperative, with Kamaladevi as its President. I volunteered to move from the refugee camp and became the ICU's first village-level organizer in 1948 at Mehrauli village near the Qutb Minar. We had little knowledge of the ground realities surrounding a cooperative. Soon the beams of the roof started collapsing on our heads day by day; the cooperative law, the cooperative rules, the cooperative department, the registrars, the inspectors, the cooperative auditors, the cooperative bank, maximum credit limits.

The departments were immune to the passion for building a new India, and also immune to the tragedy wrought by the partition on its victims – the refugees. They were indifferent to the state of mind of the refugees, of being uprooted not only geographically, but also in terms of self-confidence. How do you retain self-confidence when you are unable to save your family, children, ancestral home and property and often human life itself from marauders? All of it was snatched before your very eyes and you stood a helpless witness. How could self-confidence survive such an onslaught? The refugees were drained of their inner strength.

But the laws and the cooperative department could not care less. They had only one song – "you have to conform: we cannot bend ourselves to suit your circumstances". In that hour, cooperation, when I first experienced it as a practice, appeared as a monster which could do no more than devour you. How were the helpless then to rebuild a life through its aid, when it was more ready to bite than to build? Nevertheless, the ICU fought on and continued to build, while the system continued to bite. The ICU succeeded but only sometimes.

We are still far from the goal we set for ourselves at the dawn of Freedom. And, as many continue to pursue the goal undaunted by the frustrations of the past, it is handy to have an account of the endeavours and struggles of groups like the ICU in the formative years of Free India. This is the *raison d'etre* of this book.

Soon after Independence, there was very little government to reckon with. In the circumstances of partition, in fact, there was no government worth the name. As such, life and property were under tremendous pressure. A number of people felt that India had to be rebuilt. And that it was for the people to rebuild it. People in various spheres had to find effective means to increase productivity in agriculture and industry. So, there was an initial stimulus given to cooperative activity that was born out of the fire of the Freedom Movement. But within five years or so the government had recovered, and taken shape.

Our newly formed republic chose to use planning as an instrument for setting priorities, mobilizing resources and then directing the flow of those resources, according to the chosen priorities. It also made a broad choice in favour of what is known as the mixed economy model. It was felt that the problems India faced required multiple approaches. Private industry and trade were already on the scene, but it was felt that the State would have to intervene and set the pace and cover grounds which, it was assumed, could not be done by the market. At the same time, there was an overwhelming sense of social commitment and aspiration: that it was not mere economic development that we were pursuing, but something much larger and deeper. The fight against disparity, inequality and social stratification were all on our agenda. So a place was found in that "mixed economy" formula for cooperatives. It was felt that the three vehicles – the State, the private sector and the cooperatives – together would help us move forward.

That was also a period of clashing ideologies. No debate in those days was complete without recounting the virtues and vices of capitalism and communism, especially the Soviet model and what was happening in China. It was in that context that India's endeavour of a mixed economy was placed: we were supposed to be in neither extreme. Mixed economy was therefore, our "middle path".

What has happened since is well known. In particular, the churning that has taken place since the beginning of the 1990s has arisen partly from the policy makers' concluding that we have hitherto followed an erroneous path, and that is why we have failed to achieve the expected results. There is not much talk of mixed economy now. From the beginning, the constituents of the mixture were never really clearly determined. So, at times, it seemed that we were becoming a mixed-up economy, rather than a mixed economy. And, whoever could throw his weight in a particular way got the State to feel that not only should it control the "commanding heights", but also simultaneously be at sea, to wit, the holiday resorts at the Kovalam beach, or to start making bread. There was no discernible direction.

This little sector, called the cooperative sector, which was supposed to be one of the constituents of the mixed economy, was given the pride of place in the early debates, discussions and Plan documents. But then it simply got squeezed out. One reason was that much of the poetry about cooperatives began by saying that the middleman had to be eliminated in every sphere. So, naturally, the middlemen were not looking forward to this sector as a friendly companion within the mixed economy pattern.

But astoundingly, the State itself, which had chosen cooperatives to be an important vehicle, became in a sense its rival and competitor. For example, we started with supporting handloom cooperatives, but mid-way, the Government launched its own network of Handloom Development Corporations. Being a part of the State, these corporations became a favourite for the Government's attention and for the bulk of allocation of resources. On the other hand, the management of cooperatives was not left to their members. The State felt that it must take over their day-to-day management. A very large number of administrators were diverted from basic governmental tasks of saving life and property to go and manage cooperatives. Cooptex (the apex body of Tamil Nadu handloom weavers cooperatives), which was acknowledged as one of the most inspiring examples of dynamic cooperative enterprises is being administered not by a management elected by its members, but by civil servants nominated by the State Government for over two decades.

Today, we are faced with a drastically different objective situation at the macro level. Rightly or wrongly, the State has now come to the conclusion that in the economic sphere, it cannot play the leadership role that it played in the past. It must curtail its ambitions, its allocations, its involvement in the economic sector. It is disinvesting even existing investments. It has decided to free to the utmost the private sector from licensing, control and regulations and leave much of the economic management to the market. It has decided to reduce drastically the spheres which were, hitherto, reserved exclusively for the State to invest. The private sector is now free to enter those reserved areas. Similar freedom is extended for the first time to foreign enterprises, foreign investment, foreign technology and foreign management. In short, "globalization" of the Indian economy.

However, when the policy-makers say "liberalization" of the economy, it is important to note that they are talking merely of the tail of the economy, only one segment, and not the whole economy. The

Indian economy is a vast area. At the bottom are the marginal and small farmers, and the agricultural labourers, i.e. 70 per cent of our labour force. Next to them are the workers in the informal sector, while 90 per cent of employment generated in the manufacturing sector is in the unorganized sector, 80 per cent of the investment that we have made so far, is in, or for, the organized sector. And to make the matters worse, organized sector employment is on the decline. While the organized sector has consumed massive investments, it has choked employment. It is left mainly to the unorganized sector, which is otherwise denied access to institutional credit, to provide incremental employment.

The major instruments that were developed for regulation and control were the licences, control over capacity, foreign collaboration and choice of technology, choice of products to be made, and the product mix, import of equipment, processes, location, etc. All these adversely affected the organized sector. Surely, if the sector is producing for the economy, either by itself, or in collaboration with foreign companies (even if they be multinationals), there was no reason to put avoidable obstacles in their way. There can be no quarrel with liberalization. The problem is when liberalization stops with releasing only large industry from the shackles of bureaucracy. In the case of small-scale industry, though there are no licensing requirements, there is a battery of thirty-five inspectors who breathe down the necks of entrepreneurs from morning till evening. Under tremendous criticism and pressure from Parliament and elsewhere, the Government declared that it would abolish *Inspector Raj* affecting small industries, *within a specified period of three months.* That was in August, 1991. Over four years have passed, but the Inspector Raj remains. In the rural areas, the entire rural administration with its strangulating powers continues to function exactly as before unaffected by "liberalization". In the cooperative sector, the regime of inspectors also remains. It is as if the rural areas and co-operatives are not part of the economy, and, therefore, not in need of liberation.

Similarly, cooperatives remain highly government regulated. Government presence is very extensive and severe in the entire credit regime available to cooperatives. The same thing repeats itself in the cooperative administration. So, while everything else in the economy is being liberalized, cooperatives remain exactly the same. The bureaucratic stranglehold over them has to end to enable them to compete in the market on equal terms.

This brings us to examine the likely significance of cooperatives in the Indian economy in the foreseeable future.

If people were the focus of the policy, and the aim was to liberate the energies of the people for creating goods and services, then the agenda of liberalization sould have addressed the problems of all the important segments of the economy, including agriculture, small industry and cooperatives in the same way. Studies in India have shown that even if our foodgrain production is adequate at the aggregate level, the hunger of the poor cannot be eradicated unless these grains are produced locally or in geographically accessible areas. Even in a State like Kerala where the public distribution system is one of the most efficient in the country, a study by the Centre for Development Studies showed that the poorer households were still not able to obtain the grains they required, because neither the PDS, nor the market mechanism, nor the comfortable aggregate supply was able to reach them. Therefore, the study recommended that where feasible local production of the kind of grains which the poor require for their consumption is a necessary condition for improving their access to food. To stimulate and sustain local production for local consumption, it is necessary to have an efficient, responsive, local institution. This, given our millions of small land holdings, can only be a cooperative institution.

While the economy is important for society, it must also safeguard its political interests, its dignity, its independence and its ability for self-assertion. These are as much its capital as the cash that fuels economic growth. So, we have to remember that, as a people, with a population of over 940 million, we are dealing with a mass of humanity afflicted with stark disparities, unemployment and poverty. Stark disparities, in particular, are the enemy of any democratic society which lives by electoral equality: one person one vote. The system of one person one vote can take only so much disparity. Therefore, a significant measure of social equality and independence has to be built into our economic development endeavour. If that be so, the market and the State, at their best, cannot adequately meet this need, as has been well proven. The situation demands and offers a significant space for cooperatives in the economic domain. This necessitates an urgent need to liberate the cooperatives from their continued Government stranglehold.

It seems clear that in the emerging situation, a greater spurt to the cooperatives would probably come from a certain amount of national self-assertion at the political level, as the economy is sought to be globalized. As the economy opens itself, people will realize that decision-making power is going out of their hands. That they are not able to determine the shape their economy should take. And, therefore, there would be a rebound, there will be pressures which express the feeling that, "We cannot allow all the initiatives to go out of our hands". There will also be more severe pressures – from within the domestic economy for widening the present narrow horizon and narrower base of the new economic policy. It will have to embrace poverty eradication through food security, and base this food security on widespread local production of grains and widespread diffusion of purchasing power, and in the process improve consumption of the poor households.

Cooperatives will thus also become a platform for those who feel that there is a need to build up safeguards against havocs wrought by unrestrained globalization to ensure that we are not totally at the mercy of global winds, with little scope left for self-defence and self-assertion. Self-assertion at the political level and search for sustainable food security to the population as a whole at the economic and social levels, are certain to provide a lot of external and internal stimulus and clear-cut purpose to cooperatives.

The challenges we face today are far more tortuous than those that partition inflicted on us, or the formative post-Independence years had in store for us or those which we are contending with through the new economic policy. What are these challenges? To name the principal ones: demography, debt, besides disparities and deprivation of a large number of people on the social and economic plane.

Besides, society, which was striving 50 years ago to preserve its newly won freedom, is overcome today with uncontrollable sectarian passions. We are increasingly relying on the State, its police and para-military forces, to keep us together. The armed forces, too, are being brought in to the aid of the civil authorities. Here, again, the limitations of relying on the "khaki" force have shown themselves in abundant measure. They can quell a riot perhaps but they cannot forge the friendship, or the unity necessary, to root out the cause of the riots. The secular character of the Constitution cannot be driven into our body politic by the police. In fact, the State as a whole, as an instrument, with or without the use of the "khaki" force, is unable to cope with the challenges in this realm. The challenges we face constitute a task well beyond ministers, cabinets, bureaucracy, the police, the para-military and the military. It has also been shown that the State is not even an appropriate instrument for this task.

What all this adds up to is that India is being diminished. We cannot afford to be passive. An unprecedented mobilization by the people in an orderly manner is required. It must extend up to the remotest village to save India, to move it forward and for the people themselves to develop along with the economy and in conditions of equity.

Parliament has electrified the environment for such a mobilization. It has passed the 73rd and 74th Amendments providing for a nationwide network of Panchayats and Nagar Palikas, with mandatory elections every five years and the subsequent elections to be completed before the expiry of the five-year term. Equally significant is the provision for the massive presence of women, of a minimum one-third, in these elected bodies in rural and urban areas. Swami Vivekananda used to say that, "With five hundred men, the conquest of India might take fifty years; with as many women, not more than a few weeks." And, if they join hands with another two lakh representatives of *dalits* and other disadvantaged groups in the panchayats, India can pulsate with change.

While recognizing these possibilities, the limitations of the panchayats must also be recognized. They can promote, aid and encourage economic activity, but they cannot undertake it. Economic activity is the substance of life for the masses of our people who live by the sweat of their brow. It is here that the cooperatives have a unique role.

I see already some inspiring and encouraging examples. Samakhya in Andhra has rekindled not only my interest in cooperatives, but also my faith in the capacity of society to build cooperatives independently of the State, and resist the intrusions of the latter where necessary. Samakhya is also resisting deviations from principles and democratic practices by cooperatives themselves, and placing an accent on good principles and sound business practices at the same time. A chance meeting with Shashi Rajagopal of Samakhya at a seminar a few years ago was like my chance encounter with Kamaladevi in 1947.

Recently, I have also seen some highly analytical, instructive and thought provoking literature on cooperatives flowing out of the Institute for Rural Management, Anand (IRMA). They are producing knowledge on why cooperatives fail? They have explained sugar cooperatives have failed, even where Amul, the milk cooperative, has won hands down. These insights are a valuable capital. They must be read, debated and interacted with by anyone involved and interested in cooperative endeavour. Our support for cooperatives must be tempered by an understanding of their complex cultural, commercial and organizational context.

A new Cooperative Initiative Panel has just begun to act as a national centre for setting the agenda and for pressing for changes in law, practice and policy. It also wants to usher in a new outlook within the cooperative movement. And then there is Andhra Pradesh.

On May 4, 1995, the Andhra Pradesh Legislative Assembly passed the Andhra Pradesh Mutually Aided Cooperative Societies Act, 1995 sponsored by the Telugu Desam Party led by N.T. Rama Rao. It is a historic act which restores member control to all cooperatives which do not hold Government share capital. The Act breaks new ground in the history of the Indian cooperative movement. For the first time since the original 1904 Cooperative Societies legislation, a cooperative law respects the right of members to fully own and control their own cooperative enterprise.

The new Act guarantees cooperatives the same freedom to conduct their own affairs that other forms of enterprises presently enjoy. Elections will be conducted by the cooperatives themselves. The selection of auditors is now the responsibility of the cooperatives. The affairs of the cooperatives will be governed by their own bylaws, subject to very limited restrictions in the 1995 Act. The State Government has denied to itself rule-making powers under this Act. Staffing patterns, staff remuneration, service conditions, etc., on which cooperatives had in the past required the prior approval of the Registrar of Cooperatives, will now be entirely the responsibility of the cooperatives themselves. They will no longer need to take permission to make investment decisions, where earlier, even to invest in their own business, they needed the Registrar's approval.

The new Act applies to all cooperatives that do not have Government share capital. The earlier Act of 1964 continues to apply to cooperatives that have Government equity. However, if a cooperative wishes to come under the Act, it may do so by returning the Government's share capital.

This liberation of the cooperatives from governmental stranglehold must extend beyond Andhra Pradesh throughout India given the forces of globalization and the ground political, economic and social realities touched upon earlier.

It is in this context that we can think fruitfully of a new phase in the cooperative movement, where, through the combined strength of the people gathered together systematically from the village-level upwards, we can create a viable force to impact the economy and uphold our self-respect as a civilization. Much of what we do may not change India or subdue all its demoniac problems. But if we do not act, the demon would not even feel challenged. The first step, therefore, is to throw the challenge.

To conclude, the impulses of the Freedom Movement gave birth to many initiatives and institutions in the post-Independence period, all too eager to consolidate freedom and build a new India. The Indian Cooperative Union (ICU) was one such institution born in 1948.

Two days before he was shot dead by an assassin, Gandhiji had formally proposed that the Indian National Congress should dissolve itself, having achieved its historic task of liberation of the country from foreign rule. He wanted Congressmen to become Lok Sevaks. As is well known, Congressmen turned a deaf ear to this advice. But not all of them.

Kamaladevi and several others had already decided to opt out of party politics and prepared a blueprint to launch the Indian Cooperation Union – a voluntary organization which would provide the much-needed shoulder to the socio-economic emancipation of India through cooperation – an endeavour which received Gandhiji's blessings.

ICU was an active force with high visibility during the first two decades after Independence. In this, what may be called the First Phase, it active on both planes – practical and policy, action and advocacy, embracing the twin fields of economic and social endeavour. Its endeavours, successful and unsuccessful, yielded valuable practical results and insights. This book is an attempt to record them in one place. However, it suffers from some severe limitations. Due to the passage of time, substantial ICU records and Kamladevi's personal papers have been lost and could not be traced. Further, the book does not include the story of Faridabad – the most inspiring and instructive refugee resettlement project, in which the ICU played a substantive role. The reason is Faridabad needs a book by itself – and it is on the anvil.

In what may be called the Second Phase, i.e. after 1968, there was a metamorphosis: ICU changed from being a mover on its own to being a channel i.e. acting through the medium of other organizations. It wound up all its on "on going" projects and decided to disseminate its experience through other organizations, and to air its views on public policy issues through the media.

The resolve to put together this book was made when Kamaladevi passed away in 1988. But the idea did not make much progress, until 1994 when, quite by accident, a complete outsider to ICU chanced on the scene: Karen Coelho. Karen returned to India the previous year after doing her M.Phil at the University of Sussex, completing a scholarly dissertation on "Political and Social Impacts of Democratic Decentralization – The Case of Karnataka (1991-93)." She was gripped by the ICU story and undertook to co-edit this volume. Her unique contribution here is not only in putting the book together, but in investing ICU's experience with contemporary relevance. That is the essence of Chapter 1, "Overview", authored by her.

In the meanwhile, Amita Baviskar, also fresh after her dissertation at Delhi University, offered to prepare a historic profile of the cooperative movement during the colonial rule. It is Chapter 2.

Chapter 3 describes the birth of ICU and its place in the cooperative movement.

From here on, the book attempts to capture the major contributions of the ICU under two broad categories : *Advocacy* and *Action*.

Advocacy is of principles and perspectives relating to the cooperative movement and as applied to the goals and context of a Free India. Chapter 4 is a summary of the ICU's proposals for change in the direction of the cooperative movement. Several significant steps were being taken at the time by the Government which the ICU felt were likely to affect the very character of the cooperative movement. It was, therefore, regarded of utmost importance to study the important official initiatives, analyse and assess them in the perspective of the principles of cooperation , democratic substance and social consequence, and place them before the country for a wider informed debate.

These included official policies and plans for converting the traditional farming system in Indian agriculture to the system of *cooperative farming*. Cooperative farming was adopted as the main plank of the Congress Party. The ICU's analysis of the Cooperative Farming policy and plans and their deeper implications, if implemented, were analysed and published to generate a debate. The study was authored principally by Raj Krishna jointly with Gopikrishna and L.C. Jain and constitutes Chapter 5. It also includes a brief account of the follow-up action by the ICU to persuade and assist the Congress Party to give precedence to service cooperatives over cooperative farming.

Another major official step was to alter the *cooperative law* drastically curtailing members' control and reducing cooperatives to mainly government controlled and directed entities. Proposals for such changes in cooperative law were authored by an official committee and its report presented as a fait accompli to the cooperatives and the country. The ICU sensed a deep conspiracy to divest cooperatives of their democratic substance. It undertook a critical examination of the official report and recommendations for changes in the cooperative law. The resulting study raised a countrywide debate which did not escape the attention of Prime Minister Nehru who asked the ICU, "What are your constructive suggestions on cooperative law?" The ICU responded with two well-researched papers: (1) a perspective by which cooperative legislation should be governed; and (2) draft of a new cooperative law based on the recommended perspective. These papers, included in Chapter 6, became, and continue to be, the basis of an informed campaign by cooperatives across the country for changes in the cooperative law.

Another policy initiative by the authorities relating to cooperative credit caused deep concern to the cooperative movement. Based on the Report of the All India Rural Credit Survey (ARCS), the Reserve Bank and the Government decided on the latter's participation in the equity and management of cooperatives, and in determining the size, scope and business substance of rural cooperatives which were to replace the existing village-level multipurpose cooperatives. The ICU made a thorough review and analysis of the voluminous ARCS reports from the viewpoint of the cooperative principles and in keeping with the best interests of rural producers. The ICU study titled "The All India Rural Credit Survey vis-a-vis The Cooperative Movement," authored by ICU's Senior Research Fellow, Sita Ram Goel along with subsequent articles/papers by the ICU on rural credit constitute Chapter 7.

Yet another move by the Government to promote community development under official auspices caused serious concern to voluntary organizations in the country, particularly those which had been in the forefront of rural development. It was apprehended that the official reliance on departmental staff headed by a Block Development Officer to bring about community development would be counter productive. It would stifle community initiative and foster dependence on government.

The ICU pinpointed the issues involved and acted as a catalyst along with selected organizations to bring together the main voluntary organizations in the country. This led to the founding of the Association of Voluntary Organizations for Rural Development (AVARD). The proceedings of this conference in which ICU played a key role form Chapter 8 and, as would be seen, the issues raised then about the role of the State vis-a-vis Society are still of great relevance today.

As a consequence of the official approach to cooperative law, cooperative credit and cooperative farming were unprecedented expansion of cooperative departments across the country, arming them with draconian powers and overburdening them with matters which should have been internal to the cooperative management. The ICU regarded these as totally repugnant to a democratic system in general, and to inner democratic governance of cooperatives, in particular. Such expansion and empowerment of the cooperative departments was viewed by ICU as a relic of colonialism and thus detrimental to the healthy growth of a socially purposive and vigorous cooperative movement. Chapter 9 includes some of the ICU's papers on this theme and its advocacy that the cooperative departments should be dissolved and their functions assigned to unions of cooperatives.

Now we turn to the *action* side of the ICU's role. There is here a reversal of chronology. The ICU started as an action organization. It donned the role of advocator, only subsequently, as and when official policies and programmes threatened the environment for building a new India by the people with minimal dependence on the State. As the account will show the ICU was a pioneer in almost every sphere of its field action. It was a pioneer not only in the sense of being "the first" but also because of innovations be it cooperative farms, community development, rural credit, self-help in rehabilitation endeavours, development and management of large marketing networks such as the Central Cottage Industries Emporium and the Super Bazaar.

The ICU's major endeavours in the field were :

(a) in helping refugees in Delhi and Faridabad in their efforts for rehabilitation in rural and urban occupations on a self - help cooperative basis (as explained earlier, the story of Faridabad with its numerous socio-economic dimensions forms the subject of a book by itself).

(b) rural development through multipurpose cooperatives of farmers and landless agricultural workers; community development effort and agricultural extension;

(c) help to handicraft artisans in finding a secure place in the post-Independence economic milieu, particularly through the instrument of the Central Cottage Industries Emporium;

(d) help to consumers to protect and promote their interests through consumer cooperatives through the instrument of what have come to be called "Super Bazaars";

(e) help to Tibetan refugees in their rehabilitation;

(f) organization of social welfare services for rural and urban communities; and

(g) research studies and there publication, in aid of its efforts at both advocacy and action.

Starting in 1948, the first field endeavour of ICU was in organizing rural agricultural cooperatives to resettle refugee landless agricultural workers in villages around Delhi. Later, the ICU extended its services to non-refugee farmers also in the same villages – particularly in the provision of seeds, implements, livestock and in building minor irrigation sources and marketing support.

When the official community development (CD) programme entered these villages in the mid-50s, the ICU reoriented the scope of its services and strategy, and concentrated on tackling the observed weaknesses of the CD programme. The purposes of the ICU's programme, its focus and working experience were recorded and published by the ICU in a special report, "Community Development – Mehrauli". This report is produced here in Chapter 10. It highlighted the extent, and methods the ICU programme used to succeed in overcoming the major weaknesses observed in the official CD programme.

Subsequent to the CD programme, the Government also launched a special Intensive Agricultural Development Programme (IADP). As a result of its experience at Mehrauli, the Agricultural Ministry associated the ICU with the training and extension work related to IADP. This phase of the ICU's field work relating to IADP, etc, is captured in the section titled " Extension" in Chapter 10.

The ICU's action programme for revival and strengthening of traditional handicrafts and support to handicrafts and artisans moved on two inter-related fronts: (1) a diagnostic survey of the conditions of major crafts and artisans in the country, to evolve an informed policy framework and strategy for development of handicrafts which was recommended to the Government for adoption ; and (2) a working plan for the ICU for the development and expansion of markets including exports, for all-India handicrafts, through the restructuring of the Central Cottage Industries Emporium (CCIE) . The CCIE evolved as a pacesetter for dynamic marketing of handicrafts, exports, design and market research. A summary of the all-India survey and an account of the growth of CCIE are incorporated in Chapter 11.

From its inception, the ICU took interest in supporting consumer cooperatives to protect the interests of the consumers against unbridled market forces. At times of crisis, such as the Chinese aggression in 1962 and devaluation of the rupee in 1966, prices invariably got out of hand.

On each occasion, the ICU was approached by the authorities to help in moderating the rigour of price rise through activating consumer cooperatives. The Delhi Consumer Cooperative wholesale store, for example, was promoted by the ICU in 1962 in the wake of the Chinese aggression. It serviced over a hundred small consumer cooperative retail stores. The price rise following the devaluation in 1966, however, broke all past records and was unbearable for the ordinary consumer. The Government itself panicked. The ICU was approached again. But this time, the ICU proposed a longer-term plan and urged the Government to take sustained interest in the consumer cooperative movement. The ICU offered to initiate the implementation of the plan by pioneering the establishment of the Delhi Cooperative Store with a network of branches in the capital (popularly called Super Bazars). This was intended to serve as a model and a training ground for the promotion of a large number of similar stores by Central and State Governments and voluntary agencies, in other parts of India. Chapter 12 gives the story of the Super Bazar.

Chapter 13 is a brief account of the ICU's role in the rehabilitation of Tibetan refugees who crossed into India alongwith His Holiness the Dalai Lama in the late 50s. It also provides a glimpse of some of the initiatives by ICU to organize social welfare activities and health services for rural and urban communities.

From the day when the ICU was set up and applied for registration under the Cooperative Act, it had the most amazing and agonizing memorable encounters with the authorities, both ministerial and bureaucratic. These encounters multiplied as ICU progressed. Most of the time, it was confrontation such as on the issues of cooperative law, cooperative farming, cooperative credit, a new approach to community development, land for the landless, cooperatives versus contractors. There were also notable and helpful exceptions. Some of these episodes are recalled in Chapter 14 titled "Encounters with Bureaucracy". Most of it will sound familiar to even present-day voluntary organizations.

While the chapters upto 14 describe the ICU's role in advocacy and action during its first 20 years (1948 - 1968), Chapter 15 provides a brief view of the transformed role of the ICU in the subsequent period. The publication of selected papers on important policy issues and subjects brought out during this period is planned as a sequel to this book.

L.C. Jain

1

COOPERATIVES
A Force for the 1990s?

LITERATURE on the cooperative movement in India in the decades immediately following independence strikes some familiar chords for readers in the 1990s. The language surrounding the movement, the promise with which it was imbued, its keen mobilization of large sections of Gandhian, socialist and nationalist intellectuals, and certainly the notes of scepticism and dissent that were encountered from other, perhaps larger, sections of the society— all these carry echoes of features surrounding the Panchayati Raj legislations of today.

This is not surprising, as the two situations have much in common; they concern the deployment of a particular type of institutional arrangement with the purpose of stimulating profound alterations in the social, political and economic spheres. The cooperative movement was a vehicle loaded with activist designs. Through the practice of cooperative farming or cooperative enterprise, it was envisaged, the spirit of cooperation would permeate the members and thereby, in an expanding process, the larger society. It was hoped that the practice of cooperative enterprise would "provide for the growth of self-disciplined and self-reliant citizens capable of practizing self-government at all levels of social existence" (ICU, 1959:18). The ICU wrote in 1959, "Politically cooperation strengthens the foundations of democracy, provides for decentralization and serves as an effective safeguard against all forms of statism and concentration of power." Thus cooperatives were seen as a rehearsal ground for self-government in civil society, just as the Panchayati Raj institutions under the new legislation are expected, by the practice of regular elections, mandatory representation of the weaker sections, and the tasks of self-government, to become real units of the democratic local governments in the country.

Both sets of institutions carry significant histories, which justify the scepticism they provoke. The cooperative movement before Independence and the cooperative institutions that the republic inherited were as far from being democratic, autonomous, people-led forces for societal transformation as the Panchayati Raj bodies that came into being in the 1960s. Thus, apart from its intrinsic historical value, the cooperative movement in the 1950s and 1960s in India is particularly interesting to study for its resonances with the Panchayati Raj "movement" still sweeping the country today.

Another major aspect of the current context that may be worth considering in discussing cooperatives is their relevance in the new economic atmosphere of the 1990s in India. All movements in the country are faced with a new challenge—if they are to survive into the 1990s and beyond, they must show what they can offer in the new "liberalized" or "marketized" economy. Do they hold out any promise in the current macro-economic transformation, as vehicles for aiding or empowering the poor and vulnerable groups? The special significance of the New Economic Policies is that their impact will pervade every remote corner of the economy and society, altering the lives of rural children, of women and tribals, of pastoralists and peasants. Changes in the prices of essential commodities, market pressure for changes in land-use patterns, incentives for export of agricultural produce and changed market opportunities for various non-farm rural products will change the face of rural livelihood patterns. Through shifts in employment opportunities and, crucially, through the State's gradual withdrawal of protective measures for vulnerable sections of the population, changes will pervade. At base, patterns of power and dominance will undergo shifts according to the new alignments of market forces, impacting the intimate dimensions of culture and identity of people across the country.

In such an atmosphere, are cooperatives still relevant? The tide, as defined by macro-economic policy, is explicitly against them. As Jayathi Ghosh points out (1994: ws2-4), the loosening up of rules and restrictions under the NEP is discriminatory and "fundamentally undemocratic": while they favour foreign capital, large businesses and finance capital, "they are still as rigid and restrictive as ever for cooperatives and genuinely democratic alternative organizations" While the rhetoric of the NEP is that of a freer economy with reduced interference by the State, actual functioning, in terms of State financial measures and policies towards bank credit, is increasingly centralized, favouring large conglomerates over small enterprises. And labour market reform policies, focusing as they do on suppressing working class demands with the "exit policy," cut at the basic premise of the cooperative approach, i.e. the strengthening of opportunities for labour, working classes and consumers vis-a-vis capital in a capitalist production system.

Thus the shape and form of the current market reforms are hostile to cooperatives. Yet the real condition of the agricultural sector and the rural economy remain broadly similar to those in the years around the Green Revolution, when cooperatives were seen as the only institutional way of bridging the gap between rural realities and technological expectations. All studies point to continuing low productivity in the agricultural sector, tracing the problem to a great lack of resources for productive investment, especially of credit. The predominance of "unprogressive" medium and small peasant holdings and the existence of a vast underemployed army of landless agricultural labour speak of the failure of land reforms and land consolidation policies to transform agriculture in any significant way. Studies have also consistently pointed to the absence of accompanying institutional arrangements for access to inputs as a critical ingredient in the failure of land reform (see, for example, Lipton 1991 and Pandey 1994). Meanwhile, the non-farm sector, also for want of investment, has failed to generate enough employment or capital to constitute a viable alternative means of rural livelihood. Poverty has been and continues to be the single most pervasive feature of the rural economy.

In this situation, studies and recommendations have been pointing (often indirectly, sometimes explicitly) to the role cooperatives have played or could play in strengthening the access of the weaker groups to productive resources and in enabling them to procure and manage needed services. The approach of the policy reforms so far has been to accompany the unleashing of market forces with a set of special targeted welfare programmes for vulnerable groups. These measures run parallel to the liberalization measures instead of actually addressing the changes that the measures bring about (Shah *et al.* 1994, Ranadive 1994).

As K. Seeta Prabhu writes, "The poor have neither the skills nor the assets to respond to market signals and hence the developments in the market economy are of little relevance to them" (*EPW*, April 1994). Most studies addressing the impact of the reforms on the agricultural sector identify institutional reform as vital, besides the stepping up of productive investment in agriculture and the removal of subsidies. For example, C.H. Hanumantha Rao focuses on problems in provision and management of infrastructural services in rural areas and writes, "... Non-market institutions of representative type at the local level seem to provide the only workable alternative at this stage, whether to bureaucratic management or to full-scale privatization" (Rao 1994: 1009). He also focuses attention on the continuing credit needs of the weaker sections, while mainstream banking institutions continue to favour lending to a smaller number of big borrowers rather than a large number of small borrowers. He prioritizes the strengthening of credit institutions, improving their viability and giving them greater autonomy from administrative and political interference. These are certainly pointers to the role that cooperatives have played in Indian agriculture from their earliest days.

Meanwhile, recommendations under the "Adjustment with a Human Face" agenda include supporting initiatives which mobilize people for health and education and for greater community action in such areas as housing, water and sanitation (Fleming 1991).

More direct references to the potential of cooperatives in standing up to the market reforms on behalf of the affected groups are also being articulated. Shah, Gandhi *et al.* speak of the record of workers' cooperatives in resisting corporate take-overs, where the workers develop financially viable plans and obtain bank finance and the legal rights to take over and run the plants themselves. These represent new attempts at "reconciling modern industry with ideas of social justice and democratization." The authors note, "Efforts are now under way to develop cooperative relations at the shop-floor level as well as to transform enterprises taken over into truly self-managed cooperatives" (1994:ws46).

The relevance of cooperatives is more strongly highlighted in the context of changes wrought on women's lives by the NEP. Shah, Gandhi *et al.* examine these changes in detail and envisage a wide-ranging set of strategies to counter the negative trends. Cooperative-style strategies figure prominently in these. The strategies, they argue, must "constantly bridge the gap between the workplace, community, neighbourhood and household" and must, while supporting women in the current context, lay the foundations for a more genuine transformation of exploitative relations in the economy. They quote examples from various countries where women have undertaken cooperative action to safeguard survival needs of households, and where these actions have also shown potential for evolving into more transformative strategies. An example is the Communal Kitchens in Lima, Peru, in the 1980s. In India they cite campaigns to reform the public distribution system, organized by NGOs and women's groups under the banner of the Ration Kriti Samiti in Bombay, where attempts were made to monitor prices and distribution at ration shops. They also refer to women's credit cooperatives and women's initiatives in starting *balwadis* (childcare centres) to enable members to participate more freely in the labour market.

Jaya Jaitley who is dedicated to the cause of artisans, describing the destitute state of village artisans and village industries in general, tells how women mat-weavers in Kodungallur in Kerala, by forming a cooperative, were able to secure loans from local banks and the IDBI and to significantly increase their income and bargaining power in the local market. She sees in cooperatives the chance of keeping alive a wide range of ecologically sustainable, small-scale, employment-generating and skills-preserving crafts and industries.

In the political sphere too, the discourse around cooperatives has picked up some life and colour in this decade. The increased politicization of the district and sub-district echelons of the polity via the Panchayati Raj legislations, which mandate regular elections to village, taluka and district-level councils, have sent State political parties into a scramble to coopt existing local organizations with any political affiliations. Cooperatives in India, whatever they lack, are rich in political connections. The storm that arose around the moves of the BJP Government in Gujarat, in April 1995, to supersede elected boards of cooperatives and replace them with State-appointed custodians, proves that cooperatives are still alive politically. The move echoes attempts of the Congress Party in Karnataka in 1991 to supersede Panchayat bodies and reinstate bureaucratic control over them, in a bid to weaken the power of the Janata Party at local levels (see Krishnaswamy 1993). In May 1995, only weeks after the BJP Government actions in Gujarat, the Andhra Pradesh Government of N.T.Rama Rao witnessed the growing political significance of cooperatives in a starkly contrasting move. It won national acclaim for its passing of the Andhra Pradesh Mutually Aided Cooperative Societies Act, 1995, an Act that frees cooperatives that have no government share capital from State control and restores their autonomy in functioning. Cooperatives that have government share capital can come under the new Act by returning the capital. The Act allows eligible cooperatives to hold their own elections, appoint their own auditors and run their own affairs with no interference from the Government.

Taking all these voices together, it would seem that cooperation as an idea and cooperatives as institutional options have not vanished into the void altogether. Nor have they come onto the center-stage as recognized, tried and proven models. Writers explicitly or even indirectly referring to cooperatives as viable options in today's context remain in the minority. For the large part, although a huge institutional network of thousands of primary cooperatives and several hundreds of federal units and cooperative banks are still in place, they have not earned positive recognition by their manner of functioning over the past three to four decades. Instead, the term cooperatives conjures up, even among the cooperative activists and scholars, a tight mesh of bureaucratic and political control, corruption, distortions in resource allocation, and rank inefficiency.

Where, then, can we go with notions of cooperation and with cooperative institutions? Credibility gained from the record of past performance is at least as important in judging the viability of an institutional option as its potential as a model or an idea. The character of cooperatives as expressed through their history in India and elsewhere may yield some insights into their applicability in India's future economic and social trajectory.

Character and History of Cooperatives

Tracking the course of the cooperative movement through to the 1990s in India is something of an adventure. Like a forest spring, it is visible at one point, then vanishes down hidden, often buried, trails, to a resolution that is not yet apparent. Will it finally disappear altogether, or find its confident expression in the contemporary polity?

It is not only the result that is sought. History is seldom interesting simply as an umpire pronouncing victory or defeat. In the case at hand, it is in the stories of the struggles in praxis of an idea, the struggles of an institution against the rigidities of organizational forms, the struggles of civil society against an overweening State, that the real material for study lies, particularly for the 1990s in India. Most importantly, such a study may throw more light on the character of cooperatives than would any abstract study of cooperative principles or their economic roles.

In its heyday in India, which spanned a couple of decades after independence, cooperation was hailed with much rhetoric, seen as the only hope for the economy. It seemed to embody all that could be desired in a newly shaping economy, society and polity—the benefits of capitalistic production without its ills, "combining the advantages of private ownership with public good," the blueprint for organized and democratic units of civil society, and the vehicle for self-reliance and values of mutual aid and protection of the weaker sections. In those days, cooperation was spoken of almost as an ideology, a world-view; the language surrounding it was one of visions and dreams, of principles and missionary commitment. As the Indian Cooperative Union recalls, it became "an issue on which people have resigned (from government), an article of faith" (see Chapter 3). A whole literature developed, stressing the principles of cooperation and judging the reality of the movement against the ultimate notion of the "Cooperative Commonwealth," the aspired state of cooperation. Yet the reality of cooperatives from their inception in India has been one of pragmatic and clearly reformist economic and political design imposed from above.

As an economic concept, cooperation underpins institutional formations aimed at supporting and simultaneously containing capitalism. Cooperation as an economic instrument serves to eliminate the more undesirable elements of the capitalist production system, such as monopolies, middlemen and a fragmented and destitute labour force. It promotes the power of labour vis-a-vis that of capital in labour-abundant and capital-poor situations. In its purer form, it promotes the political, social and philosophical climate conducive to a liberal but organized capitalist economy, a scenario of individual producers acting voluntarily in their best individual interests by cooperating with other individual producers in strategic alliances to mutually strengthen their instruments of production, consumers, markets or bargaining power vis-a-vis other producers, consumers or markets. It thus embraces but qualifies the notion of competition. Its emphases are on voluntary association, productive orientation (i.e. production of the whole association must exceed the sum of production of the individual parts) and distribution of surplus or profits according to the labour contributions of its numbers. Democratic management and self-reliance are also central to the concept.

However, in practice this "associated production" concept has been employed primarily in underdeveloped economies, with weak and vulnerable farmers, craftspeople or consumers exploited by feudal landlords, middlemen, large industrialists or an extractive State. Thus, the notion of cooperation has come to be weighted with a set of protective and welfaristic overtones, edging it closer to the socialist thought. Historically, cooperation was born in capitalist conditions, conceived as an attempt to enable marginalized groups to integrate successfully into an increasingly harsh economy. Its earliest proponents were, however, socialist thinkers like William Owen and his followers. Distributive justice, principles of service and assistance to the needy, and stipulations that "mutual benefit" must not take off, leaving behind the weaker groups, came to be the doctrinal foundations of cooperation. In practice, surplus and dividends of cooperative endeavours were distributed according to the labour contribution of members, while the capital earned a small dividend at a fixed interest rate. The notion of cooperation later expanded to economic functions beyond production – management of common resources, procurement of essential commodities and organization of labour for better bargaining power – has also come into the cooperative fold. Thus in their real contexts, cooperatives became socialist-type institutions, attempting to contain and regulate individualistic advancement in favour of a broader-based development.

Hence, as an instrument of economic development, cooperation has ambiguous affiliations. In the political sphere as well, its ideological patrons, i.e. the regimes that have sponsored its establishment as an institution, have been varied enough to maintain confusion as to its real character, or perhaps to highlight what the Indian Cooperative Union refers to as "the endless plasticity" of its ideological base.

In its earliest history in the Industrial Revolution in early and mid-nineteenth century England, and a little later in Germany and France, cooperation was conceived and grew up as a purely voluntary social formation. It was a citizens' response to the hardships and disruption visited on the society by capitalist industrialization. The Owenites, and later the Rochdale Pioneers, generally regarded as the founders of the notion of cooperation, were essentially "civil society" formations in the stricter sense of the term (formations accompanying and facilitating the rooting of capitalist production systems in the social and economic spheres), as well as in its looser sense of "non-state". Cooperation as conceived by these groups was aimed at protecting, through joint social action, the interests of workers and consumers by eliminating the role of the exploitative traders in the new industrial economy. In its subsequent adaptations in other parts of Europe, this essential character of voluntary, joint action to protect vulnerable sections and facilitate their participation in the evolving capitalist economies remained. Interestingly, the set of principles and practices evolved by these early proponents have remained, essentially unchanged, to form the core of the notion of cooperation even up to the present.

Given this vein of autonomous social action in the origins and early history of cooperation, it is ironical that the manner and shape in which it was introduced in India (and, indeed, in many countries where cooperatives were instituted as developmental vehicles in the modern phase) was as a State-sponsored and top-down programme of a colonial government. These features have dogged the steps and characterized the progress of the Indian cooperative movement to this day, forming the chief impediments to its gaining popular support as an effective movement.

Anita Bhaviskar's essay on the early history of cooperatives in India (see Chapter 2) identifies clearly the British administration's motives in introducing cooperatives as a major thrust in India: "It had its roots in the colonial imperative of maintaining political control." Concerned by the growing rural unrest caused primarily by extreme indebtedness of the peasants, and interested in fostering a transformation of the peasantry into "progressive" capitalist farmers, the administration saw in cooperatives the appropriate vehicles for agrarian development. Yet despite the pragmatic overtones of this move, with the passing of the Cooperative Credit Societies Bill in 1904, the cooperative movement entered India with much of the fervour of a missionary cause, bearing the baggage of ideology, vision and principle that have never been far away from the concept. Much of the history of the cooperative movement in the earlier decades of the twentieth century is that of the struggle of idealistic sponsors (e.g. several government-sponsored Commissions and Committees making recommendations on cooperative policy) to foster an alien concept in unreceptive soil, creating what Bhaviskar calls "a history of contradiction as a colonial State tried to develop a self-reliant peasantry". While the provision of credit was the primary, explicit purpose of the establishment of cooperatives in India, its underlying notions of democratization, self-government and self-reliance soon overtook the discourse.

Yet the crux of the contradiction was never resolved. The Indian nationalist intelligentsia, many of whom saw much promise in the ideas of cooperation, could never in practice identify with this movement due to its State-sponsored character. As Jain puts it, "Just at the time the British decided to introduce cooperation, the Indian National Congress had adopted 'non-cooperation' as its basic weapon. In the eyes of the Nationalist Movement, cooperatives came to be identified mainly as a channel for distribution of official patronage" (ICU 1967; see Chapter 9).

Immediately after Independence, however, the identity of the cooperative movement altered radically. Cooperatives began to be adopted by the new national leaders as key institutional instruments in the development of the economy and in transformation of the society towards a more equitable, democratic and socialistic model. Pandey makes a telling case locating cooperatives as strategic stepping stones in the transformation of the agrarian peasant economy, from the early post-Independence land reforms toward the Green Revolution changes of the late 1960s. It is generally agreed by scholars that the cooperative mode was employed primarily to facilitate the modernization of agriculture among the vast medium and small peasantry, in a context where the policy thrusts were towards broad-basing production and retaining land in the hands of the tillers. The peasants' need for credit, for seeds, equipment and for access to post-production processing and to marketing facilities spelt out the scope for cooperatives. The Five Year Plans repeatedly revived the stress on cooperatives as "indispensable instruments of planned economic action in democracy, combining initiative, mutual benefit and social purpose" (First Plan) or as "a vital factor for stability, for expansion of employment opportunities and for rapid economic development" (Third Plan) but most of all as "an important institutional framework to ameliorate the condition of the weaker sections, particularly in providing inputs and working as a limb of the National Public Distribution Scheme" (Seventh Plan).

In these thrusts, the cooperative effort retained the character of a top-down programme under State auspices, with the Cooperative Department and the Registrars being the chief protagonists of the movement. Reports such as the Rural Credit Survey (1954) and that of the Committee on Cooperative Law (1957), identifying weaknesses in the extent, effectiveness and functioning of the movement, began recommending more stringent controls, regulations and supervision by the Department. Simultaneously, however, the movement, having captured the interest of intellectuals and activists in the new republic, began to find voices re-articulating the basic visions and principles of cooperation. The progress of cooperation after Independence thus became a history of protracted struggle of activists to claim the movement as autonomous, people-led and democratic.

These activists, who included some of the great mobilizers and political leaders of the time such as J.P. Narayan and Kamaladevi Chattopadhyay, sought to re-discover and re-assert the more radical transformative potentials of cooperation. They envisioned cooperative institutions infusing a profound value-change in the larger society by a slow permeation, carrying their spirit of democratization, self-reliance, self-governance, mutual assistance and social concern. Education of cooperators and of the larger community became a central feature. Many of the writings, speeches and exhortations of this phase of revivalism in the cooperative movement criticized the current "economism" in which the institution had got trapped — its focus on securing loans, grants or programmes, its orientation towards numbers, targets and statistics to monitor the spread of the movement, and, more crucially, its being cornered by powerful or better-off sections of the population.

The story of these struggles is the story of organizations such as the Indian Cooperative Union, which took up the role of advocacy for the cooperative movement as a transformative people's movement. (The role played by the ICU in these struggles is given in the following pages).

The discussion above attempted to trace the broad contours of the journey through which cooperatives have travelled to reach the modern phase. What do these reveal about the character of cooperatives as institutional forms?

In terms of economic ideologies, cooperation is a socialistic notion that ably serves a capitalist economy. As a political concept, its affinity to anarchic thought has not prevented it from becoming a favourite developmental implement of regimes ranging from the colonial or fascist (as in pre-Second World War Italy and Japan) to the new self-governing republics in Asia, Africa and Latin America. It appears that cooperation has no autonomous existence as an ideological construct, but is an ultimately instrumental notion, finding expression in a set of institutional forms, these in turn serving a variety of economic, political, developmental, even philosophical ends. It is a concept that, beyond the basic set of principles that have remained its core, finds its definition in praxis. ICU observes that "Cooperation has never been a dead dogma or institutional ritual unrelated to the needs of time and place. If the history of cooperative experiments, the world over, is any evidence, cooperation has shown, both doctrinally and institutionally, an abundance of adaptive capacity provided it is not called upon to surrender its basic character" (ICU 1961, see Chapter 7).

However, the extent to which its "basic character" or "core principles" have been followed in real applications has depended on the sponsoring establishment. Proponents of cooperation, including the ICU (elsewhere in the same document), continue to maintain that "cooperation is a well-defined ideology in its own right, a self-sufficient system of values which lay a limit to all social institutions including the state" (*ibid.,* see Chapter 7). In theory this may yet be argued, but in fact the history of the movement has shown that social institutions and especially the State have a greater agency in limiting or influencing the praxis of cooperation than the other way around.

This, in fact, best represents the verdict that modern scholarship pronounces on the cooperative institutional form. Modern analyses have tended to approach cooperatives from an empirical standpoint, in contrast to the "ideal-typing" or essentializing approach of ICU and other proponents. Assisting this shift in approach is the enormous body of empirical material now available on the achievements of cooperatives after several decades of application in post-colonial reconstructive tasks in developing countries across the world. From Botswana to Brazil to the Philippines, cooperatives were established, largely by governments or international agencies, to solve problems of rural development, with the expectation that they would mobilize resources, promote growth with equitable distribution of benefits, and rebuild fragmented communities. The majority of them, across the world, failed to deliver on any of these counts (Attwood and Baviskar, 1988; Esman and Uphoff 1984). The patterns of failure turned out to be rather similar across the variety of contexts. As Attwood evaluates existing cooperatives, he finds that

> "Some are empty shells, ignored by their supposed beneficiaries; others are simply arms of government bureaucracy; others are plundered by local elites, giving few if any benefits to those who most need them" (1989:5).

Yet there are resoundingly successful examples of cooperatives that have met many of the above expectations and endured the test of time. The most famous examples of these are the dairy cooperatives of Gujarat, modelled on the Anand pattern, and the cooperative sugar factories of Maharashtra. These have been subjected to intense study in recent years and have yielded further evidence of the highly specific or contingent sets of circumstances that spelled success or failure in particular cases. Variations in performance on any of the goals of these cooperatives (equity, growth, income security, community cohesion) were found to be significant even within a small geographical area or among different cooperative societies within the same sector (such as dairy). Thus modern studies emphasize the need to identify, distinguish and analyse the conditions surrounding these cases in order to understand the circumstances leading to the success or failure of cooperatives on any particular dimension. As Attwood and Baviskar maintain,

> "What is important, then, is to understand the comparative pattern of successes and failures, to see why some successes have occurred, to know whether these are the product of unusual local conditions, and

to deepen our understanding of the interconnections between cooperatives and the social systems in which they are embedded. We also need to determine just what types of cooperatives have been successful under different kinds of local conditions, and to learn whether 'success' in one sense (such as increased production) leads to better distribution of incomes and opportunities—that is, whether and in what respects it benefits the poor" (1988:3).

Thus, in the case of the dairy cooperatives in Kheda district, the seat of the renowned success story, analyses by Baviskar (1988) and George (1988) find that while the cooperatives were extremely successful in some respects, their record was grossly overstated on other counts. While the input, marketing and veterinary services they provided were unprecedentedly effective in enhancing milk production, increasing incomes and providing critical livelihood support to farmers in the area, they did not, as claimed, "overcome the three obstacles of caste, class and power which have frustrated earlier programmes of rural development" (Baviskar 1988: 346). Their success in fact rested largely on caste factors, namely, the dominant role of the Patidar caste as landowners, milk producers and leaders in the district. The majority of those who benefited from cooperative dairying in the district were those who had access to fodder (either through land ownership or purchasing power); thus, contrary to expectation, the landless or the very poor did not figure prominently among the beneficiaries. Nor did the cooperatives succeed in reducing the income gap between big and small farmers; in fact, they may have increased it (Baviskar 1988 and George 1988). In addition, a number of special features that the cooperatives of this area enjoyed–such as the availability of fertile, irrigated land and special support from the State and Central Governments and from international agencies – raise the issue of replicability of the experience in other contexts.

Attwood, in an analysis of the cooperative sugar factories in Maharashtra, also identified particular configurations of caste, agrarian relations and political opportunities that were responsible for their success, by constructing a "community of interests" among the members of the cooperative. Under these particular circumstances, he found structures of internal and external competition and political factionalism (theoretically antithetical to cooperative ideology) actually contributed to economic efficiency and organizational success of the factories. They pushed the factory leaders (who were elected representatives) towards more enterprising, risk-taking and innovative management of the factory while also demanding from them efficiency and accountability to cooperative members. Attwood contrasts these member-controlled cooperatives to less successful cooperative sugar factories, for instance in Uttar Pradesh, where factories are managed by government officials and not elected leaders. "Thus the elected leaders are not responsible for economic performance, and the officials who run the factories are not directly accountable to the shareholders" (*ibid*:21). Corruption and negligence are rampant in these factories.

Thus the issue of whether cooperatives are member-controlled or professionally managed (an issue that the ICU battled over for years, as the papers included in this book will show) continues to lie at the heart of their performance. The extent to which members control the affairs of the cooperative in turn depends upon a variety of situation – specific factors including caste configurations, educational levels of members and their elected representatives, economic stakes of members in the enterprise, presence of professional managers and their patterns of affiliation.

Parallelly, the actions of cooperative members may be governed by strategic considerations alternating with social and cultural realities. While economic calculations tend to figure significantly in their decisions (such as selling cane to private factories for better prices than the cooperative offers), other considerations such as trust and dependence, mediated by social structures and networks in the area, can often override the economic impulse (Attwood 1989).

What emerges essentially from all these findings is the hazard of assuming replicability of cooperative experiences from one context to another. This is the underlying theme of many scholars studying the successful cooperative experiences of India (George 1988, Doornbos *et al.* 1994, Baviskar 1988). Replication has been the cornerstone of the top-down cooperative movement in India from its inception to the recent Operation Flood programme, the latter designed to replicate the Anand model throughout India. Doornbos (1994), examining the development of Operation Flood, notes that bureaucratization became an inevitable concomitant of the spread of the model:

> "The apex implementing agency propagates the Anand pattern in a manner which tries to minimize the complexities arising from local differences. The NDDB (National Dairy Development Board) is responsible for programme blueprints and resource allocation.... In other words, the model which has been replicated (a) is not truly the

Anand model which arose spontaneously from grassroots organizing, and (b) is a relatively rigid construct imposed from above and therefore is not always appropriate for local circumstances" (1994:924).

Replication goals, he notes, tend to develop their own momentum and lead in unforeseen directions. Interests and processes associated with replication may not be the same as those of the original programme.

The essence of the critique of replication goals is echoed in the single most common finding among the several contemporary studies of cooperatives: that indigenous cooperative formations spontaneously arising from local initiative, and rooted in specific sets of selective alliances and political negotiations, are much more likely to be viable and enduring than cooperatives imposed from above. These local formations are rarely modelled on the cooperative ideal of favouring the weakest or ensuring equitable access, nor are they likely to bring about significant changes in income distribution or social structure. The alliances may be between unequal partners—small and large farmers—and may entail vertical as well as horizontal relations. Yet, across the world, the most successful cooperatives have been those created by local initiative. Hyden (1988) characterizes the issue by contrasting what he calls "blueprint" versus "greenhouse" approaches—the former referring to imposed models as against the latter which nurture indigenous organizations.

The challenge for cooperative activists today, then, is not to identify ingredients of the ideal cooperative institution that can fulfil all the goals of the Cooperative Commonwealth, but to discover cooperative formations in the variety of local networks and alliances that people create to support their livelihood systems, and to find ways of supporting and strengthening these in the interests of vulnerable sections.

Redefining the Cooperative Movement: ICU and its Struggles

Independence opened the doors to a new political significance for the cooperative movement. As noted above, the movement immediately shifted, from being a suspect colonial tool in the hands of the British administration, to become a mainstream strategy of nationalist leaders in building the new republic. The cooperative movement began to be perceived as a crucial vehicle in the huge task of transforming a mammoth two-hundred-year-old colony into a modern self-governing republic.

The task, essentially, was one of "consolidating freedom". Its goal was to translate freedom of a nation into freedom for its citizens from the variety of local regimes that held them oppressed—from the *zamindar*, the moneylender and the trader, the clutches of caste, class and communal systems, the various social and mental structures of being "ruled," an entire psyche that had been too long colonized. An institutional form was needed to reach the vast, unorganized and still largely unawakened population with the dreams of a free India as conceived by the leaders of the freedom movement and the new rulers of the republic. Through the existing network of institutions and organizations left by the old regime, a new spirit or meaning had to be spread: political education towards democracy, notions of self-reliance and self-governance, communal harmony and new, egalitarian/socialist notions of community. And on the developmental front, a new socialist spirit to facilitate and accompany structural changes in the economy towards more distributive equality, experience in organization and management of joint enterprises, skills in financial management, thrift and a "progressive" orientation in farming and other enterprises.

It is to the credit of the cooperative movement, or perhaps to the idea of cooperation itself, that, despite the history of the movement in India up to that time, it was still perceived as a vehicle equal to these tasks. That cooperation could be seen as capable of serving the new masters so ably also points to the ultimate flexibility and instrumentality of the concept.

However, as cooperation entered its new role in the independent nation, a whole new arena of struggle opened up around it—a tug-of-war between two very different sets of agents for definition, propagation and ownership of the movement. This struggle around cooperatives highlighted a crucial dynamic of the new republic, an evolving tension between State and Society. As statist development plans took the country over with supreme complacency, all programmes emanating from the centre and the central bureaucracy maintaining a stranglehold over the lower echelons of the federal hierarchy, i.e. district and below, activists working with the people began to voice strong opposition. The politics of centralization was one of the ingredients that began to breed a slow disillusionment with the new State among a large cross-section of activists. In practical terms, the difficulties of building up a strong base of community involvement and participation in centrally conceived developmental programmes became increasingly evident even in programmes that overtly called for community participation such as the Community Development Programme (CDP) initiated in the 1950s.

The tension between centralized, bureaucratically controlled development and people-led autonomous development was strongly expressed in the cooperative movement and formed the basis for the long and arduous battles that were fought, over many years, by agencies like the ICU. While standing for an idealized notion of the cooperative institution, and not averse to fostering such institutions on a replication basis wherever possible, the ICU adamantly opposed the target-led propagation of cooperatives by the government and envisaged the spontaneous spread of the movement as the only viable strategy.

The ICU was started in 1948 by "a small band of idealists" as its key initiator, Kamaladevi Chattopadhyaya, called them. It was conceived as a voluntary organization, committed to reclaiming cooperation as a movement of the people. Its goals were at once simple and ambitious. In terms of action it sought to carry out small, specific projects, starting with a rehabilitation settlement for refugees from Pakistan in a site outside Delhi and followed by a series of similar experiments in setting up small cooperative microcosms. In its intent and design, however, it aimed at reorienting the cooperative movement in India, giving it shape and guidance, evolving new frameworks and guidelines that would help in transforming the movement from a set of economic bodies to a webbed tissue of institutions embodying a new way of life. It saw itself acting as watchdog, advocate and lobbyist to the Government towards a redirection of the movement. Besides its specific community development projects, therefore, the ICU took up the whole set of activities aimed at guiding and facilitating such a shift. It undertook research and publication of monographs and literature on principles of cooperation. It held seminars and conferences which brought together prominent cooperators and activists, and sometimes people from the Government, to critique existing features of the movement and evolve new thrusts. It studied, simplified and commented on reports of various commissions and committees set up by the Government to make policy recommendations on cooperatives. These were unique and valuable functions. The ICU accompanied the movement with a torch held on both the movement itself, showing up its inadequacies, inconsistencies and failings, and on the surrounding conditions of the movement, the path ahead of it, the forces acting on it. Here it highlighted potential pitfalls and dangers to the movement by interpreting the intentions and moves of the Government—it predicted consequences and it proposed alternatives. It created fora at various levels, in networks, in the written word, in seminars and meetings, where these activities of critiques and proposal could be broad-based, involving other activists of the movement.

It tried to form a bridge between the echelons of policy-making and the base of the movement—for instance in the simple but essential task of reading the vast documents produced by official agencies and extracting, simplifying and interpreting them. In all its functions of commentary and critique, the ICU made no pretense of objectivity, neutrality or academic distance. It was openly and passionately polemical, consistently attacking the State's heavy interventionism not so much from the empirical standpoints of effectiveness or efficiency, but on ideological grounds.

The legislation surrounding cooperatives was one of the prime battlegrounds where the ICU confronted the Government. It developed an elaborate and detailed critique to the recommendations of the Committee on Cooperative Law set up by the Ministry of Agriculture in 1956. This report leaned heavily towards compulsory State partnership in cooperative societies and State participation in their management, and in general favoured centralization of control over cooperatives in the hands of the Registrars, in the interests of stricter supervision and closer accountability to the State. Having stringently attacked these recommendations, the ICU then undertook to develop an equally elaborate alternative proposal for cooperative legislation, in the monograph entitled "Plea for a Perspective" (see Chapter 6). Here the basic principles of cooperation are articulated, juxtaposed with their political context in post-independence India; recommendations of various other committees and commissions are quoted, and the cooperative legislation of a series of other countries is briefly reviewed, as the bases for the alternative proposed. For thoroughness, apart from anything else, the work is a model in advocacy writing.

Having worked on the foundations of the cooperative movement through its study of the cooperative law, the ICU then worked on two of the major pillars of the movement in the country at that time: cooperative credit policies and cooperative farming policies. The two documents relating to these subjects are fascinating profiles of the existing policy and the problems arising from them, with, once more, constructive proposals built into the critiques. What is interesting in both these documents is the pragmatic appraisal of the limits in the scope of cooperation and the pulls of private interest and incentive that are brought up to face the Government's blind and counter-productive rhetoric. In the case of credit, for instance, the ICU critiques the call for nationalization of commercial banks, which was issued ostensibly to ensure their lending to cooperatives, among other reasons. It traces the cooperatives' problems with access to credit more to administrative and legal restrictions and to the stranglehold of the Registrar and his Department than to the unwillingness of commercial banks to lend to them.

In the collection of monographs and papers published by the ICU in the 1950s and 1960s, then, we have a fairly rich review of the struggles of the "movement" to become a movement. The success of its endeavours is not evident. Certainly from where we stand today, there is no cooperative movement in the sense envisaged by the ICU. This, as discussed above, may be due in part to the expectations themselves, to the "ideal type" notional model of cooperation superimposed on the reality of existing cooperative institutions, with the vision that they would all one day change from being what they were to what they should be. The ICU, as the following papers show, was guided by such a vision. However, the bulk of its effort was directed toward countering the very real distortions, corruption and cooptation that marked the cooperative sector of the time.

The writing must be seen as a product of the time as well as the politics that the ICU represented. To contemporary readers the language may resound with paternalism and gender blindness. In the classic Gandhian tradition, there is also a tendency in its writings to romanticize constructs such as the family or the village community. Nowhere in its writings are the bitter rural divisions around caste, political factions, economic interests and gender ever explicitly considered. The ICU may be justifiably critiqued for its silence on the subject of women. Women hardly appear in the pages of ICU writing, even though the "first wave" of the women's movement had made a significant contribution, both to the freedom movement and to shaping the laws and policies of the new republic (see Liddle and Joshi 1986). However it must also be said that the cooperative sector of that period had hardly begun to include women; it had certain structural outlines (based on ownership of land or other productive resources, or reliant upon membership of registered societies) that made it almost automatically gendered in most areas of the country. More recently, Apte (1988) notes that even in the model Kheda milk cooperatives, women accounted for only seven per cent of the total members, as loans tended to be taken in the name of males, who generally held the titles to land.

Despite the above shortcomings, the ICU's writings and its commentaries remain valuable as records of the struggle, the striving for an alternative development, the faith and vision and commitment of sections of society to people-led and people-centred development. As noted at the start of this chapter, they are valuable because these struggles, strivings and visions are alive again in the 1990s, this time in relation to the Panchayat Raj institutions. The readings presented in this book are educative also for what they lack, highlighting the need for contemporary students of institutional performance to go beyond idealizing constructions of institutional form and purpose and towards an empirical examination of social, economic and political relations and negotiations that are the real life-blood of local institutions.

REFERENCES

Apte, D.P. (1988). "The Role of Cooperative Dairy Schemes in Rural development in India" in D.W. Attwood, and B.S. Baviskar, eds., *Who Shares? Cooperatives and Rural Development*, Oxford University Press, Delhi.

Attwood, Donald. W. (1989). "Does Competition Help Cooperation?" in *Journal of Development Studies*, 26(1), pp.5-27.

Attwood, D.W., and B.S. Baviskar. (1988). "Introduction" in D.W. Attwood, and B.S. Baviskar, eds., *Who Shares? Cooperatives and Rural Development*, Oxford University Press, Delhi.

Baviskar, B.S. (1988). "Dairy Cooperatives and Rural Development in Gujarat" in D.W. Attwood, and B.S. Baviskar, eds., *Who Shares? Cooperatives and Rural Development*, Oxford University Press, Delhi.

Doornbos, Martin, and Liana Gertsch (1994). "Sustainability, Technology and Corporate Interest", in *Journal of Development Studies*, 30(3), pp.916-950.

George, Shanti (1988). "Cooperatives and Indian Dairy Policy: More Anand than Pattern" in D.W. Attwood, and B.S. Baviskar, eds., *Who Shares? Cooperatives and Rural Development*, Oxford University Press, Delhi.

Ghosh, Jayati (1994). "Gender Concerns in Macroeconomic Policy" in *Economic and Political Weekly*, XXIX (18), April 30.

Hanumantha Rao, C.H. (1994). "Reforming Agriculture in the New Context" in *Economic and Political Weekly*, XXIX (16 & 17), April 16-23.

Hyden, Goran (1988). "Approaches to Cooperative Development: Blueprint versus Greenhouse" in D.W. Attwood, and B.S. Baviskar, eds., *Who Shares? Cooperatives and Rural Development*, Oxford University Press, Delhi.

Jain, L.C., Krishnamoorthy B.V., Tripathi P.M. (1985). *Grass Without Roots: Rural Development under Government Auspices*. New Delhi, SAGE Publications.

Jaitley, Jaya (1994). Village Industry: Struggling to Survive" in *Economic and Political Weekly*, XXIX (15), April 9.

Krishnaswamy, K.S. (1993). "Karnataka's New Steps Backwards" in *Economic and Political Weekly*, May 1, 1993.

Liddle, Joanna, and Rama Joshi (1986). *Daughter of Independence: Gender, Caste and Class in India*, Kali for Women, New Delhi and Zed Books Ltd., London.

Lipton, Michael (1991). "Land Reform as Commenced Business: The Evidence Against Stopping", Paper presented to an international conference on State, Market and Civil

Institutions, sponsored by the World Employment Program of ILO and Cornell University, December 13-14,1991.

Pandey, Vikash. N. (1994). "Agrarian Transformation and Cooperatives: Continuity and Change" in *Economic and Political Weekly*, XXIX (15), April 9.

Ranadive, Joy. R. (1994). "Gender Implications of Adjustment Policy Program in India: Significance of the Household" in *Economic and Political Weekly*, XXIX (18), April 30.

Seeta Prabhu, K. (1994). "The Budget and Structural Adjustment with a Human Face" in *Economic and Political Weekly*, XXIX (16 & 17), April 16-23.

Shah, Nandini, Sujatha Gothoskar, Nanditha Gandhi and Amritha Chhachhi (1994). "Structural Adjustment, Feminization of the Labor Force and Organizational Strategies" in *Economic and Political Weekly*, XXIX (18), April 30.

For a detailed evaluation of the performance of the Panchayati Raj bodies associated with the Community Development Programme (CDP) in the 1960s, see Jain (1985). Of the several historical assessments of Panchayati Raj now available, this book provides one of the most thorough and informative discussions.

Whether the country-wide establishment of a local government system by constitutional amendment and state legislation may be termed a movement is debated. This of course is also true of the "cooperative movement." In both cases, however, there was substantial involvement of non-governmental agencies of various types, and a degree of activist mobilization suggestive of a movement.

2

THE COOPERATIVE MOVEMENT IN INDIA BEFORE INDEPENDENCE

Before moving further into the writings of the ICU, it is useful to have a brief look at the earliest days of the cooperative movement in India. The essay here lays the ground for discussions of the post-independence cooperative movement by outlining the circumstances surrounding its entry into the country and its early lines of formation. Primarily a government-sponsored arrangement to make credit available to small peasants, it soon began to exhibit the tensions that pull at the movement to this day: that of the relationship with the State and with the non-official intelligentsia, that of external funding needs versus self-reliance; and that of social purpose versus financial soundness. The essay concentrates on cooperatives in western India, a region which saw the emergence of several strong and widespread cooperative networks such as those of sugar and milk.

THE latter half of the 19th century in British India was marked by increasing official attention to the pathetic condition of the peasantry. This concern was not motivated entirely by benevolence; it had its roots in the colonial imperative of maintaining political control. Soon after the country-wide uprisings of 1857, the Deccan region of the Bombay Presidency (comprising parts of present-day Gujarat, Maharashtra and Karnataka) was rocked by a series of revolts aimed primarily at moneylenders. The Committee on the Deccan Riots which examined the disturbances that took place in Poona and Ahmadnagar districts in 1875 reported that the incidents consisted of attacks on the houses of moneylenders by large groups of villagers. The moneylenders were generally warned of what was to come; many of them seem to have complied with the rioters' demands, which were normally limited to the surrender by the moneylenders of their "bond" and other documents — the written evidence of indebtedness – and the destruction of these documents. Little violence followed (Catanach 1970). Similar incidents occurred in 1899 and 1901 in Panchmahals district as well (Hardiman 1987).

In all these incidents, confrontations between peasants and moneylenders seem to have been precipitated by the cumulative effect of a number of factors such as the coincidence of drought with low agricultural prices which made the demands of the moneylenders unbearable. There was also the genuine threat that non-payment of dues would lead to the alienation of land from cultivators into the hands of traders-moneylenders. However, indebtedness seemed to be the perpetual condition of the peasantry, something that was usually borne stoically, and even with a degree of equanimity.

For the British, though, rural indebtedness was a serious political and economic problem. Besides being a law and order headache, the riots demonstrated that any social unrest could indirectly challenge the legitimacy of the colonial State by offering nationalist critics a target for attack. In economic terms, too, indebtedness was an obstacle in the path of the transformation of the Indian peasant into a "progressive" capitalist farmer of the Western model, quick to adopt and invest in technological innovation, capable of exploiting the market to his advantage.

Ironically, the prevalence of rural indebtedness was largely a creation of the British, who had earlier changed property institutions (making land private and mortgageable) and set up an oppressive revenue system that necessitated the sale of agricultural produce. However, after having pushed the peasantry from a largely self-sufficient subsistence economy to an increasingly monetized commodified world where control rested more with the State and the market, the British decided to "liberate" the peasant from the burden of oppressive debt. It must be remembered that the latter half of the 19th century was a time when commercial prospects for Indian agricultural produce generally looked quite bright. Large parts of the Deccan which were earlier fated to be eternally drought-stricken came to be irrigated through canal networks such as the Nira and the Godavari. The American Civil War had resulted in highly favourable cotton prices, and other commodity prices had also risen correspondingly (Morris 1966). To cash in on this boom, it was necessary that peasants have access to adequate credit at reasonable rates.

According to the Deccan Riots Committee Reports, the situation demanded that the powers of the moneylender to alienate land be severely circumscribed. In 1879, the Deccan Agriculturalists' Relief Act was passed, which attempted to halt the transfer of land from the "agriculturalist" to the "non-agriculturalist" classes by allowing civil courts to reschedule debts, and by requiring that all pertinent documents be registered. Similar steps were taken in Punjab, where the problem of indebtedness was further complicated by a communal divide between Muslim peasants and *bania* moneylenders. However, the immediate effect of these measures was a shortage of agricultural credit in the Deccan as moneylenders withheld loans in the absence of land being offered as security. At the same time, investment opportunities were opening up in the industrializing city of Bombay, leading to a flight of capital from rural areas which worsened the credit scenario in the villages. These conditions made it imperative that the moneylender be bypassed as a source of agricultural credit. Several proposals were suggested and investigated – extending the *takkavi* loan schemes, establishing agricultural banks and setting up credit cooperatives – but nothing was actually tried for about 25 years. Then the Famine Commission of 1901, reporting after one of the worst famines ever in the Deccan, added a new note of urgency to these deliberations. The Indian National Congress kept the issue alive through the exertions of members such as Gopal Krishna Gokhale, Pherozeshah Mehta, Dinshaw Wacha and Mahadev Govind Ranade, who persistently raised questions about it in the Bombay Legislative Council. The Government of India also brought pressure to bear on a reluctant Presidency which was sceptical about the chances of cooperatives ever succeeding in India. The Co-operative Credit Societies Bill was finally passed on March 25, 1904.

The New Act and the First Cooperatives

The new Act, and the Resolution which accompanied it, proposed to concentrate on the encouragement of societies for the supply of agricultural credit. It had been originally intended to limit membership to men of small means; it was now thrown open to all, though there were to be precautions against the Act's provisions being used by "persons for whom they were not intended". There was no expression of hostility against moneylenders. Cooperatives were intended to make small, short-term loans for "productive purposes". The implication was that the moneylender was to be left to handle long-term business as well as loans for "social" purposes and family emergencies. Such an emphasis was to have important repercussions. The Act also provided that unless the provincial government ruled otherwise, the liability of rural societies was to be unlimited; this, it was considered, would promote careful and thrifty habits among the members of the village societies. Only when some deposits had been collected by a society would the Government consider making it a loan. Such loans would not be granted automatically. They were to be given primarily as "an earnest of the reality of the interest taken by Government in the movement"; it was not intended to grant loans to new societies indefinitely. It was hoped that urban societies, "lending with the approval of the Registrar to rural societies", would soon come into being. As we shall see, the actual working of credit societies was quite different from the original conception of the Act.

The Cooperative Credit Societies Act provided for the appointment of a Registrar of Cooperatives who would work out the overall policy and oversee its application in the entire province. In July 1904, J. McNeill of the Indian Civil Service was appointed the first Registrar. McNeill had spent some time in his homeland learning about the Irish Agricultural Organization Society, the organizing body for Irish cooperatives, and had even assisted them in their work. He was also enthusiastic about the prospects of starting cooperatives in India. In his first year as Registrar, McNeill concentrated on gathering a staff around him, on obtaining office accommodation in Poona, and on drafting leaflets and having them translated (Catanach 1970:57). He failed to start any societies at all during this year, a fact that seemed to confirm the scepticism of the rest of the Bombay bureaucracy regarding the feasibility of cooperatives. However, McNeill found a spark of hope when he travelled to Betigeri-Gadag in Dharwar district in Karnataka. There he met Canon C.S. Rivington, an Anglican missionary, and his friend Shivaji Ramachandra Kulkarni, who eventually organized the first cooperative society in the Bombay Presidency, the Kanaginhal Agricultural Cooperative Credit Society, in Gadag taluka. The headman of Kanaginhal, Shiddangavda, helped in the organisation of several other cooperatives in the area. In his report for the year ended March 31, 1905, McNeill wrote that eight societies had been registered in Dharwar district since the close of the official year; in five of these "the work was being carried out excellently". At the end of March 1906 there were 31 societies registered in the Presidency; of these, 10 were working satisfactorily. But the Bombay Presidency still lagged behind Punjab where the Registrar had, in the same year, toured one district and had registered 85 societies there alone.

McNeill's early experience persuaded him that the Government of India's idea that societies should not be hampered at the beginning by too many rules was a false one so far as the Bombay Presidency was concerned. "Village communities, far from resenting restrictive rules, are timid about undertaking responsibility without directions as to its exercise," he wrote. There should be no ambiguity about rights and duties, otherwise few would join the societies. So detailed model rules for societies were drafted. McNeill also felt that a supervisor was essential at the level of villages to organize the societies. "Even when the people (of a village) are anxious to have a society and are willing to subscribe capital they expect to be gently pushed through every step and to be given a little breathing time between successive steps." This task could nct be entrusted to the existing village bureaucracy. Thus a system of "honorary organizers" of cooperative societies came to be evolved in the Bombay Presidency. These would be "non-officials" who lived in the rural areas, men with some education, leisure and social standing in their communities, who would voluntarily oversee the work of the societies.

Another early step of McNeill's was of great significance in charting the future course of the cooperative societies. This related to the supply of funds to cooperatives. The 1904 Government of India Resolution on cooperative societies had promised an initial loan to deserving societies, on a rupee-to-rupee basis, up to a maximum of Rs. 2,000. McNeill believed that this sum was insufficient: the amount which villagers could subscribe to qualify for this grant was, he claimed, "only a fraction" of the amount required to finance the year's agricultural operations. "I think that if less importance be attached to stimulating thrift and effort and more to testing the capacity of village communities to manage funds raised on their joint credit the results of the first few years' working may be much more valuable." This was a direct challenge to the public philosophy of the Cooperative Societies Act. C.S. Campbell, the Registrar who succeeded McNeill, continued along the same lines by stressing the spread of the cooperative movement over considerations of financial soundness and self-reliance. In 1911, at the end of Campbell's period as Registrar, there were about 300 societies, compared to 31 when he took up the position. By 1913, there were 515 societies, and by 1914 the total was 698. Indeed, by 1914 the Government of Bombay began to fear that the movement might overreach itself, and laid down the policy that no official pressure should be used to accelerate the formation of credit societies.

The rise in the number of societies was partly the result of the opening of the Bombay Central Co-operative Bank in 1911. The BCC Bank was organized and financed by a group of Bombay businessmen, led by Vitthaldas Thackersey and Lallubhai Samaldas. These men were motivated in part by the *swadeshi* movement which encouraged Indian consumers and businesses to boycott British goods and capital. A number of *swadeshi* banks were established in Bombay about this time amid a great burst of *swadeshi* commercial activity (Attwood 1952:106). The Government of India authorized the formation of the BCC Bank and guaranteed interest on its debentures. Interestingly, the Government of

Bombay did not demand to have a representative on the Bank's board of directors. Share capital for the BCC Bank was raised on the Bombay market, and the Bank was authorized to lend only to cooperative societies. The Bank was financed and directed by wealthy businessmen, primarily Gujaratis, and in the early years, most of the fixed deposits came from a Gujarati who managed investments for the princely State of Baroda. The Bank opened its branches in the Nira Canal area and affiliated credit cooperative societies with itself. It also started purchasing fertilizer in bulk, to supply as a part of the sugarcane growers' advances. In 1926, this operation was reorganized into the Nira Canal Sale-Purchase Union with an elected board of directors – the first of its kind in the Bombay Presidency.

The BCC Bank weathered the Bombay banking crisis of December 1913 and early 1914 remarkably well. However, the Government of India thought it worthwhile to appoint a committee to investigate the cooperative movement's achievements and prospects in detail. This committee was headed by Sir Edward MacLagan, Secretary of the Government of India's Revenue and Agriculture Department. R.B. Ewbank, the Bombay Registrar, was Secretary to the Committee and Lallubhai Samaldas, director of the BCC Bank, was one of its members, with his son Vaikunth Mehta accompanying him as a private secretary. The MacLagan Committee was critical of the existing structure of cooperative lending, with its heavy reliance on the leadership provided by the BCC Bank. Specifically, it held that the main defect of the Bank was that almost all its shares were held by individuals who were "mainly concerned with realizing their dividends". The Bank's directors, being unfamiliar with local needs, had to rely on the Bank's own inquiry staff and, to a greater extent, on the Registrar's staff. Supervision of this variety "provided only an outside view of the working of any particular society". Since the village societies "had not yet combined for mutual supervision and control", but relied entirely on the supervision provided by the honorary organizers, and by the Government and bank officials, the MacLagan Committee felt that some intermediary structures were essential between the provincial and village levels. This resulted in the creation of a four-tiered system of cooperative finance: the "primary society" at the village level; the "guaranteeing union", an association of several neighbouring societies, often within a taluka, which would mutually guarantee loans from banks; the "district central bank"; and the "provincial bank". In a step towards making the BCC Bank more representative of the lower order of the system, its board changed its membership from almost exclusively Bombay financiers to representatives of cooperative societies and district central banks. By 1930, one-third of the share capital of the BCC Bank came to be owned by the societies. With some energetic canvassing by Ewbank, District Central Banks came to be organized in Surat, Thana, East Khandesh and Dharwar (1916), and in Poona and Sholapur (1917). Despite these early landmarks, the expansion of cooperative societies was not an unmitigated success. From the beginning, the results varied according to different circumstances. The next section describes the people who formed the membership of cooperative societies, relating them to the success of the cooperative movement.

Profile of Cooperators

Within 10 years of the appointment of the first Registrar, wheat was being separated from chaff. In 1914 the cooperative societies of Satara district in the "famine zone" had been identified as "the plague spot of the Presidency" (Catanach 1970:96). As many as 113 societies had, at one time or the other, been registered in the district. Already 46 had been liquidated, and a further 15 would have to be wound up. The then Registrar, R.B. Ewbank, declared that "For the submerged debtor, the loafer, or the hopelessly illiterate, no system can create wealth or independence." In this way were defined the lowest income limits to which the cooperative movement would reach in the future. It was decided as a matter of policy that "the man with the economic holding who can do a little more than make both ends meet is our most promising recruit". Who were the people who formed the mass base of "promising recruits" into the cooperative societies in the villages? These were usually medium peasants, those who cultivated their land themselves, with little or no reliance on agricultural labourers. Many of them had established themselves as commercial farmers in the canal-irrigated areas. These people had fared reasonably well in the first two decades of the 20th century. They tended to belong to the *Patidar, Mali* and *Maratha* castes which were dominant in the village economy, and which often had strong corporate bonds. Significantly, the emergence of successful cooperative societies was linked to the non-Brahmin movement in the rural areas of the Bombay Presidency where precisely the same castes sought upward mobility and social reform (see Attwood 1992:88).

However, by 1920 many of the cooperative societies were in trouble. In 1920-21, overdues had climbed to Rs. 18 lakhs. At the end of March,

1923 they amounted to Rs. 31 lakhs, or over 18 per cent of the working capital of the movement. In 1929 more than half of all the societies were burdened with serious arrears. The societies in real difficulties were concentrated in a few areas in the districts of Ahmedabad, Kaira, Poona, Ahmednagar, Sholapur. Bijapur, Ratnagiri and Kolaba. In Ratnagiri, Kolaba and Ahmedabad, the cooperative movement had never been viable, largely because a very high proportion of the cultivators in those districts possessed no land of their own. Poona, Ahmednagar, Sholapur and Bijapur were all potential famine districts; even where they were irrigated, difficulties arose due to the widespread crisis in the sugar industry.

Thus cooperative societies were frequently unable to establish themselves as independent, self-reliant economic entities. This state of affairs was partly due to the economic conditions of the peasantry, and partly due to the structure of cooperative societies as created by the Government (see below). By another criterion of success – that of eliminating indebtedness – cooperative societies had again made only limited progress. By 1923, of the two million agriculturists in the Bombay Presidency, 208,000 or nearly 11 per cent were members of credit societies. The total amount lent to individuals by credit societies with unlimited liability in 1922-23 was Rs. 11,503,380. On the basis of data provided by the Department of Agriculture, the Bombay Provincial Banking Enquiry Committee concluded that the total cash requirements for cultivation in the Presidency as a whole came to about Rs. 32.5 crores. Even if only Rs. 20 crores were required by the agriculturalists annually, the cooperative societies' members would require at least Rs. 2.5 crores, since many of them came from irrigated areas requiring large amounts of capital. Therefore it was estimated that the cultivators who were members of cooperative societies were obtaining from the societies only a little over two-fifths of what they required for current agricultural operations. They were far from abandoning the moneylender.

This was a central contradiction in the credit cooperative movement. Indebtedness was so endemic that most cooperative societies simply could not raise sufficient deposits to allow them to borrow enough to overcome the problem of debt. Without large injections of funds into the cooperative societies, villages had no recourse but to approach the moneylender. This dilemma lay at the root of the gradual differentiation of cooperative societies into financially healthy and unhealthy ones. Only too often, financial soundness was determined by pre-existing levels of prosperity: cooperatives in the dry "famine belt" were the ones that were usually unsuccessful while cooperatives in the irrigated canal areas generally did better. Government policy on this issue tended to see-saw between the desire to prop up the impoverished peasantry in the famine belt and elsewhere, and the urge to invest its funds among the viable peasants with economic holdings. In that sense, the cooperative societies were caught between two models – that of extending *takkavi* loans and that of functioning like agricultural banks. That is, the welfare aspects of the colonial State and its desire for profit were hard to balance. In the event, both these tendencies came to be reflected in the cooperative policies at different points of time. The relative importance given to each depended on the particular configuration at that time between the State, the nationalists, and different classes of peasants.

Relationship of Cooperative Movement with State

There seems to be a general consensus that the cooperative movement in India was, to begin with, the creation of the State. Cooperatives were started by the Government after enacting relevant legislation, and the Registrar himself took an active part in the formation of the first and subsequent credit societies. Since there seemed to be no indigenous institutional arrangement that was similar to Raiffeisen-type cooperative societies, it was decided in India that, to begin with anyway, cooperation would have to be actively fostered from above. From its very inception, the cooperative movement was tightly hedged about by Government regulations, perhaps less so in the Bombay Presidency than in Punjab, since in the Deccan the honorary organizers mediated between the State and members of the cooperative. It was also decided that a minor bureaucracy, "of a reasonably permanent nature", was necessary to assist in the guidance and extension of the cooperative movement. Even the Royal Commission on Agriculture, which claimed in 1928 that "If cooperation fails, there will fail the best hope of rural India", still felt it necessary to recommend, "for the immediate future, a continuance of official guidance and, to some extent, of official control". They urged that every effort be made to build up "a highly educated and well-trained staff of officials" in all provinces.

In many ways, the early history of the cooperative movement is the history of contradiction as a colonial State tried to develop a self-reliant peasantry. The large numbers of cooperative societies that failed and the magnitude of arrears that burdened the bulk of them indicated that there was a fundamental problem in the way in which people perceived cooperative societies. In most cases, they functioned simply as somewhat paternalistic, slightly more benevolent replacements for money-lenders. Rarely did the majority of the members participate in the working of the cooperative societies. Matters were usually administered by the Registrar's staff, the honorary organizers and one or two prominent members. Control over the cooperatives was vested heavily with the colonial government. Ironically, cooperatives were partly encouraged by the Government because it wanted to move towards a framework of "responsible self-government" and towards "democratization"! As Catanach sardonically remarks, "Cooperation was given to the peasants of India, and of Bombay in particular, not because they asked for it, but because some of their 'Guardians' thought it would be good for them." The aim of the Government in the first 20 years of the movement's existence was always, professedly, to prepare the movement for eventual self-control; however, self-control was rarely fostered by the policies of the State.

From the institutional structure of the early network of cooperatives, it would appear that to call it a "movement" would be a misnomer if by "movement" we mean something that involved meaningful local participation and control. Although the fundamental sympathies of some British officials such as the Registrar R.B. Ewbank (in office 1911-19) were with the villager, with whom they felt that "the future hopes of the movement lay", their conception of the villager was highly paternalistic. The villager was thought to be someone slow and simple, yet hardy and in most ways basically honest. The union made up of the "little leaders of the labouring classes" was eventually to be the axis around which the movement revolved. In the meantime, official control at the top had to remain. However, the rapid spread of cooperative societies threw up opportunities in unexpected quarters. In particular, it attracted the interest of a class that the British fundamentally distrusted – the educated elite which was at the forefront of the nationalist movement. Thus the cooperative movement in Bombay at this time reflected to a remarkable degree the attitudes of the British to the whole problem of the transfer of power. Democracy must start from the bottom; "unrepresentative" elites were to be distrusted. It is with these elites and their relationship with the cooperative movement that we deal now.

Role of Nationalists

As mentioned earlier, leading Indian politicians and public men had concerned themselves with the cooperative movement from its very inception. As the network of cooperative structures spread, nationalists found that it offered them an opportunity to engage in public action that had potential to challenge the colonial State. Thus positions on the boards of the cooperative banks came to be hotly contested. In the Poona Central Bank, for instance, the provincial government played it safe by avoiding politically sensitive appointments. Yet the Government was greatly embarrassed when, in trying to raise capital, the bank accepted the promise of a substantial sum from N.C. Kelkar, Bal Gangadhar Tilak's lieutenant. At the first general meeting Kelkar was elected Chairman of the Board of Directors.

In 1917, Ewbank promulgated a draft of the new Cooperative Societies Rules which greatly increased the power of the Registrar. One of the rules read: "No society, by itself or by the Committee or any officer, may take any action which would involve the society in the discussion or propagation of controversial opinions of a political or religious character, and the Registrar may prohibit any action, or rescind any resolution which, in his opinion, is of such tendency." The new rules provoked vehement objections from a group of Bombay men who were rapidly emerging as "non-official" leaders of the cooperative movement with strong nationalist proclivities. A protest meeting was organized under the auspices of the BCC Bank at which people asserted that the cooperative movement could not be entirely divorced from the life of the nation.

Some of the people associated with these protests were drawn into the movement as a result of their personal friendship with Vaikunth Mehta, manager of the BCC Bank, who was inspired by the ideals of democratic autonomy and who consistently sought to limit government control over the cooperative movement. Mehta worked as the Bank's manager for decades, travelling widely throughout the countryside to supervise its operations and promote the ideals of cooperation. Mehta had wide practical knowledge of conditions in the villages and long-standing contacts with their leaders. Although he had never been active in politics, he was sympathetic to the nationalist movement.

Besides Vaikunth Mehta, other members of the cooperative intelligentsia included leaders of middle-class urban cooperative banks and housing societies in the city of Bombay: organizations for clerks and small businessmen, on the whole from the higher castes. There was S.S. Talmaki, a Saraswat Brahmin, who was a pioneer first in cooperative banking and then in the building and letting of blocks of tenements on a "co-partnership" basis. There were welfare workers from the Bombay mills, who saw cooperation as providing a framework for "loan societies". One of them was N.M. Joshi of the Servants of India Society who was to become a distinguished trade union leader. This set of people from diverse backgrounds was beginning to form itself into an intelligent and sometimes impatient group of commentators on cooperative matters. The Registrar eventually had to give in considerably to this group's criticism of the draft rules. Rather than antagonize them, he chose to try to elicit their cooperation. Ewbank encouraged them to produce a quarterly periodical, the *Bombay Cooperative Quarterly*, which was edited largely by Talmaki and Mehta.

At this time, Ewbank, the Bombay Registrar, also founded the Bombay Central Cooperative Institute which was intended to provide "propaganda" and, in Bombay city only, some supervision. The establishment of the Institute was thought hazardous by other cooperative officials. The Madras Registrar advised caution; otherwise, he felt, Ewbank might find that he had placed control of the whole movement in the hands of an unofficial autocracy that would be quite as unrepresentative and far less responsible than the official department. As prophesied, the Institute, given a taste of power in Bombay city, wanted a great deal more elsewhere. On two successive days in December 1919, the nationalist *Bombay Chronicle* devoted editorials to the Institute's affairs. The chief complaint of the *Chronicle* was that the Institute had no concern with the main functions of organization, supervision and audit. "It was presumed," the paper said, "that the Institute, when started, would be entrusted with certain questions relating to the development of non-credit cooperation and would be recognized as the representative association of cooperators in the Presidency." The goal of "absolute self-management in internal affairs" should always be kept in mind in the cooperative movement. "That ideal governments set before themselves when the movement was first introduced into this country, but in many a province it has been well-nigh forgotten." Instead, control was still centered in "the Registrar's department and its ornamental adjunct, the Honorary Organizers."

Ewbank, for his part, stated that "the goal of our policy is to restrict official control gradually to the functions definitely assigned to the official staff in the Cooperative Societies Act and to transfer all initiative, training, finance and development to the cooperators themselves *as rapidly as efficient, representative and democratic cooperative institutions can be created.*" [emphasis added]. However, Ewbank strongly opposed any extension of the control over the movement which was exercised by the district central bank: "The small knot of professional gentlemen and landowners at headquarters", who in practice ran these banks, "were too distant from the village societies to be able to supervise them directly." As early as 1913, Ewbank had been speaking of "democratizing" credit as well as cheapening it. In 1919, a revival of concern about the implementation of the ideals of "local self-government" appears to have spread to the cooperative sphere, which was beginning to be thought of as the training ground for political democracy. However, the cooperative intelligentsia of Bombay were not seen to have a significant place in "self-government". The Registrar observed that "the Central Cooperative Institute can do valuable propagandist and training work but is not truly representative of the movement as a whole and is not in my opinion suited at present for taking over any administrative work". Ewbank stated quite categorically that "the alternative to expert official control is not control by non-official amateurs, however philanthropic, but self-control". Since the "simple but honest" villagers were not yet deemed responsible and competent enough for self-control, power over the cooperative societies remained vested with the official "expert" staff and little "democratization" occurred. In the 1920s, the majority of the intelligentsia associated with the Institute was absorbed in "political affairs".

Around 1916 the ideology of cooperation attracted the attention of Mahatma Gandhi to the cooperative movement. At this time, he was still thought of primarily as a supporter of the war effort, the friend of the Bombay Governor, Lord Willingdon, the "philanthropist" working on behalf of the Ahmedabad mill employees. The Cooperative Department, which wanted to promote cooperative societies among both handloom weavers and factory workers, staged demonstrations at Gandhi's ashram at Ahmedabad for three months during 1916-17. Ewbank and Gandhi went together on one occasion to address a meeting of millhands, presumably to ultimately form a society among them.

In September 1917, Ewbank invited Gandhi to speak at the Bombay Provincial Cooperative Conference on the subject of "The Moral Basis of Cooperation". Gandhi's experience of conducting the Champaran campaign made him appear at the Cooperative Conference a "doubting Thomas before the Jesus of cooperation", as he put it. The "so-called agricultural banks" in Champaran had disappointed him. Cooperation conceived simply as an economic movement, he warned, was not a panacea for the country's ills. The moral as well as the economic aspects of the question needed to be emphasized. However, Gandhi saw the moneylender as not completely evil, but as someone who had good qualities which could be drawn out. It was this attitude that the problem was one of somehow reforming the moneylender, not of removing him entirely from the village, which was to characterize a good deal of the Congress thought on the problem of rural indebtedness in the 1920s.

Almost certainly, one of those who heard Gandhi speak at the 1917 provincial Cooperative Conference was his future secretary and intimate biographer, Mahadev Desai. A close friend of Vaikunth Mehta, Desai had taken up the post of Inspector for the Bank which Mehta had offered. He had travelled widely on behalf of the Bank in both Maharashtra and Gujarat, and had sent detailed reports on the societies. His experiences convinced Desai that the whole question of honorary organizers needed to be reconsidered. Men should be appointed who had "a thorough knowledge of the cooperative principles and of local conditions... men who are keenly alive to a consciousness that they are appointed, above all, to serve the people".

Since the government refused to entrust the running of the cooperative movement to such people, the problem of top-heavy decision-making and the financial problems of arrears continued to persist. Instead of decentralising control, the provincial government chose to pass another Bill in 1922 which attempted to deal with the financial problems of cooperative societies by further tightening legislative control, overriding the protests of nationalists.

The number of honorary organizers was drastically reduced in the 1920s as an acknowledgement of the powerful anti-Brahmin sentiments which were gaining strength; Brahmin recruitment to official posts was also reduced. It had been envisaged that the work of the honorary organizers would be turned over to the supervision union, but the unions were found to have neither the skilled personnel nor the financial resources to perform such a function. As Janardan Madan, the then Registrar, said in 1929 :

> The whole point is this. The Movement is based on democratic principles. But our people in the villages are not yet literate enough or competent enough to work a democratic institution and especially so when it deals with a large amount of money; and the society goes bad because the generality of members are themselves unable to control the actions of the men at the top. If the members are themselves unable to control it, there must be someone else... who

would be able to control it when necessity arises; and if that is necessary... what kind of control should it be?

In the absence of a satisfactory answer to this question, arrears continued to mount. Both the District Banks and the BCC Bank started investing larger and larger funds with commercial banks while cutting down on the loans that they made to cooperative societies. This was hardly what the banks had been set up for. The situation was exacerbated by the high rates of interest that District Banks and cooperative societies persisted in paying on fixed deposits. It was a strange situation. The work of arbitration in the matter of recovery of the societies' dues was vastly increased. In 1927 arrears were very heavy all over the Presidency, especially in the canal areas. In Poona district unauthorized arrears made up 81 per cent of the amount due for collection. It was becoming obvious that many defaulting members had no intention of paying at all. The consequence of over-generous financing and the lack of supervision was ignominous liquidation. In 1928 registration of cooperative societies in the Deccan ceased altogether. A policy of "weeding out" the bad members in all societies was followed.

The discontent caused by the arbitration and liquidation proceedings was seized by the Congress. Gandhi had lost all interest in the government-sponsored cooperative movement. "I am engaged in running the greatest cooperative society that the world has ever seen." After the floods in North Gujarat in 1927, Vallabhbhai Patel and Narahari Parikh showed signs of commencing an agitation against the government policy on cooperatives in that area. To enforce the recovery of arrears after such a calamity was, they felt, completely unjust. Patel spoke on the subject at a public meeting in Bombay. But Vaikunth Mehta visited Patel and managed to smooth matters over. But it was not so easy to smooth over the agitation about the cooperative societies in Bardoli taluka, the scene of the Congress's most concentrated efforts. "Governments have devised makeshifts in the shape of cooperative societies," wrote a Congress worker from the southern part of that taluka. "They may at best offer the riots money at moderate interest and tempt them to run into more debt. They cannot give them any relief. If it can at all be given, it can be given by the *charkha* and by taking away the temptation of Drink."

At the end of the decade, cooperation in Matar taluka of Kaira district, where many societies were slated for liquidation, came under Congress fire. Vallabhbhai Patel, Mahadev Desai and Narahari Parikh were members of a committee led by J. C. Kumarappa which investigated economic conditions in Matar taluka. Cooperation was condemned for its "lack of principle," its "want of human touch," its "lack of expedition". The committee declared that "the cooperative societies movement, which stands for a great principle and holds out a promise of making this world a much better place for all to live in, has proved itself, to us at least, a veritable curse of the Gods".

However, the weeding out process seemed to have served a purpose. After the depression of the late 1920s, surviving cooperative societies emerged leaner but sounder. In 1937, the Vaikunth Mehta-Bhansali Committee investigated the working of the cooperative movement at the request of the new Congress Government and offered a fairly optimistic prognosis. By 1930 many of the foundations had been laid in western India for those post-Independence developments which led to a considerable expansion in cooperative activity. Attempts had been made to integrate cooperative credit with marketing, on the understanding that the problem of indebtedness could not be dealt with in isolation but demanded more complex responses from the State. In many ways, the administration of the movement after Independence had its origins in the battles that were fought before 1930. The State was able to be the 'dominant partner' in the movement because, in the early part of this century, the urban intelligentsia, the cooperative banks and the village societies had all lost, sometimes by default, in the contest for the control of the movement.

REFERENCES

Atwood, Donald (1952) In *Raising Cane: The Political Economy of Sugar in Western India,* Westview Press, Boulder, Colorado.

Catanach, I.J (1970) *Rural Credit in Western India, 1875-1930.* Rural Credit and the Cooperative Movement in the Bombay Presidency, University of California Press, Berkeley.

Hardiman, David (1987) "The Bhils and Shahukars of Eastern Gujarat" in *Subaltern Studies V: Writings on South Asian History and Society,* Oxford University Press, New Delhi.

Morris, D (1966) "The Labour market in India" in Wilbert E. Moore and Arnold S. Feldman (ed) "Labour Commitment and Social Change in Developing Areas", Social Science Research Council, New York.

The debate about the feasibility of cooperatives in India covered a wide range of issues, including whether the 'spirit of cooperation' existed in Deccan villages, whether there was statistical evidence of land alienation on the scale of Punjab, whether cooperatives would succeed in the Deccan "famine belt", and so on. (For more details see Catanach 1970:38-50).

The position of the honorary organizers was a contested one. At different times, organizers faced charges of fomenting nationalist agitation in the countryside, or of partisanship in the anti-Brahmin movement. The changing position of honorary organizers in the movement in Bombay over time reflected different government attempts to control the cooperatives.

The opposition to the Bill in the Bombay Legislative Council was led by L. B. Bhopatkar, the Chitpavan Brahmin chairman of the Poona Central Co-operative Bank and a man who later became prominent in militant Hindu Mahasabha politics. But Bhopatkar and his men could not gain the support from the non-Brahmins and, of course, from the official elements in the Council.

3

THE EARLY YEARS OF THE ICU: PIONEER AND ADVOCATE FOR A NEW COOPERATIVE MOVEMENT*

In the fraught year of 1948 when everything was up for grabs, but when to dream required an inordinate amount of courage and faith, Kamaladevi Chattopadhyaya, one of the more versatile and energetic socialist leaders of the day, managed to inspire a small group of activists, including Dharanı Pal, Srinivas Malliah, Kitty Shiva Rao, B. Shiva Rao, M.L. Sodhani, Jaikishori Handoo, Anusuya Gyanchand, P.M. Mathai, L.C. Jain, Gopi Krishna, Padam Singh, Onkar Nath Sharma, Dr. N.R. Deobhankar, R. Veerapan and M. Natesan, to promote the ICU.

SYMPATHIZER members included M. Ananthasayanam Ayyangar, Achyut Patwardhan, R. Venkataraman, Ramalingaswami Chettiar, B.N. Rau, Prof. Gyan Chand, O.V. Alagesan, Lala Shri Ram, C.M. Poonacha, M.O. Mathai and Malati Ramakrishnan Rao to launch and support the Indian Cooperative Union. The following excerpts tell of this endeavour in Kamaladevi's own words; only the most minor changes have been made for this volume. This piece formed the introductory chapter to a small monograph entitled "Ten Eventful Years," published in 1958 by the ICU, which chronicled the activities of the organization over the decade since its inception.

1947 was the year of decision. The land lay in fragments, India stood in disarray. Across the borders populations in their millions exchanged places in history's greatest mass migration. The unit of this human torrent was the refugee, uprooted from his ancestral home, defeated, dejected, demoralised. The refugee came with the smouldering psychology of the dispossessed. The political argument held no validity for him. He was no chooser. Alone he was a tragedy, in combination human dynamite. The task was to cool his impassioned mind, assuage his griefs, and bring him to understanding, to acceptance – to new ways of life. In

*This chapter presents a broad profile of the Indian Cooperative Union, with the aim of contextualising the ICU's writings which are presented in later chapters.

such times of travail did the Indian Cooperative Union come into being, to add one more shoulder to carry the heavy burden.

Ten years later those troubled times have given place to a certain serenity. The refugee has transformed himself into a new being – a part of the home and a member of the family that is India. His urgent problems have been replaced by the less pressing but equally imperative needs of all who form the family.

The work of the Indian Cooperative Union in refugee rehabilitation through cooperation has now expanded into broader areas of national development – in rural cooperation, small industries, handlooms, handicrafts, social welfare – wherever need exists to help people help themselves. The story unfolded in these pages is not so much a catalogue of organisational achievements as a testament of collective endeavour, not so much a glorification of an organization as a reflection of the transition of the times through the small life and works of a voluntary body.

Journey Through Cooperation

Cooperation has today become a political factor. It is, in fact, becoming the hallmark of political parties. It is regarded as almost an article of faith in the Congress Party, an issue over which several people have resigned to form new alignments. At no time in the history of this country has cooperation been highlighted as it is today, pressed with a kind of feverish urgency, like a house-building programme.

In the time of the British it was a different story. Cooperation was then the hallmark of service to the British regime. For, in all the British colonies, cooperation was part of the government and cooperatives were sponsored, administered and run by the Government as one of its Departments. Cooperation was doled out to the people as one of the many "benefits of British rule," and those non-officials who helped in this task were duly rewarded with titles by the British Raj. Nevertheless, this situation did throw up cooperative personalities who were genuinely devoted to cooperation. Whatever success the cooperative credit movement achieved was largely due to these faithful cooperators who, though to us may seem to have worked in a groove, certainly laid the foundations of cooperation and for that period broke new ground. During the Second World War industrial cooperatives received a fillip, largely from the acute pressure for increased production. But it was more the symptom of an emergency rather than the flowering of a seed and much of it died away as the pressure relaxed.

For most of us who grew up in opposition to the British regime in India, cooperation had no special significance excepting as a means of winning the favour of the rulers. It was a visit to Scandinavia and seeing cooperation at work in Denmark, Sweden and Norway that first revealed to me its potential. There, one saw it not just as an economic lever for providing a means of livelihood or raising income but rather as a social factor, and a way of life. It had been evolved out of the dreams and aspirations of idealists. The strategic and heroic role of the cooperatives in war-torn China under very grim conditions further enriched my own concept of cooperation.

After the 1942 struggle, cooperation came to have a more important place in the socio-political programmes of younger groups like the socialists. Cooperatives seemed to point the way to resolving many problems that were besetting the country, and cooperators were getting endowed with the new idealism, stripped of the scepticism of the British days. The stage was thus propitiously set for a newly oriented cooperative movement when August 1947 dawned. In a way, an edge was provided to this by the partition upheaval and the uprooting of millions.

It was against this background that the Indian Cooperative Union was born. A small band of idealists, who had talked of cooperation as the ideal middle path, saw a great opportunity for putting these dreams into practice and giving them some tangible shape. Thus, while the problem of providing elementary relief to the refugees from Pakistan weighed on the country like some colossus and the thought of rehabilitation seemed almost irrelevant at that time, some did give weight to rehabilitation and cooperation seemed to point the way. To these families, torn away from their age-old environments with not the remotest hope of going back, who had to re-make their homes in strange surroundings, find new vocations, and adjust themselves to unaccustomed things, cooperation had everything to offer. Whatever resources they could muster could be pooled. They had no properties or possessions to part with or share, only their hopes, struggles and labour. They could accept this corporate life with greater ease and less inhibitions. But the refugees had no organization of this quality and nature. The ICU found its first niche in this juncture of need and opportunity.

It was during Gandhiji's last days that he went over the blue print for this organization. The idea held great appeal for him. He studied and discussed it in its various aspects. He even thought it worthwhile to commend it to the Prime Minister, newly in office. But it was characterized as too utopian, one of those new-angled impractical schemes.

Gandhiji was a little regretful but thought it a blessing in disguise. He said, "I shall help and identify myself [with the effort] on one condition. You promise to work on the strength of your idealism and the labour of the co-operators; let it remain a people's organization, not identified with the administration and not dependent on the Government." Cooperation, he explained, was self-reliance where people came together to help each other.

The first problem was to get some cultivable land to start a co-operative farm. All evacuee land was in Government possession. It was hard to convince the administration of this new movement and its experiments. Gandhiji was hopeful of getting land from a private person with whom he opened negotiations. It was being finalised the very week he was taken away from us.

For a while it looked too dark and hopeless and there seemed no way except to abandon it. But that looked like a betrayal, since he had decided to help and identify himself with it. He seemed to have left behind an unfinished task. The Indian Cooperative Union had many travails to go through. The Cooperative Department did not take kindly to it and would not agree to register it. The very concept of such an independent Union seemed like a challenge from a rival body. But the Union soon began to win friends from all sections including the officials. The Union was finally registered after eight long months.

A New Beginning

The first cooperative farm at Chattarpur, twelve miles from Delhi, marked the beginning of a new epoch in the history of cooperatives. Many more were organized. They did not all run to pattern. Some of the experiences were trying and disillusioning. Idealism called for clock-less days and calendar-less periods, infinite patience and faith, whereas refugee rehabilitation compelled urgency, quick results and dealing with people whose faith had been shattered. All the same, there were several landless farmers ready to work through this new medium. No doubt their land hunger was greater than their understanding of cooperatives. We learnt through hopes and heart-breaks that pooling resources for securing services is attractive and feasible, but it is far harder when it comes to pooling land and jointly cultivating it. We realized that cooperation needs a social approach, not merely an economic one. The cooperators have to appreciate and accept the principles through experience, not books or lectures.

The Indian Cooperative Union got a real break when it was invited to participate in the construction of the refugee township of Faridabad for rehabilitating 30,000 Pathans from the North-West Frontier. This was the kind of challenge one faces with the cry, "do or die." The ICU did it. All the big things it had talked of as feasible it demonstrated in achievement. People who had never laboured with their hands, or shouldered a burden, or turned a wheel, gladly and willingly turned the soil, broke stones, made bricks, and sawed wood. The township sprang up like a magic city. The traders, moneylenders and shopkeepers became producers, manufacturers and servicemen. It was not all that easy. The skies were often overcast, the air rent by thunder. But these troubles all passed. Faridabad showed the way to new possibilities in community undertakings and evolved the pattern for community projects in the reconstruction of this country.

The Indian Cooperative Union today covers a wide variety of co-operatives, from rural to urban, from farming to up-to-date department stores, from multipurpose to housing. It is still the dream world of a small group of irrepressible idealists who refused to be disillusioned or dejected and who rejected the thought of defeat. The Union has long since moved on from the refugees to the normal farmer. This journey over the decade has been a long one, but looking back it seems like a brief span, dotted with memorable events, specked by pitfalls, all the same a rich and abiding experience that has filled us with thrills, excitement, expectations, and an occasional disappointment, but above all an unflagging courage to keep on the track, forward on the march to greater and richer experiences and achievements.

The publication, *Ten Eventful Years,* ended with the hopeful verse:

Behold, I scatter this seed broadcast
and flowers shall grow,
And from the flowers fruit
and the fruit shall bear seed.

In the decade that followed, the activities of the ICU expanded and diversified from the setting up and running of refugee cooperatives (co-operative farms for displaced persons or urban resettlement townships) which had occupied its first few years. It moved on to broader issues of agricultural development, regeneration of handicrafts and handlooms, social welfare and research.

Indeed right from day one, Kamaladevi oriented the ICU to adopt socio-economic surveys of the communities to be served as a precondition for planning action. The starting point had to be what the communities perceived to be their goals, problems and likely solutions

It started with a door-to-door survey of landless workers who were settled later in the Mehrauli villages. Then a similar survey of refugees at Faridabad wanting to a build a new life, researching for new avenues of work and income. This was tougher. Landless workers wanted land and they knew the art of agriculture. But, over 90 per cent of the ten thousand families of Faridabad refugees had previous experience only in petty trading, money-lending or shop-keeping. They were at a loss to think of what to do in the new situation. Yet the very process of survey helped them to reflect on their conditions and options or the lack of them – and it turned out to be an important factor that made them accept manual work (as construction workers) in spite of the severe hardship involved which ultimately opened for them many unforeseen new gainful avenues of employment.

Such surveys also helped to link ICU workers intimately with the community who imparted their knowledge about what the community worked for and what its strengths and limitations were. They were thus better able to help in formulating a plan of action and practical steps required to achieve the goal.

As the ICU's sphere of activities expanded, it had also to undertake formal systematic research with good academic backing and specialized knowledge. This led to the setting up of the Research and Publications Divisions led by Rajkrishna and Som Benegal respectively. The quality and distinction they lent to the ICU's work in this field is reflected in the studies/publications reproduced in this book. Then there were a series of monographs on selected topics. The type of research areas chosen by the ICU and the eminence of Rajkrishna attracted some of the brightest young scholars including Balbir Singh, P. C. Joshi, R. K. Madan, K. K. Lamba, Tilak Nijhowne, Shaila Ambegaokar, M. A. Devaki, Kanta Nangia, Malathi Bolar, K. Kaushal, G. P. Srivastava, Ranjit Gupta; N. C. Jain (Statistician in Marketing Research), Dr. Anand Prakash and Dr. D. D. Joshi did short stints. Later, the ICU decided to put the entire Research Division in the fold of an independent organization. It gave birth to the Institute of Social Studies (known as ISST).

Since education is the bed-rock of any cooperative programme, the ICU found it necessary from the very earliest days to conduct systematic educational and training projects for its workers and members, with the help of its Research Division.

Early in its history the ICU began to take up networking activities, such as the first All India Exhibition of Cooperative Products held in 1951 and the Convention of Cooperatives in 1952, when 3,000 workers met to discuss new guidelines for a "creative partnership between producers, consumers, organizers and workers". This Convention located itself and the section of the cooperative movement it spoke for squarely in the socialist camp by adopting the motto "Land to the Tiller" and "Factory to the Workers". It also called for an amendment to the cooperative laws and declared cooperatives a force for radical changes towards a new social order.

In these years, the organization also became a key actor in handicrafts development. It strove to popularize, promote and support handicrafts and cottage industries through the cooperative approach, in order to face the onslaught of mechanization that was sending this sector into retreat. The ICU organized an All India Exhibition of Handicrafts and Products of Cottage Industries Cooperatives in 1952, and in 1952-53 took over management of the Central Cottage Industries Emporium in New Delhi from the Ministry of Commerce and Industry, on the invitation of the Government of India. In the following years, the ICU promoted Indian handicrafts abroad and built up relationships with cooperative and welfare organizations in Britain, USA, Canada and other countries.

By 1953-54, having handed over much of its work with displaced persons to local boards and societies, the ICU began to focus more attention on research and education, taking up national development issues for consideration. It also set up a Publications Division in 1954-55 to take care of its increasing output of documents and writing. Between 1955 and 1958 the ICU produced a series of major documents studying key development sectors in depth and articulating policy thrusts and concrete programmes. In 1955-56 it published a *Report on the Marketing of Handicrafts*, the result of a two-year nationwide survey. Its recommendations were accepted by the Central and State Governments. Studies on consumer co-operatives were initiated.

In 1956-57, the second major research study, *Co-operative Farming – Some Critical Reflections*, stimulated a debate across the nation as it unambiguously attacked government efforts towards joint ownership and management of land and declared that the only cooperatives likely to help farmers were those that assisted them in access to services, implements, credit or marketing without expecting them to pool their lands.

In 1957-58 the ICU once more stirred up a national debate with its thoroughly researched and detailed critique of the Report of the Committee on *Cooperative Law* set up by the Government. Other expanded studies covered *rural credit* and small industries, the Delhi milk supply, co-operative banking, handlooms, and other subjects.

The chapters that follow cover the substance of the ICU's writings on most of the above-mentioned themes. Taken together, they form a comprehensive commentary on the cooperative movement in the early years of independent India.

ADVOCACY

This section of the book presents some of the major contributions of the ICU in terms of a wider advocacy of the principles and perspectives relating to the co-operative movement and as applied to the goals and context of a free India.

It starts with the ICU's proposals for changes in the perspective of the principles of cooperation, democratic substance and social consequence. This is followed by the ICU's advocacy on specific issues such as cooperative farming, cooperative law, cooperative credit, cooperative administration and for forging a united front of voluntary organizations in rural development.

4

A PROFILE OF THE MOVEMENT AND PROPOSALS FOR CHANGE

TEN years after its birth, the ICU, in 1959, held a stock-taking event. Characteristically, the organization examined its existence and identity in terms of the larger reality of the cooperative movement. The event addressed the state-of-the-art in cooperative thought and action in the country and the conditions obtaining in the movement.

> The ICU recognized that in terms of figures there were a large number of cooperatives with their membership running into crores. Yet it felt that there was no real cooperative movement, created, controlled and sustained by the people who have faith in and an understanding of cooperative principles.
>
> As an organization interested in seeing the cooperative movement based on a truly voluntary and democratic basis and eager that the subject should be considered by the movement itself and by those associated with it, the ICU decided to help in arranging a forum for cooperative and other workers to come together to discuss the various ways in which cooperation could be an effective instrument of India's social aspirations.
>
> In line with this desire, the Union sent out invitations to 20 cooperative organizations, 13 other voluntary organizations working in the field of economic and social development, the Ministry of Community Development and Cooperation and the Planning Commission to join in a Seminar on Cooperation.

The Seminar was held at the Vigyan Bhavan in New Delhi on August 21-23, 1959. Besides the cross-section of cooperative organizations and institutions from across the country, a number of key national organizations such as the All India Women's Conference, Association of Voluntary Agencies in Rural Development (AVARD), Indian Adult Education Association and the Bharat Sewak Samaj were present. All the political parties were also represented: Congress Party, Communist Party, Praja Socialist Party, Socialist Party, Swatantra Party and Bharatiya Jan Sangh. Individuals from movements such as Bhoodan also attended. The discussions at the seminar are presented here in digest, as they reveal the essence of the ICU's advocacy work in the cooperative movement.

In welcoming the gathering, L. C. Jain, General Secretary of the ICU, drew attention to the fact that

> . . . the cooperative movement is no more the preserve only of existing cooperative societies. It has today become a matter of national aspiration throughout the country.
>
> So far matters pertaining to cooperation have been discussed at conferences and seminars where a predominantly official opinion was present or prevailed. Even in official circles, however, it is being increasingly realized that cooperation is a much more broad-based movement. The recent policy decisions of the Ministry of Co-operation, for instance, have a very encouraging content and tone which strike a new note in the whole field of cooperative development. We, however, thought the initiative rested with the cooperative movement itself in discussing some of the issues that face it. Both in respect of cooperation and in respect of movement, there is much that is missing. It would be no exaggeration to say that in its true purposes the movement is nearly in a state of stagnation. One does not feel that it is a force which embraces the weaker sections of our society, tries to help them to build themselves up. Its benefits have been largely absorbed by the well-to-do classes in society. We have to face the question squarely whether or not these benefits will ever reach the weaker members of the society for whom they are primarily intended. If the movement should continue to miss the broad masses of our people, the history of the past fifty years will repeat itself. This is one of the basic questions that are among the many before you on the agenda.

J.P. Narayan chaired the seminar and delivered the opening address. The following are extracts from his speech:

> I look upon cooperation from the point of view of, shall I say, the whole of life; cooperation does not, for me, cover only certain special spheres such as the economic. I personally believe in a type of social

organization which one might call a Cooperative Society, i.e. the whole of society to become a *cooperative* society. I believe in that idea and I also believe that the cooperative movement as it is being run in our country and, more so, as it is being run in some other countries, is one of the means by which this "cooperative society" might be brought into existence.

Our society is based largely on the values of competition. Whether it is the educational system, a system of examinations, or whether it is the competitive services, or whether it is business, competition seems to be one of the fundamental bases of our life. I should like this to be changed into a cooperative basis – a new attitude towards life to be developed in which the incentives that competition gives today would come from cooperation. This, I am sure, will be a very difficult kind of a psychological revolution to be brought about. But I think that if cooperation has to come into its own, such a revolution would be essential.

In those countries where cooperation has developed into a big economic movement as, say, in Scandinavia or Great Britain, cooperators are concerned with the loss of the original driving idealism of cooperation in the course of the gigantic development of the movement and its societies. They have become organizations beyond the human scale. Cooperative societies with millions and millions of members who do not even participate in the elections to their committees, to whom the membership of the society really means some sort of economic or other benefit, are no longer cooperative. I believe there is concern in such highly developed cooperative communities also about the decline in the values of cooperation.

We in this country are far behind the West and you have all assembled here to discuss among other things why, in this sense, the movement is so backward. But I hope that all of you will keep in mind the ideals and the values of cooperation and will try to ensure, as far as it is possible to do so, that in the course of the development of the movement these values on which I have laid stress are not lost. Efforts are being made in the country to bring about a psychological revolution much beyond the framework of cooperation as it is generally understood. Our whole freedom movement — at least during its later stages when it really became a movement (a mass movement as distinct from a political agitation) during the time when Gandhiji took the leadership — came to be under the psychological climate of this cooperative ideal of society as distinct from the competitive ideal. And briefly we might say that was the Gandhian social philosophy behind the whole national movement. I think it was for this reason that the Indian National Congress adopted the ideal of the *Cooperative Commonwealth* as its objective which later on was changed to the objective of socialism or the *Socialistic Pattern of Society*.

Personally I believe that the earlier ideal of the Cooperative Commonwealth expressed much better the whole philosophy which Gandhiji tried to popularize in our country. The freedom movement has been fulfilled but the movement for social reconstruction, according to the ideals of Gandhiji, really began after the 15th of August 1947. That movement did not directly link with the cooperative movement as it is called or understood in its narrow sense. But since Vinobaji took up its leadership, the movement has developed out of local efforts at rural reconstruction into a general national movement. An attempt is being made to inculcate among those committed to cooperation in life the idea that it is not enough only to form cooperative societies and register them and carry on some business through them. The outlook of the people towards life has to be changed and they should be persuaded to look upon it as a cooperative venture in which every individual, according to his own ability and equipment and resources, helps others in building a common life.

I should say that one of the best allies of the cooperative movement in its narrower sense is this *Sarvodaya* movement — the movement which is based on love and non-violence, the movement which emphasized cooperation in all aspects of life. Economics are only a part of our life and while we all agree that, in the economic sphere, the highest ideal is cooperation for mutual benefit, today in this age of horror weapons cooperation has become a matter of survival for the human race. It is this aspect of cooperation, this larger aspect, which I thought I should place before you.

In one of the documents of the Indian Cooperative Union, I saw a reference to the *sarkari* and *sahkari* aspects of the movement. I think that was a very beautiful description. It brings out the fundamental problem: whether the movement should remain, as the British Government conceived it, a *sarkari* movement – an official movement – or whether it should really become a *sahkari* movement – a cooperative movement.

Next, the participants in groups and then in a plenary reviewed the present situation of the cooperative movement. The following digest of their report gives a succinct and critical picture of the movement at that juncture in history.

REVIEW OF THE PRESENT POSITION

The cooperative movement in India displays impressive statistics regarding the number of societies registered, membership enrolled, capital invested and business concluded. But the quality and content of the movement can be determined only by evaluating the existing cooperatives as well as their environment, in terms of cooperative ideology and principles.

General Consciousness

Our people in general have no knowledge or appreciation of the prevailing cooperative methods and forms. Generally, the cooperatives that exist have not been formed by them but for them. Psychologically, cooperation today is frequently identified with government grants and loans rather than with self-help and mutual aid.

Sponsorship

Cooperation is a non-political voluntary movement. In India sponsorship of the movement has so far largely rested with the State. State sponsorship kills popular initiative which is the key to all voluntary effort. There are instances where cooperative societies have been formed and used for politically partisan purposes.

Viability

A cooperative is also a business proposition which succeeds only if preliminary assessment of prospects and proper planning precedes its registration. At the same time, even a properly planned cooperative is likely to fail unless it obtains the technically necessary capital and other facilities at the right time.

In India, most cooperatives are formed without any assessment of prospects or proper planning. The general objective is to score a departmental target or use available funds. Cooperatives which have been properly planned are frequently denied the technically necessary capital and other facilities in time and are thus allowed to fail.

Membership

Cooperation is primarily a movement of the underprivileged and weaker sections of society. However, in India, no direct and determined effort has yet been made to take cooperation to these sections. Generally, cooperatives are organized by better-placed people to augment the privileges and benefits they already enjoy as individuals. There are instances of spurious cooperatives where the poorer members serve as dummies in the hands of influential or resourceful persons.

Management

A cooperative is a self-governing and democratic institution in which the day-to-day business is conducted by a duly elected management which holds office only so long as it enjoys the confidence of its members. At the same time, no one who is privately engaged in the same business as the cooperative is elected to the management so that cooperative business may not be wilfully made to suffer.

In India, there are instances where the management is appointed or directed by the Registrars without reference to the General Body. The Registrars are also empowered to suspend, remove or change the management arbitrarily. There are cooperatives which have become pocket organizations of entrenched cliques and vested interests. Sometimes the management of cooperatives includes people who are privately engaged in the same business as the cooperatives concerned.

Supervision

Cooperation is basically a self-governing movement in which the higher levels of a democratically raised federal structure assist as well as supervise the lower levels. Usually the federal bodies also undertake research and education which the primaries cannot afford to do. The health of the primaries is largely dependent upon continuous evaluation and guidance by the federal bodies. In India these hardly, if ever, happen. The primary as well as the federal cooperatives are generally supervised and controlled by the Cooperative Department. The primaries do not create and wholeheartedly associate in the federal bodies, which in turn remain artificial structures without a supporting base.

Audit

Audit is a specialised and technical service to be performed by trained and qualified personnel. In so far as it is intended to inspire public confidence it should be undertaken by an agency which is independent of all parties interested in a cooperative. And if it is to serve its purpose of properly publicizing the performance and prospects of cooperatives, it should be prompt and regular. In India, audit of cooperative accounts is generally in the hands of ordinary departmental employees, most of whom are hardly qualified for the job. Audit is not independent. It is entrusted to the same departments which are responsible for registration of societies, recommending of financial aid and general supervision. As a result, it is widely felt that many acts of financial irregularities, in which departmental officials are involved together with certain members of cooperatives, generally remain undetected. As the cooperative departments have too many executive responsibilities and functions, the audit work is generally neglected and remains in arrears.

State Aid

Cooperation is based on the principle of self-help and mutual aid. But that does not imply that the members of a cooperative should raise all the resources needed for the business of the cooperative. It only means that they shall contribute to these resources to the best of their capacity. For the rest, every State which accepts cooperation as a public policy is obliged to make the necessary resources available without strings attached.

In India, State aid, wherever available, is made conditional on acceptance of departmental control or State participation in the management of cooperative societies. State aid is provided mechanically in accordance with some generalized conventions or departmental rules rather than related to the concrete needs of the business which a cooperative has undertaken. State funds for promotional purposes are almost entirely spent by cooperative departments and seldom made available to the movement itself.

Cooperative Law

The function of cooperative law should be to enable a cooperative to acquire a legal personality on the basis of cooperative principles. Once the cooperative character of a society has been ensured, the law should leave it alone to grow and live its own life. The law should also be simple so that a society does not require the help of an expert every time a legal matter arises.

In India, the cooperative law goes far beyond its essential function of enabling cooperatives to acquire a legal personality. It lays down too many and too rigid rules for the conduct of cooperative business itself. It vests the Registrar and his department with too many statutory and non-statutory powers of interference in the internal life of societies. It is also too complex and has far-reaching implications which legal experts alone can decipher. Under the existing law, cooperatives have to observe too many formalities and maintain too many records.

Summing Up

These problems from which the cooperative movement in India suffers at present are, in fact, organically related to each other and ultimately are the symptoms of a single malady — excessive State interference and bureaucratic control over the cooperative movement. Historically this state of affairs was, to a very large extent, inevitable. Whatever cooperative principles and forms we possess at present were brought into this country from outside and introduced from above by an alien government which was in no position either to explore and experiment with indigenous forms and traditions or to sponsor a broad-based popular movement. Cooperative institutions, therefore, had to remain borrowed devices mechanically imposed on an unprepared and unreceptive soil rather than the organic creations of a popular movement projected along the curve of our specific national genius.

Worse still, these imported forms have lost most of their original idealism in the process of transplantation. In India, these forms were introduced merely as alternative techniques of economic enterprise. The meaning and significance of cooperation were thus narrowed down to a very great extent. The larger vision in which the individual human being was to be encouraged as well as enabled to grow morally and spiritually together with his community came to be completely ignored. As a result, we have in India today a vast structure of cooperatives but they hardly add up to a movement of high social order, inspired and imbued with a distinct purpose. It is not suggested that all existing cooperatives suffer from the defects and drawbacks listed above. The general depressing picture is no doubt relieved by brilliant patches of good growth. For, in spite of the obstacles and hurdles created by the bureaucratic departments, the existing cooperative law and political and other opportunities, some very good cooperatives have managed to come up purely due to the sincere devotion of the cooperative workers and organizers in the field.

In the next phase of discussions, the desired direction of the movement was articulated, before moving on to specific tasks of reform. The report of this section is presented in some detail here, as it provides a statement of the philosophical foundations, rationale and broad parameters of the reformed movement, as envisaged by a substantial cross-section of the non-official part of the movement in the 1950s and 60s.

LINES OF FUTURE DEVELOPMENT

The task before us after independence is not one of merely rebuilding the economy of the country but of bringing about a spiritual, moral and social regeneration. The individual human being must rise and with him the society. We have to provide for the growth of self-disciplined and self-reliant citizens capable of practising self-government at all levels of social existence. It is with this goal in view that the future role of cooperation in India can be properly appreciated.

Cooperation in Life and Living

Today, the idea and practice of competition is acquiring an increasing hold on all spheres of our life. But competition can only breed selfishness and perpetuate imbalance in society. We have, therefore, to encounter competition with a superior idea. And that idea is cooperation. Cooperation brings out only that which is best in a man, allows for its growth, checks any unhealthy tendency towards individual self-seeking and develops a sense of social responsibility. At the same time, cooperation is basically concerned about the individual human being and his all-round welfare. It respects individual freedom and yet accommodates harmoniously a *communitarian* outlook where all are for each and each is for all.

Cooperation does not believe in the survival of the fittest. Its ideal is the family in which the stronger and more influential members practise self-denial in favour of the weaker and less influential members. In an imbalanced society, cooperation is also a unique instrument of the underprivileged and the weak whom it seeks to strengthen by releasing their inner strength and initiative.

Politically, cooperation strengthens the foundations of democracy, provides for decentralization and serves as an effective safeguard against all forms of statism and concentration of power. It encourages the growth of a structurally richer social system in which the voluntary efforts of small communities tend to replace universal coercion of State law.

Cooperation is thus a whole philosophy of life. The future of the movement in India depends upon its being able to persuade thousands of men and women to accept it as a way of life. It is in this perspective that we have to bend our energies to realize our goal of a Cooperative Commonwealth.

Cooperation and Indian Society

Independent India has inherited a social structure which is overwhelmingly composed of small village communities. There are attributes of these communities, such as poverty, ignorance and apathy, which have to be fought and removed. But there is also a great deal of good which obtains there. Life in our villages allows the individual to be near to his community, near to his religion, near to nature and near to himself. We are called upon to make a conscious and deliberate effort to preserve these values and rebuild round them. And here cooperation can play a very important role in both human and economic terms. There is a danger that, in our enthusiasm for increasing the gross national product, we may disintegrate our village communities and destroy these great values. The mass migration to urban areas entailed by indiscriminate industrialization is bound to deprive the individual of these essential conditions of his growth as a fuller, harmonious and contented human being. Here too, cooperation can intervene effectively by pointing out ways and means of increasing our wealth and productivity without doing any violence to that social fabric.

Tapping our Tradition

In order to be able to play this momentous role in the rebuilding of the nation, the cooperative movement will have to draw more and more upon our indigenous traditions and do away with a large part of its alien attire. It is well known that Indian society, since its immemorial dawn, has experimented with a variety of cooperative principles and forms. In fact, the history of the Indian village community is an unbroken record of cooperative aspirations and achievements. Also, the various urban communities, particularly the urban artisans, have developed their own methods and modes of cooperation. It will certainly be worthwhile to investigate and evaluate these traditional forms as well as the principles underlying them. The Seminar, therefore, suggests that suitable research should be organized and undertaken in this direction.

The health of our village communities has noticeably suffered a decline and loss of vitality in recent times. Large sectors of village life no longer present that picture of a harmonious social whole for which they have been reputed down the ages.

A serious inquiry to unravel the real causes behind this decline and loss of vitality has to be made. The Seminar, therefore, recommends that such an enquiry be taken up at the earliest.

Evolving of New Norms

It has been observed by experience in the field that the exclusive use of monetary norms for cooperative business has been partly responsible for giving to cooperation the distorted direction it has taken in this country. Monetary norms are *par excellence* norms suited to a predominantly urban and competitive economy in which capital is more abundant than labour. Cooperative enterprise in the midst of a predominantly rural economy, such as we have in India, cannot confine itself to monetary norms without suffering a serious shrinking of its field of operation and undergoing an unhealthy distortion. Moreover, we have a scarcity of capital and an abundance of labour. It is, therefore, incumbent upon our cooperative movement to devise and experiment with other types of business norms more appropriate to our actual social situation.

Attempts should be made to replace the present monetary norms of cooperative business by labour norms. Labour banks should be established to capitalize the plentiful supplies of labour available all over the country. Norms in kind should also be evolved and implemented. *Dharma golas* in which the farmers can deposit their surplus produce can go a long way towards stepping up the cooperative campaign for small savings. Some experiments in these new norms have been made in the villages under the Intensive Area Scheme. These may be studied for implementation by the cooperative movement at large.

Diversified Development

Ever since its inception, the cooperative movement in India has been rather tightly tied down to the concept of "one village, one cooperative." The multipurpose idea has further intensified this concept. The dominant motive all along has been business expediency rather than the broader values of cooperation. Cooperation implies a certain degree of homogeneity as well as mutual knowledge amongst its members. Also, a cooperative can easily perform functions which are not integrally related to each other. Both these criteria put a limit on the size of the cooperative as well as on the number of its activities.

It will, therefore, be better if large villages which are set up more than one cooperative for the same purpose or purposes. Similarly, neighbouring communities which are too heterogeneous to allow for much mutuality should set up separate cooperatives. On the other hand, several small villages which have a homogeneous population practising occupations which are integrally related may have a single multipurpose cooperative.

Broadly speaking, the cooperative movement should not accept or implement any uniform pattern of institutionalization.

The cooperative device of federalism is always available to bring about whatever degree of coordination may be needed for pooling cooperative strengths and resources. Cooperation is, therefore, not called upon to sacrifice multiplicity and decentralization for the sake of unity and centralized direction.

Mutual Aid Groups

In the procedure adopted so far for the development of cooperatives, institutionalization has generally preceded consciousness. Generally, cooperatives are registered before the members are educated in cooperative principles and methods, tested for their capacity for undertaking cooperative business and allowed to grow into as large and homogeneous a group as is practicable in a particular situation.

A better method of launching cooperatives would be to encourage homogeneous teams of people in a locality, as a first step, to start working as mutual aid groups. The groups can add to their functions as they develop cohesion and efficiency. And then at a suitable stage the groups should be given a legal personality as full-fledged cooperatives entitled to all the responsibilities and privileges under the cooperative law.

Practice of Targets

Letting cooperatives grow in stages and in a diversified manner along natural and organic lines would definitely rule out the present practice of fixing departmental targets for development of cooperatives. Targets, if necessary, should be fixed in respect of volunteers to be trained and put in the field for promotional, educational and organizational work. They can also be fixed in respect of the number of people to be rehabilitated, assisted and provided with employment. But there should be no place for targets in terms of the number of cooperatives to be launched and the number of members to be enrolled.

Cooperation and Planning

That does not mean that planning for the development of cooperatives is ruled out. Planning is important because the various cooperatives operating in a particular area have to be coordinated and provided with a certain common direction in respect of their multifarious functions as also for the allocation of available resources: It is recommended that a population of about 25,000 is a scale on which some kind of local planning should take place. The distance involved between various villages within this population range should be the walking distance with which people are familiar. The various villages under every local plan should know each other, know their environment and know the total available resources. Wherever these conditions of mutual and general knowledge are obtainable over a larger or a smaller population the scale of planning may be accordingly adjusted.

Primary Concern of Cooperatives

The cooperative movement must primarily concern itself with the rehabilitation and welfare of the underprivileged and weaker sections of our society. It should safeguard against the advantages being absorbed by well-to-do persons and vested or political interests. It should immediately start a "clean-up" campaign to purge itself of spurious and unprincipled cooperatives, while all existing cooperatives of the underprivileged people deserving attention and assistance should be revitalized, reorganized and strengthened.

Cooperation and the State

The State should facilitate and assist the growth of this movement with "delicacy of touch and firmness of purpose" so that it can fulfil its promise. The State should remove its multiple and suffocating control; it should halt the expansion of its bureaucratic organs for the promotion and control of cooperation; and it should lay its trust in the ability of the common people to help themselves by erring, if necessary, on the side of freedom which includes the right to make mistakes.

The basic concepts and attitudes underlying State aid to cooperatives should be fundamentally revised so that State aid flows to cooperatives, as far as and as long as it is necessary, without compromising the character of the movement.

State partnership in the management of cooperatives or in the capital of cooperative societies should be avoided except in very exceptional circumstances, purely as a temporary measure, and should be strictly confined to the higher levels of the cooperative edifice. At the same time, the concept of self-help should be better understood. Self-help should be understood to mean that the members have contributed to the maximum of their capacity.

A Cooperative Sector

At present, the totality of our national enterprise is demarcated into two sectors: enterprises owned by the Government are called public enterprises while all sorts of non-government enterprises, including cooperatives, are indiscriminately lumped into the category of private enterprise. This erroneous classification should be given up in favour of a three-pronged one, viz. government, cooperative and private. The Seminar suggests that in all future planning the cooperative sector should be accorded as distinct and well-defined a place as the public and private sectors. As a logical implication of this new classification, the cooperatives should be recognized as *social bodies* instead of *private bodies.*

The next step in the Seminar was to draw up concrete proposals and initiate measures by which the reform of the movement could be carried out.

REFORM OF THE MOVEMENT

The objective is to promote a popular, principled and democratic cooperative movement which becomes increasingly capable of extending and looking after itself by developing its own agencies for sponsorship and supervision.

Grain and Chaff

As a first step, the existing cooperatives should be evaluated in terms of cooperative principles. In consultation with non-official cooperative opinion, existing cooperatives in various States should be classified into the following three groups:

(a) Those following cooperative principles and working well;
(b) Those showing a reasonable promise of qualifying for the first category after a reasonable period of time;
(c) Those working against cooperative principles, or dead or obviously spurious in character

The societies classed in the first category should be declared free from departmental control. The normal functions of supervisions in respect of such cooperatives should be vested in the unions. The societies classed in the second category should be helped and assisted by the movement to qualify for the first category as early as practicable after a proper inquiry.

General Consciousness

Education in the cooperative method is essentially of the nature of adult education. In the midst of prevailing mass illiteracy, no large-scale reliance can be placed upon printed publicity material. The task of educating the common people in cooperative methods should, therefore, be entrusted to various social and educational institutions of a voluntary character, in addition to cooperative institutions and the rural institutes. Educational work should precede actual formation of new cooperatives so that people may own and take pride in what they regard as their own creation.

The need for self-help and mutual aid should be emphasized to the maximum and promises of Government grants and aids should be minimized. The subject of cooperation should receive greater attention in schools, colleges and universities. Students' cooperatives should be organized and steps taken to prepare textbooks on cooperation for school and college students. An appeal should be made to the national executives of all political parties and other social organizations to resolve that they will not use the cooperative movement for political or partisan purposes. At the same time, the political parties may be asked to take a greater interest in spreading cooperation with the clear understanding that this is a constructive work above all party politics.

Sponsorship

The pivot of the movement is sponsorship which entails educational, organizational and promotional work. In so far as cooperation is a voluntary movement, the responsibility relating to sponsorship should rest primarily with non-official organizations, especially with voluntary organizations like the Bharat Sevak Samaj, All India Women's Conference, Harijan Sevak Sangh, Indian Adult Education Association, and the Association of Voluntary Agencies in Rural Development which are concerned about the weaker sections of our society. The overall aim should, however, bè to organize Block, District and State unions of different types of cooperatives. As these federal bodies grow in number and size, the work of sponsorship can be taken up by them entirely.

Important functions of a promotional agency would include :

- examination of preliminary prospects and planning cooperative education and publicity
- promotion and organization
- training of cooperative workers and managers
- research and evaluation.

Membership

Concrete steps should be taken to ensure that the weaker sections of our people are drawn into the movement and that most of the State benefits available are given first and foremost to cooperatives of such people. It should be clearly defined as to who constitute the weaker sections of our people. A workable definition may be:

(a) *Agriculture* : all landless labourers and all farmers cultivating or owning an area of five standard acres or less,

(b) *Industry*: all working artisans, craftsmen and workers engaged in small industries,

(c) *Urban Housing*: all families who are not assessable for income tax purposes.

Management

Every measure, legal and other, should be taken to see that the cooperatives are member-controlled rather than controlled by Registrars, Government officials, influential cliques or private business. The Registrar and his department should not be allowed to interfere in any manner with the election of the management of a cooperative by its General Body in accordance with the bylaws. Nor should the Government be allowed to nominate members on the management committee body of a cooperative.

No member should be allowed to hold more than one elective post at a time in the same cooperative. No member who is privately engaged in the same business as the cooperative should be entitled, under its bylaws, to hold any elective post in the management of the cooperative.

Suitable provisions may be made on the revised cooperative law for safeguards against exceptional cases where there may be maladministration, misappropriation or complete violation of the cooperative law. In such cases, reliance should first be placed on the supervisory unions which should act in this matter. On their recommendation, the Registrar or any other authority provided may take suitable action.

Audit

As far as possible the normally available services of chartered accountants should be utilized by the cooperatives. There are, however, a large number of societies which are situated in the interior where access to chartered accountants is not easy. For assisting such cooperatives, the unions exercising supervisory functions over them should maintain panels of approved chartered accountants. There are also likely to be cases of cooperatives which cannot meet the costs of auditing for various reasons. For all such exigencies audit service should be subsidised by the State.

Functions of Unions

The supervisory functions which are at present exercised by the Registrars and their departments should be entirely vested in the unions. The unions should enjoy a statutory recognition under the cooperative law and be responsible for helping constituent cooperatives in following cooperative principles and conducting their affairs in accordance with their bylaws. The unions should be encouraged to undertake promotional activities as outlined above. In addition the unions may:

- Aid and advise cooperative societies in business management, technical, organizational and legal matters .
- Supervise member societies to ensure observance of the provisions of the cooperative law, bylaws and resolutions of the general meetings of societies.
- Promote harmonious relations between the member cooperatives and help in the settlement of disputes among member cooperatives and between a cooperative society and its members.
- Investigate, where necessary, the working, business, accounts and other affairs of an affiliated society.
- Provide counselling services to all member cooperatives.

Summing Up

The core of all reform measures suggested is greater internal autonomy for cooperatives, promotional and supervisory roles for unions of cooperatives and a minimum of State control and interference. Cooperative law should be simplified as well as purged of all provisions which give control of the cooperative movement to the Registrars and their departments.

ROLE OF THE STATE

The State has played in the past and will continue to play in the future an important role in the development of cooperation in the country. We have, therefore, to consider what may constitute a principled and purposive relationship between the State and the cooperative movement. The State comes into contact with the cooperative movement at two points. First, it regulates the movement by means of cooperative legislation and the departments created by such legislation. Second, it finances the movement for its developmental and business activities. The relationship between the Movement and the State should, therefore, be redefined in respect of these two points of contact.

Revision of Cooperative Law

Cooperative legislation in India was founded on statutes which were already in disuse in Britain for over fifty years. During the last fifty-five years the original law has been changed or modified invariably in a manner as to make it more rigid and authoritarian. The statutory powers and the non-statutory (assumed) functions enjoyed by the Registrar and his department combine to prevent the establishment or growth of cooperative societies enjoying voluntary character and internal autonomy. Cooperative legislation, as it exists in India, therefore, requires not just a few modifications here and there, but a fundamental and comprehensive revision.

Terms of State Aid

While it is envisaged that through reforms in the cooperative law, the movement will become autonomous, self-directing and self-expanding, it is not likely to become self-supporting for some years to come. In the transitional period the movement will have to depend on financial aid from the State. And it is here that the danger of State control by the backdoor has to be spotted and guarded against. It has been observed that the Registrars and the Reserve Bank exercise much better control and influence over the movement and its constituents in the process of giving financial aid than is envisaged by the much criticized cooperative law and its authoritarian provisions. We have, therefore, to devise certain principles so that State aid becomes available without compromising the basic character of the movement.

State aid should be accepted by the cooperative movement as temporary and transitional. The aim of the movement should be to develop its own resources as fast as possible. No thought of permanent dependence on the State should be permitted. The cooperative movement should be prepared to accept supervision of its accounts only in so far as it relates to the proper utilization of State resources.

The Centre and the States

Under the Constitution of India, cooperation is a State subject. The various States provide funds annually for development and other purposes, and their resources are annually augmented by the Union Government. The Seminar recommends that the Union Government should provide funds directly to the movement for all development purposes. The State Governments should continue to shoulder the main responsibility of assisting the cooperatives to stand on their own feet and accomplish their business in a satisfactory manner.

Cooperative Grants Commission

The development work proposed for unions and other voluntary agencies has no profit or commercial content. The work has, therefore, to be supported by the State as a part of planned development expenditure. A Cooperative Grants Commission should be set up by the Union Government for purposes of providing State aid for developmental purposes. The Commission should be an autonomous and statutory body, serving the Union Government. It should give grants to promotional bodies for the range of promotional activities enumerated above. The grants given by the Commission together with the purpose for which they are given should be regularly published in a Gazette. An annual report of the Commission's work should be placed before the country. The commission should not interfere in the internal working of the grantees, who should be left free and unhampered to carry out their mission. Any rules made by the Commission for the issue of grants or other general conditions imposed on the grantees should be published in the Gazette. The grantees on their part should submit to the Commission annual audited statements certifying the use of funds as well as annual reports of work done.

State Cooperative Development Boards

The responsibility of providing assistance to cooperatives should be entrusted to a Cooperative Development Board set up in each State by its Government. The Boards should be autonomous bodies, considering applications from the cooperatives on the recommendation of the promotional bodies. Before any finances are actually advanced to a society, the Boards in consultation with the promotional bodies should make sure that members of the society concerned have themselves made the maximum contribution they are capable of. In cases where the banks hesitate or hedge in providing adequate loans to deserving societies, the Boards should take suitable steps (including advances out of their own funds) to help the cooperatives stand on their own feet. The State unions should be encouraged to take over the functions of the Boards within the next five to ten years.

Summing Up

Under the present dispensation, the cooperative law as well as State financial aid to the cooperative movement are administered departmentally. A substantial part of the total funds available are spent on staff and establishment of the departments which have grown enormously since Independence. In the new scheme of things, all this should be taken away from the departments and vested in special bodies set up by the Central and State Governments and consisting predominantly of non-officials having knowledge of and faith in cooperation.

These, then, were the changes that the participants of the Seminar proposed. A further stage of the Seminar went into discussions of changes needed in specific sectors such as cooperative credit or farming. These sectors are discussed in detail in the later chapters.

Recommendations for changes in the cooperative legislation are covered in detail in Chapter 6.

5

COOPERATIVE FARMING

ONE sector of the post-Independence economy where the ICU had hands-on, practical experience was in the initiation and management of farming cooperatives. These experiences had a particularly experimental character as they involved cooperative farms set up for the refugees from Pakistan. The resettlement farms were creative entities, in social, economic and political terms, of an uprooted people thrown together in a new context. They offered ample scope for innovation and experimentation in community development as well as in the technical aspects of farming and the running of cooperatives. In 1955 the ICU undertook evaluation studies of the working of three of these cooperatives and submitted its findings to the Ministry of Food and Agriculture in the form of monographs. (Regrettably, these monographs are not included as they could not be traced.)

In 1956 the ICU brought out a more general document on cooperative farming, drawing on its own experiences, but also on observations and studies of farming in the rest of the country and abroad. Characteristically, the document addressed an aspect of recent government policy and took up a polemical position against it. It dissected the basis of the policy and assembled scholarly as well as empirical material to counter these hypotheses. The ICU reports that this paper evoked considerable controversy all over the country when it was published.

Reading it today, one is not surprised. The document is a fascinating piece of argument, in terms of what it reveals about the ICU's precise standpoint (and, presumably, that of a section of the cooperative movement) within the complex applications and affiliations of cooperative philosophy, both in general terms and in the particular context of the political economy of India in the 1950s. In contrast to the intense idealism that characterized the ICU's stances on most subjects to do with cooperation, here its arguments are stubbornly pragmatic. They also stand on a solid empirical ground. The land reforms of the 1950s had the effect of securing ownership rights in the hands of a vast mass of tenant-cultivators but failed in the enforcement of ceilings legislation and in outright redistribution of land to the landless and marginal peasants. As Charan Singh notes,[1] "millions of tenants were made secure on their land and freed from a host of illegal exactions". The benefits of the reforms were significant, given the pre-Independence agrarian structure, where the colonial administration had explicitly countered absolute rights in land to cultivators, while giving surplus- and rent-extraction powers to non-cultivating intermediaries, with the result that production suffered greatly. In the post-Independence period, cooperatives formed an important institutional support for the movement of the peasantry towards modernized, capitalist farming.

However, as Lipton (1993) points out, the beneficiaries of the 1950s land reforms were not usually among the poorest; the reforms' main effect was to broaden the base of middle peasantry and a dominant proprietary class of owner-cultivators, albeit with a limited capital base. These classes formed the coalition that embraced the Green Revolution measures and began to win extensive support and privileges from the State. The functions of cooperatives in this context, as analysed by Pandey (1994)[2] and others, were to protect the newly acquired land rights of these classes by rendering crucial assistance in access to inputs for cash-crop farming, and to prevent them from slipping into the hands of rich gentry and moneylenders. Pandey writes of "the exact nature of land reforms and cooperatives under 'mixed economy' which are quite distinct from collective/communal ownership, farming and distribution. In the Indian context both (land reforms and cooperatives) were, conceptually and operationally, based on the idea of private property and protection offered under the agenda of 'freedom to the individual'

In the document "Cooperative Farming," the ICU, although composed of some prominent socialists, explicitly upholds this agenda. It does this in opposition to the State which, in a thrust of somewhat confused democratic socialism, was experimenting with "cooperativized" farming (involving the pooling of land by peasants) as an alternative means of moving towards modernized (mechanized) agriculture.

Cooperation in this chapter appears for us in some of its extremely contradictory guises: as a State-sponsored socialist instrument, with coercive undertones, and as an instrument of a capitalist proprietary class struggling to protect their individual property rights. The ICU clearly throws its weight behind the notion of cooperation as founded on the individual as the inalienable ultimate protagonist of progress and societal well-being, on respect for the individual rights and individual freedom as its basic value.

I. COOPERATIVE FARMING: SOME CRITICAL REFLECTIONS

Policy of the Plan

The term "cooperative farming" is often used indiscriminately to denote all kinds and degrees of agricultural cooperation. But in the Second Five Year Plan and in a resolution of the Conference of State Ministers for Cooperation held in Mussoorie in July 1956 it had been given a categorical meaning. It has been stated that "cooperative farming necessarily implies pooling of land and joint management" (*Second Five Year Plan,* p. 201). It is to be distinguished from "other forms of cooperation in agriculture such as cooperation in non-farm operations, that is, marketing, processing, obtaining special services ... without surrender by each farmer of his right to manage his field as he chooses". Such cooperation is to be called "better farming". While all cultivators in the village can avail themselves of the general departmental services and the common facilities offered by the multipurpose "better farming" or large-sized credit societies, those who pool their lands in cooperative farming societies are to get special subsidies for administrative expenses, credit on specially liberal terms, preference in consolidation proceedings, preference in technical assistance, preference in the supply of seeds, fertilizers and construction materials, and special financial and technical assistance for developing ancillary occupations. The target provisionally recommended is to have at least one cooperative farm in every National Extension Block (or about 5,000 covering the whole country) during the Second Plan period (*Second Five Year Plan,* pp. 203-204). Resolution No. 5 of the Mussoorie Conference, "All India Cooperative Review", August 1956, pp. 292-93).

The programme proposed for the immediate future is admittedly "experimental". The need for flexibility in respect of the internal organization of cooperative farms is recognized. Land may be pooled but the owners may be given ownership dividends or shares of the value of land pooled or agreed rents.

The farm as a whole may be managed as a single unit for all purposes or for some selected purposes. Groups of families may form sub-units within the cooperative farm. Or, as is likely, in the first stage of cooperative development there may be family holdings supplemented by joint work for specific purposes (Second Five Year Plan, p. 202).

Thus the real purpose of pooling land, namely, the joint conduct of all or most farming operations, may not be immediately realized. The so-called cooperative farms may still be merely associations of family farms joining in partial cooperation to secure government assistance or some common facilities.

But it is clear that the long-term aim of the planners is general "cooperativization" of farming (with pooling of land and joint management)[3] not only in individual cooperatives but in the village as a whole. In the *First Five Year Plan* itself "cooperative village management" was suggested as the "more comprehensive goal towards which the rural economy should be developed" (p. 195). Land management legislation was recommended to enable the village community "to manage the entire area of a village, both cultivated and uncultivated, as if it were a single farm" (p. 197). In the *Second Five Year Plan,* again, cooperative village management in this sense remains "the main direction of reorganization in the rural economy" (p. 223). The aim is "to enlarge the cooperative sector until the management of the entire land in the village becomes the cooperative responsibility of the community" (p. 206).

Though, therefore, the policy recommended by the planners for the time being is termed experimental there can be little doubt that they have already decided upon general "cooperativization" of farming as their settled long-term policy. The purpose of experimentation seems to be merely to evolve appropriate techniques for implementing this policy in terms of detail — incentives, methods of pooling, methods of assigning and evaluating work and distributing proceeds, etc. It is necessary, however, that the merits of the basic policy itself are closely examined. It would be a mistake to adopt a policy of general cooperativization merely because it has some theoretically conceivable economic advantages. Its deep and far-reaching social implications should also be taken into account. We have to analyse the benefits expected from the cooperativization of farming and see how far they are really realizable in Indian conditions.

Some Basic Facts

The basic facts about the size and productivity of farming units in India are well known. Fifty-nine per cent of the farms in India, covering 15 per cent of the total cultivated area, comprise five acres or less. Ninety-four per cent of them, covering 66 per cent of the total cultivated area, have 25 acres or less. In many States,[4] including U.P., Bihar, Madras and Travancore-Cochin, more than 80 per cent of the holdings are below five acres. A recent enquiry in Bihar revealed that 33 per cent of the holdings were less than half an acre, 50 per cent below one acre, 69 per cent below two acres, 78 per cent below three acres and 87 per cent below five acres *(Indian Journal of Agricultural Economics,* August, 1954, p. 25).

The Rural Credit Survey has brought forth new evidence about the average earnings of Indian farmers. About one-third of the cultivating families were found to have a gross produce of the value of less than Rs. 200 per year, and about half of them a gross produce of the value of less than Rs. 400 per year. The farm expenses of the former exceeded the value of gross produce by 25 per cent. All farming families have to supplement their farm income with other income, the most important source of which is wage employment. But cultivating families of the lower strata are more dependent on wage receipts than those of the upper strata. Cash wages constituted about half of the total cash receipts of the former (*The Survey Report*, Vol. I, p. 72).

Thus it is obvious that at least half of the cultivating families in India are not able to earn even their barest subsistence from farm operations alone. "It is futile to consider them as independent units of land exploitation...". (Gadgil, D.R, *Indian Journal of Agricultural Economics,* 1955, p. 20).

Enforcement of a Floor

The smallness and continuous subdivision of holdings is usually regarded as the chief cause of farmers' incomes being so low. Therefore, numerous proposals have been made from time to time to secure the integration of small holdings. One of the suggestions frequently made is that holdings below a specified minimum size be compulsorily combined by law. The Agrarian Reforms Committee suggested compulsory cooperativization of holdings below the "basic" size (after a period of experimentation with voluntary cooperativization).

Professor Gadgil has suggested the enforcement of a "floor" by legislation. The floor should be determined "in relation to the ability of the State to pool the holdings of uneconomic holders". Professor Dantwala has also recommended that "with the least possible delay, production on such (sub-marginal) units must be banned. To be able to cope with the administrative problem we may keep the limit fairly low". He suggests that the sub-marginal farmers may either sell out their land or surrender it and take employment. Or they may merge their holdings with those of their neighbours and agree to joint cultivation. Or they may undertake cooperative joint farming (*Indian Journal of Agricultural Economics,* 1953, p. 97, and 1955, pp. 29,31).

No State in India has so far taken action on these lines. In Bhopal, Madhya Bharat and Hyderabad some provision has been made in the land reform legislation to the effect that holdings of less than a specified size cannot be sub-divided in the future. But the concept of a "floor" has nowhere been used to enforce the combination of existing small holdings. The Bombay Small Holdings Bill of 1927, containing provisions to this effect, had to be dropped on account of the strong opposition it aroused.

In many countries of Western and Southern Europe also the problem of small holdings is very acute. But because of their socio-political background very little has been done so far to solve it directly. In France, Denmark and Germany some steps have been taken to prevent further sub-division of holdings. Only in Sweden (and, very recently, in Norway) has some action been attempted to combine existing holdings into larger units. But the process of combination is strictly voluntary. Small holders continue to receive substantial subsidies. They may pool their holdings in cooperative farming societies, but the societies receive government loans on the same terms as individual farmers. So the process of combination is not making much headway. The actual decline in the number of farms in the 2-10 hectares group between 1944 and 1951 was only one per cent in Sweden (Gullander, *Farmers' Cooperation in Sweden,* p 134; *Economic Survey of Europe,* 1955, p. 139).

In Southern Europe, again, "experience shows that it is difficult under the pressure of land-hunger to avoid excessive sub-division" (*European Agriculture,* FAO, p. 48). In Eastern Europe, in spite of the redistribution of land, the density of the agricultural population did not permit the allotment of more than an average of four to five hectares of cultivable land per family. Since postwar collectivization affected only a small proportion of the total agricultural area (except in Bulgaria), small holdings continue to predominate. Thus wherever the density of the agricultural population is high and the population is rapidly increasing the problem of small holdings remains and becomes progressively more serious. Considering the requirements of rational agriculture, the persistence and multiplication of small holdings appears to be exasperating. But as European experience shows, until industrial growth brings about a substantial reduction in the manpower dependent on agriculture, it is difficult to do much to solve the problem directly within a democratic framework. Although many economists continue to favour it in India, the proposal to combine or cooperativize all holdings below a specified size by law seems to be utterly impracticable in view of the experience in other democratic countries as well as the probable opposition it is likely to encounter in a peasant democracy like India (not to mention the magnitude of the administrative task involved).

At best, further sub-division may be prevented, though it would require great administrative vigilance to secure that provisions to this effect are really observed in practice. It must be realized that the enforcement of a "floor" is an enormously more difficult affair than the enforcement of "ceiling" — for it would affect almost half of the peasant families in India. We are very far yet from the imposition of ceilings on further acquisitions throughout India; we are farther still from ceilings on existing holdings; and quite remote from the enforcement of a "floor," no matter how imperative it may seem to many of us on logical economic grounds.

The imposition of ceilings as proposed in the Second Five Year Plan is, in any case, not going to facilitate the imposition of "floors," for it would not release more than five per cent of the total cultivated land for redistribution. If landless workers are given a prior claim on it, as they ought to be, the land likely to be available for enlarging the smallest holdings would be negligible.

Estate Farming

If economic considerations only were supreme, the imposition of ceilings would be very questionable. An enlargement of the scale of cultivation could conceivably have been achieved through an extension of capitalist estate farming — had no ceilings been imposed. Big landowners could have evicted and expropriated the small farmers or purchased their holdings and started modernized farming on large contiguous estates. A process analogous to the enclosure movement in Britain could have taken place. Millions of small farmers would have been turned into wage-workers or destitutes but the size of the farming unit would have increased. To a small extent this has been happening already on a number of estates resumed by zamindars for personal cultivation after the abolition of *zamindari*. Substantial investments and improvements have been made on many of these "resumed" estates. The point is that if estate farming is universally rejected on considerations of social justice and harmony, in spite of its economic merits, such considerations cannot be ignored in determining the role of cooperativization.

Cooperativization and Economies of Scale

When the integration of small holdings through legislation or through an extension of estate farming seems to be impracticable, a programme of "voluntary" cooperativization on a large scale appears to many as the next best alternative. Such a programme is advocated partly on the basis of the theory of economies of scale and partly the experience of cooperative farming. It is, therefore, necessary to examine very carefully both the theory of economies of scale as applied to agriculture in Indian conditions and the experience in foreign countries.

Man-Land Ratio and Mechanization

It needs to be recognized that the reorganization of agriculture – whether it takes the form of cooperativization or any other form – cannot alter the basic man-land ratio significantly. It cannot alter the unhappy situation in which a large number of people have to draw their livelihood from a small area of land for want of alternative avenues of employment. This basic problem can be solved only through an expansion of industrial employment opportunities. All that agricultural organizations can be expected to do is to increase the produce, and hence the income, from that small area. Since land is the scarce factor, "the objective of economic policy is to maximize output per acre, and not output per worker" (Lewis, *Economics of Growth,* pp. 129-30). Therefore, the merit of any proposal for agricultural reorganization should be judged primarily in terms of its effectiveness in raising the output per acre.

The enlargement of the size of the farming unit would be more important and imperative if land and capital were abundant relative to labour and it were feasible to mechanize agriculture on a large scale. But in India, as the Planning Commission has stated, "In agriculture, except under certain conditions in the present stage of development the possible economic advantages of mechanization may be more than offset by the social costs of unemployment that such mechanization would involve" (*Second Five Year Plan,* p. 113). It has been estimated that the working force in agriculture is likely to increase from 109.5 million to 111 million during the next five years in spite of the rapid industrial development envisaged in the Second Plan and the creation of non-agricultural employment of the order of 7 million (*ibid*, p. 115; "Tentative Framework", p. 28). Mechanized methods may need to be used for bringing under the plough new land which could not be cultivated otherwise. For the rest, hand cultivation would have to continue for a long time. It may be pointed out in this connection that though the Chinese have launched upon collectivization, they do not "propose to have mechanization of agriculture for the next 10 to 15 years" (P.N. Thapar, p. 20). And in Japan, while post-harvesting processes like threshing, hauling, etc., are being extensively mechanized, other operations such as seeding, planting, weeding and reaping continue to be performed by hand (*A General Survey of the Agriculture of Japan,* Ministry of Agriculture, Japan, March 1956).

Economy of Labour

One of the points usually made in discussions of cooperativization is that it would "bring into the open the disguised unemployment inherent in owner-operated dwarf farms. The cooperatives will soon be faced with the problem of surplus labour. This isolation of the phenomenon of surplus labour is a necessary step in the programme for its reabsorption in the non-farm occupations" (Dantwala, *Indian Journal of Agricultural Economics,* March 1953, pp. 97-98). In other words, a more rational use of labour made possible by cooperativization would bring out the underemployed. But it is difficult to understand how the mere "isolation" of the problem brings us any nearer its solution, when the rate of labour absorption in industry is severely limited due to other factors. In this matter we must learn from the experience of collectivization in Eastern Europe. One of the aspects of the economic crisis it created there was that industry was not "capable of immediately absorbing redundant agricultural labour" (*European Agriculture,* p. 59).

The scope for the rationalization of work is in any case limited in agriculture. A high degree of specialization is ruled out by the nature of operations. As Cohen says, "There are few operations in agriculture which must be repeated for all of every day, so that a man has no opportunity of concentrating on one small motion. A farm worker can only plough, harrow, and harvest the crops at the right seasons of the year, and must be able to perform all these operations. Cows must be milked twice each day, and pigs fed; but the stockman cannot spend all his time on these tasks, and must perform others as well.... In variable climates ... it will be extremely difficult to reduce production to a routine since the work to be done will vary from field to field, and alter as the weather changes. For this reason such farming generally involves a number of detailed decisions, which must be made rapidly and cannot be easily delegated to anyone other than the farmer himself" (*Economics of Agriculture,* pp. 54-56). Thus in agriculture much labour may be saved through mechanization but not much can be saved through the introduction of a minute division of labour. Labour costs on family farms are often lower than on (not very mechanized) large farms, for family labour is better able to adjust itself to the peculiar nature of agricultural work than paid farm labour working to a rigid routine.

Problems of Management

As the size of the unit increases, the difficulties and cost of management also increase faster in agriculture than in industry. The workers are spread over a much wider area and the supervision required is much closer than in industry. Thus it becomes necessary to have supervisors for every small group of workers. But again because of the nature of the operations the supervisors cannot be fully occupied merely in supervision. In other words, a complete separation of managerial and manual functions is very uneconomical in agriculture (Cohen, *op. cit.,* p. 56). This accounts for the excessive costs of supervision and management in the Soviet collective farms about which there has been continuous criticism in Soviet economic literature.

It is due to the diseconomies of large-scale management in agriculture that the size of the optimum unit is relatively low in agriculture in most countries — except where the abundance of land and shortage of labour make the existence of large mechanized farms unavoidable. These diseconomies begin to offset the other economies of scale fairly soon. That is why money returns per acre on smaller family farms are often higher than on large-scale farms. In countries suffering from an acute shortage of competent managerial personnel and general illiteracy of farmers, the disadvantage of large-scale farming is even greater.

Thus, in labour surplus countries where the scope for the mechanization of agriculture is limited, and economization of labour is unimportant, the realizable economies of scale, so far as farming operations proper are concerned, are insignificant. Therefore, the argument for cooperativization in so far as it rests on the theory of economies of scale applied to farming operations is very weak.

Work Assignment in Joint Farming

It becomes weaker when we consider the practical difficulties of running a joint farming cooperative. As a UN study says,

> ". . . to assign tasks among members and ensure that they are carried out effectively is often difficult because the managers and foremen who are selected by majority votes . . . must act in a way to win general favour and this is often not the way that achieves the highest standard of production. Correctly to compensate individual members for work done is also difficult. Differences in skill and conscientiousness are wide, and since most workers cannot wait until the end of the farming year, advance payments, which many come to regard as wages, have to be made. Their own feelings of responsibility for the economic efficiency of the cooperative are therefore reduced. Jealousies between efficient and inefficient workers can be serious. The distribution of profits at the end of the year is likewise difficult to make fairly".
>
> (*Rural Progress Through Cooperatives,* p. 81).

The essential dilemma is that if the numerous heterogeneous and often discontinuous farm operations, requiring varied degrees of exertion and skill, are valued and paid for without much differentiation, inefficiency and light work get a premium and labour costs are inflated; if accurate differential evaluation is attempted, overhead costs are inflated. The measurement and evaluation of different types of farm work is extremely difficult. Even after twentyfive years of experience with differential work evaluation in the Soviet kolkhozy we still hear of grave "shortcomings in the standardization of work, in the laying down of standards of production and the valuation of the labour involved in workdays" (N. Barou, *Cooperative Group Living,* p. 76).

Where management is democratically elected, discipline is poor and efficiency suffers. Where management is authoritative, the cooperatives lose their cooperative character, overhead expenditure increases while the discontented members go slow. On all accounts, the cooperatives are afflicted with discontent and dissension. For this reason, "large cooperative enterprises run by the workers themselves have seldom been successful in history" (Lewis, p. 135). In India, dissensions which would normally arise due to purely economic reasons multiply manifold on account of casteism and the indiscriminate mixing of landless labourers, tenants, and small and medium owner-holders which must take place in cooperative farms.

The Peasant Mind

The greatest drawback of cooperativization, however, appears when we consider the psychology of the peasant. Productivity depends much more on the personal interest of the worker in agriculture than in industry. In industry a worker can be "functionally" efficient even if he is utterly uninterested in the work, because work is highly routinized, impersonalized and mechanized. But intensive farming is not a matter of routine. The yield of the land depends directly on the care with which the farmer cultivates and conserves the soil and protects the crop. Hired workers or members of large cooperatives can hardly be expected to cultivate the soil so intensively as well as peasant proprietors or tenants with secure long-term rights. Peasants the world over have consistently demonstrated their reluctance to work wholeheartedly under any collective arrangements which deprive them of a sense of secure personal possession of the land they cultivate and the crop they harvest. Under all such arrangements many of the expected economies are outweighed by the diseconomies of peasant indifference and sloth, the diseconomies of constant dissension and the diseconomies of bureaucratization necessitated by the situation.

The sense of property is so deep-rooted in the psychology of the Indian peasant and his attachment to land is so strong (because the social prestige attached to landholding is so high) that any proposal which deprives the farmer of independent rights of cultivation and cropping in land arouses his deep and instinctive hostility. Lately, the fact that the Indian peasant is too individualistic to pool his land in cooperatives has been ridiculed as a prejudice of those who mention it. But the fact nevertheless remains a brute fact discovered again and again by administrators, social workers, cooperators, economists and sociologists. The very fact that at every succession a joint family holding is subdivided among the descendants is enough proof of its truth. Where the members of a joint family — a natural cooperative — would seldom keep their holdings together for joint cultivation, would large numbers of unrelated families pool them? Peasants stick to their small plots of land even when they barely yield their minimum subsistence, even when they are heavily in debt, sometimes even when more remunerative employment is available elsewhere. The hunger for land for individual cultivation is so acute that forty per cent of the total reported credit needs of the lower half of the cultivating families covered by the Rural Credit Survey were stated to be for the purchase of land. As Professor Ranga says, "It is difficult to understand how the National Planning Commission thinks that the villagers who could not successfully work cooperatives created during the past half a century could be persuaded to take to and work successfully cooperative farming which is certainly more complicated" (*All India Cooperative Review,* August 1956, p. 235).

It is not enough for the success of any form of productive organization that the intelligentsia should be convinced of its value from the point of view of efficiency or idealism. It is also necessary that it should be able to evoke the sustained enthusiasm of those who would work in it. There is no evidence that farmers have been or can be enthused about joint-farming — except under extraordinary conditions, and for short periods. If we view the attitudes of the Indian peasants realistically, if we realize that persuasion and propaganda can modify them only in certain respects and to a limited extent, if we assume that coercion (and administrative preferences and pressures amounting to coercion) should be ruled out in a democracy, then we have to think of those types of cooperatives which can help the small farmer to raise his income without straining his socio-psychological make-up to the point where it evokes his active or passive resistance. Supply cooperatives, credit cooperatives and marketing cooperatives — in short, common facility "service cooperatives" — are eminently suitable for this purpose.

Service Cooperatives

The "economies of scale" expected from cooperativization are often referred to without necessary distinction being made between operational, commercial and financial economies. The operational economies — the economies of mechanization of farm operations, and the economies of labour specialization and nationalization — have, as we have seen, less significance in agriculture than in industry, and a negligible scope in the agriculture of labour surplus countries. But the commercial and financial economies — the economies of organized bulk buying and selling, and cheap credit — are of crucial importance. In fact, apart from mechanization, it is mainly, if not wholly, due to these economies that large farms are superior in respect of money returns to small farms. In respect of yields per acre, overhead costs and sometimes even labour costs, the large farms are seldom superior. If, therefore, the commercial and financial economies of scale could be brought to the small farmers by purchase, sale, credit and service cooperatives while their incentives remain unimpaired and cultivation remains intensive, they could not only raise more produce per acre but also reduce their money costs and increase their money returns substantially. As Professor Lewis says,

> "The small organization can succeed just as well if it is surrounded by agencies — private, cooperative, or statutory — which will take over all that part of the work which needs to be done on a large scale, so that the small farm can concentrate on those activities which are adequately done on a small scale. Thus the small farm can get its specialist advice from an agricultural extension service, its standardized seeds from seed farms or its tractors from the tractor hiring agency, and can dispose of its product to any agency which bulks it with that of other farms, and grades, processes, advertises and sells it in bulk".

It is true that "except as a member of a cooperative the small farmer can never be in a position to avail himself of technical, financial or other external aid of which he stands in need more than anybody else" (Gadgil, *Indian Journal of Agricultural Economics,* 1955, p. 31). But it is not true that the cooperative must be a joint farming cooperative. The scale of commercial operation may be enlarged without it being necessary to raise the scale of cultivation. Cooperatives are needed to serve the small farmer but not to supplant him. The role of service cooperatives — whether they are called multipurpose or better farming or credit cooperatives — which merely serve the individual farmer is very often belittled. They do not appear to many to be "radical" enough because farming remains individual. The assumption is that "collectivism" of any kind is necessarily more radical than individualism regardless of its acceptability to the individuals concerned and the real benefit which it eventually brings to them. "Collectivism" thus comes to be regarded as an end in itself rather than a means to the fuller growth of the individual. The approach is clearly inconsistent with the basic tenets of cooperation and democracy. In a democracy only such a degree of cooperativization is legitimate as would be willingly accepted by the people and help them to raise themselves as free individuals.

A very radical socialist economist rightly complains that "far too much emphasis is placed in current discussion on other institutional matters — especially fragmentation, size and marketing — and much too little upon other means of increasing efficiency — especially water supplies, seed farms for improved seed, fertilizers and agricultural extension services" (Lewis, p. 136). We must concentrate in the immediate future on establishing a really effective extension service and network of purchase, sale, processing and credit cooperatives geared to serve the small farmers quickly, cheaply and adequately. This task alone is big enough to engage all our administrative, financial and moral resources. If it is accomplished, agricultural productivity and incomes can be raised manifold without alienating the peasants.

Size and Yield

The case of Japan is an instance in point. The cultivated land per capita in Japan is only 0.07 hectare as compared with 0.29 hectares in India. On an average, a peasant family in Japan cultivates only 2.5 acres as compared with 3.43 acres in overcrowded Bihar. While in India 59 per cent of the holdings are less than five acres in size, in Japan 95 per cent are less than five acres and more than 40 per cent less than 1.25 acres in size. And yet the yield of paddy in Japan is 48.1 quintals per hectare as compared with 12.2 quintals in the USA and 21.5 quintals in the USSR. Between the 1880s and 1930s the yield was doubled as a result of technical and financial assistance extended by the government and service associations, without any noticeable change in the size of the farms.

In India, too, small cultivators have time and again demonstrated their capacity to multiply their yields if technical advice and credit are made available to them. Economist R. K. Hazari, for example, while advocating estate farming on the basis of his study of the estate farms at Walchandnagar points out that good cultivators in the region have been able to raise on their farms as much sugarcane per acre and sometimes even more than at Walchandnagar (45 tons). These were unaided small farmers. Very conceivably, if a comparison had been made between yields of average estates and those of farmers receiving the necessary technical and financial help from the State and the multipurpose cooperatives, it would be found that the small farmer can consistently obtain comparable and sometimes even higher yields. It is the lack of an efficient extension service and the credit needed to raise output that negatively offsets the intensiveness and strong personal motivation of small peasant cultivation.

So far there have been other institutional handicaps as well — the prevalence of absentee landlordism, gross inequalities in land holdings, fragmentation of holdings, insecurity of tenancy and the exorbitance of rents. These handicaps have affected the creative energies of the peasants, and thereby their productivity. But now that these difficulties are being removed through land reforms legislation, peasant incentives can come into full play and the help of service cooperatives would be more eagerly sought and prove more fruitful. Now that the environment is becoming favourable it is necessary that our limited resources are devoted only to the promotion of such cooperatives as have a reasonable chance of succeeding in the immediate future, instead of launching a campaign to promote cooperatives of the most "comprehensive" type.

As service cooperatives become effective the spirit of cooperation will grow. Customary arrangements between related or neighbouring farmers for the common use of wells, ploughs, bullocks, etc., may be further strengthened by the utilization of common services. In due course small farmers (groups of five to six families) may be persuaded to develop arrangements for coordinating more operations particularly those involving the use of improved equipment like drills, threshing equipment, etc., while ownership and other operations remain strictly individual. Agreements may also be reached, if possible, about the crops to be grown. But it is necessary that the degree of cooperation is allowed to increase naturally and spontaneously without any pressure and only up to the point to which willingly the peasants wish to carry it. And Government help should be available to all small and medium farmers without discrimination.

As Professor Ranga says it would be dangerous to launch

> ". . . any campaign against the non-exploitative peasant family economy, as if it is inimical to socialist ideals or cooperative commonwealth. For such a campaign will discourage peasants from ploughing back their savings into their land improvements. It will prevent any more investments in land . . . . It will induce the highly educated and more enterprising elements among peasants to give up agriculture . . . . It will set in motion the disintegration of villages, rural life and family economy"
>
> *(All India Cooperative Review,* August 1956, p. 238).

Foreign Experience

It would be useful at this stage to see if any lesson can be learnt from the experience of joint farming in other countries and in some States of India. Foreign experience is often cited in India to support the case for cooperative farming. It is necessary, however, to study the precise "degree of cooperation" that prevailed in them, the conditions under which they succeeded and whether similar circumstances exist in India. Certain conclusions clearly emerge from the experience of agricultural cooperatives abroad. In most countries only those forms of cooperation have succeeded which have enabled the peasant proprietors to buy their farm requisites and sell their products on more favourable terms than they could individually do, without affecting their rights of ownership in land or product. Joint farming has succeeded only in a few places and only when it has been backed by a strong religious faith or necessitated by conditions of extreme distress or political pressure. And even in these places as soon as there has been a relaxation of circumstantial or administrative pressure a tendency to revert to individual farming, with limited cooperation, has appeared.

After a survey of agricultural cooperation in different parts of the world, Professor J.A. Venn of Cambridge concluded as far back as 193? that

> ". . . purchase and sale, or supply, societies . . . appear to be the only ones that can meet with success in all countries and among all types of agriculturists . . . . Cooperative agriculture, pure and simple, ha

everywhere proved a failure from the philanthropic efforts of individual land owners of the early 19th century down to the post-war colonies provided for ex-servicemen by the State"

(*Foundations of Agricultural Economics,* p. 349).

Twenty years later we are again informed by a UN survey of European agriculture that "while cooperation in buying, selling and processing has long been practised in many Western European countries, and cooperative ownership and use of machinery is gaining ground in a number of countries, cooperation in the process of farming exists only in rice production, or as isolated experiments with cooperative stables or as a remnant of old-time common cultivation in some Southern countries (*European Agriculture, Food and Agriculture Organisation,* Geneva, 1954 p. 43).

In Western Europe there are some mountain pasture cooperatives, but their members only pool their mountain use rights and some labour. Stock breeding is common but the livestock are private property and lowland arable farming is strictly individual. The Welsh land settlement societies, the first cooperative farms to be established in Britain with Government assistance "despite favourable prices since 1939 and substantial outside contributions of capital and aid, have not made any notable progress and have no more members than in 1939" (*Rural Progress Through Cooperatives,* United Nations, p. 32). A recent study of these societies concludes that "as farming enterprises they have succeeded. From the point of view of cooperative organization they have not shown much progress (*Farm Economist,* Vol. IV, No. 8).

In the land settlement schemes in England, on the other hand, it has been possible to raise the incomes of small farmers through the provision of cooperative services without the pooling of land (A.R. Richmond, "Proceedings, International Conference of Agricultural Economists", 1949). In the Italian "braccianti" the group spirit is relatively strong because of shared adversity but lands are allotted to individual families; some farming operations (ploughing, sowing and manuring) and marketing are jointly carried out while others (pruning, weeding, thinning, dressing, picking, etc.) are performed by individual families (*Joint Farming Cooperatives,* ILO, 1948, p. 13). In Austria "the independence of the single-farm enterprise and its management is completely safeguarded. The collaboration applies only to certain activities of a commercial and technical character which are taken over by the cooperative, that is, such activities as cannot be adequately and efficiently carried out by the individual farmer. The Hutterite communities in the United States have been successful mainly due to their religious fervour and their self-imposed asceticism and insolation (Infield, *Cooperative Communities at Work*, pp. 22-24).

In the cooperative farms set up under the Farm Security Administration in the United States in the 1930s, even economic adversity failed to create the cooperative spirit. These farms "did not achieve much success in the cooperative field for the reason that members were mainly drawn from the low strata of society; they had no sufficient training or education; they were not imbued with the ideals of cooperation and there was no common bond or ideal inspiring them to carry out their mission" (Reserve Bank of India, *Cooperative Farming*, 1949, p. 33). The cooperative feature was regarded as a meaningless legal device. It did not exist for either members or managers who had no share in planning it. There was, in other words, a great gap between the intentions of regional and national officials and the way they were carried out by subordinates, who did not understand or approve of the policies" (Infield, *Cooperative Group Living*, p. 9). The government lost enormous funds and most of them were disbanded after 1943. On the other hand, the FSA Land Leasing Associations which were simultaneously organized on the basis of individual tenant farming succeeded in developing cooperation in many activities spontaneously, particularly in the use of machinery, processing, purchasing and marketing (*Cooperative Farming*, Reserve Bank of India, 1949, p. 34).

The agricultural settlements in Israel are often, and deservedly, referred to as models of cooperative community development. But it should be remembered that they have been established under very extraordinary circumstances. The Jewish refugees constituting them had suffered prolonged persecution all over the world. United by this common distress, a common religious faith, and a common desire to find a new homeland, they were ready to sacrifice all individualism for the sake of the collective success of the new settlements in a difficult and hostile region and for facilitating the settlement of the largest number of immigrants in the shortest possible time. The Israel experiment can only be regarded as an extreme case, not a model for general application. It is significant that even in Israel, besides the Kvutzot settlements in which ownership, work and consumption are collective, other types of cooperatives have grown in which individualistic elements are prominent, e.g. the Moshavim and the Meshveiovdim in which the members work on their own plots of land on an individual basis and are personally entitled to the products of their labour, although purchase and marketing facilities are cooperatively provided. Such settlements have been no less successful than the Kvutzot and their number seems too be increasing. "If we take the Kvutza alone, its members, living under conditions of extreme comprehensive cooperation, comprise only a seventh of the total rural and about a twentieth of the whole immigrant population" (Infield, *Cooperative Communities at Work,* p. 177).

Similarly about the famous "ejidos" of Mexico we learn that:

(a) Their members were originally bound together mainly by antagonism to the large estates on which they were employed as labourers and by the fact that the agrarian laws of Mexico gave them as local communities the rights of use of these estates" (*Rural Progress Through Cooperatives,* UN, p. 30).

(b) "Neither the spirit of cooperation nor that of enterprise has been so great as in the Kvutza. This has aggravated the commonest fundamental difficulties and weaknesses of collective and communal farming" (*Rural Progress,* p. 81).

(c) Only "one-third of these ejidos were jointly cultivated: the others were worked along individual lines..." (*Joint Farming Cooperatives, A Preliminary Survey,* ILO, Geneva, 1949, p. 39).

Contrary to common belief "even in Africa only a comparatively few tribes retain fully collective farming where fairly large groups of families pool all their land use rights" (*Rural Progress,* p. 81). The success of the fully collective farms in Saskatchewan, Canada, is mainly due to abundance of prime land, shortage of labour, and the consequent advantage of extensive, mechanized cultivation. Nevertheless, "of the ploughed area of the province only about one per cent is farmed collectively" (*Rural Progress,* p. 85).

In the USSR, the man-land ratio is, again, highly favourable for extensive mechanized cultivation. But the process of collectivization was carried out by ruthless force and resulted in near-famine conditions for about two years and the slaughter of livestock on a mass scale. Livestock losses following the forced collectivization were not made good until about 1938. Fodder shortage is chronic. In 40 years grain production per head has not increased significantly. Yields are still low in comparison with those in Western Europe where small-scale peasant farming predominates. (Jasny, *The Socialised Agriculture of the USSR*, p. 793). Both labour costs and overhead costs are very high. "If we calculate on the basis of West European norms of labour requirements in farming operations, the normal labour input of approximately 100,000 large-scale farms composing Soviet agriculture today with about 1,500 hectares of crop land each, considering their actual present intensity of farming and their actual degree of mechanization, we arrive at an excess farm population of at least 30 million." (O. Schiller, *Farm Economics,* May 1956, p. 306). Since the death of Stalin these facts have been more or less frankly admitted and a series of measures have been taken to increase agricultural production by making more use of individualist incentives to peasants. They have been encouraged to grow more on their private plots and to breed their own stock, although there have been endless complaints that farmers spend more time on their private plots than on collective work.

By far the most eloquent proof of the ineradicable individualism of the Russian peasant is furnished by the fact that

> ". . . in 1941 during the first months of German occupation, in remote villages where, after the retreat of the Soviet Army, the peasants were not disturbed by orders of the German authorities and felt free to act according to their own wishes, in all cases they dissolved the Kolkhoz farms at once and turned to individual farming. The young Kolkhoz members were no exception"
> (Schiller, *Farm Economics,* May 1956, p. 308).

Thus the only achievement of agrarian collectivism in Russia has been the introduction of mechanized farming over large areas and the effective appropriation of the rural surplus for rapid industrialization and militarization at the expense of a rise in rural living standards, and sometimes even at the expense of subsistence.

In Eastern Europe during the last three years a process of de-collectivization has been going on. In Czechoslovakia some 40 per cent of the farms were not paying their way and a large number of them were permitted to disband in the autumn of 1953. In Yugoslavia, more than half of the collective farms have been dissolved since 1951 under the new policy which permits peasants to withdraw from them. The number of collectives declined from 7,000 in 1951 to 2,500 in September 1953. In Hungary, again, "peasant dissatisfaction was so great that even with a Police-State, normally equipped to handle discontent, it constituted an element of such basic instability that almost half of the collectivized households have left the 'socialist sector'" (Praeger, p. 123). Under the New Course, greater use is being made of material incentives rather than administrative pressure for increasing agricultural production. The policy of the elimination of the so-called kulak has given way to a policy of the limitation of the kulak. (*ibid.*, p. 122).

The phenomenal growth of farmers' cooperatives in China during the last three years has aroused much interest. A very earnest effort has been made by the Government of India through two high-level delegations to study this development. The ultimate aim of the Chinese Communist Government is, of course, the establishment of completely collective farms run by the State.

During 1951 and 1952, Mutual Aid Teams were organized on a massive scale. There is abundant official Communist evidence, however, that many of these produced only proforma results. Groups of families cooperated on particular tasks at particular periods of the harvest year, but the individual family, not the Mutual Aid Team, remained the basic production unit. And, when a serious team use of labour, tools and farm animals was attempted, a variety of unsatisfactory results emerged: quarrels among the families interfered with efficient output; no one assumed responsibility for the upkeep of communal property; the claims of inefficient members violated the sense of equity of the more efficient, and when shares were fairly allocated the less efficient lost economic ground" (Rostow, *The Prospects for Communist China*, p. 84).

The peasants have been and are being made to join these cooperatives mainly through force or the threat of force, or irresistible administrative pressure exercised through discriminatory taxes and other measures. An increasing number of "elementary" cooperatives are being converted into "advanced" collectives in which even the theoretical ownership rights and land dividends are abolished.

"There is ample evidence that the Chinese peasant, however grateful he may have initially been for land distributions, does not wish to enter collective arrangements.... In this respect he fully shares the outlook of Russian and Eastern European peasants; and the peculiar intimacy of intensive Asiatic agriculture may well heighten his reluctance." (Rostow, p. 152). "The post-Stalin leaders of Communism in Moscow have openly indicated that the course of output under Soviet collectivization has been distinctly discouraging, and throughout all other parts of the

(Communist) bloc they are putting forward a programme which emphasizes the need for peasants' incentives on the one hand and increases of output in consumers' goods on the other. It is at just this moment–when past Communist failures are revealed and current pressure on the peasantry apparently relaxed – that the Chinese Communists appear to have decided to collectivize substantially in the course of the First Five Year Plan.

Shri P.N. Thapar has rightly concluded that it is too early to say whether cooperative farming itself as distinct from the various kinds of assistance that has been given by the State has led to any increase in production. Some of the agricultural experts told us that they expected from the introduction of cooperative farming alone an increase of yield to the extent of 10 to 15 per cent. There is, however, no experimental or scientific basis for this statement . . . . In India, where social and political conditions are different, where the Government works through persuasion and not force, and where the small peasant has not been prepared for such a change, it would be a mistake to press them on the people on a very large scale.

(*AICC Economic Review*, Sept. 15, 1956, p. 21).

A democratic country can hardly learn much from a political system which rides to political power on the response of the land-hungry peasants to the slogan "land to the tiller" but, as soon as the expropriation of the landlords and the redistribution of land are completed, proceeds to deprive the peasants.

From Foreign Experience Back to Indian Experience

Although more than a thousand cooperative farming societies are said to exist in India, most of them have been established on Government land, with Government capital for the settlement of refugees or landless workers. There are a few of them in which land-owning peasants or tenants have pooled their existing holdings for joint cultivation. It is evidently easier for the Government to impose the cooperative pattern of farm organization when its adoption can be made a condition for the grant of land and capital and the people settled are in distress, have no resources of their own, and have never held and cultivated their own land before.

There is little indication of the pattern being acceptable to the millions of farmer families who have been cultivating owned or rented land on their own for generations. There are a few societies in India which have yet demonstrated that these latter can take to cooperativization. All the evidence proves that contrary is the case. What is more, even in the settlement societies joint cultivation has been rarely undertaken and still more rarely continued after a few crops.

The Agrarian Reforms Committee which visited some of the settlement farms of the "joint farm management type" in the Ganga-Khadar area found that

> ". . . for Kharif sowing means of production were pooled and harvesting was done jointly. When, however, Rabi ploughing and sowing commenced every settler family worked individually on its own 10 acres, and there was no cooperation in the operation of cultivation and harvesting. The reason given was that joint farming did not work well, and there were disputes about one individual working harder and the other avoiding work. Further, the distribution of the harvest caused heartburning amongst people who were otherwise living together on most friendly terms . . ."
>
> (*Report,* pp. 69-70).

In the Darauna and Nanwara societies in Jhansi district "the peasants complained of coercion and threats. One of them alleged that he was threatened with imprisonment if he refused to join the cooperative farm. There was also a widespread complaint about non-payment of wages".

In Madras

> ". . . some success has been achieved through the land colonization societies, which, again, are not a real venture in cooperative farming. It is observed by Shri Sathianathan and Shri Ryan that although the ideal of joint cultivation, joint harvesting and profit-sharing have been recommended to the colonists, nowhere has it yet found favour. Each colonist prefers to cultivate his land on his own account, and to keep to himself the fruits thereof".
>
> (Thirumalai, *Post-War Agricultural Problems and Policies in India,* p. 157).

The same is true of the land colonization societies in Orissa.

The Planning Commission recently carried out a survey of 20 cooperative farming societies. They were not a representative sample by any means; in fact, the State Registrars selected them as they were among the best organized. In six of the societies the land has been obtained from the Government; in one of them the land has been obtained in one block on lease from a Raja. There are 13 societies in which members have pooled their own land but in 10 of these 13 most or all of the members do not perform any farm work. It appears, therefore, that the so-called cooperative farming societies are merely either settlement societies or societies run on capitalist lines by groups of absentee land-owners having all the work done by hired agricultural workers — a kind of joint-stock estate farms (of 100 to 200 acres) established to secure the concessions given by the Government to cooperative farms. Farming operations are conducted jointly in only three of them (in one of which continuous pressure from the members for allotment of individual plots is reported).

In only three cases the members have contributed bullocks and implements. These have been in most cases purchased and provided by the societies. In most societies wages are paid to hired workers and to working members at 12 annas to Rs. 1-3 per day. No attempt has been made to differentiate between different types of farm work done by members for purposes of wage payment. As a result, where members work there are continuous disputes about the quantity and quality of work put in by different members. Or else work is done indifferently and members' interest is no more than that of hired workers. Where members work, the wage bill forms a very high percentage of, and sometimes exceeds, the proceeds. In two of the societies where owned land was pooled and under the bye-laws was withdrawable after five years, some of the members withdrew their land immediately after the expiry of the period. Two of the societies are reported to be on the verge of dissolution. In two societies a reversion to individual farming has taken place after an initial period of joint farming. In many others litigation and disputation is continuous and members wish to revert to individual farming as soon as possible. In two societies the bigger land-owners are reported to have appropriated an unfair proportion of the proceeds as land dividends and wages (for their servants) and the small farmers wish to withdraw.

Experience in some of the refugee resettlement societies organized by the Indian Cooperative Union since 1948 in the villages of Delhi State has been similar. The first two or three crops were raised on a collective basis, the next two on a group basis, and all the rest on an individual basis. The continuation of joint cultivation became nearly impossible because of factionalism among the members and the executive committees' disputes about the relative intensity of work put in by different members, mistrust regarding the use of funds by the executives, etc. Gradually, implements and cattle had to be distributed on an individual basis although they were obtained on a collective basis. In the beginning produce was distributed equally among the members after deducting expenses and reserves. But after reversion to individual farming this had to be given up. There has been constant pressure for individual allotment of land and complete individualization of farming although land was initially allotted for joint cultivation.

On the basis of a study of cooperative farming societies in Gujarat in general and in Baroda in particular, Shri C. Patel concludes "that attachment for one's own land is very strong and the question of measurement of quantity and quality of work of members is complicated. So in the beginning in order to generate an atmosphere for cooperative farming, we should first organize better farming societies. We should leave the initiative to the cultivator for his individual cultivation" (*AICC Economic Review,* 15 September, 1956, p. 26).

In Bombay where the most determined efforts have been made by the Government to introduce cooperative farming, out of about 350 farming societies all except 40 have been organised on government lands for the settlement of landless workers. Out of the remaining 40, cultivation is collective only in about 20. Where collective cultivation has been tried in settlement societies "it has been the experience in the Bombay State that in a large number of cases, the wages distributed or the maintenance advances given in the course of a working season have far exceeded the total produce of the society" (P.D. Kasbekar, formerly Deputy Registrar, Cooperative Farming, Bombay, *All India Cooperative Review,* September 1956, pp. 310-11). The members regard the society "as something external to themselves like some kind of government farm where they are merely employees" (*ibid.*). If any lesson has been drawn upon the joint farming in the Bombay State so far it is that even the organization of such a society and the preservation of such a society after organization presents considerable difficulties.

Kasbekar concludes that

> ". . . in the case of most of our cultivators their only important possession is their piece of land. It is naturally a cherished possession. It is no mean sacrifice to a cultivator to be told to give

> up that possession for pooling it with a society for the sake of supposed benefits of a way of living with which he is not familiar. If people have to be persuaded to offer themselves as guinea-pigs for experiments the least that the State can do for them before they are asked to take the plunge is that they are fully insured against the failure of the experiment . . . ."
>
> (Kasbekar, *op.cit.*, p. 314).

Cooperation, "Experimentation" and Democracy

We stated at the outset that the whole programme of cooperativization is being described by the planners as "experimental" although, notwithstanding the failure of almost all experiments in every State, the planners' policy of cooperativization remains unaffected and, at every successive review of policy, the "targets" of the number of cooperative farming societies continue to be multiplied. This hardly indicates that the "experiments" are really experimental, for in that case failures would lead to an abandonment of the policy rather than an upgrading of numerical targets. It may be said that so far experiments have not been "planned" enough. But in U.P., Delhi and Bombay at least they have been as well-planned and well-financed as they could be. Apart from this, however, the truth is that experimentation, at least in this field, is not likely to reveal anything startlingly new — anything, that is, which experience all over the world and in India has not already brought out. Given the well-known fundamental conditions in which experiments must be conducted in India — the highly unfavourable man-land ratio, the individualism of the Indian peasant rooted in centuries of tradition, the paucity of first-rate leadership, and the bureaucratism of the Indian administration at the village level — one could safely infer what is likely to happen.

It seems, therefore, that experimentation cannot, and indeed is not, really intended by the planners to guide us in deciding whether the pooling of land should be insisted upon or not. It is a basic question of policy which should be — and which perhaps is being — decided on the basis of some other preferences. The danger is that every failure of a fundamentally unsound policy of cooperativization may be used by the planners, convinced of its soundness *a priori*, as an argument not for abandoning it but for pursuing it with even greater vigour in the post-experimental stage — which, in effect, means pursuing it with coercive methods. Thus it is that a well-meant but impracticable policy of democratic cooperativization may imperceptibly degenerate in future into a policy of undemocratic regimentation of the peasantry by the State machine. Therefore, the time to guard against this danger is now and not when the thousands of targeted experiments fail.

That these fears are not imaginary is indicated by the fact that in certain authoritative documents a more and more complacent attitude is being taken about the use of compulsion for purposes of cooperativization. The Congress Agrarian Reforms Committee had quoted with approval a resolution of the Cooperative Registrars Conference to the effect that cooperative joint farming should be compulsorily introduced if 66 per cent of the owners of land or owners of 75 per cent of land should agree to such a scheme of joint farming. Provisions to this effect had already been included in the Bombay Cooperative Societies (Amendment) Act of 1928. The Committee added "that in urgent social and economic reforms there is less and less aversion to the use of compulsion" (*Report,* p. 52). The Planning Commission again stated in the First Five Year Plan that "while the controversy between voluntary and compulsory formation of cooperative farms may at this stage be avoided, it can be suggested that in any area where a majority of holders representing at least half of the total area under cultivation desire to establish a cooperative farm, legislative means should be at their disposal to proceed with the formation of a cooperative farming society for the whole village".

It is doubtful whether it has yet been possible in any State in India to persuade a majority of land holders to pool their land (except perhaps in some Bhoodan villages). But even if a majority agree to pool their land, a cooperative farm could hardly be run if it contains within its membership a significant minority which is opposed to its very basis. Apart from this, however, the whole approach of extending the principle of compulsion for cooperativization seems to be unjustified. It may be legitimate for the State to use moderate compulsion to consolidate holdings, to prevent further subdivision, to regulate tenancy rights and rents and to impose ceilings. But it would be wholly illegitimate to compel farmers to pool their lands. If the principle of compulsion is extended to the pooling of land one does not know where it may lead to. (Since this was drafted the Prime Minister has hinted at the possibility of collectivization if cooperativization fails.)

The very notion of fixing targets for the development of cooperative farming in terms of the number of societies to be established during a year or five years assumes that such pressure may be applied. It is inconceivable that the field cadres of our cooperative departments would be able to persuade, educate and psychologically prepare tens of thousands of Indian peasants to pool their lands "voluntarily" in the required number of societies. Either the peasants would be made to join them through administrative pressure, or the societies would be paper societies and the progress would be statistical. The creation and multiplication by government departments of cooperative societies which are cooperative only in name has been the bane of the Indian cooperative movement so far and has given it a very hypocritical character.

Capital Formation and Cooperativization

One of the arguments advanced for cooperativization is what may be called "the capital formation argument," that it would increase and make it possible for the State to appropriate more of the rural marketable surplus which is the chief source of investible industrial capital in underdeveloped countries. But this argument — assuming that it is legitimate to let the State appropriate the bulk of the rural surplus — only proves the necessity for State control of the *marketing* of produce and not of production. For this purpose, if the warehousing and marketing programme is effectively implemented, with state partnership in the agencies established, the Government should be able to acquire a large proportion of the commissions and profits of marketing. The millions of small peasants have to sell, as a rule, their entire produce over and above their barest subsistence because of the desperate need for cash. Unless, therefore, it is intended to extract from them a greater surplus than is left after bare subsistence is kept back, there is no case for the cooperativization of production as such.

In the Soviet Union, Eastern Europe and China, the State forced down the actual consumption level of the peasantry in the name of capital formation. If cooperative farming societies are really to be used for capital formation, the State will have to be in a position to appropriate the bulk of their surpluses — which shows how "voluntary" these societies would be. In short, the distinction between democratic cooperativization and State collectivization would have to be obliterated altogether. More mansions would have to be added to the growing citadel of statism in this country.

Sociology of Peasant Farming

Socialism is generally regarded as synonymous with statism in this country — against the best tradition of socialist thought, which has always insisted on the gradual "withering away of the state". If in a feudal village the small peasant is a slave, a serf of the landlord, the moneylender and the merchant, he is much more so in a state-cooperative or State-collective system which can only be described on the basis of its record in many countries as a Higher Feudalism, no less exploitative than the old one. The peasant can be free only when, in an appropriate land-rights environment created by the State, he can independently cultivate his land and harvest his crop with the assistance of service cooperatives — an arrangement that may be called Cooperative Individual Farming or Cooperative Peasant Farming. Cooperative Peasant Farming gives the peasant the freedom that is his due after centuries of oppression. Besides, it has an inherent sociological value which, though eclipsed at present by the urgency of increasing production, should not be lost sight of in the formulation of agricultural policies.

As Dr. Sigmund V. Frauderfer says,

> "Let us even assume — although reliable evidence is entirely lacking — that this kind of "cooperation" which too closely resembles collectivization results in higher living standards and higher income on account of increased productivity per unit of labour, would the fundamental change of transforming a free independent small holder into a bondsman serving the bureaucracy of a totalitarian state really lead to genuine progress? We believe, on the contrary, that the preservation of property rights and individual management of our peasants is a fundamental requisite for the maintenance of Western civilization. The European peasant farm is more than just a business unit; it is a source of biological and cultural values which are essential for our civilization which, without them, would be doomed to disintegration and breakdown. Agriculture is not only the backbone of the national economy, but a very important reservoir for the most vital biological and cultural forces of a nation. How then, we have to ask, is European peasantry to be rescued from the double attack from Western capitalism and Eastern collectivism? The answer is cooperation in the true

conservative sense of combining individual forces without prejudicing individual property and individual freedom, and as a second equally important factor, rural education. . ."

(Measures for the Rehabilitation of Low-Income Farmers, pp. 46-47).

Thus much more is at stake in the current debate on cooperative farming than many participants in the debate realize — not only the growth of agricultural output but the freedom and dignity of the peasant, the relationship between the peasantry and the city gentry, social stability, the future of our nascent democracy and the vital rural roots of our culture and civilization. And, as we said before, the time to measure our steps is now. The time has come for cooperators to have the courage to say where cooperation shall stop, and where the State shall stop, lest in the name of cooperation, and using its terminology and apparatus, the State gradually reduce the peasant to a new servitude.

II. SERVICE COOPERATIVES: POSTSCRIPT TO NAGPUR RESOLUTION

The ICU was attacked "politically", by the Congress Party and the left for its critical views on "Co-operative Farming" which had been adopted by the Congress as its main plank at its Nagpur session at the initiative of Mr. Jawaharlal Nehru. He himself shrunk back (for the first time) from contributing to the ICU's Endowment Fund, on the ground that given the surrounding controversies, it was not the appropriate time. However, within a short time after the Nagpur Resolution, and heeding the criticisms that followed the Resolution, the Congress Party itself modified its position and decided that in the first phase the emphasis will be on service cooperatives. This was also the ICU's approach.

The ICU offered active cooperation to the Congress for promoting service cooperatives. Extracts from the Congress Party's proceedings, notes exchanged between the ICU and the then Congress President Indira Gandhi on service cooperatives are given at the end of the chapter. But the pity is that the interest of the Congress in the service or farming cooperatives was short-lived. The training programmes started by it for its workers failed to attract the latter. The Congress Party did little further to pursue even its amended Resolution.

This section provides a view of the interaction between the Congress Party and the ICU in the attempts to promote service cooperatives.

Indian National Congress Proceedings (February, 1959)

In particular, the Congress is of the opinion that:

(1) The organization of the village should be based on village panchayats and village cooperatives, both of which should have adequate powers and resources to discharge the functions allotted to them . A number of village cooperatives may form themselves into a union. All permanent residents of the village, whether owning land or not, should be eligible for membership of the village cooperative which should promote the welfare of its members by introducing progressive farming methods and improved techniques of cultivation, developing animal husbandry and fishery encouraging cottage industries. In addition to providing credit and discharging other servicing functions, it will arrange for pooling and marketing the agricultural produce of the farmers and for storage and godown facilities for them. Both the panchayat and the cooperative should be the spearheads of all developmental activities in the village and, more especially, should encourage intensive farming with a view to raising the per acre yield of agricultural produce.

(2) The future agrarian pattern should be that of cooperative joint farming, in which the land will be pooled for joint cultivation, the farmers continuing to retain their property rights, and getting a share from the net produce in proportion to their land. Further, those who actually work on the land, whether they own the land or not, will get a share in proportion to the work put in by them on the joint farm.

As a first step, prior to the institution of joint farming, service co-operatives should be organized throughout the country. This stage should be completed within a period of three years. Even within this period, however, wherever possible and generally agreed to by the farmers, joint cultivation may be started.

(Working Committee, New Delhi, March 15, 1959)

Agrarian Organizational Pattern

The Working Committee considered the question of taking effective steps for implementing the Nagpur Resolution on the new agrarian organizational pattern. They were of the opinion that the two immediate tasks which must receive the full attention of the Congress organization and the country were : (1) increased agricultural production, and (2) formation of Service Cooperatives. There has been an attempt on the part of the opponents of the Nagpur Resolution to concentrate their attack on Joint Cooperative Farming and divert the attention of the people from Service Cooperatives which were essential for a number of reasons and whose success would also open the way for the introduction of Joint Cooperative Farming. Joint Cooperative Farming was envisaged in the Nagpur resolution as the ultimate pattern. For a period of three years our main task should be the formation of Service Cooperatives. Joint Cooperative Farming was vitally connected with the success of Service Cooperatives which would inculcate among the people the attitude and habit of co-operation in many spheres of rural life. Joint Cooperative Farming would then be but an extension of cooperation to the process of production. Some such farms already exist and others may be started where agreed to by the farmers even during this period of three years. But the emphasis at present has to be on Service Cooperatives.

A well-thought-out programme of training is necessary for large numbers of workers who would be needed for manning as well as guiding the large number of Service Cooperatives. The training could be at the Central as well as State level. The State Governments have an important and vital responsibility in the matter of training. They should create facilities for training of workers belonging to any political party or to no party to receive this training. There should be full co-operation between the State Government and the Congress Party in the formation of Service Cooperatives.

Both the State Governments and the Congress Organization should undertake to produce necessary literature for the education and guidance of workers.

NOTES

1. Charan Singh in Cooperative X-rayed.
2. Vikas N. Pandey, "Agricultural Transformations and Cooperative Continuity and Change", *EPW*, Vol. (15), April 9, 1994.
3. The term "cooperativization" is used hereafter in this sense.
4. References to States throughout this monograph refer to States before reorganization.

REFERENCES

Agrarian Reforms Committee (Prof. Gadgil and Dantwala : Suggestions).

All India Rural Credit Survey, *The Survey Report*, Vol. 1, RBI, 1955.

Barou, N, Cooperative Group Living.

Cooperative Farming, RBI, 1949.

Gadgil, D.R., *Indian Journal of Agricultural Economics*, 1955.

Gullander - Farmer's Cooperation in Sweden in Economic Survey of Europe, 1955.

Indian Journal of Agricultural Economics, 1953 & 1955.

Indian Journal of Agricultural Economics, August 1954.

Infield, Henrik F, *Cooperative Communities at Work*, 1947.

Lewis, *Economics of Growth*

Lipton (1993)

Richmond, A.R. Proceedings of International Conference of Agricultural Economists, 1949.

Second Five Year Plan, Resolution No. 5 of the Mussoorie Conference. *All India Cooperative Review*, August, 1956.

INDIAN COOPERATIVE UNION

10th February, 1959

Dear Mrs. Gandhi,

I have just read the Press account of your most inspiring call to the nation. If I may be presumptuous enough to say, you have struck the right note. This is specially so, for the Indian Cooperative Union which is strictly a non-political organization. During the last 10 years the Union has earned the confidence and respect of all parties.

In your message this morning you have broadened the scope of the Congress in asking for national support for the two major programmes, i.e land reforms and the development of service cooperatives. This makes it possible for us without hesitation to assure you of our fullest and utmost cooperation. As you know, we are an organization doing actual field work both in the rural areas and in handicrafts. Our offer of service is thus more than a mere expression of sentiment and we would like to bend all our energies to the attainment of these national objectives.

(L.C. Jain)
General Secretary

Mrs. Indira Gandhi,
Congress President

ALL INDIA CONGRESS COMMITTEE
7, Jantar Mantar Road
New Delhi - 1

February 16, 1959

Dear Mr. Jain,

Thank you for your letter and for your offer of help which I am sure will be most useful to me.

The Nagpur Resolution on Cooperatives was necessarily of a general nature. We must now fill in the gaps in our thinking and produce a clear-cut plan to be worked out by our Mandal Committees. I find that there is no suitable literature on the subject. I am told also that the Law on Cooperatives is defective.

I should like to have the I.C.U's views on these matters.

The literature we must provide must be in the simplest of language and understandable to the village-level workers as well as to the peasant, as nothing like this is available – perhaps this could be in the shape of Question and Answer. Could you help directly or put us in touch with people who might be able to prepare brief notes rather quickly.

Yours sincerely,

(Indira Gandhi)

February 19, 1959

Dear Mrs. Gandhi,

Thank you for your kind letter of 16th February. The Indian Co-operative Union is engaged for the last two months on drawing up its recommendations for the changes required in the cooperative law. As cooperative law is only one of the hurdles in the further development of this movement we are also suggesting other concrete measures. We hope that by the end of this month our report will be ready.

We would be very glad to help in drawing up a clear-cut programme to be followed by the various Mandal Committees. I am getting into touch with Shri Sadiq Ali to find out what thinking has been done so far in the AICC.

We would also be in a position to help in regard to the educational material required for the organizers as well as for the village community. I am having this work started by our research unit immediately.

(L.C. Jain)

Mrs. Indira Gandhi

21st February, 1959

Dear Mrs. Gandhi,

This is further to my letter of 19th February.

I got into touch with Shri Sadiq Ali to find out what thinking had been done on the idea of service cooperatives. I understood that there was no available material as yet. He suggested that we might put down our own ideas on paper. Here is a short note on the promotion of service cooperatives. This is not meant to be exhaustive but only to clear our thinking on some of the essential points.

(L.C. Jain)

Mrs. Indira Gandhi,
Congress President

PRIME MINISTER'S HOUSE
NEW DELHI - 2

April 24, 1959

Dear Kamaladeviji,

I am in Delhi just for one day between tours.

Thank you for sending me the booklet on Cooperative Law. It is sure to be of interest and use to us.

Yours sincerely,

(Indira Gandhi)

Kamaladeviji,
President, ICU

2nd March, 1959

Dear Mrs. Gandhi,

Here are two drafts: one in Hindi and one in Urdu about service cooperatives. This is in the form of a discussion between an organizer and the farmers. If you find these drafts satisfactory and as representing your approach, we would finalize them.

The present draft is only the first of the series of such pamphlets which could be brought out in succession.

Yours sincerely,

(L.C. Jain)

Mrs. Indira Gandhi,
Congress President

6

COOPERATIVE LAW IN INDIA

The ICU's 1964 omnibus document "Cooperative Law in India: a Disquisition" is a compilation of three monographs "A Review of the Report of the Committee on Cooperative Law", "Plea for a Perspective" (both of these were first published in 1959) and "Proposed New Features" (published in 1960).

The 120-page compilation (substantially edited and compacted for this chapter) is a thoroughgoing study of cooperative legislation in India and includes some historical background of related legislation in England. It is a rich assembly of extracts and quotations from a wide range of commentators on the cooperative movement. It also contains ICU statements on Cooperative Principles as relative to the larger aspirations of post-independence India.

I. A REVIEW OF THE REPORT OF THE S.T. RAJA COMMITTEE ON COOPERATIVE LAW 1957

Introduction

There is a growing realization in the country that cooperatives are neither developing nor fulfilling the larger social, economic and democratic aspirations expected of them. Among other causes the existing Cooperative Act of 1912 and rules and bylaws are considered as major obstructions. In its resolution on Cooperative Policy, the National Development Council (November 1958) declared:

> The Central and State Governments have been considering measures for simplifying the present procedure for registration of cooperative societies, grant of loans and management of cooperatives. Many of the existing procedures impede the development of cooperation as a popular movement in which small groups and communities can function freely and organize their work and activities without excessive official interference and red tape. The restrictive features of the existing cooperative legislation should be removed.

In this context, the Report of the Committee on Cooperative Law appointed by the Ministry of Agriculture merits close examination

The Law Committee, its Membership and Terms of Reference

The Committee was appointed in 1956 and its Report was submitted in 1957. The eight members of the committee were all officials of the Central and State Governments and the Reserve Bank. Not a single non-official was drawn from the cooperative movement. The Committee was called upon to review the existing cooperative legislation and to make recommendations for a simple legislative measure generally suited to the whole country to facilitate coordinated progress of the movement. It was also to examine, in the light of the recommendations of the Rural Credit Survey Report, the modifications necessary in the Cooperative Societies Act and rules for giving effect to the concept of *state partnership in share capital and State participation in management* of cooperative societies.

The examination of the present rules and bylaws, and suggestions for modifications were to be made to enable the societies to "play an increasingly important role in the economic development of the country". It was also to suggest standard sets of byelaws to facilitate the proper and smooth working of the "new types of societies which are sought to be encouraged under the changed economic and social policy".

Principles Adopted by the Committee in Modifying the Existing Cooperative Laws

Although repeated reference is made in the Report to the broad principles but are not mentioned anywhere in the Report.

Further, the terms of reference of the committee used the phrase "changed economic and social policy." which is nowhere explained or elaborated either in the terms of reference or by the committee itself.

In the Model Bill recommended by the committee, it emphasizes the principle of State partnership as it is one of the most important recommendations of the Rural Credit Survey. Except for this, no clue is given as to other principles which guided the committee.

The committee hopes that the statement of objects and reasons, to be published along with the Bill, will contain references "to principles of State partnership in cooperative societies and State participation in their management as also to the principle of self-help and mutual-help and to the objectives of promoting better business and better methods of production". The committee itself does not provide any draft statement. But this observation of the committee is very significant and provides a key to the understanding of the rest of the Report. The committee has laboured hard to introduce provisions to give legal sanction to State partnership and State participation in management of cooperative societies. Nowhere are the principles of self-help and mutual help manifested in its recommendations. If anything, these have been undermined, as we shall show later.

The only factors recognized by the committee which necessitate revision of existing cooperative laws are the implementation of the Rural Credit Survey and of the schemes of cooperative development under the Second Five Year Plan.

In discussing the various phases in the growth of legislation in India it refers to the attainment of Independence by the country in 1947, but the only significance of that fateful event which attracted the attention of the committee was "the emergence of new States in the Indian Union".

Again, among the six "landmarks" regarded by it as important in the history of cooperative legislation in India, the Constitution of India, embodying the Directive Principles of State Policy and Fundamental Rights of the citizens guaranteeing their sovereign and democratic life does not find mention. (The Report of the Rural Credit Survey and the Second Five Year Plan are, however, included in the six landmarks.) The committee has missed the entire significance of India's independence, and the adoption of a democratic Constitution which has paved the way for developing cooperatives with a view to strengthening the base of democracy by development of individual initiative and sense of responsibility.

The committee's recommendations are obviously not governed by any principles of either cooperation or the changed economic and social policy or by the Directive Principles of State Policy as laid down in the Constitution.

The Indian Constitution replaced the India Act of 1935 so as to reflect the dawn of a new life of sovereignty and the aspirations of the Indian people to live and grow in the spirit of democracy. A whole series of subsidiary Acts in operation when the Constitution was adopted were not replaced but were revised, changed and modified in the context of the Constitution.

As it is, good, bad or indifferent, there are several lakhs of people who are members of different cooperative societies; and many millions more are hoped to be drawn into it to find the fruits of freedom, democracy, increased economic opportunities and prosperity. One would not compare the task of framing an appropriate legislation for the cooperative movement (from which so much is expected) with that of the framing of the Constitution. But between the Constituent Assembly and the Cooperative Law Committee the gap is astounding and one is forced to the conclusion that its appointment was made with complete lack of responsibility towards millions of people whose life the cooperative law is to embrace.

It is necessary to stress this point, for, in a democratic society, the individuals are expected to obey the law. This imposes a serious and sacred responsibility on the law-makers to take their task seriously and with thoroughness of method, and to frame laws in conformity with the political, social and economic aspirations of a free and democratic people.

Methodology Followed by the Committee

The committee decided to take two steps:

(i) to undertake an "objective analysis" of the existing Act, rules and byelaws; and
(ii) to issue a questionnaire to various persons, institutions and authorities.

The committee does not report having held any discussions with representatives of the cooperative movement at any stage on any matter.

The questionnaire issued by the committee was sent to a cross-section of official agencies, including all State Governments, all Registrars of Cooperative Societies, the Reserve Bank of India, the State Bank of India, the Planning Commission, various Central Ministries, the Houses of Parliament and the State Legislatures, the All India Khadi and Village Industries Board, the Community Projects Administration, the All India Handloom and Handicrafts Boards, the Cooperative Training College at Poona and other Cooperative Training Institutions (run by the Reserve Bank and the Government). In terms of representation from the cooperative movement, only the All India Cooperative Union was canvassed.

The Registrars of Cooperative Societies were requested to circulate copies of the questionnaire to all the important cooperative institutions in their States.

The contact with the most valuable and important source of information was thus made indirectly through the Registrars of Cooperative Societies. As earlier mentioned, the committee itself did not have a single non-official member from the cooperative movement; and it did not apparently resort to any personal discussions with the cooperators to solicit information.

Replies to the questionnaire were received primarily from registrars and officials (24); from Cooperative Banking Institutions (36) and from officers of the Cooperative Training Institutions (11) run by the government. Replies also came in from 11 cooperative bodies, out of over 2 lakh societies in the country, federated into 3,398 district-level and 91 State-level societies

If nothing else, the committee could have at least given a summary of the important problems brought to its notice by (a) cooperative societies and (b) the Registrars and others in the replies it received. One could have then examined whether the recommendations of the committee really met the problems that were brought to its notice.

The methods followed by the committee were bound to be weak and uncertain, in the absence of any guiding principles, but the casual manner in which it obtained data and information is very regrettable.

Some Important Recommendations of the Committee: Model Bill

(a) Authority and Control of the Registrar

1. *Single Authority*

The Cooperative Act of 1912 provides that the Government may, if desired, appoint a Registrar for only a portion of a State. This was to facilitate the appointment of more than one Registrar where necessary. The Cooperative Law Committee has deleted this provision as such a provision in its view "would be inconsistent with the concept of a single authority in the entire State". Imagine a State like Uttar Pradesh or Bombay where a large number of cooperatives already exist and thousands of new ones are to be promoted. Again, the societies are to embrace practically all fields of economic and social endeavour: agriculture, cottage and small-scale industries, consumers' stores, housing, thrift and credit, labour contract, transport, etc., involving several million members. The concept of a single authority in such a situation could hardly be in the best interests of the movement.

2. *Conditions of Registration of Societies*

Firstly, the committee recommends registration of a society which has as its objects the promotion of the "economic" interests of its members. Why only economic? Or are the cooperatives to be reduced to mere commercial units? Especially in the context of the changed economic and social policy in which new types of cooperatives are to be fostered, one would have thought that the definition would be broadened and not made narrower than it has been hitherto. This is immediately followed by another condition that the "proposed society complies with the requirements of sound business".

It is left to the Registrar to be satisfied on these points as a condition precedent to registration.

The Registrar is also to be satisfied that the aims of the society are not "inconsistent with the principles of social justice". The principles of social justice are not defined by the framers of the Report thus leaving them to be interpreted by the various Registrars.

The committee states that it had to lay down these conditions so as to prevent the registration of cooperative societies which are not genuinely cooperative in character. It felt that "the provisions of the 1912 Act have not been adequate in preventing the registration of societies which are not genuinely cooperative in character". It does not show which of the existing provisions lend themselves to abuse, nor does it anywhere define what the committee considers to be "cooperative in character".

It appears to us, however, that it was not so much because of any inadequacies in the existing laws that doubtful cooperatives could get themselves registered, but because of the failings of the registering authorities.

A society seeking economic success should be able to comply with requirements of sound business. But will the Registrars be competent to determine this, when each society will have a different nature of business, when the level of members' skills of management, marketing, manufacture, etc., would vary from society to society? The Registrar may advise and persuade them before registration. But this is primarily for the members to decide. The members may genuinely hold another view of their business prospects and ability. It is too much to give statutory powers to the Registrar to refuse registration on such grounds.

3. *Amendment of byelaws*

The conditions to be imposed statutorily for registration of societies are to apply for registration of amendments also.

4. *Limited or unlimited liability*

The Cooperative Planning Committee had recommended that "a society may adopt limited or unlimited liability". Again a provision should be made in the Act enabling societies to change their liabilities.

The Committee on Cooperative Law, on the other hand, recommends that:

> no cooperative society shall be registered with limited liability, if (i) its primary object is the creation of funds to be lent to its members; (ii) the majority of its members are agriculturists; and (iii) none of the members is a cooperative society.

The committee, however, faced some internal dissension on this point as it records that "There was, however, another view forcefully expressed" that "making unlimited liability compulsory would deter persons from becoming members of cooperative societies". Despite this the committee retained the provision quoted above but agreed to leave the matter to the State Governments.

5. *Supersession*

In one paragraph the committee expresses itself against the Government having power to veto or give directives to cooperative societies but it adds that the State Government or the Registrar should take "suitable administrative measures in this behalf". It proceeds to amplify these "administrative measures".

> Supersession of a committee — There is no provision in the 1912 Act (enacted by the British Government) for the removal by the Registrar of the committee of a cooperative society, if it mismanages its affairs. Such a provision exists either in the Act or in the Rules in most States. We consider that it is necessary to invest the Registrar with power to supersede the committee of any society under certain circumstances and that this power need not be confined only in respect of such societies in which Government has major financial interest.

The person or persons appointed by the Registrar to manage the affairs of a society where a committee is to be superseded by the Registrar will "manage the affairs of the society for a period not exceeding *two years* specified in the order, which period may, at the discretion of the

Registrar, be extended from time to time; so that the aggregate period does not exceed *four years*".

Even in the case of the President's rule being extended to a State there is a safeguard that after eight months a government of elected representatives should be installed. A cooperative society is an institution of people and it is for them to elect, suspend and appoint their managing committee or managers. If the Registrar finds any defects in the management he can, under the laws, bring them to the notice of the general body of the society which consists of all its members—personally or through a written communication. The Report also says "the final authority in a cooperative society shall vest in the general body of members" but wherever it proceeds to vest extraordinary power in the Registrar, undermining the autonomy of a cooperative, it completely ignores the "final authority" of the society.

6. *Inspection made Statutory*

The Registrars, in view of their immense power over the societies, have made a custom of "inspecting" cooperative societies—a practice which was not supported by the Cooperative Act of 1912. The Law Committee has seized this opportunity to make a statutory provision for a practice which cooperators have throughout resented and abhorred. The committee states "we consider it desirable to give statutory recognition to this practice". It certainly was an advantage to have no representative of the cooperative movement on the committee. The very use of the word "inspection" in relation to cooperative societies is highly questionable.

7. *Inquiry by the Registrar*

The committee recommends that :

(I) The Registrar may of his own motion, by himself or by a person authorized by him by order in writing, hold an inquiry into the constitution, working and financial condition of a cooperative society

The cooperatives cannot have any internal autonomy, so long as the Registrar is allowed to hold an inquiry of "his own motion".

It further recommends :

The Registrar or any person authorized by him under sub-section (I)

shall, for the purposes of an enquiry under this section, have the following powers, namely :

(a) he shall, at all times, have free access to the informative documents, books, accounts, documents, securities, cash and other properties belonging to or in the custody of the society and may summon any person in possession or responsible for the custody of any such books, accounts, documents, securities, cash or other properties, to produce the same at any place at the headquarters of this society or any branch thereof;

(b) he may summon any person who, he has reason to believe, has knowledge of any of the affairs of the society to appear before him at any place at the headquarters of the society or any branch thereof and may examine such person on oath; and

(c) (i) he may, notwithstanding any rule or byelaw specifying the period of notice for a general meeting of the society, require the officers of the society to call a general meeting at such time and place at the headquarters of the society or any branch thereof and to determine such matters as may be directed by him and where the officers of the society refuse or fail to call such a meeting, he shall have power to call it himself;

(ii) any meeting called under clause (i) shall have all the power of a general meeting called under the byelaws of the society and its proceedings shall be regulated by any such byelaws except that no quorum shall be necessary for such a meeting.

These are sweeping executive and judicial powers which would completely subordinate the cooperative to the Registrar's control, especially if he is also allowed to hold such enquiries of his own motion. If the state of affairs of a society reaches such a point, the enquiry must be held under judicial auspices. The power to hold a meeting without quorum amounts to the inquiry officer taking the decision himself; this is indeed an extraordinary provision.

8. *Winding up of a Cooperative Society*

The committee recommends :

(2) the Registrar may of his own motion make an order directing the winding up of a cooperative society:

(a) where it is a condition of the registration of the society th the society shall consist of at least ten members and the number of members has been reduced to less than ten; or

(b) where the cooperative society has not commenced working or has ceased to work.

(3) The Registrar may cancel an order for the winding up of a cooperative society, at any time, in any case where, in his opinion, the society should continue to exist.

Section (b) is very omnibus, provides for no safeguards and may be open to misuse.

The powers suggested for the Registrar of winding up of a cooperative society and appointment of a liquidator, show no regard for autonomy of the cooperative society.

9. *Appeals*

The Cooperative Planning Committee had recommended as early as in 1946 that

> The 1912 Act does not provide any right of appeal against the decision of the Registrar refusing to register a society. We feel that a specific provision for appeal against such refusal should be made in the Act. The 1912 Act gives unlimited powers to the Registrar to reject amendments to the byelaws of a registered society. We are of the opinion that he should ordinarily register all amendments which are in conformity with the Act and Rules. In cases where he rejects an amendment he should assign reasons therefore, and an appeal to Government may lie within two months after the rejection which shall be intimated by registered post.

The Law Committee has indeed provided for appeal in both these and other matters. But by another provision it has been ensured that in actual practice no appeal could be made to the State Government if the Registrar so desires. It lays down that an appeal shall be made:

(a) to the State Government, if the decision or order was made by Registrar; or

(b) to the Registrar, if the decision or order was made by any other person, or a cooperative society.

No further appeal shall lie under this section from any decision or order by the Registrar, in appeal. Where the catch lies is in the following:

> *Explanation* : For the purposes of this section, the Registrar shall not include any person exercising all or any of the powers of the Registrar.

On page 72 it lays down that "Every person appointed to assist the Registrar" on whom the State Government may "confer all or any of the powers of the Registrar" shall exercise the powers conferred on him "subject to the general superintendence and control of the Registrar".

Technically, therefore, the Registrar should be held responsible for any decisions taken by his subordinates and there can be no escape from appeals going to the State Government under the cover that the decision was taken by a subordinate officer. The Registrar can conveniently ensure that all orders are given by his subordinates whom he can cover in appeal, thus defeating the very purpose of providing for an appeal.

(b) Control Over Audit

In addition to his executive control the Registrar is also in charge of audit of societies. The Cooperative Planning Committee had observed in 1946 that "the practice of combining the functions of audit and supervision in one person is undesirable as it is likely to lead to inefficiency. If the person who supervises the working of a society also audits its accounts many defects in the working are likely to remain undetected". The Cooperative Law Committee, on the other hand, observes that "the important point to be borne in mind is that the Registrar of Cooperative Societies, who is responsible under the law for the proper conduct of Societies, cannot fulfil his responsibility satisfactorily unless he keeps in close touch with the working of these societies by getting their accounts audited *under his direction and control,*" and that "the Chief Auditor" appointed for this purpose "will be responsible to and work under the control of the Registrar of Cooperative Societies". Even for the Government of India or State Governments such a freedom does not exist and the Comptroller and Auditor General and the Accountant General are given statutory safeguards to be free of executive control.

After declaring in paragraph 18 that the Government should not interfere in the day-to-day administration and working of the societies, the committee recommends in para 35 that "it is necessary to empower the Registrar under the Act to give a *directive* to a cooperative society to rectify the defects indicated in the audit report". This is *de facto* interference. The Registrar ought only to call the attention of the society to the defects indicated in the audit report and request rectification or ask the Society for its explanation. Where no rectification or explanation is forthcoming and there is proved incidence of maladministration of accounts, other remedial measures are available. A *directive* on first motion seems to us unwarranted.

(c) Judicial Powers of the Registrar

In para 38 the committee recommended that to avoid prolonged and expensive litigation, no court should have jurisdiction to entertain any suit or other proceeding in respect of disputes of cooperative societies.

The committee states that in several States the law at present permits reference of disputes to three or more arbitrators, one each to be named by the parties to the dispute and one to be named by the Registrar to serve as Chairman of the Panel of Arbitrators. The committee recommends that "as reference of disputes to more than one arbitrator is likely to hinder a speedy settlement of disputes, we have not provided in the Model Bill for the reference to a panel of arbitrators of a dispute". The Registrar may now "settle a dispute himself or appoint another officer of the Cooperative Department to do so or appoint an arbitrator".

Thus the Registrar, already empowered fully with powers of control, supervision, audit, issue of directives and supersession of committees of cooperative societies, is also armed with all the judicial powers. In one stroke the jurisdiction of the law courts of the land over cooperatives is withdrawn, appointment of arbitrators by the parties is withdrawn, and full power is vested in the Registrar to arbitrate "any dispute touching the constitution, management, or the business of a cooperative society".

The delegation of such powers to the Registrar in the very first instance is a violation of the Constitution, as one of the Directive Principles of State Policy requires that judicial powers should be separated from the executive.

(d) State Partnership and State Nominees

The committee recommends that a State Government may become a member of a cooperative society and "each person nominated by the State Government on the committee of the cooperative society shall have one vote".

This is a total violation of cooperative principles and under no circumstances can the Government be allowed to nominate persons on the managing committee of a society.
Where the Government has lent money, it can as a lender ask for its representative to be associated with the management of a cooperative society, if necessary.
The committee recommends that "sections 39 to 49" of the chapter on state partnership "shall have effect notwithstanding anything inconsistent therewith contained in any other law" thus making these Sections supreme over everything else.
The committee has subordinated all its deliberations to shaping cooperatives in the image of the Rural Credit Survey. In doing so it has served the requirements placed on it by its terms of reference to incorporate the recommendations of the Rural Credit Survey Report in the Cooperative Law.

The document here quotes at length from the Prime Minister's address to the Third Indian Cooperative Congress in April 1958, wherein he expresses his own strong reservations regarding some of the recommendations of the Rural Credit Survey Report, in particular those relating to State partnership and State management in cooperatives. These sections of the Prime Minister's speech are contained in the next chapter.

Recommendations of the Committee: Model Rules

Not content with the powers proposed for the Government and the Registrar under the Model Bill, the committee envisages complete autocratic control through the assumption of the following further powers which the administration would be able to lay down as it wishes from time to time.

The State Government is to make rules to carry out the purposes of the Model Bill, and some of the subjects on which it may make rules are stated in particular, without prejudice to its general power to make rules, e.g.

1. Matters in respect of which the cooperative society shall or may make byelaws;
2. The qualifications or disqualifications of individuals who may be admitted as members of cooperative societies;
3. The election of members of the managing committee by the general body of a cooperative society;

4. The qualifications and disqualifications for membership of a committee of a cooperative society;
5. The qualifications of employees of cooperative societies;
6. The mode of investment of funds of a cooperative society.

These are a few of the 40 subjects listed in respect of which the State Government may make rules, in respect of any society.

Under the Model Rules drafted by the committee for recommendation to the State Governments, we may cite just two to show the trend of authoritarian control :

Management of Societies (Clause 17)
Officers and Employees of Cooperative Societies

(1) No cooperative society shall appoint any person as its paid officer or employee in any category of service, unless he possesses the qualifications and furnishes the security as specified by the Registrar from time to time, for such category of service in the society, or for the class of societies to which it belongs.

(2) No cooperative society shall retain in service any paid officer or employee, if he does not acquire the qualifications or furnish the security as is referred to in sub-rule (1) within such time as the Registrar may direct.

This would mean that in addition to the powers of the Registrar to control a society in ways earlier discussed, he will also be able to interfere in the employment of staff of cooperative societies.

The power to lay down the qualifications of lakhs of employees of cooperative societies is a power open to dangerous abuse.

Conclusion

The committee which was set up to simplify the Cooperative Law and to modify it to enable cooperative societies "to play an increasingly important role in the development of the country" has ended by setting up the Registrar's rule. The powers of the Registrar have been made absolute.

Under the existing laws the Registrar was at best called a "benevolent dictator" or a "trustee" but the revisions suggested by the Law Committee turn him into an absolute autocrat.

Here was an assignment of historic importance. The opportunity could have been utilized to carry democracy further than the five-yearly elections to Parliament and State Legislatures. Democratic values and precepts—the essence of cooperation—could have been made part of the day-to-day life and business of the people. With some social vision, the laws could have been so revised as to place the people in a position appropriate to a free democratic people on whom the Constitution has already bestowed political sovereignty. The effect of the Law Committee's recommendations would be to subvert this sovereignty through unprecedented control and interference in the peaceful pursuit of economic activity—especially of a section of our people already too inarticulate and oppressed.

We suggest rejection of this Report by the Cooperative Movement by cooperatives and the Central and State Governments.

The Indian Cooperative Union also hopes to submit shortly a memorandum to the Government and the public embodying some of the general considerations and guiding principles relevant to the framing of a new Cooperative Law.

In fulfilment of the above undertaking, the ICU presented the following report to the Government in 1959.

II. COOPERATIVE LAW: PLEA FOR A PERSPECTIVE

Introduction

Every idea that seeks to get translated into social reality has to throw up an institutional form which can adequately embody and express it. But very soon the institutional form acquires a life of its own which increasingly tends to become independent of the idea. The order of primacy is then reversed. A belief arises that the idea, instead of being the source and sustainer, is a consequence of and dependent on the institution. Henceforth, the institutional form receives all attention and the idea none, until, in due course, the idea is completely replaced by a mass of institutional ritual. At this stage, the institutional form becomes dead, and a fetter on further social progress.

We, in India, have lived for many years in the suffocating company of a medley of such dead forms. Some of these forms we have inherited from our ancient and medieval past while others were brought in more recently by the British administration.

Now that we are a free nation with our own government chosen by a free vote of the people, we have to see not only that all dead matter is cleared off the social stage but also that all our institutional innovations throb with life and a creative impulse. This is possible only if we constantly keep in mind the ideals and values we cherish as a nation.

We hope this report which is conceived in that spirit will prove useful in framing suitable legislation for the cooperative movement and in generally advancing the cooperative cause.

The document begins by laying out, as a foundation for its proposals, the lines along which the independent republic of India was sought to be constructed:

Objectives of Freedom

Our national struggle for political freedom was all along inspired by certain definite social, economic and cultural aspirations. In 1931 Gandhiji declared: "Let there be no mistake as to what *Purna Swaraj* means to the Congress. It is full economic freedom for the toiling millions." In 1946 a resolution passed by the Meerut Congress declared:

> In the opinion of the Congress, Swaraj cannot be real for the masses unless it makes possible the achievement of a society in which democracy extends from the political to the social and economic sphere... fullest scope for every citizen for the development of his personality.

Immediately after the attainment of independence, in November 1947, the All India Congress Committee reaffirmed this objective in the following words:

Political independence having been achieved, the Congress must address itself to the next great task, namely, the establishment of real democracy in the country and a society based on social justice and equality. This can only be realized when democracy extends from the political to the social and economic spheres.

The paper goes on to quote several passages from the Constitution of India, stressing the orientation towards a democratic order based on justice, equality and concern for the weaker sections. Some of the fundamental rights written into the Constitution are mentioned, especially the right to form associations or unions, and to practise any profession, trade or business. The State is obliged to ensure the right to an adequate means of livelihood to all its citizens; its policy must also ensure that the ownership and control of the material resources of the community are so distributed as best to subserve the common good; and that the operation of the economic system does not result in the concentration of wealth and means of production to the common detriment.

The State is obliged to secure for all its workers :

> A living wage, conditions of work ensuring a decent standard of life and full enjoyment of leisure and social and cultural opportunities and, in particular, the State shall endeavour to promote cottage industries on an individual or cooperative basis in rural areas.

As regards the weaker sections of the nation, Article 46 of the Constitution announces:

> The State shall promote with special care the educational and economic interests of the weaker sections of the people... and shall protect them from social injustice and all forms of exploitation.

The political basis on which the social and economic principles are to be worked out is stated in Article 40 which says:

> The State shall take steps to organise village panchayats and endow them with such powers and authority as may be necessary to enable them to function as units of self-government.

Finally, Article 50 of the Constitution states:

> The State shall take steps to separate the judiciary from the executive in the Public Services of the State.

Socialist Pattern of Society

The same aspirations are inherent in the socialist pattern of society which we are out to build. Explaining this pattern, the Second Five Year Plan says:

> The socialist pattern of society is not to be regarded as some fixed or rigid pattern. It is neither necessary nor desirable that the economy should become a monolithic type of organization offering little play

for experimentation or as to forms or modes of functioning. Nor should expansion of the public sector mean centralization of decision making and of authority. The accent of the socialist pattern is on the attainment of positive goals; the raising of living standards; the enlargement of opportunities for all: the promotion of enterprise among the disadvantaged classes and the creation of a sense of partnership among all sections of the community.

Summing Up

We may now formulate more concisely a statement of objectives to be promoted:

1. The first and foremost consideration is the individual and his fuller and richer growth in an atmosphere of freedom.
2. His relationship with fellow human beings should be governed by mutual respect and consideration, all enjoying equality of status and opportunity.
3. The political, economic and social institutions of national life should be informed by principles of democracy, justice and equality and should maintain the dignity and sovereignty of the individual.
4. The political, economic and social organs of society should be decentralized ... to ensure that the individual does in actual practice enjoy freedom so that his initiative and self-reliance may grow and develop further.
5. Matters in which the individual and the community have the right of self-government should not be encroached upon or controlled by the bureaucracy.
6. Special measures of assistance and protection are to be extended to those whose conditions of life—economic and social—are far from the order of society envisaged by the Constitution.
7. For proper administration of justice, the powers of the judiciary and the executive should not be vested in the same persons.

The foregoing in our view represent the ideological aspirations of free India. All measures, legislative or otherwise, undertaken to promote economic and social welfare in India today must be guided by these aspirations. Finding a satisfactory institutional answer to these aspirations calls for the best of imagination and idealism. It is in the search of that answer that we turn to the cooperative movement.

COOPERATIVE PRINCIPLES AND PRACTICES

Our public policies and plans have repeatedly emphasized that cooperation is the best method for translating into social reality the ideals enshrined in our Constitution. Cooperative ideology brings into harmony the best elements of liberalism as well as socialism—the two powerful modern philosophies which have often warred with each other to mutual detriment.

Self-Government

A cooperative society is based on the free will and voluntary association of a group of people. The supreme authority is vested in the general body of all members. All matters of policy, programme, management, investment of funds and distribution of profits are subject to the approval of the general body.

The day-to-day management of the cooperative is entrusted to a committee elected by the general body of all members, each exercising one vote. The elections are held annually for the membership of the entire committee, or, in some cases, of one-third or one-fourth of the members at a time where a system of retirement of a proportion of members is followed.

The cooperative society is thus a voluntary association of people having common objects. It is a self-governing institution. Its governance is carried on strictly on democratic lines.

Social Democracy

In a cooperative, mutual aid is the core of personal relationship amongst the members. It accords equal social status to all members. No distinction is allowed as between master and servant, employer and employee, and no discrimination on grounds of religious belief or on account of caste or political difference.

Economic Democracy

Cooperative principles allow only one vote for one member, thus neutralizing the disparities caused by ownership of capital and as a consequence establishing economic equality amongst its members. This economic equality is further secured by relating profits primarily to work. Earnings on capital are rendered nominal. In fact, a number of cooperative societies pay no interest on share capital. Means of economic activity and business are subscribed by each, according to capacity, to the common pool which is employed for the benefit of all.

Unions of Cooperatives

The federal formations of cooperatives and their unions represent a "centralized-decentralized" structure where the powers of the Centre are determined by the constituent members.

It is actually through the active and vigorous functioning of Unions and Federations that the cooperative societies become part of a movement. The movement stands to bring greater life and strength into the working of individual societies by commanding greater spokesmanship and resources; at the same time, it serves to correct lapses and weaknesses on the part of the members in matters of principles.

In countries where the movement is young and which follow mixed economy patterns, the federal cooperative institutions are able to protect the movement and cooperative principles from trespass or harm by individuals or institutions opposed to cooperation, or from excessive interference by the State. According to an ILO study:

> The purpose and effect of this federal structure, rising gradually from local societies to national and international organizations, is to place at the disposal of its smallest component units all the benefits normally conferred by large-scale financial, administrative and technical concentration.
>
> It is characteristic of the cooperative structure that it is built upon the most numerous and smallest economic units. These units are the individual households—the peasant farms, the small family workshops of rural industries and of the multiple forms of home industry, the little undertakings of artisans, small shopkeepers and fishermen. Each cooperative society, large or small, is a free federation of primary economic units, which have united for some definite common purpose, but are not merged into a new organism. The units retain their full identity and autonomy. Indeed, the cooperative society which unites them not only respects, but even tends to strengthen, their independence and sense of their own responsibilities.
>
> ...Throughout the ascending scale of the federal structure, each higher organization is created and administered by and for those below it. In

the final analysis, it is not the top organization but the small basic units that are sovereign.

As Dr. Fauquet has written, "It is, of course, possible that at some particular moment and in some particular branch of the cooperative movement the tendency towards concentration may appear to outweigh (perhaps excessively) the tendency towards democratic decentralization, or vice versa. But over a sufficient range of years and countries the general picture will be one of unceasing readjustments designed to restore the equilibrium which is the distinctive mark of genuine federalism."

An Economistic Misconception

Because most cooperative societies are ostensibly engaged in economic undertakings of various types, some people have the impression that cooperation is simply an alternative form of business organization. This is a dangerous misconception because it tends to put a premium on expediency as against fundamental principles.

E. Hosselman writes:

> Cooperation has higher objectives than increase of economic advantages, which are what most people probably seek when they join a cooperative society. It evidently also implies a conception of economic organization quite different from that prevailing at present... it is urgently necessary to re-introduce ethical motives and practices into the economy and that their reintroduction is the intent and most fundamental and far-reaching endeavour of the cooperative movement.
>
> It is claimed that the cooperative movement, through its machinery and through cooperative education, the guardian of its social content, is a successful attempt to ensure in economic life freedom from obsession with profit, the abolition of exploitation of man by man, and the dignity of self-help combined with mutual aid—revaluation of man himself.

Dr. Fauquet says:

> The primary aim of the cooperative institution is to improve the economic situation of its members, but by virtue of its methods and

of the qualities which it demands of and develops in the members, it achieves a higher aim. The goal, then, of cooperation, is to develop men– men imbued with the spirit of self-help and mutual aid, in order that individually they may rise to a full personal life and collectively to a full social life.

Conclusion

We can now say without fear of contradiction that cooperative principles are in complete accord and harmony with the objectives of freedom we have placed before ourselves in this country. Further, the cooperative form of organization answers well the requirements of a social institution of our seeking which would respect and provide the practical means for advancing our natural aspirations.

Cooperation, therefore, is not a matter which can be entrusted to a committee of experts in the hope of obtaining a foolproof recipe. Nor can it be left in the hands of an administrative hierarchy, howsoever devoted and efficient, to be percolated from the top through a set of rules and procedures. We envisage that, in due course, cooperation will embrace a significant sector of the lives of a majority of our people. It is, therefore, in the fitness of things that the people themselves should deliberate over its philosophy and approach, experiment with its methods and give a verdict over its promises and achievements.

No amount of statistics about the number of societies formed, members enrolled, capital amassed, business concluded and accounts audited can ever be a substitute for a living movement created, sustained, controlled and put to effective use by masses of awakened people.

REVIEW OF THE PRESENT SITUATION

The history of cooperation in countries where it took birth and shape is a witness that popular movements and organizational work preceded legislation and departmental set-up at the government level. In India, however, the process has been the reverse. Cooperation was first brought into India by an alien government which was hardly in a position to sponsor a popular movement. Cooperative institutions had, perforce, to be borrowed devices mechanically imposed on an unprepared and therefore unreceptive soil.

It was no wonder, therefore, that the power and control of the Registrars and other departmental functionaries over these institutions as well as official interference in their day-to-day life went on increasing year after year. There was no democratic life inside the institutions themselves to object to undemocratic interference. In the minds of the people cooperatives had become associated as a *sarkari* and not a *sahkari* movement. Worse still, there was no democratic opinion outside sufficiently concerned with the health of these institutions to challenge the growing departmental control which, once established in practice, was recognized by subsequent legislation. One has only to examine the comparatively liberal Cooperative Act of 1912 side by side with the Cooperative Acts passed by various provincial governments after the Reforms of 1919 to realize the inroads of the Registrars' powers even in the routine affairs of cooperative societies.

All this cramping legislation and the resultant official stranglehold still presides over our cooperative endeavour. More, there is a tendency further to departmentalize the movement, as is amply evident from the recommendations made by officials who constituted the Committee on Cooperative Law. As a consequence, cooperation, which, as we pointed out earlier, symbolizes the marriage of two live movements remains for all practical purposes a stillborn child. The common people have not yet owned it as their own offspring. Nor does this "departmental prodigy" directly know the common man who alone can breathe life into it.

We are not alone in stressing that there is something seriously wrong with our present cooperative set-up. The feeling has been voiced from a number of quarters, official and non-official.

Impressions of Principal Kaji in 1945

In 1945 the Government of India of the time had appointed the Cooperative Planning Committee to review the situation. Although it was unable to come up with a clear diagnosis, one of its members, Principal Hiralal L. Kaji, a distinguished cooperator, submitted a minute of dissent, a penetrating commentator which was incorporated in the Report.

Extracts from his writings:

> More than 40 years have passed since the movement was launched under State auspices and official control, and the success that was hoped for is not attained. The Registrar of Cooperative Societies, far from being merely the registering officer as in the case of joint stock companies, was to be friend, philosopher and guide, and soon

> constituted himself into the trustee of the societies. From him came the drive for a rapid multiplication of societies in the earlier years of the movement; with him rested, directly or indirectly, the extent and availability of finance for primaries from the central and provincial banks; with him rested supervision, inspection and audit; from him came continual streams of circulars giving advice and guidance which soon acquired the force of law; with him remained the power to interfere with the day-to-day working of societies.
>
> And yet despite this complete control, on him rested not the responsibility for failures! If a society failed it was the members' sins of commission and omission that were responsible; Government and its officers were immune from all liability and blame; the sense of security that the public had, because of State control, turned out to be more a fancy than reality.

Review by the Congress Agrarian Reforms Committee in 1949

Perhaps, the first all-India committee that commented on the cooperative movement inherited by independent India was the Congress Agrarian Reforms Committee appointed in 1947-48 by Dr. Rajendra Prasad, then President of the Indian National Congress. The Committee, headed by Shri J.C. Kumarappa, submitted its report in 1949. The report states:

> The Royal Commission on Indian Agriculture in 1928 observed that if cooperation fails there fails the whole fabric of Indian agriculturists. During the two decades since the Royal Commission made its report, the cooperative movement, however, has made little progress in tackling the problems of Indian farming.
>
> By and large it is true that the cooperative movement on account of the bureaucratic control and rigidity of administration has failed to attain the tempo of a popular movement.

The committee also records its detailed findings of visits to some of the cooperative farming societies. One of the incidents recorded by it is very revealing:

> The committee met with peasants separately in the absence of the government officials attached to the farm, with a view to finding out their free and frank reactions. Some of these peasants were the elected *Panchs*. Hardly one or two among them could sign their names and

the ignorance and backwardness was indeed colossal. It was evident that the officers had taken meticulous care to keep the records in very good shape so as to impress any visitor, but the records were not indicative of the real position. The peasants complained of coercion and threats. One of them alleged that he was threatened with imprisonment if he refused to join the cooperative farm. There was also a wide-spread complaint about the non-payment of wages.

Findings of the All-India Rural Credit Survey in 1954

In 1951,the Reserve Bank sponsored the All-India Rural Credit Survey to examine and recommend suitable policies in the sphere of rural credit. The Report of the survey, submitted in 1954, also covered cooperative institutions engaged in rural credit.

As the findings of this survey are covered in detail in the following chapter, we only mention here briefly the essence of the extracts quoted by the ICU: that

"...the place occupied by cooperative credit in the rural finance of the country is very insignificant,... that the class-wise distribution of cooperative finance is preponderantly in favour of the large cultivator—as compared with the medium and the small," and that "the magnitude of its three-fold inadequacy (i.e. inadequate geographical coverage, inadequate coverage of the agricultural population, and marginal fulfilment of the credit needs of even members of cooperative societies) is such as to warrant, from the quantitative aspect, only one judgment, namely, 'failure,' on the fifty-year record of the cooperative credit agency in this country".

Observations of Sir Malcolm Darling in 1957

Early in 1957, the services of Sir Malcolm Darling were secured by the Government of India to "review recent developments in the field of cooperation with reference to programmes in the Second Five Year Plan". In his Report, published in the middle of 1957, he observes:

In the Draft Outline of the Plan it is rightly said that "if strong primary unions exist at the base, effective organizations can also be built at higher levels". It follows conversely that without strong primary units effective organizations cannot be built. Yet it is proposed to add an imposing new storey—for cooperative manufacturing, marketing and processing—to a structure, as I shall show later, nowhere very strong and in some States deplorably weak, and to do this without any systematic strengthening of its foundations. This is sooner or later to risk partial, perhaps even in some areas total, collapse. And if that were to happen, experience shows only too clearly that rebuilding is extremely difficult—also very costly. Bihar and Bengal are conspicuous examples of this; indeed in every other State the path of cooperation is strewn with wreckage.

Comments by the Survey of Handicraft Associations

The Report of an All-India Survey of Handicraft Associations says, after visiting as many as 63 handicraft cooperative societies all over India :

> Most of the cooperatives are controlled and managed by departmental officials, who, although paid by the cooperatives out of subsidies received from the Government, nevertheless behave as masters and employers. The craftsmen-members generally have no knowledge about their intimate affairs such as finances, marketing, accounts, profits and losses. The official managers are frequently sceptical and occasionally contemptuous about the craftsmen's capacity ever to manage their own affairs. And, as if in exchange, the craftsmen develop a sense of suspicion towards these managers and frequently complain that funds provided by the Government for the good of "poor people" are being embezzled and misused.

Indictment by the Third Cooperative Congress, 1958

Finally, we have a judgement expressed in the Third Annual Cooperative Congress held in April 1958. In his presidential speech Shri K.D. Malaviya said:

> The Britishers have gone but the legacy of their methods still binds us... With the strait-jacket methods of control and administration of the movement, with government nominees and government managers in cooperatives, how can we expect to call forth popular initiative and enterprise in cooperative institutions?...

Conclusion

The existing cooperative structure must be judged according to the following criteria. Firstly, cooperation should be able to introduce the understanding and practice of democracy and self-government amongst its members. Secondly, it should be able to establish equality in economic and social status amongst its members. Thirdly, the movement should be able to provide economic and social opportunities to the weaker sections of the people. On all these counts, however, the cooperative movement in India has failed.

In presenting such an overall assessment of the cooperative movement we are not overlooking individual instances of good cooperatives. But they are no more than exceptions. They are like oases in a vast desert.

COOPERATIVE LEGISLATION

The first cooperative law, viz. the Cooperative Credit Societies Act was passed in 1904; it was modelled largely on the English Friendly Societies Act of 1793.

> It was however soon found that the Act was restricted in its scope in that it permitted registration of primary credit societies alone and left non-credit societies and federal organizations of primary credit societies outside of its purview. These shortcomings were removed by the Cooperative Societies Act 1912, which, however, retained the simplicity and elasticity of the earlier Act.

Under the Constitutional Reforms of 1919, cooperation became a transferred subject under the Provinces. From that time the various Provinces in India passed their own Cooperative Acts beginning with Bombay in 1925, Madras in 1932, Bihar in 1935, Orissa in 1945, and so on. "Although the new Acts were thus enacted in these States, the essential features of the 1912 Act were still retained in every one of them".

In the post-Independence period between 1947 and 1954 the various Indian States "either adopted the 1912 Act or such other Act as was in force in another State, or enacted new legislation, which was based more or less on the existing legislation which was in force in States like Bombay or Madras."

Thus, the Friendly Societies Act of 1793 has obviously occupied a central position in our cooperative legislation till today, despite occasional modifications here and there. It may, therefore, be useful to study the purposes for which that Act was passed by the British Parliament. We may also study the experiences of the cooperative movement in Britain in regard to the Friendly Societies Act, as also in the development of cooperative legislation in that country in general.

Outmoded Foundations

Describing the history of cooperative legislation in Great Britain, Laszlo Valko observes:

> The great misery and distress during the eighteenth century created serious problems for Parliament. The several Poor Acts, however, did not solve the basic problems of these economic conditions. Even the next step of the affected people in uniting in certain kinds of self-help organizations was a modest aid.
>
> The act for encouragement and relief of Friendly Societies (1793) assured the interested people the right to establish voluntary associations for the mutual help and benefit of their members during hard times of sickness, unemployment and other need. "Their purpose was to bring aid in emergency cases, and their number grew very rapidly.... Although they were very popular, the scope of their activity was limited to charity actions".

During the first half of the nineteenth century public opinion in Britain became sharply aware of the ineffectiveness of the Friendly Societies in meeting economic distress. Valko adds :

> The beginning of the nineteenth century was filled with energetic pressure and desire to change the economic and social backwardness of the employed classes. The first primitive cooperatives or mutual trading societies were organised at various places of England... The first cooperatives were legally put in the same category as the Friendly Societies.

Some amendments were, however, made in 1834 to the Friendly Societies Act, and the mutual trading societies continued to be registered under that Act, including the first successful cooperative store of the Rochdale Pioneers. But, says Valko :

> This uniformity created several limitations for the first cooperatives.

They could not buy land, trade with non-members or make investments, except in government securities.

In 1846, the British Parliament introduced another amendment to the Friendly Societies Act to include a clause for the "frugal investment of the savings of the members to better enable them to purchase food, firewood, clothes, and other necessities, or the tools or implements of their trade or calling, and to provide for the education of their children...". This gave the movement some fillip and more cooperatives came up as a result. Again, we quote Valko :

> But the new cooperative societies differed considerably from the Friendly Societies in purpose as well as in construction. They were organized for the economic strengthening of weak individuals by self-help: not to provide for charitable assistance and protection extended by the Friendly Societies, against the ordeals of sickness, unemployment, and other unexpected emergencies.
> The legal form provided by the Friendly Societies Act did not fit the economic postulates of cooperative societies. This legal dress was either too tight or too loose for cooperatives. They obviously needed their own particular legal uniform.
> The cooperative societies were specifically legalized when the world's first cooperative law was passed by the British Parliament in 1852 in the form of the Industrial and Provident Societies Act. This opened the way for the development of cooperative legislation, which closely followed the practical progress of the movement.

Thus, in 1852, long before the cooperative movement was first introduced in India (in 1904), the inadequacy of the Friendly Societies Act in developing the cooperative movement had been fully realized.

Subsequent Deformation

What besets cooperative legislation in India today, however, cannot all be blamed on the unfortunate decision made 55 years ago to import the Friendly Societies Act from Great Britain. For, the Cooperative Act of 1912—the last of the Central enactments on cooperatives—is still today the most liberal piece of legislation compared with the various Acts passed by the various Provinces after the Constitutional Reforms of 1919. We give below several instances (these are quoted from the *Report of the Committee on Cooperative Law*, pp. 7-10) from some of the State Acts which show the many excesses that have been committed by the present legislation.

The Bombay Cooperative Societies Act passed in 1925 empowers the State Government to bring about amalgamation of societies compulsorily.

The Madras Cooperative Societies Act, which followed in 1932, provides for the supersession of the committee of a cooperative society by the Registrar. With a view to promoting speedy collection of arrears of cooperative societies, the Act provides the Registrar with powers to recover amounts due to societies under decree or awards by attachment and sale of property. It enables the financing bank to inspect the books and accounts of the society indebted to it. It also provides for compulsory amalgamation of societies.

Similarly, the Bengal Cooperative Societies Act, passed in 1940, provides that the financing bank, to which the society is indebted, can direct the latter to amend its bye-laws. Under this Act, a cooperative credit society can serve notice on any creditor of a member requiring him (creditor) to furnish a written statement of his claims against the member.

In other instances taken directly from the State Acts we find the following in Punjab :

> The Registrar may direct the general meeting convened at his instance or postpone the consideration of any item on the agenda, he may issue such directives as he considers necessary for regulating the nature and extent of security which society or class of societies may demand in respect of loans advanced by it, (and)...may, from time to time, issue such directives as he considers necessary for the successful conduct of the business of a society or class of societies. The Registrar has, power to suspend the Managing Committee.
>
> (Section 43)

Out of 101 Rules framed under the Act, the Registrar's powers of approval, sanction and interference appear in 55 Rules. In Uttar Pradesh:

The Registrar has powers to compel societies to change the bye-laws. If a society does not change the bye-laws, the Registrar can issue the amendment himself which shall be treated as a duly registered amendment. (Section 11-A).

Rule 175—The Registrar may disallow any resolution passed or any action decided upon by an officer or a committee or a board of directors or a general meeting of any society, if such resolution or action is, in his opinion, foreign to the objects of the society or against the Act and the Rules.

The Registrar has powers to suspend the Managing Committee (Rule 31).

This sort of cooperative legislation has produced results which sound very anomalous in the context of what is intended to be a voluntary movement. Here we have cooperative societies with power over non-members to require the latter to submit information, etc. Here we have Registrars with powers to enforce compulsory amalgamation of cooperative societies and, what is shocking, here we have banks with powers to "direct" a cooperative society "to amend its bye-laws". It will be very hard to find a similar piece of legislation anywhere in the world.

Under the Acts, the Registrar has been given authority to frame model bye-laws which a society must adopt before its registration is allowed. Model bye-laws are invariably so worded as to include a provision requiring a society to submit money matters to the Registrar "for his prior approval". This is another legal device through which the control of the Registrar over cooperative societies is further heightened.

Non-statutory Powers of the Registrars

The various Acts represent only a part of the picture in showing how the original Act of 1912 has been deformed beyond recognition. These Cooperative Acts, after all, represent what may be called the statutory powers of the Registrar. The real control of the Registrar, however, emanates more from non-statutory powers exercised by him over the cooperative societies. In the words of Principal Kaji :

> It is the gradual encroachment by the Registrar in other matters, it is the non-statutory functions taken up by him which constitute what is properly regarded as vexatious interference and demands attention. There is organization, supervision and periodical inspection. Nowhere does the Cooperative Societies Act of 1912 confer these powers on the Registrar and yet he performs these functions and exercises, if he chooses, a great measure of control even over the day-to-day management. At the time of registration, the bye-laws of a society are pressed into conformity with a standard pattern; the registration of amendments of bye-laws gives a further occasion for

changes; and often the words "with the approval of the Registrar" are added to some of the proposed amendments so that the Registrar secures powers not conferred on him by statute and prescribes, regulates, supervises and inspects the affairs of cooperative societies.

Summing up

Cooperative legislation in India was founded on statutes which were already in disuse in Britain for over 50 years; and during the last 55 years statutes have been changed or modified invariably in a manner as to make them more rigid and authoritarian. The statutory powers and the non-statutory (assumed) functions combine to prevent the establishment or growth of a cooperative society enjoying democratic status, internal autonomy or a voluntary character—the basic attributes of a cooperative society.

Cooperative legislation as it exists in India, therefore, requires, in our view, not just a few modifications here and there, but a basic and fundamental change. The new Cooperative Law should embody not only the principles of cooperation, but also provide for safeguards against non-statutory interference by authorities.

Cooperative Department

Under the scheme of things established by our cooperative legislation from time to time, the cooperative departments in the States have been the main agencies set up by the Government to introduce cooperation and to promote and organize cooperative societies. In view of the importance of the functions assigned to the cooperative departments, it was felt that the heads of these departments, i.e. the Registrars of Cooperative Societies, should possess special qualifications.

Registrar's Qualifications Defined

As early as in 1915 the McLagan Committee had laid down the essential qualifications which a Registrar should possess in the following words :

> In order to fulfil his duties he must be continually studying cooperative literature, which is now most extensive; he must make himself acquainted with economic conditions and practices both throughout India and in his own Province; he must know the principles and

methods of joint-stock banking; and must examine the systems of developing thrift and inculcating cooperation which have been tried in other countries. He is also head of a teaching establishment and must devise effective means of impressing a real knowledge of cooperation on the bulk of the population. He has further to control a large staff, to draft model bye-laws and rules, to collect statistics and write reports, to advise Government on various subjects, and keep in close touch with the higher finance of the movement as managed by provincial banks and central banks. In addition to this he must attend conferences, cooperative and agricultural, must keep in constant touch with markets, with honorary organizers and other well-wishers and various departments of Government, and must undertake a certain amount of writing and reading the official press and cooperative journals. It must further be remembered that there is no finality in the Registrar's work and he can never feel that it has been cleared off and brought up-to-date.

New means and methods to attain fresh ends must constantly be discussed and devised. His work is, moreover, highly responsible, involving a watch over large sums of money deposited by the public and a share in the responsibility for the economic fate of a Province. It can well be realized that few officers are entrusted with work more serious or more exacting.

The Cooperative Planning Committee, in 1946, re-emphasized this advice :

He (the Registrar) should not only be a man of outstanding ability but should also be temperamentally suited for the work of running a popular movement of this kind. Before he assumes charge of the post of the Registrar, he should undergo a thorough training and should work for at least two years as Deputy or Joint Registrar. During the course of his training as well as during his tenure of office he should be allowed opportunities to study the working of the movement in other Provinces and outside India. In view of the responsible nature of the duties of the Registrar, he should enjoy a higher status than he does at present . . . .

We observe that in some Provinces Registrars are changed at short intervals. The work in connexion with the cooperative movement is becoming increasingly technical and it is necessary that sufficient time should be given to the Registrar to study it and to formulate and execute policies. In our opinion, therefore, his tenure should be for about 10 years. He should be fully compensated for holding the post till the end of the term.

Departments Full of Unqualified Personnel

The actual situation was, however, very different. Reviewing it in 1957, Sir Malcolm Darling wrote :

> Again and again I found officers from outside the department appointed Registrar, Joint or Deputy Registrar without even a day's training. In the case of the Registrar, the policy is, I venture to say, inexcusable considering the weight of authority against it. And when it is combined with frequent transfers, it is dangerous in the extreme, since it deprives the movement of experienced leadership at a critical moment of its development...
>
> It is still the rule rather than the exception for Registrars to be appointed without any training at all. Uttar Pradesh, West Bengal, Bombay, Orissa, Kerala and Bihar are all examples of this. In Rajasthan it applies to the last three Registrars.
>
> What I have said about the post of Registrar applies only less strongly to other gazetted posts. Case after case came to my notice of men appointed Joint Registrar or Deputy Registrar with little or no training, most of them without any at all.

Responsibilities Divorced from Competence

Yet the functions which were intended to be entrusted to specially qualified people were neither reduced nor modified and continued to be discharged by unqualified staff. Naturally the departments could not be expected to do justice to the job assigned to them. They registered cooperatives without any adequate investigation into the nature of business that was to be undertaken, the economic viability of the enterprise proposed and the availability of capital resources and managerial skill needed for a successful outcome. They seldom remembered that cooperation could not be fostered by getting certain forms filled and signed and, therefore, hardly ever cared to educate the members whom they mechanically herded into departmentally devised constructions.

It is true that most of them performed this institutional ritual in a conscientious manner. But mere conscientiousness, in the absence of vision and a grasp of fundamental principles, could not produce satisfactory results. With the coming of the Plans and the acceptance of the principle that rapid industrialization in certain sectors was to be achieved on a cooperative basis, this very conscientiousness became a source of grave danger. The departments were now in a hurry to set up as many cooperatives as they could within a fixed period of time and against the background of fixed targets. Noticing this trend, Sir Malcolm Darling wrote :

> Owing to a natural human tendency for those below to wish to please those above, I found many disposed to regard the targets under the Plan as aims to be achieved at all costs.

Spurious Cooperatives

One of the most harmful effects of this official sponsorship has been the formation of spurious cooperatives. According to the Report of the Rural Credit Survey, the departments have associated themselves with undesirable elements to bring about this deplorable state of affairs. Says Sir Malcolm Darling :

> In the Punjab—it may also be the case elsewhere—there has been a tendency to register societies whose members have joined together solely to take advantage of Government's financial and other concessions to Cooperative Societies; perhaps to borrow from Central Banks at a comparatively low rate of interest. A typical example is the cooperative transport society formed by its promoters for their exclusive benefit with no regard to those who use the transport. I even heard of a cinema society formed on similar lines.
>
> This applies to all societies whose dealings would be mainly with non-members. It is not always remembered that the facilities and benefits conferred by the Cooperative Societies Act are primarily intended for persons of moderate or slender means.

Misuse of Power

The powers of control and regulation were given to the departments in response to certain functions they were expected to perform. They have failed to perform those functions. But they have exercised their power to the extreme limit set by law.

Having got thoroughly mixed up with the internal affairs of the societies in a manner not free from abuse, the departments have been unable to act as watch-dogs of public interest. Malpractice in the cooperatives, misuse of privileges and resources have either not been brought to light or have been concealed from public knowledge. Apex cooperative institutions have been unable to act as brakes or checks on the Registrar's unfettered control over the cooperative societies because until recently the Registrars in most States were also Presidents of the apex institutions.

NEED FOR A DECISIVE DEPARTURE

Circumscribed by inappropriate legislation and mismanaged by incompetent and authoritarian departments the cooperative movement remains for all practical purposes a departmental fossil. Our Constitution has given to the common man the right to vote and choose the government he likes. The two General Elections have shown the admirable manner in which the common man has responded to this new status and responsibility. Can there now be any justification in keeping the cooperative movement in sterilized isolation from the common people?

A momentous decision is needed to turn our backs on the last 50 years of the "cooperative movement" so that we can lay firmly the foundations of a new movement which is both popular and principled. For, what is at stake is not the dilapidated house that we have today but the new edifice we aspire to build. Perhaps we can consider a sound municipal practice in dealing with a house which endangers the lives of its inhabitants as well as those of its neighbours: to pull it down with special care, clear the debris and start all over again.

In recommending this, we have, uppermost in our mind, the objective of restoring the people's confidence in the cooperative movement. Most of the time, people refer to cooperation as the "latest method of enticing public money into private pockets". It is becoming daily more difficult for people who believe in cooperative principles and who have not been discouraged by the current mess, to defend the movement.

If we insist upon keeping the old order intact, we shall have corrupted the new order that is fast emerging all around us. For, as Goethe says, "there is nothing more dangerous for a new truth than an old error".

Precedents from Japan and Italy

The situation in which we find our cooperative movement today is not without parallel. In fact its symptoms closely resemble the disease developed by cooperative movements in other countries which did not possess a democratic form of government. The state of the cooperative movement in imperialist Japan and fascist Italy provide a good study in comparison.

When Japan adopted a democratic way of life after the war, it was found that the cooperatives which had developed before and during the war were not cooperatives in character and were under too much official control.

> All farmers were forced to join a town or village agricultural association and all the town or village agricultural associations to join a prefectural agricultural association and all (the latter) to participate in the National Agricultural Association and in the Central Cooperative Bank for Agriculture and Forestry.
>
> Heads and officers of agricultural associations were appointed by the respective administrative agencies, thus losing their self-governing functions and becoming an integral part of the administrative organ.
>
> On December 9, 1945, a memorandum was issued by General MacArthur, the Supreme Commander of the Allied Powers, to the Japanese Government to take appropriate measures to ensure the farmers a more equal opportunity to enjoy the fruits of their labour and to develop "a programme to foster and encourage an agricultural cooperative movement free from domination by non-agrarian interests and to the economic and cultural advancement of the Japanese farmer".
>
> After the war, a democratic idea began to spread rapidly among the Japanese and the elimination of the war-time control was set about in every field. The Japanese Government took temporary measures to democratize the government-dominated Agricultural Organization Law and provide new legislation authorizing member-controlled cooperative associations and dissolving existing agricultural associations.
>
> This was accomplished by enacting in the Diet the Agricultural Cooperative Association Law, and the Agricultural Organization Liquidation Law, promulgated on November 19, 1947.
>
> The Agricultural Cooperative Association Law was enforced from December 15, 1947, but in the absence of true democratic ideas on the part of farmers there was a strong tendency that the new agricultural cooperatives might be dominated by non-agrarian interests and

> bosses. Hence the Government undertook a policy to place restrictions on the establishment of agricultural cooperatives until knowledge about the fundamental principles and purports of democratic agricultural cooperatives was fully disseminated among the farmers. In practice, the establishment of agricultural cooperatives under the new law was set about from February 1948.

Another example relevant to our problems is provided by Italy :

> In 1926 when cooperatives came under the direct influence of the Fascist Government, the National Fascist Institute of Cooperatives (ENFC), a government-established and government-controlled body, was entrusted with these functions for all cooperatives.
>
> After the Second World War, it was an urgent task to restore the democratic and autonomous status of cooperatives. However, on the other hand, there arose a serious problem brought about by inflationary economic conditions. Several profit-seeking private business enterprises were using the cooperative form. A great number of pseudo-cooperatives operated under the protection and privileges of the prior cooperative laws, but for the private profit of a small group of businessmen. These conditions led to the creation of a new cooperative law pertaining in particular to supervision and inspection, in 1957.
>
> The new law had to restore the original autonomous legal status of cooperatives and protect their characteristic principles by refusing the admittance or registration of the increasing number of pseudo-cooperatives. It was very important to set up the supervision and inspection in a democratic way, avoiding direct control by the State as was characteristic of the Fascist regime. Experience indicates that this intention was realized. Leaders of the Italian cooperative movement feel that the present system provided by this law is not at all anti-democratic. It recognizes the rights of cooperative societies to self-control and self-government, and states that the State should act only in a few exceptional cases. This consideration was included in the new Constitution of the Italian Republic which came into force on January 1, 1948.

The Future Task

The experiences of Japan and Italy have a relevance to our problem, and we believe that solutions similar to the ones adopted by those countries are most likely to meet our requirements.

In order to pave the way for the development of our cooperative movement along right and principled lines, the first and foremost step required is to subject the existing cooperatives to a searching inquiry in the light of the national aspirations stated earlier. We recommend that an inquiry commission consisting primarily of judges, cooperators and public men should be appointed in each State for this purpose. We hope that in future the Government will not appoint committees and commissions to advise on cooperative matters, composed entirely or mostly of officials.

Here the ICU'S recommendations are that cooperatives should be categorised and dealt with in the manner described in Chapter 3.

We also recommend a similar searching probe into the working of the cooperative departments and the suitability of their personnel.

THE STATE AND THE COOPERATIVE MOVEMENT

There are countries, notably Denmark, where cooperation is flourishing without a cooperative law or a cooperative department. But due to historical circumstances, we are at the other extreme. The State has played in the past and is likely to play in the future an important role in the development of cooperation in this country.

There is a close parallel between our problem in India today and the problem of reconstruction and rehabilitation in a number of countries after the Second World War. These countries had not only to rebuild their shattered economies but also to rehabilitate, psychologically and socially, their people who had been afflicted by the abnormal conditions of the war. In some countries like Japan and Italy, even the political order underwent a change and the advancement of democracy became an added objective of national policy.

It was obvious that the State would have to play an active and important role to achieve these objectives as people's efforts by themselves could not be enough.

Most of these countries sought a solution of their reconstruction problem through the cooperative movement. Cooperation was not considered a panacea for all national problems, but it was acknowledged as the best means of popular participation in the process of national reconstruction. This naturally raised the question of relationship between the State and the Cooperatives. The problem engaged the attention of various national and international organizations and thinkers all over the world.

Statement of Basic Policy

In January 1946 the Central Committee of the International Cooperative Alliance adopted the following resolution :

> Considering that the evolution of liberal capitalism into a capitalism of cartels and trusts, as well as the situation resulting from the war imposes on the States the task of ensuring, by deliberate measures of organization, the restoration of national economies and of international economy;
>
> Considering that this imposes on the Cooperative Movement the necessity of defining its position with regard to those changes which the action of the State is bringing about in the structure of economy;
>
> Recognizes that there is a convergence of aims between cooperative action and action of the State, provided that the latter be freed from any coalition of private interests, and that it corresponds to the necessity of an organization which places an economy of service above an economy of profit, both from a national and an international point of view.
>
> The Cooperative Movement is aware that the State is being led to take measures in order to assume the direction of the whole sphere of economy. But the action of the State necessarily has limits, and in its efforts towards the general organization of economy it cannot do without the collaboration of cooperative institutions of all kinds. Cooperation, being an organization built up from below and which groups, in federated organizations, units of a personal and family character which are at the basis of economic and social life, both in towns and in the country, is the only organization capable of linking those units organically with any plan embracing the whole economy. Therefore the Cooperative Movement is entitled to claim from the public authorities the liberty of its full development in the large fields of economic life where cooperation succeeds in reconciling order, efficiency and liberty by a freely accepted discipline and by putting into practice the principles of self-help and mutuality.

Commenting on this resolution, an ILO study observed :

> The point of junction between State and cooperative activity to which reference is made in the above resolution may be placed high or low, nearer the base of the joint structure or nearer its apex, according as the one or the other system has developed further; but the higher that point lies, the more completely organizations of the economy will be free from authoritarian and bureaucratic connections. The cooperative system may perhaps be regarded as appropriate for the transmission of directives from above; there is no doubt that owing to the reactions from below arising out of its very structure, it is equally suited to correct such directives and to lessen the effect of the errors they contain. Indeed, if planned economy is supplemented by, and can rely on, a cooperative system, it may recover the sensitive and reflex qualities of a living body.
>
> The stronger the cooperative organization are—in numbers, in achievement and also in quality of membership —the more fully and the more successfully will the State be able to use them in fields distant from itself, fields which its authority reaches only in an enfeebled and diluted form, where compulsion fails but cooperative discipline succeeds.
>
> If, however, the public sector is to obtain from this alliance the standard of service it is entitled to expect, the cooperative institution must retain their original characteristics, on which their peculiar virtues depend. It is essential that their connection with government should not involve degeneration into mere additional cogs in the administrative machine.
>
> This eventuality—dangerous both to the cooperative institutions themselves and to the success of their alliance with the authorities—will only be avoided if the bonds which hold cooperators together are not weakened; if the links between them and their representatives also hold firm; if the cooperative spirit is kept alive and strengthened; and if members of the cooperative association can continue to feel and act in that spirit.

State Help—Temporary and Transitional

In India, the entry of the State in the field of economic and social reconstruction on an unprecedented scale is largely due to the attempt to remove a backlog of economic and social backwardness in a short time.

As these circumstances change, and development is effected, the instruments of development created by the State should disappear or be reduced to the minimum.

Accordingly, the presence of the State in the field of cooperation should be viewed as a temporary and transitional measure. The long-term objective should be to minimize the burdens of the State and maximize the capacity and the contribution of the people.

We believe that this also represents the general approach of the Government of India, the Planning Commission and the National Development Council, even though they have made no special declaration of policy on the role of the State vis-a-vis the cooperative movement as such. This approach is also shared by the cooperative movement in India. The only note of dissent to this approach has been struck by the All-India Rural Credit Survey which initiated a doctrine of State partnership in and State participation in the management of cooperative societies.

Although the Government of India at one time (1955) accepted such a doctrine, it seems to be undergoing a reappraisal. We hope that the Government will take early steps to announce their clear and firm rejection of this doctrine which is now in a State of suspended animation.

Self-Government versus Good Government

The arguments for and against these two propositions must still be fresh in our memory. Until 1947 they were the subject matter of considerable debate. But the Indian people overwhelmingly resolved in favour of self-government. Good government, however benign and efficient, was not accepted by the Indian people as an alternative to self-government. On the other hand, it has been conclusively demonstrated, if demonstration were at all needed, that self-government has, in fact, also meant good government. India is not only a sovereign republic today but also one of the best governed States in the world.

Social Bodies versus Private Bodies

Since public policy requires that the weaker sections of the people should be assisted through cooperative endeavour, funds and aid must be provided to the cooperatives for various purposes and varying degrees. But as the officials regard cooperatives as *private* bodies and the funds are *public*, the administrative mind cannot see how a private body can be trusted with the public funds. Firstly, it needs to be clarified that though cooperatives are not public bodies, they are also not private bodies. They are social bodies. They are the instruments of social and economic democracy as Parliament and State Legislature are instruments of political democracy. Cooperatives are governed by social purpose and policy. Their operations are open, recorded, democratically controlled, subject to a constitution and with a legal status under the law.

Once cooperatives are declared as "social bodies" the Government should be concerned about the conscientious use of resources by the cooperatives, in accordance with the cooperative law and with the rules governing a society. These are, however, regulatory functions which the State should be able to perform without any objection in principle or difficulty in practice.

As Principal Kaji writes :

> Really there is no inconsistency between cooperative autonomy and State assistance. The State makes large grants to private educational institutions and to local self-government organizations. It has, besides, a programme of subsidies and tariff protection for the development and fostering of large-scale industries. And yet no claim has been made for control over these institutions, organizations and industries which continue to enjoy autonomy in their internal affairs. The grant of ample State assistance to which agriculture and small-scale industries have as great a claim as any other sector of national economy cannot, therefore, be urged as a justification for greater and permanent control.
>
> India has to borrow today from foreign countries and international agencies to implement its development plans. They lend us funds because they regard us as an honourable and capable nation. They do not ask for their representatives to be nominated on our Central or State Cabinets or on the Planning Commission or the boards of Public Corporations. We want aid but without jeopardizing our independence, self-respect and operating freedom. We vehemently object to any kind of strings attached. Is it too much to extend this principle to dealings with small groups of our own people? Some waste and losses may occur in the process, but surely not more than what happens today under the guise of supervision, State partnership and caution.

Following on the above analyses, the ICU detailed its proposals for reform of the movement in a section entitled "A New Order". As these proposals are substantially the same as those contained in the "Seminar on Co-operation" (Chapter 3), they are not repeated here.

In fact the Seminar on Cooperation, under the chairmanship of J.P. Narain, was held soon after the publication of the above paper; it served to broad-base and win consensus for these proposals, and its report was circulated very widely (nearly 3,000 copies) among cooperative unions, societies and their members, among MPs, MLAs and ministers, and among other prominent economists, activists and scholars in the country. Guided by the Seminar, the ICU in 1960 published the following document, suggesting important changes in the existing cooperative legislation, with the basic thrust towards a more "member-controlled, self-regulating and democratic" movement.

> Effective measures (were also) suggested for an internal regulation of the cooperatives to ensure their proper management, audit and functioning. The measures suggested for solving disputes would minimize unnecessary litigation.
> The report refrained from commenting upon routine provisions in existing legislation as there (was) very little controversy about them. The measures suggested (could) easily apply to practically all types of societies: joint farming, service, credit, consumers, industrial housing, transport, etc.

The document was prepared by Shree Hukam Singh Lather, Research Adviser and consultant to the ICU, who had formerly served as Deputy Registrar of Cooperatives for five years, and as Principal of the Block Level Cooperative Officers' Training Centre at Dhuri, set up by the Reserve Bank.

The original document contains, as appendix, comments on existing cooperative legislation in various States in India and some foreign countries.

III. COOPERATIVE LAW: PROPOSED NEW FEATURES

Chapter I: Registration and Bye-Laws

1. *Societies which may be Registered*

(1) Subject to the provisions of this Act, a cooperative society which has as its objects the promotion of the economic and social interests

of its members or a cooperative society established with the object of facilitating the operation of such, may be registered under this Act.

(2) A society established under this Act shall observe the following cooperative principles :

(i) It shall be a voluntary association based on the consent of its members;
(ii) Its supreme authority shall vest in the general body of its members;
(iii) No member shall have more than one vote;
(iv) Its management shall be carried on democratic lines, i.e. through a board of management elected by the general body;
(v) It shall promote thrift, self-help and mutual aid;
(vi) It shall allow only limited interest on capital; and distribution of its surplus shall be made in proportion to business done or services rendered by its members; and
(vii) It shall not discriminate against any member or person on account of religion, caste or political beliefs, in matters of administration or in any other matter.

2. Registration with Limited or Unlimited Liability

(1) A cooperative society may be registered with or without limited liability depending upon the choice of its members.
(2) The word "limited" or its equivalent in any Indian language shall be the last word in the name of a cooperative society registered with limited liability under this Act.

3. *Registrar*

(1) The State Government may appoint a person to be the Registrar of Cooperative Societies for the State or any portion of it and may appoint other persons to assist him.
(2) The State Government may, by a general or special order, confer on any person appointed to assist the Registrar, or on any cooperative society or recognized institution all or any of the powers of the Registrar under this Act.

4. *Application for Registration of Cooperative Societies*

(1) An application for the registration of a cooperative society shall be made to the Registrar in the form as given in "Schedule A" of this Act and the applicants shall furnish to him all such relevant information about the society as he may require for purposes of this Act.

(2) Every such application shall conform to the following requirements, namely,

(a) the application shall be accompanied by three copies of the proposed bye-laws of the cooperative society;
(b) where all the applicants are individuals, the number of applicants shall not be less than seven;
(c) every one of the applicants who is an individual shall be above the age of 18 years;
(d) the application shall be signed by every one of the applicants in the case of individuals; by a duly authorized person in the case of a cooperative society; and by each individual and duly authorized persons in the case of an application from both.

(3) The bye-laws of a society shall provide among others the following:

(a) The name, address and area of business operation of the society;
(b) The objects and functions of the society;
(c) Qualification and disqualification for membership, admission, non-admission and expulsion of members;
(d) The value of each share, payment for such shares, maximum number of shares a member may be allowed to own; withdrawal and transfer of shares, nominees in case of death of members;
(e) The liability of members and the extent of liability if it is limited;
(f) The meetings of the General Body and the Board of Management, the maximum period between two meetings, the minimum notice for calling of the meeting; place of the meeting, agenda and quorum;
(g) The number of office-bearers and Board of Management, the division of their duties and their election and removal;
(h) Maintenance of accounts, books, records, custody, raising and

investment of funds of the society and operation of its bank accounts;

(i) The auditing of accounts of the society, the appointment of auditors, fixing of fees of the auditors;

(j) The business year, annual and periodical reports, plans, budgets and balance-sheets and statement of accounts;

(k) Appropriation of profits or the meeting of losses;

(l) The Reserve and other funds, their amount, accumulation and purposes for which they may be employed;

(m) Employees of the society;

(n) Membership of other organizations;

(o) Method of public notice;

(p) Amendment of its bye-laws;

(q) Settlement of disputes; and

(r) Dissolution or liquidation of the society.

5. *Registration*

(1) Where the application for registration and the bye-laws of a proposed society are in conformity with the provisions of this Act, the Registrar shall register the society and its bye-laws and issue to the society, within two months of receipt of its application, a certificate of registration which shall be conclusive evidence that the society therein mentioned is duly registered under this Act.

(2) Where the Registrar refuses to register a cooperative society, he shall within two months of receipt of its application communicate, by registered post, the order of refusal together with the reasons therefore to the applicants specified in such application.

6. *Cooperative Societies to be Bodies Corporate*

The registration of a cooperative society shall render it a body corporate by the name under which it is registered, having perpetual succession and a common seal, and with power to hold property, enter into contracts, institute and defend suits and other legal proceedings and to do all things necessary for the purposes for which it was constituted.

7. *Amendment of Bye-laws of a Cooperative Society*

(1) No amendment of any bye-law of a cooperative society shall be valid unless such amendment has been registered under this Act.

(2) Where the proposed amendment is in conformity with the provisions of this Act, the Registrar shall régister it and issue a registered copy to the society within two months of receipt of its application.

(3) The copy of the registered amendment shall be conclusive evidence that the amendment has been duly registered.

(4) Where the Registrar refuses to register an amendment of the bye-laws of a cooperative society, he shall, within two months of receipt of its application, communicate by registered post the order of refusal, together with the reasons therefor to the society.

8. *When Amendments of Bye-laws come into force*

An amendment of the bye-laws of a cooperative society shall, unless it is expressed to come into operation on a particular day, come into force on the day on which it is registered.

Chapter II: Cooperative Unions

9. *Cooperative Unions*

(1) Cooperative Unions, consisting of primary and secondary societies as members, may be established and registered under this Act at State, District and Block levels to undertake promotion and supervision of cooperative societies.

(2) The unions may perform the following functions:

(a) Promote and organize cooperative societies;
(b) Provide cooperative education, training and information;
(c) Undertake research and evaluation, case studies, problems and prospects of development of cooperative societies and evaluation of working results;
(d) Aid, advise and counsel cooperative societies in business management, technical, organizational and legal matters;
(e) Ensure observance by the member-societies of the provisions of this law, the bye-laws and resolutions of their general meetings:
(f) Promote harmonious relations between the member-cooperative and help in the settlement of disputes among member-cooperatives and between a cooperative society and its members;
(g) Investigate, where necessary, the working, business, accounts and other affairs of an affiliated society; and

(h) Undertake any other business to attain the objects of the unions.

(3) Unions may from time to time give advice to the Government and others in matters related to development, specially pertaining to cooperatives, or may collect and provide useful data relating to the growth and progress of cooperatives.

(4) Every society shall be entitled, after its registration, to become a member of the Union of the Block in which its head office is situated, and the Block Union to become a member of the District Union and the District Union to become a member of the State Union; and shall be subject to such guidance of the block, district and State Unions as provided by this Act and their bye-laws.

Chapter III: Management

10. *Final Authority in a Cooperative Society*

The final authority in a cooperative society shall vest in the general body of its members:

(a) Provided that, where the bye-laws of a cooperative society permit for the constitution of a council consisting of delegates of members of the society elected in accordance with such bye-laws, the council shall exercise such powers of the general body as may be specified in the bye-laws of the society;

(b) Provided further that nothing in this Section shall affect any powers conferred on a committee or any officer of a cooperative society by its bye-laws.

11. *Annual General Meeting*

A General meeting of a cooperative society shall be held once in a year for the purpose of –

(a) approval of the budget and programme of work of the society;

(b) election of the members of its board of management or any other committee in accordance with the procedure laid down in its bye-laws;

(c) consideration of the statement of accounts, the audit report and the annual report;

(d) disposal of the net profits;

(e) appointment of auditors; and
(f) consideration of any other matter which may be brought forward in accordance with its bye-laws.

12. *Special General Meetings*

(1) The committee of a cooperative society may, at any time, call a special general meeting of the society and shall call such a meeting within one month after the receipt of a requisition in writing from such number of members or a proportion of the total number of members, as may be provided in its bye-laws;

(2) If a special general meeting of a cooperative society is not called in accordance with the requisition referred to in sub-section (1), the applicants may ask the Union to which the society is affiliated to take appropriate action as provided in this Act.

Chapter IV: Properties and Funds

13. *Funds not to be distributed*

No part of the funds other than the net profits of a cooperative society shall be paid by way of bonus or dividend or otherwise distributed among its members:

Provided that a member may be paid remuneration on such scale as may be laid down by the bye-laws for any services rendered by him to the cooperative society.

14. *Disposal of Net Profits*

(1) A cooperative society shall, out of its net profits in any year

(a) transfer an amount not being less than 25 per cent to the reserve fund; and
(b) transfer an amount not being less than 5 per cent to the Cooperative Education Fund of the Union to which it is affiliated.

(2) The balance of the net profits may be utilized for all or any of the following purposes, namely,

(a) payment of dividend to members on their paid-up share capital at a rate not exceeding 6 per cent per annum;

(b) payment of bonus to members and employees to the extent and in the manner specified in the bye-laws;
(c) constitution of or contributions to such special funds as may be specified in the bye-laws; and
(d) donations of amounts not exceeding 10 per cent of the net profits for any cooperative or social purpose or any charitable purpose as defined in Section 2 of the Charitable Endowment Act, 1890 (6 of 1890).

(3) No part of the funds or profits of a cooperative society shall be utilized for or contributed to any political party.

15. *Investment of Funds*

A cooperative society may invest or deposit its funds

(a) in Government Savings Bank; or
(b) in any of the securities specified in Section 20 of the Indian Trust Act, 1882 (2 of 1882); or
(c) in the shares or securities of any other cooperative society; or
(d) with any cooperative bank or scheduled bank; or
(e) in any other mode permitted by its bye-laws.

16. *Borrowing*

A cooperative society shall receive deposits and loans only to such extent and under such conditions as may be specified in its bye-laws.

17. *Loans*

(1) A cooperative society shall not advance a loan to any person other than a member:
Provided that a cooperative society may advance loans to another cooperative society, as may be specified in its bye-laws.
(2) Notwithstanding anything contained in sub-section (1), a cooperative society may advance a loan to a depositor on the security of his deposit.

18. *Other Transactions with Non-Members*

Save as is provided in Sections 16 and 17, the transactions of cooperative society with persons other than members shall be subject to such restrictions, if any, as may be specified in its bye-laws.

19. *Provident Fund*

(1) A cooperative society may establish a contributory Provident Fund for the benefit of its employees to which shall be credited all contributions made by the employees and the society in accordance with the bye-laws of the society.

(2) A contributory Provident Fund established by a cooperative society under sub-section (1)

  (a) shall not be used in the business of the society;
  (b) shall not form a part of the assets of the society; and
  (c) shall not be liable to attachment or be subject to any other process of any court or other authority.

Chapter V: Audit

20. *Audit*

(1) Each cooperative society shall get its accounts audited at least once in each year by any of the following:

  (i) a chartered accountant or accountants registered under the Indian Chartered Accountants Regulation Act; or
  (ii) any other person approved for this purpose by the State Cooperative Union; or
  (iii) any official of the Cooperative Audit Service to be established by the State Government under this Act in accordance with the following provisions:

  (a) The Cooperative Audit Service shall be under the charge of a Chief Cooperative Audit Officer;
  (b) No person shall be appointed as a Chief Cooperative Audit Officer, unless he is registered or is eligible for registration as a chartered accountant under the Indian Chartered Accountants Regulation Act;
  (c) The State Government may appoint a person or persons under the Chief Cooperative Audit Officer for conducting the audit of

cooperative societies. The person or persons so appointed shall possess such qualifications as may be prescribed; and

(d) The Chief Cooperative Audit Officer shall function under the State Government and independent of the Registrar.

(2) In case a society fails to get its accounts audited within one year of the closure of its accounts for a particular year, the Chief Audit Officer shall audit or cause to be audited its accounts by any of the persons mentioned in sub-section (1).

(3) The auditor shall at all times have access to all the books, accounts, papers, documents, cash balance, securities or other properties of a society, and every officer and member of the society shall furnish such information in regard to the transactions and working of the society as the auditor may require.

(4) The fees of the auditor shall be paid by the society. In cases where audit has been conducted under sub-section (1), clause (iii) and sub-section (2), the scale of audit fees shall be fixed by the Chief Audit Officer in consultation with the State Cooperative Union.

(5) The auditor shall furnish one copy of his report and audited statement of accounts to the society and another copy to the Chief Cooperative Audit Officer. If the audit discloses any defects in the working of a cooperative society, the Chief Cooperative Audit Officer may bring such defects to the notice of the society and if the society is affiliated to another secondary or State cooperative society, also to the notice of that other society.

Chapter VI: Investigation

21. *Investigation*

(1) (1) (i) A Union shall have the power and may investigate the working of a member-society if the latter is deemed to have violated any provisions of this Act, bye-laws or agreements with financing agencies or improper conduct of elections or non-compliance with any resolutions of the general body meetings at the request of any of the following :

(a) one-fourth or any 50 members, whichever is less, of at least one year's standing of a society;

(b) a creditor of a society, whose debt exceeds five hundred rupees and has become overdue, and in respect of which he has demanded payment but has not received satisfaction within three weeks;

(ii) Any request for such an investigation shall be submitted in writing stating full reasons and the union may require the applicants to furnish additional information as it may consider necessary, and may also require them to give security for the cost of scrutiny and may ultimately apportion the costs between the applicants, or the society, or any person acting on its behalf who may be held responsible; and

(iii) A society shall, when such an investigation is undertaken of its affairs, furnish all relevant information and facilitate the inspection of its books, records and documents.

(2) If, on investigation, the union is satisfied that there has been violation of any provisions of this Act, bye-laws or the resolution of the general body meeting of the society in question, the Union may ask the society to take corrective action within a reasonable time.

(3) If a society fails to comply with the provisions of sub-section (1) (iii), or sub-section (2), the Union may order a re-election of its office-bearers or Board of Management within a reasonable time or may move for the dissolution of the society after giving it proper notice.

(4) If a society or an applicant mentioned in sub-section (1) is aggrieved by any decision of a Union, it may appeal against the decision of the Union to the State Union and to the Cooperative Tribunal if the decision has been given by the State Union or on the advice of the State Union. The period of appeal in each case will be two months from the date of communication of the decision by registered post.

(5) If the complaint or representation as provided in sub-section (1) is against a primary society it shall be made to the Block Union, if against a secondary society, to the District Union, and if it is against a District Union or a State society, to the State Union.

(6) If the complaint or representation as provided in sub-section (1) is against a State Union, it shall be made to the Cooperative Tribunal and the Cooperative Tribunal in such a case shall exercise all the powers of the Union as provided in this Section.

Chapter VII: Settlement of Disputes

22. *Disputes which may be Referred to Arbitration*

(1) Notwithstanding anything contained in any law for the time being in force, if any dispute, other than a dispute regarding disciplinary action taken by a society or its managing committee against a paid servant of the society, touching the constitution, management or business of a cooperative society arises

(a) among members, past members and persons claiming through members, past members and deceased members, or
(b) between a member, past member or persons claiming through a member, past member or deceased member and the society, its committee or any officer, agent or employee of the society, or
(c) between the society or its committee and any past committee, any officer, agent or employee, or any past officer, past agent or past employee or the nominee, heirs or legal representatives of any deceased officer, deceased agent, or deceased employee of the society, or
(d) between the society and any other cooperative society,

such a dispute shall be referred to the Union to which the society is affiliated.

(2) Every Union shall maintain a panel of names of suitable persons out of which a committee of three arbitrators shall be constituted in the following manner, as and when a dispute is referred to the Union:

(i) both parties to the dispute shall nominate one arbitrator each, and the third, who will act as chairman of the committee of arbitrators, shall be nominated by the President of the Union;
(ii) if a party fails to nominate its arbitrator within 15 days after receipt of notice from the Union, or where an arbitrator so nominated refuses to act, the President of the Union shall have the power to fill up the vacancy;
(iii) any two members of the committee of arbitrators shall form a quorum for the disposal of its business.

(3) For the purposes of sub-section (1), the following shall be deemed to be disputes touching the constitution, management or the business of a competitive society, namely,

(a) a claim by the society for any debt of demand due to it from member or the nominee, heirs or legal representatives of a deceased member, whether such debt or demand be admitted or not;

(b) a claim by a surety against the principal debtor where the society has recovered from the surety any amount in respect of any debt or demand due to it from the principal debtor as a result of the default of the principal debtor, whether such debt or demand is admitted or not;

(c) any dispute arising in connection with the election of any officer of the society.

(4) The committee of arbitrators shall, on receipt of the reference of a dispute under this section decide the dispute in accordance with justice, equity and good conscience.

(5) The committee of arbitrators or any other person to whom a dispute is referred for decision under this section may, pending the decision of the dispute, make such interlocutory orders as they may deem necessary in the interests of justice.

Chapter VIII: Winding up and Dissolution

23. *Winding up of Cooperative Societies*

(1) The Registrar may issue an order directing a society to be wound up in the following circumstances :

(a) on receipt of requisition under Section 22 (3) from the Union to which the society is affiliated;

(b) on receipt of an application made by not less than three-fourths of the members of the cooperative society.

2) The Registrar may on receipt of a requisition from the Union to which the society is affiliated make an order directing the winding up of a cooperative society

(a) where it is a condition of the registration of the society that the society shall consist of at least seven members and the number has been reduced to less than seven and is not increased again within three months thereafter to seven or more in spite of a notice from the Union to which it is affiliated;

(b) where the cooperative society has not commenced working or has ceased to work and does not start working within six months thereafter in spite of a notice from the Union to which it is affiliated.

(3) The Registrar may cancel an order for the winding up of a cooperative society, at any time, in any case where, in the opinion of the Union to which the society is affiliated, the society should continue to exist.

(4) Where the Registrar has made an order under this Section for winding up a cooperative society, he may appoint a liquidator for the purpose in consultation with the Union to which the society is affiliated and fix his remuneration.

Chapter IX: Appeals, Revision and Review

24. *Cooperative Tribunal*

(1) The State Government shall, in consultation with the State Cooperative Union, constitute a Tribunal to be called the Cooperative Tribunal to exercise the functions conferred on the Tribunal under this chapter.

(2) The Tribunal shall consist of not more than three members. No person shall be qualified to be a member of the Tribunal, unless he

(a) is a District Judge or has exercised the powers of a District Judge, or is an advocate of at least 10 years standing, or

(b) is a person who has had at least 10 years experience in the cooperative movement.

(3) Where the Tribunal consists of three members, any two members shall form the quorum for the disposal of its business.

(4) Any vacancy in the membership of the Tribunal shall be filled by the State Government in consultation with the State Cooperative Union.

(5) The Tribunal shall frame regulations consistent with the provisions of this Act and the rules made thereunder, for regulating its procedure and the disposal of its business. All such regulations shall be published in the official gazette and shall come into force from the date of such publication.

25. *Appeal to the Tribunal*

Any person aggrieved by–

(a) an order of the Registrar made under sub-section (2) of Section 5 refusing to register a cooperative society;
(b) an order of the Registrar made under sub-section (4) of Section 7 refusing to register an amendment of the bye-laws of a cooperative society;
(c) an order made by the Registrar under Section 23 directing the winding up of a cooperative society;
(d) any order made by the Liquidator of a cooperative society in exercise of the powers conferred on him by the Act;
(e) any award or decision of the Committee of Arbitrators or any other person made under Section 22,

may, within two months from the date of the decision, award or order, as the case may be, appeal to the Tribunal.

26. *Revision by Tribunal*

The Tribunal may call for and examine the record of any proceedings in which an appeal lies to it for the purpose of satisfying itself as to the legality or propriety of any decision or order passed and, if in any case it shall appear to the Tribunal that any such decision or order should be modified, annulled or revised, the Tribunal may pass such order thereon as it may deem fit.

27. *Review of Orders by Tribunal*

(1) The Tribunal may, on the application of any party interested, review its own order in any case and pass in reference thereto such order as it thinks fit :

(a) provided that no such application shall be entertained unless the Tribunal is satisfied that there has been a discovery of new and important matter or evidence which, after the exercise of due diligence, was not within the knowledge of the applicant or could not be produced by him at the time when its order was made, or that there has been some mistake or error apparent on the face of the record or for any other sufficient reason;

(b) Provided further that no such order shall be made under this sub-section unless notice has been given to all interested parties and they have been given a reasonable opportunity of being heard.

(2) An application for review under sub-section (1) by any party shall be made within 90 days from the date of the communication of the order of the Tribunal.

28. *Interlocutory Orders by Tribunal*

Where an appeal is made to the Tribunal under Section 25 or where the Tribunal calls for the record of a case under Section 26, it may, in order to prevent the ends of justice being defeated, make such interlocutory orders pending the decision of the appeal or revision as it may deem fit.

Chapter X: Miscellaneous

29. *Power of Union to be exercised by Registrar*

Where there is no Union or where a society is not affiliated to a Union the powers and functions of the Union under this Act shall be exercised by the Registrar.

30. *Powers to make rules*

The State Government may, for the whole or any part of the State and for any class of cooperative societies, after previous publication and after inviting the opinion of the State and District Unions, make rules to carry out the purposes of this Act. If the State Cooperative Union objects to the making of any rules, the State Government shall obtain the decision of the State Legislative Assembly and act in accordance with it.

REFERENCES

Bengal Cooperative Societies Act, 1940.

Bombay Cooperative Societies Act, 1925.

Cooperative Law in India -- A Disquisition, ICU, 1964.

Darling, Sir Malcolm, Report on certain aspects of the Cooperative Movement in India, 1957.

Hosselman, E., Cooperative Education in the Period of Transition, *Cooperative Productive Review,* August 1943.
International Handbook of Cooperative Legislation, 1954.
International Labour Review, July-December, 1948.
Madras Cooperative Societies Act, 1932.
Malaviya, H.D., *Land Reforms in India,* 1955.
Memorandum submitted by ICU to the Government in 1959.
Report of the Committee on Cooperative Law, Ministry of Agriculture, 1957.
Report of the Cooperative Planning Committee, Government of India, 1946.
Report of the Congress Agrarian Reforms Committee (2nd Edition), 1951.
Report of the Congress Agrarian Reforms Committee (J.C. Kumarappa Committee), 1949.
Report of the All India Rural Credit Survey, RBI, 1951.
Report of the All India Rural Credit Survey, RBI, 1954.
Report of Third Cooperative Congress, 1958.
Report of the Committee on Cooperative Law, 1957.
Report of the Committee on Cooperation in India, 1915.
Report of the Proceedings of the Sixteenth Congress of the International Cooperative Alliance.
Resolution on Cooperative Policy, National Development Council, November 1958.
Second Five Year Plan, 1956.
Survey of Associations of Handicraft Artisans, Dealers and Exporters. ICU, 1960.

7

COOPERATIVE CREDIT

To begin with this chapter contains edited versions of three separate pieces of the ICU's writings on cooperative credit. The first and most substantive is its critique of the Report of the All-India Rural Credit Survey (ARCS). The second is the report from its Seminar on Planned Production Credit and the third an extract dealing with credit from the 1961 "Seminar on Cooperation".
To these is added a subsequent piece of ICU writing – nearly a decade after the implementation of the recommendations of the ARCS by the Reserve Bank of India. It reviews the changes in Cooperative Credit and 'Who Benefits?'

I. THE ALL INDIA RURAL CREDIT SURVEY VIS-A-VIS THE COOPERATIVE MOVEMENT IN INDIA (ICU, NEW DELHI, 1961)

(Its contents are: General, History of Rural Credit in India, Nature and Scope of the Survey, Findings of the Survey, Why Cooperation has failed, The Recipe for Rejuvenation, Device without Doctrine, Practice without Principle, Rationalization of Realities, Bankers and Bureaucrats, Semantics of Size, The Fundamental Fallacy, and Conclusions: Cornerstone of Cooperation)

General

The All-India Rural Credit Survey was set up by the Government in 1951; its report, published by the Reserve Bank of India in 1954, was a landmark in the statement of the official position and policy regarding rural credit in the country. A significant portion of the report deals with cooperative credit, and as a majority of cooperative institutions in India are credit societies, "the Survey can very well be regarded as the first major post-independence enquiry into the Cooperative Movement as it has functioned and developed during the last 50 years" (ARCS).

The significance of the Report lay partly in the status it was accorded from Ministries and official agencies and from sections of the cooperative movement itself. It was seen as comprehensive and unique, and projected as a model for other Asian countries. The document was a thorough and detailed study, and its findings were a sweeping indictment of the achievements of cooperative credit institutions in India over almost 50 years. The real significance of the document, however, lay in its recommendations, which formed the major point of contention in the report. It unequivocally proposed State partnership in cooperative societies and State representation on the management committees of cooperatives as imperative for salvaging the movement and reviving the utility of cooperative institutions for the purposes of agricultural credit. The report won immediate acceptance in all the significant quarters and was hailed as "a New Testament to the cooperative world" (S. Sahaya, Chairman, Bihar State Cooperative Bank, quoted in *All-India Cooperative Review*, August 1955).

The ICU writes:

> It was, therefore, in the fitness of things that the Report of the All India Rural Credit Survey and its far-reaching recommendations vis-a-vis the Cooperative Movement should have been subjected to a searching enquiry and a serious discussion before any attempt was made to implement the policies implied in those recommendations. But a glance at the timings of the various committees and conferences which endorsed the recommendations of the Survey gives an interesting insight into how the decisions were arrived at in haste and without a full scrutiny of the issues involved.

One of the unique features of the ICU'S 97-page published critique of this report is its scrutiny and detailed commentary on the process and methodology of enquiry employed in the report, alongside its examination of content. The first 10 pages of the critique deal with the manner in which the report was endorsed and accepted, both officially and in some sections of the movement. This scrutiny of behind-the-scene methods of passing resolutions and manufacturing consent is revealing for a public accustomed to the bland, broad and opaque statements emanating from so-called deliberations of the Government.

To summarize here, it found that the massive three-volume manuscripts of over 3,000 large-sized pages, containing radical recommendations with serious long-term implications, was endorsed by a series of committees and congresses in no more than four months. Published in December 1954, it was approved by the Reserve Bank's Standing Committee on Agricultural Credit in January 1955, by the All India Cooperative Union (ICU) at its Congress in Patna in March 1955, and by a conference of State Ministers in charge of Cooperation in April 1955. This haste and over-readiness to endorse the report's findings are suggestive of a measure of predisposition.

It was widely publicized, especially by sources associated with the Reserve Bank, that the recommendations of the report had been thoroughly deliberated upon by a large cross-section of official and non-official agencies relating to the cooperative movement. The ICU, however, delves into the published proceedings of these various meetings to discover that the process of deliberation was far from thorough. In the meeting of the Reserve Bank's Standing Advisory Committee on Agricultural Credit, at least three important participants strongly advised that the recommendations should not be accepted until opinion from within the cooperative movement was consulted on a regional and State basis. Next, in the meeting of the Executive Committee of the All-India Cooperative Union, there were serious misgivings repeatedly expressed about the new proposals. Shri B.J. Patel, General Secretary of the All India Cooperative Union, went so far as to say that "if they accepted the recommendations as they stood, there was a possibility of their being disaffiliated from the International Cooperative Alliance and they would be discredited by posterity".

It was, therefore, decided that no rigid conclusions would be arrived at before further discussions at the Cooperative Congress at Patna. But strangely enough when the same resolutions came for discussion before the Subjects Committee of the Patna Cooperative Congress held in March 1955, the Chairman, Shri R.G. Saraiya, advised the members not to devote much time and attention to them as they had been already "discussed" in the Executive Committee meeting!

> We had the benefit of the views of the Reserve Bank of India representatives and most of the leading cooperators in India were present. *It was after a good deal of discussion and heart-searching that this resolution was ultimately passed and, therefore, I hope that due importance would be attached to it.*

The ICU quotes extensively from the proceedings to show that the Congress had an ambitious agenda in urging the participants along to an early acceptance of the report:

> The published proceedings of the Patna Cooperative Congress show that these hurried performances were inspired by one single objective: to get the recommendations of the Survey incorporated in the "plan frame" of the Second Five Year Plan which was scheduled to be finalized by May 1955. The objective of catching up with the "plan frame" overshadowed all other considerations in the minds of those who were responsible for piloting the relevant resolutions through the Congress.

The ICU reports that the proceedings of the Conference of State Ministers do not contain any discussions either; they only report a series of resolutions, conclusions and recommendations.

Further, the ICU notes that:

> The proceedings, wherever available, of the aforementioned meetings leave an unmistakable impression that even though the resolution affirming the report was hustled through, quite a number of participants instinctively felt that the Cooperative Movement was being led in an uncharted, perhaps an undesirable, direction. To prevent such doubters from raising pleas for a further and deeper study of the Report, the advocates of the Survey seemed to have followed the strategy of tendering profuse and repeated assurances that the "cooperative character" of the cooperative institutions would not be tampered with and that the new principles were being introduced only in order to "strengthen the Cooperative Movement".

The Rural Credit Survey Committee, for instance, had recommended vesting the State with the power of veto and the power to impose certain decisions relating to the working of cooperatives. When fears and reservations about this were expressed at the Executive Committee meeting of the AICU, B. Venkatappaiah of the Reserve Bank of India, a member of the Survey Committee, discounted the fears of the Committee Members and pointed out that there was no sinister motive of destroying cooperative autonomy behind the recommendations and their sole aim was to conform to the cooperative spirit everywhere. He remarked that all their suspicions and doubts arose because of their piecemeal reading of the Report and the construction put on some of the statements without looking into the particular context in which they were made.[1]

At the Patna Congress, there were similar assurances.

> There may be some apprehension in the minds of cooperators that the recommendations tend to officialize the Movement in a greater measure. A careful study of the Report will, however, disclose that the provision of representation of Government Departments and offices on the Boards of the Banks is more with a view to assist the Movement than with the intention of actual interference.
>
> This point was very carefully considered by some economists of repute and by some prominent cooperators at a meeting called by the Reserve Bank of India. The Reserve Bank authorities, after the conclusion of the deliberation, issued a Press note which should allay misgivings on the point of official control.
>
> Occasionally, the assurances were combined with what sounds like a veiled threat. The proceedings of the Reserve Bank's Standing Advisory Committee on Agricultural Credit state: "Prof. Gadgil pointed out that the subject of their Report was Rural Credit and not Cooperation as such. It dealt with Cooperation as it thought that cooperatives would be the most suitable agencies for State policy in respect of rural credit. It was possible to think of other alternatives, as for instance the Agricultural Finance Sub-Committee did in recommending the establishment of Agricultural Credit Corporations. When action was taken following that report in Bombay, the cooperators had to choose between the two alternatives of acting as closed associations cherishing certain spiritual values or functioning as agencies of State policy embracing all creditworthy agriculturists. *If cooperators could not accept the type of Cooperation envisaged, the State would have to think of alternative arrangements to implement its policies.*
>
> Moreover, a liberal use was made of certain value-loaded labels to portray the opposite sides in the controversy. Delivering his inaugural address at the Patna congress, Dr. Panjabrao Deshmukh said: "*I am sure in your approach to the question of the re-organization of the Cooperative Movement, likewise, you will not allow canons of orthodoxy to stand in the way of progress*, but will unhesitatingly adopt new forms of action and new principles of conduct if the larger interests of the country demand the change. The resolution which you adopted in the Bombay meeting of the Executive Committee of the All India Cooperative Union, I am happy to say, bears evidence of this *practical sense and capacity for adjustment to new situations and the*

> *same spirit of healthy adaptability* will, I am sure, enable this Congress to give a *fresh lead to the Movement*."[2]

In this way, the process of pushing through the report constructed its criteria of orthodoxy and progressiveness, its own polemic.

Meanwhile, as the ICU remarks, the cooperators who opposed the report had no empirical grounds on which to argue, as the recommendations were yet untried; their objections were thus unavoidably characterized as purely theoretical.

> But by the time the cooperators met in the Third Congress at New Delhi in April 1958, many of them had first-hand experience of how the recommendations of the Survey were shaping in practice. The Report of the Committee on Cooperative Law had also been published, enabling discerning cooperators to envisage what State participation was likely to mean in the day-to-day functioning of cooperative societies.[3]
>
> The Resolution of the Patna Congress had explicitly demanded that "the powers and rights of the State Government or their nominees should not be used for the internal administration of societies, appointment of paid staff, elections, etc". But it seems that the State Governments or their nominees had not cared to abide by any such self-denying ordinance. So the new Resolution of the Delhi Congress "exhorts all State Governments to *honour the decisions of the Patna Congress* that such participation will not extend to day-to-day working of societies".[4]
>
> The nominees, according to the Delhi Resolution, "should not have the power to veto" and "*should be selected solely for their* ability to promote business consistent with the objectives of the Cooperative Movement".[5]

The Delhi Congress brought out a range of experience related by leading cooperators from different States regarding the growth of official interference in cooperative institutions: the rising percentages of Government nominees on Boards of Directors (up to 50 in some cases), Government taking over audit functions where they were formerly performed by panels of independent moderators as in Bombay States, etc.

> The situation as it had developed between the two Congresses was summed up by Shri N. G. Ranga in the following words: "When we considered this matter at Patna, we were aware of the evils of

interference, Government as well as Ministerial, in the Cooperative Movement. Some of us had grave misgivings over the proposals of State partnership.

Nevertheless, we took that risk. What are the results? If you look into the resolutions placed before you — Resolutions Nos. 3 and 4 — you would get an idea of the dangerous trends that have developed during the two years that have passed since we met at Patna.

The Third Cooperative Congress put on record not only its dissatisfaction with developments that had taken place since the Second Congress, but also a fundamental questioning of the policies that were responsible for those developments. These policies had been dictated by the All-India Rural Credit Survey.

The pride of place for questioning the recommendations of the Survey in a fundamental manner goes to the Prime Minister of India. Delivering his Inaugural Address before the Third Congress, he said:

> I see from your four years' report or survey that there is a reference made in it to the important decisions taken about three years or less ago, when the Rural Credit Survey Committee presented its report to the Government. In it the Committee referred to the Cooperative Movement and asked for far greater association of the State with that Movement financially and otherwise so as — it said — to vitalize it. Subsequently, the proposals of the Rural Credit Survey Committee in this respect were broadly accepted by our Government and are being progressively given effect to.
>
> Now, I want to make a confession to you, and that is that I think our Government was quite wrong, in accepting some of the decisions of the Rural Credit Survey Committee — not all but some. I am sorry for it. It is as much my fault as anybody else's. The more thought I have given to it, the more I have realized that the approach of the Rural Credit Survey Committee in some respects was not a right or sound approach and they tended to push the Co-operative Movement in this country in the wrong direction.
>
> What was this wrong direction? There was a tendency on the part of that Committee to distrust our people, a tendency to think that they are not competent enough, that they cannot do a job by themselves: that, therefore, Government officials must come in and help, that Government money should push them up. If Government money comes, that money is followed by Government officials. The small

cooperative has not enough resources or money or competent technical personnel: therefore, you should have large cooperatives, which can be started and helped by Government and so on. Now, I believe that approach, which has certainly something to say for it — it may be argued that there is some reason behind it — was, nevertheless, a wrong approach, and it has given a wrong turn to our Cooperative Movement.

Ever since I realized this, I have been trying to point this out: that approach, even though it might bring some results locally and temporarily, pushes the Cooperative Movement in a direction which is not cooperative at all, which is something else, and which offends against the whole philosophy which, I believe, has grown up round this Movement. Because if it is to be a state-sponsored Movement, with Government officials running it, it may do some good if the Government officials are competent enough, but it does infinite harm in the sense that it does not allow the people to learn how to do things for themselves, how to develop a spirit of self-reliance, self-dependence, and even to make mistakes if they have to make mistakes.

Another question is about the size of the cooperatives. There has been a tendency also — derived, I believe, from the reasoning of the Rural Credit Survey Report — to put an end to the small cooperatives and establish bigger ones, the argument being that the bigger ones would have larger resources and can pay the employees who have been trained somewhat and, therefore, can do much better work. Again, possibly this will do permanent harm and will again come in the way of the development of the spirit of self-dependence, of self-reliance, of cooperating with each other, and will encourage something which, I believe, is completely wrong and which is so prevalent in this country — of just looking up to the Government for everything."

K.D. Malaviya in his presidential address before the Congress pointed out:

The Reserve Bank has constituted the National Agricultural Credit (long-term operations) Fund and is contributing out of this to the share capital of the credit cooperatives. Another institution, the National Cooperative Development and Warehousing Board, has been set up in order to participate in the share capital of marketing and processing societies. The State Bank of India is also to be responsive to the credit needs of cooperatives. These three powerful institutions and the State

> Governments are expected to assist the cooperatives in many ways. Loans and subsidies in addition to share capital are being given.... In the process of recent thinking and reorganizing of our thoughts, we the cooperators have got many more masters than we had during the British days; besides, there is already great official domination over the Movement and it is likely to increase with the increased financial assistance.

Shri Raj Krishna (Delhi) then recommended, "If we feel, as I feel, that in 1955 the Patna Congress made a grave error in accepting the principle of State partnership and State participation in management, then why should not this Congress take courage and rescind that decision. Let us say that we repudiate these principles, which have proved to be the thin end of the wedge and which are leading to the complete officialization and bureaucratization of the Cooperative Movement."

This new evaluation of the Rural Credit Survey was not incorporated in the form of a resolution passed by the Third Congress. But at the same time, it brought to the public platform a series of questions about the Rural Credit Survey that had no opportunity to come to light in the previous meetings.

History of Rural Credit in India

The report of the Survey was not the first document to consider the possibility and advisability of channelling rural credit on a large scale and in a planned manner through the cooperative agency.

The principle of Government finance being made available to the agriculturists for purposes of improvement was first accepted by the Land Improvement Act of 1871. The Land Improvement Loans Act of 1883 confirmed it. The Agriculturists' Loans Act of 1884 defined the scope of State finance for agricultural purposes in such a way as to cover all purposes. At the same time, this Act "expressly provided for loans being made available to village communities or associated agriculturists and for facilitating their settling among themselves the shape in which such loans should be recovered".[6] This was the first recognition of the cooperative principle as applied to rural India, though in a rather rudimentary form. Nothing substantial resulted from these various enactments, mainly because of the indifference and failure of the Government of the day to implement them.

Credit cooperatives for our rural population were suggested by Sir F.

Nicholson in 1895 in his *Report Regarding the Possibility of Introducing Land and Agricultural Banks into the Madras Presidency.* He recommended that the credit which the agriculturist got "must indeed be cheap, and facile in that it shall be ever at hand, but it must be credit which shall only be so obtainable that the act and effort of obtaining it shall educate, discipline and guide the borrower; it should be granted only to those who have learned to think, to plan, to save; the method of providing it must teach the lesson of self and mutual help, and suggest the extension of those lessons to matters outside of mere credit".[7] Elsewhere in the same report he wrote: "The future of rural credit lies with those who, being of the people, live among the people, and yet by their intelligence, prescience and energy are above the people...." The whole of this report might be summed up in two words: "Find Raiffeisen".

It was against the background of these positive suggestions that the first Cooperative Law in India, the Cooperative Credit Societies Act of 1904, was passed by the Government of India. We can say that the concept of cooperation arose in this country almost simultaneously with the concept of government-sponsored rural credit. Rural credit and cooperation have, therefore, been twins and any discussion of the one has inevitably occasioned a discussion of the other.

A decisive landmark in the development of thought on these related concepts was reached when the Agricultural Finance Sub-Committee recommended that "the work of debt adjustment should be accompanied in every region by the provision of agencies of credit alternative to the private financier".[8] Such agencies were intended to provide "finance for all reasonable purposes on reasonable terms" to all "solvent agriculturist producers".

But while reviewing the possibility and desirability of credit cooperatives functioning as the contemplated alternative agencies, the Sub-Committee came to a negative conclusion. They wrote, "A number of considerations rule out this possibility. In the first instance, cooperative banking organizations in all the provinces are not equally strong.... Secondly, the cooperative organizations have to be essentially autonomous bodies ruled largely by their own members.... It would not be possible to use them as instruments for implementing government policy unless their autonomy was interfered with to such a large extent as essentially to change their cooperative character". The Sub-Committee, therefore, recommended that "Agricultural Credit Corporations set up in each province should provide all types of agricultural finance".

Nevertheless, reflecting on the role of cooperation in this country, they observed: "We are in general agreement with the view that the spread of cooperation would provide the best and the most lasting solution for the problem of agricultural credit in particular and of those of the rural economy in general. The present position of the Movement, however, is not such as to inspire much hope that it can be made to play a substantial part in financing agriculture, much less to become the sole supplier of such finance in the immediate future. Nor is it possible to depend on voluntary cooperation for achieving definite results within a specified time, which planning involves.... The Cooperative Movement can, however, be made to play a greatly increasing part in agricultural finance if it is reorganized and run on sound lines and we recommend that systematic and intensive development of the Cooperative Movement should form an integral part of the plan of reconstruction.

To this end, it recommended, "it is the smaller cultivator especially in the less developed tracts whose needs of short-term finance a State Corporation might find it difficult to meet. There is little doubt that the best solution for this problem would be to induce such cultivators to form themselves into cooperative credit societies which are financed by the Cooperative Central financing agencies or, if need be, by the state Corporation. In case it is impossible to form cooperative credit societies in all such areas it will be necessary to create some kind of borrowers' organizations to form as a link between the local agency of a State Corporation and the large numbers of agriculturist producer borrowers scattered over the countryside".

Secondly, "We suggest that the corporation may finance cooperative societies where the appropriate higher cooperative organizations do not exist and that where the cooperative banking organization is not in a position to give adequate finance the Corporation might supplement the resources of the Cooperative Organization".

Thirdly, "In (those) provinces (where) ... cooperative financial agencies are strong and have the capacity to undertake all work indicated as in the sphere of the Agricultural Credit Corporation, there would be no objection if a separate State Corporation is not set up. It follows that the cooperative structure in this case would obtain the same measure and type of aid as those recommended to be given to the Agricultural Credit Corporation".

Simultaneously, the Sub-Committee emphasized the need for envisaging cooperative credit in the context of reconstructing our agricultural economy as a whole: "The attempt to raise a sound system of finance should be only a part of a general programme of reconstruction to place the agriculturist producers in a state of normal solvency." Again: "The efficiency of cooperative finance would be considerably increased if a cooperative society has control over the produce of the members.... We would here suggest that the operations of credit societies should be closely linked to those of sale societies.... We also anticipate that cooperative organizations will try to develop processing activities which would result in better prices and lead to better marketing finance for the producer.... The development of marketing finance will require the establishment of godowns and licensed warehouses".

On the Cooperative Movement *per se*, the Sub-Committee wrote: "If the Movement has not been successful in realizing its purpose, it was not because the principles on which it was based were wrong. The causes in our opinion lie elsewhere. For one thing the Movement has had to contend against structural defects in our economy.... Secondly, it has not been worked on right lines strictly in keeping with its principles."

We have quoted somewhat extensively from the report of the Agricultural Finance Sub-Committee because we find that all the committees that followed it including the Cooperative Planning Committee and Agricultural Credit Organization Committee have based their observations mainly on the findings and recommendations of this committee. The recommendations of the All-India Rural Credit Survey were, in fact, generally anticipated by the Agricultural Finance Sub-Committee in a comparatively very small but rather tersely written report.

The main recommendations of the Agricultural Finance Sub-Committee (more popularly known as the Gadgil Committee after the name of its Chairman, Prof. D. R. Gadgil) regarding setting up of State-controlled Agricultural Corporations were not endorsed by the Cooperative Planning (Saraiya) Committee which submitted its report in 1946.

We are of the opinion that not only in some provinces where the Cooperative Movement has attained a high degree of development, but also in other provinces and States the Provincial Cooperative Bank or other central cooperative financing organizations can provide the agriculturist with all the facilities which are intended to be given by the Agricultural Credit Corporation. The same measure and type of aids as those recommended to be given to the Agricultural Credit Corporation should be given to the provincial cooperative bank and there would then be no need to start a separate organization for this purpose.[9]

In explanation of their stand against Credit Corporation, the Committee stated: "In the first place, much time may be lost in preparing a scheme for the new Agricultural Credit Corporation ... while the provincial cooperative banks and other central cooperative financing organizations are already in existence and can, where necessary, be suitably reconstituted to shoulder the additional burdens which will be imposed on them. In the second place, the Agricultural Credit Corporation is intended to deal with the agriculturist also through the medium of cooperative organizations where they exist. A provincial cooperative bank which has already acquired experience in dealing with these societies will, in our opinion, be better suited for the task. Thirdly, the anxiety of the Gadgil Committee for providing a larger number of agriculturists with institutional credit as an alternative to money-lenders' credit will be met if the provincial governments adopt the targets fixed by us for the increase in the number of rural credit societies and the recommendations made by us for the expansion of their number and functions. Fourthly, an Agricultural Credit Corporation which does not provide adequate representation in the management to those in need of credit is likely to be dominated by lenders."

The financial responsibility, however, of enabling the cooperative movement to cope with the problem was to be borne by the State. The Committee recommended: "In reorganizing a provincial cooperative bank, it will be necessary for the State to provide a good deal of the share capital, and for providing finance at such a rate of interest as will help it to advance loans to the ultimate borrowers at not more than 6.25 per cent per annum for short-term loans and at about 4 per cent per annum for long-term loans."

The Agricultural Credit Organization (Nanavati) Committee appointed by the Government of Bombay in February 1947 supported the line taken by the Saraiya Committee. The report of the Committee stated: "The existing cooperative agencies can, with suitable reorganization and State aid, carry out the work of the agricultural credit corporation and in view of this it is not necessary to start an agricultural credit corporation."[10]

At the same time, however, the Committee observed: "Although we have come to the conclusion that, generally speaking, the cooperative organizations offer the best agency for supplying rural credit in this province, we feel that it would be wrong to recommend them simply because they are already in existence.... As the progress of the cooperative movement in this province has not been uniform and as conditions vary from area to area, there is quite a real danger that *if the local central financing agencies insist on unfettered autonomy, they may not be able to play the role visualized for them*.... To satisfy these standards and to carry out efficiently the functions envisaged by the Agricultural Finance

Sub-Committee, with regard to agricultural credit corporations, the cooperative credit movement in this province will need considerable reorganization and State help."

The Committee envisaged State aid to primary societies in the following forms:

(1) Assistance towards meeting the expenditure on the cost of secretaries of rural credit societies.
(2) Subsidies to multi-purpose societies.
(3) Increased expenditure over the departmental staff, both for organization and administration of the cooperative societies.

As regards District Central Banks and Banking Union, the State aid "may take one or more of the following forms:

(1) Contribution to the share capital.
(2) Grant of subsidies to meet the management expenses.
(3) Guarantee of losses to meet bad debts.
(4) Assistance in effecting recoveries."

On the issue of Government contribution to the share capital of these higher organs of the cooperative credit structure, the Committee observed, "For Government to contribute to share capital ... will not be necessary in case of most central banks in the province, but *in exceptional cases,* Government may contribute to the share capital of financing institutions. We, however, do not recommend that Government should forgo dividend in these cases."

The report of the Committee did not recommend State participation in the management of the cooperative societies at any level. Regarding the management of banks the Committee said:

"Some reorganization of its directorate would be necessary in order to make the Bank properly representative of all the interests involved in the cooperative structure of the province. *In suggesting these changes, we have no desire to officialize the directorate.* What we want is that all the elements in the movement should be brought together in a well-balanced organization".

But strangely enough, the Rural Banking Enquiry Committee appointed by the Government of India in 1949 recorded in its report that "following the recommendations of the Nanavati Committee" the Government of Bombay have amended the constitution of the Bombay Provincial Cooperative Bank "providing for subscription to its share capital by the provincial Government to a substantial extent and *representation on its board of directors by three nominees of the Government*".[11]

That brings us to the threshold of the All-India Rural Credit Survey which was undertaken by the Reserve Bank of India in 1951. By that time, the one opinion that had crystallized as a result of the findings and recommendations of the various committees was that finance on a large scale and in a planned manner should be made available to the Indian agriculturist through the agency of the cooperatives which could be developed and strengthened, wherever necessary, with certain types of State aid. None of the Committees had considered it advisable or necessary to suggest that the State enter into participation in the management of cooperative institutions, even at the apex level, in lieu of extending any type of assistance, including contribution to the share capital.

Nature and Scope of the Survey

The Rural Banking Enquiry Committee which submitted its report in 1950 had "envisaged much larger accommodation from the Reserve Bank to the cooperatives" and suggested that "the cooperatives might take a little more advice from the Reserve Bank". In order to "define concretely to itself the policy changes, procedural reforms and other steps necessary for enlarging the volume of agricultural finance that passed from the Bank to the cultivator through the cooperative credit system", the Reserve Bank convened in February 1951 "an Informal Conference of certain cooperators, economists and others including the Registrars of some States". Among other things, the conference recommended that "the Reserve Bank should undertake a Rural Credit Survey which should include all strata of the rural population and cover problems of capital formation in the rural areas as well as the credit requirements of both economic and indigent farmers".[12]

In August 1951, the Governor of the Reserve Bank appointed a Committee of Direction "(a) To direct the planning, organisation and supervision of the survey, (b) to interpret the results, and (c) to make recommendations".

Explaining "the nature and scope" of the proposed Survey, the Governor of the Reserve Bank wrote to the Government of India :

The issues (with which the Committee is concerned) and, therefore, the data on which they must be decided are economic and administrative and not just statistical; and they have arisen ... directly out of the recent efforts to reorient the policies and activities of the Reserve Bank in the sphere of rural credit in response to reiterated demands in Parliament and elsewhere that a more constructive role should be adopted by the Reserve Bank in this context. The Programme accordingly drawn up (by the Reserve Bank) is threefold. Firstly, there are certain steps which can be taken forthwith, that is to say, without having to await either long-term policy or far-reaching organizational development.... Secondly, there are other important measures which, while not needing to await long-term policy, are at the same time dependent on organizational development and reform, such as the setting up of apex banks where they do not exist, strengthening of the intermediate and primary credit structure of the cooperative movement in particular States and arrangements for the training of the personnel of both cooperative departments and cooperative banks.... Thirdly, there is the question of the long-term policies of the Reserve Bank in the sphere of rural credit.... The Committee of Direction is concerned with the collection of only such data as will enable it to recommend practicable policies for the future.

The "problem" which the Survey was seeking to solve has been stated by it in the following words :

> Agricultural credit is a problem when it cannot be obtained; it is also a problem when it can be had but in such a form that on the whole it does more harm than good. It may be said that, in India, it is this twofold problem of inadequacy and unsuitability that is perennially presented by agricultural credit....
>
> It is, however, not to the nature of the credit agency alone that have to be ascribed the main differences between finance for agriculture and for other industries. There are several features of the agricultural industry itself which, in this context, distinguish it from all other forms of industry. Owing to the conditions in which agricultural production takes place, the cultivator finds it impracticable to make use of capital with the same degree of efficiency as does industry generally.
>
> [Here are listed a number of conditions, such as the size of the agricultural unit (usually small), dependence on vagaries of season,

> perishability of produce, relatively long duration of operations and of gestation periods for crops, relative inflexibility of production in response to market changes.]
>
> Lastly, there is the question of yield on capital invested. "The farmer does not fix the prices of his produce: they are imposed upon him, so that his profits are limited and he often suffers a loss. Consequently the rate of interest on loans granted to him should be lower than on credit granted to merchants. As long-term capital brings in an even lower yield than short-term capital, it is necessary that the rate of interest on long-term loans should be lower than on short-term loans, although this is contrary to normal banking practice".
>
> These difficulties, common to agriculture everywhere, are peculiarly great for "subsistence", as distinguished from "commercialized", agriculture.... Subsistence agriculture, whether it exists by itself or side by side with the commercialized variety, is disadvantageously placed for attracting the finance necessary for its business. The economic standard of its farm operations is very low. Moreover, a large part of the working funds which the subsistence farmer needs has the appearance of being related to his consumption rather than to his production ... where policy is conceived in terms of raising the standard of living, the problem becomes one of economic reconstruction and rehabilitation and not of credit alone ... further and more complicated elements are introduced into the problem by reason of the socio-economic structure of the villager, with its characteristics of caste and inequality, with the result that among the main elements of the problem of agricultural credit in this country today may be not only the financial aspect of providing the needed capital — short, medium and long — for the agricultural industry, but also the economic aspect of development and the social aspect of countering and correcting the repercussions on credit of a markedly unequal distribution both of status and of possessions.

Among the matters to be kept in view, then, are on the one side the different types of borrowers and on the other the different agencies of credit; there are, besides, the periods and purposes of credit; it will be clear from this that one of the main elements of the problem of rural credit as a whole in India may be described as the aspect of coordination, e.g. coordination of need and purpose with period, coordination between the agencies themselves, and coordination of the system as a whoie with the objectives of governmental policy.

Next, the "objectives" which the "solution" was to be intended to achieve against the background of this "problem" have been conceived by the Survey as follows:

> In the devising of the system, in prescribing who shall control it at different levels, and in providing for the personnel who are to run the system, it will, therefore, be of paramount importance to ensure that the interests of the weaker producer are at every stage safeguarded to the maximum extent possible and that adequate finance is made available to him on conditions not more onerous than to the bigger cultivator or the larger owner of land....
>
> The reorganization, both financial and administrative, will have to be of an order which will conform, not merely to existing requirements of production, but to the much larger ones envisaged in the national programme of development ... there is reason to believe that the growth of population in the country will make it incumbent to raise food production to the highest level feasible. The main directions in which increased production is to be effected include much larger irrigation as well as the more intensive employment of better seed, better fertilizers, etc. All these will multiply very substantially the several types of credit needs of each of the main categories, short, medium and long, of all classes of cultivators. Even more important is the effective linking of credit with purpose. From this point of view it may be said that perhaps the most pressing need in regard to the credit system is to ensure the productive character of the finance it supplies.
>
> We have elsewhere referred to one of the objectives embodied in the Constitution of India, viz. reduction of inequalities, and pointed out its special relevance to the designing of a system of institutional finance which not only provides adequate credit for the medium and small cultivator but also protects him against the socio-economic disadvantages to which he is today subjected. Along with the agricultural producer must be considered the other important rural producer, namely, the rural handicraftsman, whether in his individual capacity or as a member of a cooperative organization. The system to be devised will, if possible, have to cater not less for him than for the cultivator. This is dictated quite independently by economic considerations; but it is also relevant to recall in this connection Article 43 of the Constitution of India which lays down as a Directive Principles of State Policy that, among other things, "the State shall

endeavour to promote cottage industries on an individual or cooperative basis in rural areas".

Finally, the nature of the "problem" faced as well as of the "objectives" sought to be attained, provides the key to the type of "solution" that should be attempted. The Survey says:

> Since ... rural credit today is largely private, and the creditors themselves mostly individuals controlled by, but otherwise unassociated with, the State, the institutional system devised to carry out state policy must be an effective alternative to — not necessarily a complete substitute for — the private agencies of credit. It follows that it has to have the strength of adequate resources and of well-trained personnel as distinguished from the weakness which, subject to further analysis, may be provisionally noted at this stage as a characteristic of cooperative credit whether in finance, administration or supervision. Further, the system has to be coordinated not only internally in relation to the different institutional sectors pertaining to short-term and medium-term credit but also with complementary institutional arrangements for marketing, processing and other important economic activities of the cultivator. While providing adequately for essential items of consumption, its main concern should be with loans for production. Among these latter, again, the period and rate of interest of different types of loans should be related to the purposes for which they are borrowed. Lastly, the type of security should be such that, consistent with its adequacy from the point of view of the creditor, as large a number of solvent producers as possible (and not merely, for example, those who own land) can avail themselves of credit on the basis of security such as strength of the producer's anticipated crop, for example, rather than of the more usual and more tangible forms of security. Moreover, the credit agency should be one which is in a position to coordinate its activities with those of all the important institutional agencies, including the Government, which may be engaged in guiding the villager, improving his methods of cultivation, supervising his operations or educating him to avoid wasteful practices.
>
> For any institutional arrangements of this type to be effective, there has to exist, in the village itself, some form of association of the producers who borrow.... Obviously, such an association has many advantages not only for the disbursing agency but also for the

borrowers themselves. Where the creditor is Government, or an institution carrying out State policies, obvious advantages in dealing with an association are that administration is less complicated, matters are brought out into the open, and the better elements in the village can be entrusted with some degree of positive responsibility both for pursuit of policies and discharge of obligations. Moreover, the recovery of amounts advanced is also likely to be easier. From the point of view of the borrowers, the advantages include the possibility of the more well-to-do assuming joint responsibility for the less fortunately placed. In its simplest form, this type of association can be the basis for giving loans to different individuals on the joint responsibility of several.

An association of borrowers obviously ought to depend as much as possible on mutual aid, develop their own strength and at the same time cultivate the habit of thrift among themselves.

The findings and recommendations of the Survey, according to its authors, are largely mounted in this theoretical framework and should be evaluated as such.

Findings of the Survey

The investigations made and the data collected by the Survey cover a very large field and relate to many credit agencies besides the cooperatives. But here we are interested only in its findings about the cooperative credit structure in the country. However, in so far as the Survey concluded that the cooperative agency constituted the only suitable agency for purposes of extending rural credit in future, its recommendations regarding the reorganization, strengthening and development of cooperatives cover the most extensive as well as the most important part of its report. So, in analysing the findings of the Survey with regard to cooperation, we shall be, in fact, considering its major contribution to the old, yet ever-new, subject of rural credit as such.

Before taking up the "record of the cooperative agency" for review, the Survey makes an important reservation. "In this Report", says the Survey, "we are concerned not so much with the record as a whole as with the lessons to be learnt from it; nor with the Movement as a whole, but such of its aspects as have a bearing on credit.... None of the comments or appraisals should be construed as directed to other and unconnected features of the Movement".

The Survey reveals that the private credit agencies — the professional moneylenders, the agriculturist moneylenders, traders and commission agents, landlords, even relatives — still (1951-54) reign supreme in the field of rural credit, supplying nearly 93 per cent of the total requirements. Of the institutional agencies, the cooperatives supply only 3.1 per cent as against 3.3 per cent by the Government and 0.9 per cent by the commercial banks. And even this meagre contribution by the cooperative is largely concentrated in the "commercialized and monetized areas" so that the backward regions of the country "characterised by a subsistence economy" are generally neglected.

Regarding the performance of the existing cooperative credit structure in relation to short- and long-term agricultural credit, the Survey records the following findings :

(a) State Cooperative Banks: "In general, and barring two or three of the States relatively well developed in this respect, state cooperative banks have yet to become effective units of a coordinated structure of cooperative credit".

(b) Central Cooperative Banks and Banking Unions: "It may ... be said as a general statement of the problem that the capital structure of central banks is very weak, their owned resources meagre and their dependence upon apex banks necessarily large; and

(c) Primary Agricultural Credit Societies:

(i) As a rule, membership per society is small, so that the vast majority of societies are uneconomic as business units;

(ii) The average amount of deposits per society was as low as Rs. 408 and the average working capital per society was Rs. 4190. It may be noted that, for their finance, the majority of societies depend to a very great extent upon external sources;

(iii) There is little specific provision for medium-term finance, e.g. to buy a bullock or purchase a pump. Moreover, few societies conform to those principles of cooperative finance which require (a) that loans should be matched to productive purpose, and repayment to fulfilment of purpose, (b) that, consequently, repayment should not be out of further borrowing but from genuine savings or out of annual earnings, and (c) that, as a further consequence, repayment — if necessary in instalments — should be so timed as to be convenient from the point of view of incomings. The picture which emerges is the strikingly different one of an arrangement whereby the borrower is in effect allowed a limited permanent advance which is based on the security of his land and which he usually carries over from year to year. There is little or no relation between credit and purpose and, therefore, little or no observance of the distinction between short-term and medium-term loans. Sometimes, when the administration happens to be insistent on compliance with the formal proprieties, it is not unknown for devices to be adopted such as plausible 'book' adjustment, or temporary 'repayment' followed by immediate re-borrowing, in order to make it appear that loans are being repaid annually. These and other considerations must be kept in mind for a realistic appraisal of the 'overdues' position of the primary cooperative societies. For all India, the percentage of overdues to outstandings was 25 in 1951-52. For Madras, it was 24 and for Bombay 25. In some of the other instances the percentages were: 91 for Vindhya Pradesh, 49 for Assam, 44 for West Bengal and 41 for Bihar; and

(iv) Many factors contribute to the delay: (a) Inadequacy of owned capital and consequent need to wait for funds from the central financing agency, (b) multiplicity of stages through which loan applications have to pass, (c) inefficiency of the cooperative *panchayat*, often amounting to inability to get the application forms properly filled in, (d) consequent need to await the arrival of the supervisor, who is busy elsewhere with one or another of a number of similar societies under his charge, and (e) dependence on the supervisor, not only for filling in forms, but for specifying credit limits, recording sanction of loans and writing up accounts.

(d) Central and Primary Land Mortgage Banks :

(i) Land mortgage banking has made little progress in India. Whatever development there has been is largely confined to Madras (including Andhra). Out of a total of 289 primary land mortgage banks, as many as 130 were in Madras. More than half the States are without a single land mortgage bank;

(ii) Loans given by land mortgage banks are predominantly for discharge of prior debts and redemption of mortgages;

(iii) Land mortgage banks may have a fairly efficient machinery for the valuation of land (as in Madras and Andhra), but even so be completely lacking in the machinery for coordinating their loan policies with that of a programme of land development in one or more areas. Thus they have little or no specialized staff for assessing the technical soundness of schemes and inadequate supervising staff for verifying that schemes are in fact being executed;

(iv) Land mortgage banks as a rule find it difficult to raise long-term funds for their operations. Even though guaranteed by the State Governments, their debentures have only a limited market; and

(v) Finally, central land mortgage banks and State cooperative banks not only remain legally, financially and administratively distinct, but make little or no effort to coordinate their activities.

Summing up, "The Rural Credit Survey ... reveals that the place occupied by cooperative credit in the rural finance of the country is even more insignificant than ordinarily supposed. Organizationally and financially, there has, at the apex level, been considerable expansion in the recent past; even so, the central banks still remain weak and largely uncoordinated; *but the weakest link of all in a chain which is weak at almost all points is the primary cooperative credit society. It satisfies none of the requisites of either good cooperation or sound credit.* Its failure to promote thrift and savings is followed at not too great a distance by its failure to provide in the village a system of credit which is at once adequate, prompt and productive. Even in the two States in which cooperative credit may be said to be less ill-developed than elsewhere, viz. Bombay and Madras, the Survey reveals that a disproportionately large share of the benefit goes to the big and large cultivators.

According to the Survey's statistics, the proportion of different types of cultivator families which reported borrowing from cooperatives was as follows :

Big	5.1 per cent
Large	4.5 per cent
Medium	3.3 per cent
Small	1.9 per cent

In terms of actual amounts borrowed from the cooperatives by the different types of cultivators, the proportion was as follows :

Big	Rs. 21.0
Large	Rs. 13.5
Medium	Rs. 4.7
Small	Rs. 1.9

In explanation, the Survey says :

> Cooperation hardly shows any cognizance of produce from land, as distinguished from the ownership of land, as an appropriate basis of credit. Another factor which tends to bias the system in favour of the big and large cultivators is connected with "consumption" finance. The medium and small cultivators are, proportionately, in more need of consumption credit than, with their greater resources, are the big and the large.
>
> We have here the curious position of cooperatives departing from cooperative principle, where security is concerned, by adopting ownership as the basis instead of personal character and repaying capacity; and of their adhering to principle where "the exclusion of consumption" as a purpose of credit is concerned. What is noteworthy is that, in either case, the result is a bias of the cooperative credit system towards the big and the large and away from the medium and the small.

Taking into account all these facts and features, the Survey concludes:

> "It is generally recognized that the development of the cooperative credit movement in India has been inadequate in three important respects. There are large parts of the country which it has hitherto not covered; even in those areas to which it has extended, there are large sections of the agricultural population which still remain outside its membership; and even if attention is confined to those who are members of cooperative credit societies, the large bulk of their credit requirement is met from sources other then cooperative. *What is not as widely recognized is that the magnitude of this threefold inadequacy is such as to warrant, from the quantitative as distinguished from the qualitative aspect, only one judgment, namely, 'failure,' on the fifty-year record of the cooperative credit agency in this country.*"

Why Cooperation has failed

The causes, according to the Survey, can be divided into three categories: (a) reputed causes, (b) deeper causes, and (c) fundamental causes. The first set of causes the Survey terms "non-economic," while the next two sets are together designated as "economic" or "socio-economic". In the opinion of the Survey, "The causes more generally mentioned are non-economic, though recent findings of committees and individuals tend to lay more and more stress on the social and economic factors, especially the latter, as underlying the inadequacy of development".

Taking up the "reputed" or "non-economic" causes for analysis in the first instance, the Survey says: "These may be classified as structural and functional, in so far as they relate, respectively, to the organization and working of cooperative credit societies and banks. In addition, the low level of education generally, and the lack of training of cooperative personnel in particular, are two considerations which need mention if only because of the frequency with which they are put forward; and lastly, the degree of intervention by the State in the policies and working of the Movement is an item which often figures in discussions on the subject". As regards the structure of the cooperative societies, the "two important aspects are the size of the society and the nature of the liability (limited or unlimited)." The Survey does not think that any of these aspects is of importance in causing the failure of cooperative credit.

In terms of functions, "one issue concerns the relative merits of single-purpose and multi-purpose societies and another relates to the degree of coordination between central cooperative banks and primary societies". To the survey, however, "it does not appear that it is defective... functioning, whether in the matter of coordination or in some other respect, which is at the root of the undeveloped state of cooperative credit". For, "In quantitative terms, e.g. proportion of the total borrowings of cultivators met by cooperatives, some of the poorer records pertain to States that possess credit structures which are relatively well-organized and well-coordinated".

The "level of education and the standard of training," so much emphasized by the various committees before the Survey, may be regarded as "important factors in the situation," but neither of them can explain "why as little as 3 per cent of the total borrowing of cultivators is forthcoming from cooperatives, not only as an all-India average, but even in a relatively advanced State such as Madras". Lastly, the explanation that official sponsorship of the Cooperative Movement in

India has "been among the main causes of lack of development does not seem *prima facie* valid and is not a proposition which has found acceptance with Indian cooperative thought".

The "reputed" or "non-economic" causes, says the Survey, are only symptoms of "economic" or "socio-economic" causes. In its own words, "It is in the factors which condition the cultivators's economic activity and the social background against which the activity takes place that we believe will be found the real explanation.... The administrative, structural and functional weakness and the educational and technical backwardness by which they are accentuated will then be seen to be subsidiary forms of symptom and ailment rather than the main disease itself".

Of the "economic" or "socio-economic" causes, the Survey first takes up what it calls the "deeper causes". These are related to "a fundamental statement of cooperative and economic objectives, viz. 'better farming, better business, better living".

Better farming includes "legislative reform such as the modification of tenure, tenancy, rent, etc., in the direction of individual incentives for better production; the reconstitution of the farm by consolidation as a better-managed cultivating unit or by cooperative farming, as a much larger one; the creation of larger facilities for irrigation; the supply of better seed and manure, etc...." These, the Survey admits, are tasks which a cooperative organization, even if it had no other weaknesses, "would not by itself be able to take on". The State alone can take an effective initiative in these matters. But, until quite recently, these tasks have been "by and large also outside the state's priorities, interests and activities except as limited and uncoordinated features of policy".

Better business has two aspects: "(1) credit and (2) the economic activity which follows production, e.g. processing, storage and marketing". On both these scores, the cooperatives, which are as a rule financially and structurally weak, have to face not only an unequal competition but virtual opposition "from a private set-up of trade and finance which is not only much better organized in regard to its technical services but also much more adequately and powerfully financed from above". Further, there are "inhibiting factors within the cooperatives themselves.... Cooperative credit, at a very early stage, gravitated to ownership and landed security," as against character and repaying capacity as judged by local knowledge and kept under review by local vigilance". In this, they have taken "the line of least resistance". Further, their loans are more concerned with the liquidation of past debt than with the improvement of land and the increase of production.

The failure on the part of cooperatives to promote better farming and better business has naturally resulted in the failure to achieve better living for their members. But our cooperative theory has not yet tried to understand that "want of success is much more due to forces beyond cooperation than to weaknesses within it". Our cooperators have, instead, "tended to seek refuge in the hypothesis that if only the functions and activities of the society are directed to all aspects of life, instead of only to farming and business, the Movement will have much better chances of success". This, says the Survey, "can only be described as escapist".

But the "deeper causes," in their turn, emanate from a set of "fundamental causes" which the Survey describes as "the unique combination of the following features: (1) a socio-economic structure largely based on caste within the village itself, (2) the linking up of the upper parts of that structure to a cash economy and an administration centralized in the urban sector, and (3) the fact that the linking up took place as the outcome of three processes which historically happened to operate together in India, viz. colonial rule and administration, commercialization of agriculture and urbanization of industry".

"The bigger landlord has ways which conform with those of the moneylender, and indeed, as we have said, he is often the moneylender or trader himself. The village headman is also drawn from the same class, and it is usual for these to have connections which link them not only to the sources of finance but to the seats of administrative power. Subordinate officials, revenue and other — including those of the relatively low-paid cooperative department — have often no alternative but to stay with the village leaders and be dependent on them for ordinary amenities when they visit the village or camp in it for a few days. In this and other ways is initiated a process of association with those who wield power and influence in the village and so for that reason have their own uses as the local instruments of an administration which resides in towns and cities and which in varying degrees is inaccessible to the ordinary villager."

"The location of both power and finance continues to be largely 'urban,' and the institutions so located tend inevitably to be urban-minded in the sense that their directors and executives respond much more readily to urban than to rural interests. The urban-mindedness is not confined to private institutions of finance; it usually also extends to the more significant institution of the State.... To these seats of power and sources of finance, public and private, is established a chain of contact, influence and, where relevant, financial interrelation. At the far end of the chain, that is to say the village, are the village leaders, such as *panchayatdar* and *patel*, who occupy the local seats of power, and the village financiers such as moneylender and trader who are the local sources of finance. In view of their being a part of the channel of power and finance, they are also the recipients of power and finance from sources and reservoirs higher up the channel.... When this leadership happens to be outside the local village institutions — the cooperative society in the present context — it is a danger; when it is inside these institutions it is even more potently and more presently a danger. The danger partly arises from the fact that, while the State has a vested interest in the success of cooperation, private banking and private trade, particularly at the village level, have a vested interest in the failure of cooperative credit".

"This may be regarded as largely the heritage of a colonial economy, which, seated in the bigger ports and cities, drew to itself for export abroad the raw materials — the 'cash crops' — of the rural areas. In its relations with the rural areas, it drew sustenance from the hoary iniquities of caste and class and privilege.... Where there was self-sufficiency before, these forces of commercialization worked for the larger production and outflow of the particular commodities — cotton, jute, etc. — which were originally needed for export to the big manufacturing centres abroad and at a later stage for the urban industries which had meanwhile grown up within the country itself.... In its industrial aspect, rural self-sufficiency had been affected even earlier, since, for one thing, the products of cottage industries had to compete with those of organized industry, foreign and indigenous." Against the background of this "grave disparity within the village itself and an equally grave disparity between the village on the one hand and the town and the city on the other", cooperative effort could not but fail.

Summing up, the Survey says: "The failure of cooperative credit is explicable in terms of the total impracticability of any attempt to combine the very weak in competition with the very strong and expect them by themselves to create conditions, firstly for their emancipation from the interests which oppose them, and secondly for their social and economic development in the context of the severe disadvantages historically imposed on them by a structure of the type described."

Recipe for Rejuvenation

As in the case of its findings, the recommendations of the Survey also cover a large field. Here we shall confine our attention only to those recommendations which concern reorganization of cooperatives, which form the core of the Survey's suggested scheme.

The Survey emphasizes at the very outset that "our principal recommendations are vitally related to one another.... If one or more recommendations are taken out of the total context, the results are not likely to add up to the minimum of achievement needed, nor will the scheme be the integrated Scheme of Rural Credit". Further, it notes, "it is of the utmost importance that no delay should occur in implementing these proposals for the widening and strengthening of rural credit".

To start with, the Survey affirms its faith in the cooperative form of organization for purposes of channelling rural credit on a large scale and in a planned manner. "For several important reasons, borne out by the experience not only of India but of many other economically undeveloped countries, it may be regarded as axiomatic that at the rural base, that is to say, in the village itself, no form of credit organization will be suitable except the cooperative society. Where larger production is the aim, the moneylender's credit is obviously unsuitable.

The alternative is institutional credit, private or other; but this tends more than ever to confine itself to the bigger cultivators if it is not channelled through some form of cooperative association of the borrowers.... The problem of future policy may, therefore, be thus summed up in the context of credit; cooperation has failed, but Cooperation must succeed."

"But it was not the fault of the leadership of the Movement that an approach which had to be at once scientific and missionary, village-minded and country wide, failed to be adopted on any significant scale. It may be that the time itself was not ripe for such techniques. In any case, for a non-official agency the task was stupendous. For Government, as till recently constituted, the task was impossible".

"The prescriptions for the reorganization of cooperative credit hitherto made or tried may be described as attempts to rectify the internal weaknesses of the credit structure without taking into account the weaknesses of the rural structure as a whole, much less its maladjustment to the external mechanism of urban trade and finance. Most reforms of the cooperative movement, attempted or effected, have, therefore, been in the nature of inevitably futile attempts to combine the weak against the strong in conditions in which the weak have had no chance. Thus, effort has been concentrated on thrift, better living, multi-purpose, etc., without the prior preparation needed for correcting the maladjustment between the two economies. The arena was cleared for a fight between the weak and the strong with the rules of the game heavily weighed in favour of the strong."

It is unrealistic, says the Survey, to expect the Cooperative Movement to function under conditions that are hostile to its very existence. "The problem is not so much one of reorganization of cooperative credit as of the creation of new conditions in which it can operate effectively and for the benefit of the weaker.... The prevailing conditions cannot be transformed by the very persons who are oppressed and rendered weak by their existence. The forces of transformation have to be at least as powerful as those which are sought to be counteracted. Such forces can be generated not by Cooperation alone but by Cooperation in conjunction with the State".

"The State's way of help hitherto has been to over-administer and under-finance. But that is no remedy for a total problem which may now be seen to be one, not of rural-minded credit alone, but of rural-minded credit in conjunction with rural-minded development of agriculture and rural-minded organization of marketing, processing, etc. The total programme needed may be described as one of rural reorientation of the operative forces of the country's administrative and financial organization.... In Cooperation we have what may be described as a combination of the weak at the bottom. The State is or ought to be a combination *for* the weak at the top. An effective programme is possible only if the State at one end joins hands with cooperatives at the other in an effort to bring about the rural-mindedness that is needed."

The Survey, then, puts forward the "main features" of its "integrated scheme". The "main objects, concepts and methods of organization and development" should be as follows :

(i) "State partnership, including financial partnership, in cooperative rural credit in order that such credit may be expanded and strengthened for the positive purpose of production and for the positive benefit of the rural producer;

(ii) "State partnership, including financial partnership, for the benefit of the rural producer, in a programme for the organization of processing and marketing on a cooperative basis and for the development of storage and warehousing; and

(iii) "State partnership, including financial partnership, for the benefit of the rural producer, in a programme for the organization on a cooperative basis of such of the other economic activities of the village as are of importance to him as cultivator, agricultural labourer or handicraftsman, these activities including farming, irrigation, provision of seed and manure, transport, fisheries, milk supply, dairying, livestock-breeding and cottage industries".

The "main lines of reorganization and development" are indicated as follows :

(i) "Financial, administrative and technical strengthening of State cooperative banks at the apex of the cooperative credit organization of the State. Similar strengthening at the district (or 'central') level, either by establishment of branches of State cooperative banks or expansion and consolidation of central cooperative banks. The maximum possible coordination of both these categories — at the apex and district (or 'central') levels — with land mortgage banks. The organization, within this framework, of new central and primary land mortgage banks in the several States which lack these institutions. At the primary base, gradual establishment of larger-sized primary credit societies with a financial and administrative structure adequate for their effective functioning. Channelling of not only agricultural credit, but eventually also rural industrial credit, through this structure. Realistic devices (e.g. a modified form of chit fund) for the utilization of the primary credit structure for meeting also, to a limited extent, the consumption needs of agricultural labourers, handicraftsmen, etc., besides those of the member cultivators themselves.

(ii) "The progressive organization, on a cooperative basis, of marketing and processing ... with the needed financial, administrative and technical assistance from the State, and the development of storage and warehousing through State-partnered organizations at the all-India and State levels, and, at other levels, through cooperative institutions of the appropriate type with the needed financial and the assistance from the all-India and State organizations.

(iii) "The progressive organization on a cooperative basis of as large a sector of rural economic activity as possible, e.g. farming, irrigation, transport, milk supply, dairying, livestock breeding, cottage industries, and so on ... with the needed financial, administrative and technical assistance from the State".

Next, the Survey defines the extent and duration of State partnership in various types of cooperatives :

(i) As regards credit cooperatives: "In extent, it should be major partnership. In duration, no specific term should be set to it. The reverse process by which the State as the larger partner gradually becomes the lesser partner, and perhaps even eventually withdraws from partnership, cannot be expected either to start or to proceed as a matter of mechanical and scheduled uniformity. The point of commencement of this reverse process must differ for different institutions and areas. It can begin only when, and to the extent that, the purpose of major State partnership at the higher levels has begun to be fulfilled".

(ii) As regards non-credit cooperatives: "Major state partnership is necessary in this case as in that of credit. There should therefore be state participation in the share capital of marketing societies — this also applies to processing societies, dairying societies etc. — from the apex to the primary level at not less than 51 per cent and for an indefinite period".

What shall be the form of this partnership at various levels of the cooperative structure? "At the apex level, such partnership would be direct. In other words, the State Government would directly contribute to the share capital of the institutions concerned. At the district level, the State partnership would be through the apex institutions; in this instance, the State Government would provide funds (e.g. in the shape of additional share capital) to the apex institutions to enable them to contribute to the share capital of the institutions at the district level. At the primary level also, State participation would be indirect; it would take the form of similar contributions to the apex institutions to enable them to provide funds to the organizations at the district level, which in turn would contribute to the share capital of the institutions at the primary level. In certain cases, e.g. marketing and processing societies, State partnership... might be direct at all levels".

In order to make the concept of "major" partnership a little more concrete, the Survey proceeds:

"We recommend that each State Government should, as early as possible, draw up in consultation with the Reserve Bank (or, as the case may be, the National Cooperative Development and Warehousing Board) a phased programme for the reorganization, on the basis of State partnership, of its cooperative institutions ... at all levels. The programme should provide for each of these institutions ... an initial minimum level of share capital which, over a period of years, will be raised to the optimum level. At the apex and central levels invariably (and at the primary level, generally) not less than 51 per cent, of the share capital of these institutions should be held by, or derived from, the State Government in the manner described above; the percentage may have to be more than this if contributions from the cooperatives, etc., do so, along with the Government's 51 per cent, come up to the initial minimum level. Another possibility is that, as long as the process of the increase from minimum to optimum goes on, the Government may have to make additional contributions, directly or indirectly, in order to maintain the level of its partnership at 51 per cent."

At the same time, the Survey recommends a phased programme of "retiring State-partnership" from cooperatives at levels of the structure:

"Until the optimum level is reached, it should be obligatory on members to increase their share holding in conformity with the detailed requirements of the programme as worked out. Such compulsory contributions would first be for increasing the level of share capital from the minimum to optimum. In the case of marketing and processing societies, the compulsory contributions from members should be fixed as percentage of the turnover of the sales made through the society by each member; alternatively, they should be related to the size of the loan taken by the member from, e.g. a credit society with which the operations of the marketing or processing society are coordinated.

"Even after the optimum level of share capital is reached, compulsory contributions should continue for the purpose of 'retiring' the State or State-derived contribution to share capital in the following manner :

"The objective at the rural base, i.e. at the primary level, will be to retire the whole of the State-derived contribution to share capital within a period of time to be fixed after taking into account all the circumstances, so that at the end of that period the societies at the primary level become fully cooperative.

"At the apex and central levels, however, replacement of Government-derived share capital would proceed until it is reduced to 51 per cent, but not beyond that, so that the major partnership of the State will be retained for as long a time as necessary to enable the institutions at this level to give strong and effective support to the rural societies."

And State partnership in the share capital shall, so long as it lasts, entail State participation in the management of cooperative societies. The Survey recommends :

(i) *Regarding State Cooperative Banks*: "We consider that, despite holding major partnership, Government should not be allotted more than a third of the seats on the directorate for nomination of its representatives. *At the same time, Government should, on certain specified matters, have overriding powers, e.g. power to reverse or modify decisions on those matters, or power to impose decisions of its own in so far as they are relatable to those items.* These reserve or special powers of Government, arising from its position as major partner, may in a few instances coincide with, but in all other instances should, in principle, be kept separate from the powers of Government and the Registrar arising from the normal provisions of the Cooperative Societies' Acts.... Special care should be taken in the selection of the chief executives of the bank (managing director or manager). His appointment should be subject to the approval of Government."

(ii) *Regarding Central Cooperative Banks*: "In this case too, State partnership should not imply the nomination of more than a third of the directors by the State cooperative bank. As with State cooperative banks, Government should have special powers to reverse particular decisions of the bank, as also to impose certain decisions, on items falling within the categories of policy already specified."

The Survey does not mention State participation in the management of central and primary land mortgage banks, credit cooperatives at the primary level and non-credit cooperatives at various levels, as explicitly as it does in the case of State and Central Cooperative Banks. But the trend of the whole series of recommendations regarding these institutions leaves no doubt that State participation in their management is implied.

At least that was the assumption on which the Committee for Cooperative Law based its recommendations.

The operations of these reorganized cooperatives of different types are to be coordinated at various levels:

(a) "We recommend that, while the State cooperative bank and the central land mortgage bank should continue to remain separate entities for legal and financial purposes, direction and management should be common to the farthest possible extent and the same administrative staff operative under the two types of institutions. Thus, the State cooperative bank and the central land mortgage bank should have a common board of directors or at least some directors in common, common administrative machinery and a common building to house them."

(b) "The coordination of the State cooperative marketing societies with the State cooperative bank will have to be as effective as that of the central land mortgage bank with the State cooperative bank. Nevertheless, the coordination has to be less formal ... unlike the central land mortgage bank, the State cooperative marketing society has to be distinct from the apex bank in the administrative aspect as well, this being rendered inevitable by the extremely specialized nature of the business. Nevertheless proximity, frequent consultation and exchange of information and above all the sharing of common programme and policies so that marketing and credit may develop together is necessary."

(c) "The central land mortgage bank should, in the first instance, operate in the district through a 'section' of the central cooperative bank or the branch of the State cooperative bank, functioning as an agent of the central land mortgage bank for the disbursement of long-term loans to individual agriculturist borrowers, all of whom will have to be direct members of the central land mortgage bank. This should, however, be treated as a transitional arrangement. When the long-term loans are sufficiently numerous and the size of business, actual and potential, represents the minimum necessary for the economic working of a separate branch, the section may be converted into a branch of the central land mortgage bank. It is of the utmost importance to ensure coordination at this level also between the short-term and long-term credit structures."

(d) "There should, therefore, be a close link between primary

> agricultural credit societies and marketing societies. The primary society should finance its members on the condition that the produce of the member is sold through the marketing society with which it works in coordination."

Another very important, though related, recommendation of the Survey is regarding the size of the primary credit society. It says: "It is our considered view that the formula 'one society to one village and one village to one society' has failed in India as the basis for the organization of cooperative rural credit ... *we recommend that the future line of development of cooperative credit at the level of the village should be unhesitatingly in the direction of bigger societies covering larger areas,* i.e., covering groups of villages with a reasonably large membership and a reasonably adequate share capital.... As a rule, the area of operation of the society should be such as to provide it with adequate business."

The Survey then goes on to recommend changes in the staffing of the Government's Cooperative Services, including, among other features, the deputation of "selected officials to serve as secretaries of the larger-sized primary agricultural credit societies wherever that is necessary and feasible. Such an arrangement, viz. deputation of properly trained personnel to suitable larger-sized societies, would be particularly useful during the difficult period of initial reorganization".

Further, "The training of all these services should be organized by, or under the guidance of the Central Committee for Cooperative Training, working in conjunction with State Governments." The Central Committee which is financed and controlled by the Reserve Bank of India is also expected to organize training for "members, directors and office bearers of cooperative societies, cooperative banks and the cooperative institutions," so that there opens out "the prospect of the eventual growth of a wholly non-official State-strengthened Cooperation out of the proposed partly official State-partnered Cooperation." The term on which the All India Cooperative Union can "collaborate" with the Central Committee is stated by the Survey as follows :

> We would make the definite suggestion that the headquarters of the Union be located in Bombay and, if possible, in the same building as the Reserve Bank's Agricultural Credit Department with which the Central Committee is intimately connected. *Provided the Union shows itself ready to collaborate on these lines,* we recommend (i) that the Reserve Bank give every assistance in the matter of accom-

modation as well as of coordination of organizational machinery, and (ii) that the Central Government make more funds available to the Union for activities falling within its sphere.

Summing up, we can say that the recommendations of the Survey regarding reorganization of cooperation boil down to one basic device — major State partnership in the share capital, and State participation in the management of cooperative societies at all levels, and for an indefinite period, together with whatever the device dictates in terms of size, operation, coordination, administration, personnel, training and finance.

REVIEW

Device Without Doctrine

The Report of the All-India Rural Credit Survey has aroused such a controversy within the fold of the Indian Cooperative Movement as the report of no other committee had ever done. (Yet there) is nothing very new about its findings except the statistical scaffolding. Similarly, some of the recommendations made by the Survey are merely elaborate repetitions of what had been proposed by one or the other of the earlier committees in a much more concise and cogent manner.

The controversy has been occasioned mainly by the recommendations of the Survey regarding State-partnership in the share capital and consequent State-participation in the management of cooperative societies. What the Agricultural Credit Organization Committee had recommended as an "exceptional measure" the Survey has turned into a general rule and remedy. To a lesser extent, the concept of large-sized primary agricultural credit societies formulated by the Survey has also come in for criticism.

Before we evaluate these controversial recommendations of the Survey, we think it desirable to find out if the Survey has tried to deduce them logically from any cooperative doctrine or evidence of cooperative practice. We shall take up cooperative doctrine in the first instance.

In Chapter 10 of its *General Report*, the Survey discusses different views relating to the appropriate degree of association between the State and the Cooperative Movement in expanded credit operations. One unambiguous view, associated with what may be described as the socio-ethical school of Cooperation, is well expressed in the following sen-

village to one society" does not stand lost even in terms of purely economic considerations. Here it should suffice to point out that in the context of cooperation the criteria of "large size," "adequate share capital" and "adequate business," etc., cannot command any authority unless supplemented by other criteria such as "mutual knowledge" which are basic to cooperative philosophy. For, if "adequate share capital" and "adequate business" were the only hallmarks of a successful cooperative, we would not know how a cooperative society could be distinguished from a joint stock company or a State-managed corporation.

We admit that a cooperative which does not succeed in its business enterprise does not deserve to be called a cooperative. Even so, success in business does not by itself constitute the core of its cooperative character. That core lies elsewhere — in the cooperative principles which it embodies and on the basis of which it functions. The cooperative movement had its roots in the aspiration to run business enterprise within the framework of certain basic social values.

By formulating the possibility of a conflict between business requirements and certain basic cooperative principles, the Survey has created a sense of choice which is purely academic. And by giving priority to business requirements over cooperative principles, the Survey has reduced cooperation to an institutional shell empty of the special spirit it was devised to enshrine.

Practice without Principle

Are the recommendations, then, deduced from any evidence of actual experience, as provided by the Survey?

In Chapter 19 the Survey describes with great approval the achievements of cooperative credit in Bombay, where State participation had been put into practice in 1948-49, four years before the Survey was actually taken up by the Reserve Bank of India. The relevant portions are reproduced:

> It is necessary to examine why in Bombay alone, relatively though not in absolute terms, both the volume and the coverage of cooperative agricultural credit are strikingly large. A comparison between Bombay and Madras should be particularly significant. Both of them are usually regarded as well developed in the cooperative sense, and both of them certainly have well-administered cooperative departments. But the comparison perhaps stops there. Madras is "orthodox"

from the cooperative point of view. That is to say, in the principles of the Movement as in the practices which now dominate the system, cooperative credit in Madras runs true to old pattern. Bombay, on the other hand, especially since 1948-49, has been experimenting with a system of "crop loans". This, perhaps, cannot be said to be unorthodox; in fact, it may even be regarded as a going back from present cooperative practices to original cooperative principles. But what is "unorthodox" in Bombay Cooperation is mainly the other development which has taken place in the form of State participation, both direct and indirect, in the finances and organization of cooperative credit.

(The survey assembles statistics to demonstrate the significant growth in volume and coverage of loans by primary agricultural societies in Bombay as compared to Madras, between 1946 and 1952.)

It is clear that Bombay has recorded very much quicker progress than Madras during the last few years, and that this period has, in Bombay, also been one in which the crop loan system has been sought to be gradually established in deliberate replacement of the older pattern in which creditworthiness and ownership are more or less interchangeable. The system of crop loans has been in different stages of experimentation since 1939 when the Bombay Agricultural Debtors' Relief Act was first introduced, and it received an impetus when the revised Act was extended to the entire State in 1947. This period saw the emergence of a class of "adjusted" debtors who could not alienate their lands without the consent of the debt adjustment boards and who therefore found it difficult to obtain credit from the usual sources. Government then came forward with a scheme under which it agreed to provide a guarantee against losses up to five per cent and to bear the entire cost of supervision of cooperatives which were expected to be the main agencies for the supply of crop finance.

The system of crop finance assumed new significance when in 1948-49 the cooperative credit movement in the State was reorganized with the active support of the cooperators of the State. Under the new arrangements the reorganized Bombay State Cooperative Bank and central financing agencies, together with the primary credit societies, were expected to provide short-term finance to all creditworthy agriculturists. Instead of fixing credit limits on the basis of land security, special attempts were made to provide short-term finance on the basis of crop acreages and to link the time of repayment to the harvesting season.

> In connection with this new set-up, reference may be made to the Government contribution to the share capital of the Bombay State Cooperative Bank and also to the central banks through the State cooperative bank. Such contributions as on June 30, 1953 amounted to 43.3 per cent of the share capital and 31.0 per cent of share capital of the central financing agencies concerned respectively. Further, the Government also agreed to subsidize the uneconomic branches of the central financing agencies, especially those opened in the relatively undeveloped areas.
>
> It is not our intention to suggest that Bombay is by any means the last word on either the design or the operation of the crop loan system. It is merely to draw attention to the fact that the only State in which significant progress has been made in both volume and coverage of cooperative agricultural credit is also the one State in which a system of crop loans has been introduced and, along with it, the need for State participation has not only been recognized but also translated into practice by a reorganization of the cooperative credit structure of the State at the apex and central levels, with the State Government as an important partner in the financial structure and an effective participant in the policies of business and risks of operations.
>
> As the next stage in Bombay, there should also be considerable reorganization of the agricultural credit society at the primary level, coupled with similar strengthening and reorganization of the cooperative marketing structure at different levels. But no other State has so far attempted to reach even the first stage.

Now let us, for the time being, forget that, as stated by the survey itself in an earlier chapter, "a disproportionately large share of the benefit" of this expanded short-term credit in Bombay "goes to the big and large cultivators". Here we are mainly concerned with the actual cause of expansion in the total amount of short-term loans advanced by the primary credit societies in Bombay between 1948-49 and 1952-53. In the account presented above, the Survey refers to three new measures introduced in the operation of cooperative credit in Bombay: (a) a system of crop loans, (b) State participation in the finances and organization of cooperative credit, and (c) Government's willingness to subsidize the uneconomic branches of the central financing agencies, especially in the relatively undeveloped areas.

The Survey does not state positively and explicitly which of these measures was in its opinion mainly or wholly responsible for the expansion in credit operations. It mentions all of them as jointly responsible for a better state of affairs. We have, therefore, to assume that, for the Survey, all the three measures are indissolubly bound together. In other words, if the credit cooperatives are to operate a system of crop loans and if the Government has to subsidize the uneconomic branches of central financing agencies in undeveloped areas, the State must be enabled to enter the cooperatives as a partner in share capital and participant in management.

But the Survey does not try to explain how the "orthodox" and "unorthodox" measures are indissolubly bound together and why a system of crop loans cannot be introduced without State participation in cooperative finances and organization. It is clear, as the Survey has itself stated, that most cooperators are only too ready to accept and operate a system of cooperative loans. If they have not been able to do so up to now, it is not because they have lacked the necessary will and vision; the greatest obstacle in their way has been the paucity of finances at their disposal. Provided the finances are made available, the cooperators can, in every State, take to a system of crop loans and expand the volume of cooperative credit immediately. The real question, therefore, is: Can the State provide the necessary finances to the cooperatives for enabling them to do what is "orthodox" without insisting on their acceptance of what is "unorthodox"? The Survey has neither raised nor tried to answer this question.

Thus the principle of State partnership and State participation in cooperative societies fails to emerge logically even from the evidence of practical experience which the Survey has presented. On the other hand, the same evidence goes strongly in favour of a return to original cooperative principles which our Cooperative Movement has not yet been permitted to practise.

Rationalization of Realities

Thus we see that neither the cooperative doctrine nor the evidence of actual experience as presented by the Report of the All-India Rural Credit Survey logically supports the device of State partnership or larger-sized credit cooperatives recommended by the Survey. Nevertheless, we discern a clear tendency on the part of the Survey to draw a uniform conclusion in every instance, no matter whether the facts or the premises given warrant it or not. We are, therefore, led to infer that the Survey started with a conclusion rather than came to it in the course of its investigations and deliberations.

Chapter 23 of the *General Report of the Survey* discusses the record of the Reserve Bank of India vis-a-vis agricultural credit. The Report mentions "certain considerations, many of them arising from factors outside the control of the Reserve Bank, which set a limit to the efficacy of any programme of rural credit in which the Bank's policies and measures are not supported and complemented by corresponding policies and organizational effort elsewhere". The factors which "retard the Reserve Bank's programme" are as follows :

(a) If that particular canon of prudent banking which relates borrowing to owned funds as a multiple thereof is to be observed, then the total amount by which it is able to supplement other resources is obviously limited to the extent of such owned funds at different levels of the structure. Relaxation of the maximum borrowing limits, if any where appropriate, will help only to some extent; unless the owned funds themselves are very largely increased, the fullest possible use will not have been made of the accommodation which the Reserve Bank can make available.

(b) Connected with the weakness of the financial structure is the extremely weak and inefficient organizational set-up of many State and central cooperative banks and, of course, the primary societies. The bank can only help positively by going to the maximum possible extent in the matter of subsidizing and providing training facilities for cooperative personnel.

Next, the Report says that "the Reserve Bank's recent record, as set out in the previous paragraphs, reveals in our opinion many lines of development of great significance for the formulation of a more comprehensive plan of rural credit, rural banking and rural finance"

(a) Whether the problem was one of establishing a new apex bank or of reorganizing an existing one, the *Reserve Bank has in all suitable cases advised a policy of State partnership including contribution to share capital.*

(b) Obviously, no cooperative development even if only credit development of the order envisaged would be possible without organizing efficient training arrangements on an extensive scale, at all levels, and for a large personnel, existing as well as

> new, and pertaining to cooperative institutions as well as cooperative departments.... Accordingly, at an early stage, the Reserve Bank provided both the finance and the initiative for organizing such training, and in collaboration with the Bombay Provincial Cooperative Institute organized an all-India training centre for cooperative personnel at Poona. Two courses are provided at the centre. One is a short-term course of six months for training the higher officers of cooperative departments and the executives of State Cooperative Banks, etc. The other is a long-term course of one year for training officials and non-officials, a step lower in the rung of responsibility, i.e. the "intermediate" staff.
>
> There is one other scheme of training also sponsored by the Reserve Bank and proposed to be largely subsidized by it. This scheme relates to the training of certain grades of the personnel of commercial banks, broadly corresponding to the "supervisory" level. The training is intended to be essentially practical and, therefore, supplementary to the theoretical courses already available in the country; thus, arrangements are proposed to be made for the candidate familiarizing himself with the practical aspects of commercial banking through a demonstration, with actual forms and documents, of the problems and situations likely to arise in practice.
>
> Acting conjointly, the Government of India and the Reserve Bank have set up a Central Committee for Cooperative Training in November 1953.

The first thing that strikes the reader of these passages is that State partnership and the complementary hyper-bureaucratization of the Co-operative movement are no new innovations suggested by the Survey after detailed investigations, theoretical and statistical, in the field concerned. *The Reserve Bank had already perfected this pattern and pressed it into practice whenever and wherever it could, several years before the field survey was actually taken up.*

This impression is fully confirmed by what we read in the various reviews of the Cooperative Movement in India published by the Agricultural Credit Department of the Reserve Bank from time to time. In the two earlier Reviews, covering the years 1939-46 and 1946-48 respectively, the nature of relationship between the State and Cooperation is concretely, though briefly, discussed, and the problems and dilemmas acknowledged, while in the Review for 1948-50, the discussion is dropped in favour of a definite position.

The Review for the years 1939-46 says :

> From small beginnings the Movement has grown rapidly and now represents an influence vitally affecting a large section of the people. This development has taken place without excessive State aid on the one hand or absolute freedom from State intervention altogether on the other. The State's monetary assistance was certainly small, but its role on the moral side and in the provision of supervision, assistance, counsel and control has been in no small measure responsible for the present position of the Movement. Suffice it to say, it has reached such a stage now that it could be counted as a factor in the economic, social and political development of rural India.
>
> It is difficult, albeit necessary, to define the exact relationship that should prevail between the State and the Movement in the future planning of India's economy. The stage has not yet come when complete de-officialization would be possible, and perhaps it may take a long time before the Cooperative movement becomes the absolutely democratic organization, free from alien control and influence it ought to be.[14]

The Review for the years 1946-48 concludes :

> The facts given in this chapter would go to show that, in spite of the very intense drive to make the movement self-contained, it has not been possible to do away with Government help to any appreciable extent and there has not been any great deviation from the position that existed before; on the other hand, there has been a continuance of Government aid on the same lines and to the same degree if not greater. The question, therefore, arises as to whether State aid should necessarily be followed by State control.
>
> This is rather a delicate issue. It is difficult to support the view that financial and other help should be unaccompanied by any controlling voice. In this connection it is also worth remembering that in several parts of the country the Movement is in a rather moribund condition and is being resuscitated by State support except in certain areas such as Madras and Bombay and naturally, expert guidance and official control would be absolutely necessary, even were there to be no financial help.[15]

The next Review which covers the years 1948-50 does not discuss the theoretical issue at all. It takes for granted that the controversy has already been decided in favour of State control and, therefore, proceeds to give a detailed picture of how that control is being actually exercised.

Thus the decision for bringing the Cooperative Movement under increasing State control had already been taken inside the Reserve Bank of India as early as February 1952, when the Review for 1948-50 was published. The Survey was not supposed to re-open the closed question. It was, on the contrary, intended to confirm and advocate the dominant trends inside the Reserve Bank of India.

The proceedings of the fourth meeting of the Reserve Bank's Standing Advisory Committee on Agricultural Credit also confirms this conclusion. They record :

> The Chairman then referred to the example of Bombay where, since 1948, State partnership in the cooperative credit institution of the state had led to considerable development.... The Bank's officers had been sent to the various States to study the state of the cooperative movement and *on the advice of the Bank new apex banks have been established in a number of States on the basis of State partnership.* In the light of the developments during the last few years, *the Committee's proposals were in fact a continuation of the trends that were already in operation*; the proposals should, therefore, be regarded as of an evolutionary rather than revolutionary character. The country would, however, no longer be satisfied with slow progress. From every point of view, rapid development was imperative and if this was to take place, there was no alternative to State partnership.[16]

Thus it turns out that thc "long-term policies" suggested by the Survey for future implementation are the same which the Reserve Bank had been following in the past. Had the Survey been appointed and directed by an institution other than the Reserve Bank of India, this outcome could have been treated as a coincidence. But in the circumstances of the Survey, its report sounds like a long and laboured defence for the policies already being pursued by the Reserve Bank.

Bankers and Bureaucrats

In order to vindicate the trust placed in it, the Survey should have subjected the past practices of the Reserve Bank of India to a critical examination in the light of the cooperative principles. But instead of doing that, the Survey accepted those practices as axiomatic and built up a whole superstructure on that basis, dressing up those practices with a number of justifications. The needs that figure uppermost in the justifications are the needs of bankers and bureaucrats, rather than the needs of a self-governing movement of the people.

The problem stated by the Survey is, in spite of a very tortuous presentation, simple enough. The credit cooperatives at different levels are unable to raise a sufficient amount of owned funds in the shape of share capital and reserve funds, etc. As a consequence, their maximum borrowing capacity, which, according to present practice, has to be a certain conservative multiple of their owned funds, remains rather limited. The cooperative banking structure, therefore, is never in a position to command adequate finances for large-scale lending operations at any level.

Obviously, the way out is either to multiply appropriately the multiple which controls the maximum borrowing limit of the cooperatives or to augment their owned funds by bringing in finances from outside. The maximum borrowing limit can be redefined as something more purposive than a mechanical multiple of owned funds. The Survey itself objects to current definitions of creditworthiness wherein the tangible assets of a cultivator rather than his productive capacity are given priority. The same vision can be extended to the credit cooperatives which are, after all, only combinations, direct and indirect, of those very cultivators. The maximum borrowing limit of a cooperative can very well be fixed not as a multiple of its own funds but according to the production need and repaying capacity of the cultivators who form the cooperative. Similarly, there are methods, such as providing interest-free share capital loans to individual members or giving a Reserve Fund loan to the cooperative itself, by which the owned funds of a cooperative can be appropriately augmented.

The Survey, however, rejects both these alternatives. The maximum borrowing limit cannot be relaxed to the requisite extent because "that particular canon of prudent banking which relates borrowing to owned funds as a multiple thereof is to be observed". The intending members cannot be granted share capital loans because the Survey is "not in favour, except in special circumstances such as we shall mention below, of the idea of 'sponsored' cooperative membership of the so-called non-creditworthy".[17] And the idea of giving Reserve Fund loans to the cooperative is not at all discussed by the Survey.

Instead, the Survey adopts a threatening posture and says that "the only other way in which it (the Reserve Bank) can influence the situation is for it to say, as it is often compelled to say, that it will not lend or that it will lend less unless certain specified reforms are carried out by the administration or institution concerned". A device cannot become acceptable to cooperation simply because it has been put into practice by or suits the convenience of an important and powerful banking institution.

What amazes us most is that the Survey should ask the Cooperative Movement in India to throw all canons of orthodoxy to the winds while endorsing, all along the line, the Reserve Bank's orthodox canons of "prudent banking". Of course, an orthodox banker is welcome to have his opinion as to how cooperative institutions should be managed and run if they want to be accommodated as borrowers on a large scale. The banker is also entitled to refuse credit facilities to cooperative institutions if they refuse to operate in terms of those opinions. But a banker cannot assert that those opinions constitute the best statement of cooperative principles.

The same predilection for using compulsion from a purely banking point of view is noticeable in another notable recommendation of the Survey, viz. the mobilization of rural savings. The Survey has explicitly linked the retirement of State partnership in all sorts of cooperatives with compulsory savings on the part of all those who join the cooperatives. Says the Survey :

> Another important way in which we consider that savings may be mobilised by cooperative organizations at the village, taluka and district levels is by the operation of the process of retirement of that part of their capital which is directly or indirectly subscribed by Government. Until the optimum level of share capital is reached, there should be a compulsory increase in the shares of members, in some relation to the borrowings, together with a proportionate additional contribution to the share capital by Government (either direct or through the relevant apex or other institution). After the optimum level is reached, there should still be a compulsory contribution of share capital. This should be an important means of attracting savings from the members of cooperative societies provided it is not, as a method, confined to credit societies, but is part of a system which extends to, and is in particular intended for, those

other cooperative societies, at all levels, which are concerned with processing, marketing, etc.

We know that, as a consequence of State partnership in the share capital of cooperatives, State nominees will be on the managing board of every cooperative. The nominees of the State will see to it that this compulsory contribution from the members is meticulously enforced. But what does it all boil down to in the last analysis?

Either it is assumed, as has been done by the Survey, that aided by share capital from the State, the cooperatives will promote better production and better business to such an extent that the members will have enough to spare for contribution to share capital even after providing for a certain degree of improvement in their own living standards. In that case, there should be no provision for "compulsory contribution," at least in the context of cooperation. And it should be clearly stated that contribution to the share capital will be dependent upon actual improvements taking place.

Or, it is envisaged that "compulsory contribution" will be levied irrespective of whether better production, better business and better living are achieved or not. In that case, the Survey is not justified in saying, as it has, that better farming and better living are the aims of Cooperation. For cooperation in this context becomes another name for coercion for purposes of extracting "surplus value" from the peasants no matter whether they are poor or prosperous.

As the Survey has nowhere stated clearly that contribution to the share capital shall be dependent upon actual improvement taking place, we are left with a banker's point of view, pure and simple. The immediate aim of State partnership in the cooperatives is to generate large savings in the countryside. The Survey also admits, "In this Report we are concerned not so much with the movement as a whole, but with such aspects of it as have a bearing on credit".

Arguing in the context of re-organization of the cooperative structure, the Survey postulates as follows :

> Whatever may be the transitional stages by which the reform is effected, there is eventually no effective alternative to a cooperative form of institution, at any rate at the village level and for dealing direct with the cultivator. In that sense, the main requirement is to make the cooperative credit organization in its primary form, whether short-term or long-term, a much more effective institution than it is

at present, i.e. strengthen its structure, increase its financial resources and extend its membership so as to cover a much larger section of the rural population.

However, if our diagnosis is correct, the weakness at the most important of the levels, viz the base, is mainly attributable to the fact that the cooperative form of organization has to face not merely the competition but also in a large degree the positive opposition of a powerful array of non-cooperative private individuals and institutions. To expect such a base to produce, by the process of federation at different levels, a strong superstructure is, as we have pointed out, likely to prove as futile in the future as it has in the past.... *The prior requirement, so far as credit by itself is concerned, may be said to be strengthening of the upper levels of the structure, i.e. those above the primary society, by such measures of State participation, and for so long as necessary,* in order that a powerful helping hand may be held out, capable of guarding the primary structure against the dangers and weaknesses inherent in the present functioning of the cooperative credit system as a whole. What has to be available to the primary credit society is not an "orthodox" cooperative banking system at the district and State levels, but a strong institutional support at these levels.

So far as the first half of this statement is concerned, it is an excellent statement of cooperative methods and objectives. A strong base is essential to sustain a vital superstructure at the higher levels. In India, the base has so far remained very weak. It has, therefore, not been able to raise a strong superstructure.

It logically follows from the above premises that the base should be strengthened so that in due course it can create a superstructure which shall, in turn, further add to its strength. But, at this point, the Survey reverses the argument altogether. It postulates that the superstructure should be strengthened first so that the base may draw support and strength from it! This is a typically bureaucratic way of looking at things.

To the typical bureaucrat, all problems are ultimately problems of administration directed from the top and proliferated below by a set of rules and procedures. He generally fails to understand movement which creates consciousness and strength at the base before it rises upwards through a series of broad-based institutions.

This impression is confirmed if we look at the list of agencies recommended by the Survey for promoting cooperation in the country.

The Report says: "Besides the State Governments and the Planning Commission the main agencies are: (i) Reserve Bank of India, (ii) Ministry of Food and Agriculture of the Government of India, (iii) National Cooperative Development and Warehousing Board, the All-India Warehousing Corporation and the State Warehousing Companies, (iv) the State Bank of India, (v) the Central Committee for Cooperative Training, and last but not least, (vi) the Cooperative Movement itself". In this list all agencies except the last are State agencies.

The Report of the Survey devotes whole chapters to the various State agencies which are assigned most of the important roles in the task of re-organization. But the Cooperative Movement is dismissed in a brief para in the context of cooperative training. The All India Cooperative Union, the national organ of the Cooperative Movement in this country, is offered an opportunity to "collaborate" with the Central Committee for Cooperative Training provided the Union moves its headquarters to the same building which houses the Reserve Bank's Agricultural Credit Department!

As a nation we have been upholding the unimpeachable principle of "aid without strings attached" as the only basis for a democratic give-and-take between nations. There is no reason why this principle should not be observed and implemented in the course of democratic give-and-take at home. It has been a settled policy of the Government of India to rebuild the country on the basis of democratic decentralization. The policy implies that Government authority will part with power rather than re-acquire it. But the Rural Credit Survey seems to function in an altogether alien ideological atmosphere. It wants the Reserve Bank, a Governmental and centralized institution, to re-absorb into its bureaucratic entrails whatever elements of a democratic cooperative movement in this country have struggled into existence in the face of overwhelming odds.

Semantics of Size

The Survey advocates that the primary credit cooperatives should have "a reasonably large membership," "a reasonably adequate share capital" and "adequate business." And, in the opinion of the Survey, the only way to achieve this objective is that the societies should cease to be one-village organizations, as hitherto, and extend their areas of operations to cover "groups of villages". The point to be examined here is whether an expansion of membership and share capital, etc., of credit cooperatives is possible without necessitating a corresponding expansion in the area of their operations. The Survey has not tried to establish this correspondence at any place in its lengthy Report. It has simply assumed that the correspondence exists.

But the statistics regarding the membership, etc., of credit cooperatives in 1951-52, cited by the Survey, do not support such an assumption. On the contrary, they indicate very clearly that a considerable expansion in the membership, etc. of existing credit cooperatives is possible without involving, except in rare cases, an expansion of their area of operation beyond one village.

Says the Survey: "The average membership of societies was 44; separate figures for some States are 18 for Madhya Pradesh, 22 for Madhya Bharat, 24 for Ajmer and West Bengal, 25 for Bihar and Delhi, 26 for Assam, 33 for Uttar Pradesh and 34 for Orissa as compared with 79 and 88 for Bombay and Madras respectively". That this meagre membership is a mere fraction of the rural population is also stated by the Survey. Table 7.1 shows the relationship between membership of agricultural credit societies and rural population in some of the States.

TABLE 7.1: Membership of agricultural credit societies

State	One member for so many rural inhabitants	Percentage of members to rural inhabitants	Percentage of members to rural families
Punjab	30	3.3	21.0
Madras	31	3.2	16.6
Bombay	2	.1	7.5
Uttar Pradesh	61	1.6	8.7
Orissa	101	1.0	5.2
Madhya Pradesh	126	0.8	4.0
Rajasthan	352	0.3	1.6
Bihar	477	0.2	1.1
Assam	507	0.2	1.1

All this goes to prove that even in the case of those cooperatives which show a relatively large membership, there is considerable scope for enlarging the membership from within their own village population and without extending the area of operation. The question of extending the area of operation should arise only when a society has enlisted within its fold all possible members from within a single village and yet remains economically unsound. Otherwise, we may have societies which cover more than one village but with a membership which, with an effort, can be enrolled within the confines of a single village. To give the name of "large-sized societies" to such cooperatives will be tantamount to giving currency to a semantic confusion.

The Survey was expected to give, in its Technical Report, village-wise or district-wise comparative tables establishing the relationship, in terms of total membership, of existing credit cooperatives to the total number of agricultural families involved. But such tables have not been provided. The relevant information is scattered all over the Technical Report and it is not an easy job to put it together. We are, therefore, compelled to draw conclusions on the basis of averages for different areas (see Table 7.2).[18]

TABLE 7.2: Potential members of credit cooperatives

Region	Average number of		
	A Villagers per village	B Self-supporting agri-culturists per village (potential members of cooperatives)	C All self-supporting villagers per village
North India	489	113	142
East India	433	100	126
South India	1052	244	305
West India	708	164	205
Central India	31	00	24
North-West India	447	103	129

A comparison of this possible membership with the actual membership in 1951-52 reveals that in all cases there is considerable scope for expanding the size of credit cooperatives without expanding their area of operation. The continued rise in village population ever since 1951-52 should have further extended this range of possible membership. The Survey, however, does not discuss these possibilities.

The same mistake is committed in respect of the share capital, deposits and working capital of societies. The Survey reports an average share capital of Rs. 827 for an average membership of 48. Supposing that all self-supporting villagers become members of the cooperatives, the average share capital per society will increase considerably without any expansion in the area of operation.

All this is possible on the basis of a village economy which is not yet prosperous. As prosperity increases the share capital, deposits and working capital of society are bound to show still larger averages.

With regard to the possibilities of business, the Survey's sin of omission is still more glaring. According to the survey, out of the 58.6 per cent of cultivating families which reported borrowing from different agencies, only 3.2 per cent had borrowed from the cooperative agency. The average amounts borrowed from the cooperatives by the 3.2 per cent of all cultivating families are shown in Table 7.3.[19]

TABLE 7.3: Average amounts borrowed from cooperatives by families in select states

State	Amount borrowed from cooperatives per family (Rs.)
Bombay	28.2
Uttar Pradesh	4.3
Punjab	8.8
Madras	8.9
West Bengal	1.7
Orissa	2.3
Assam	XL
Bihar	0.1

The "overall credit requirements" of the cultivators as computed by the Survey amounted to Rs. 1,300 per family for upper-strata cultivators and Rs. 800 for lower-strata cultivators. If the societies in various villages are enabled to fulfil even a part of these credit needs, they will become sizable units in terms of business as well.

The actual organization of the so-called "larger-sized" primary credit cooperatives when the Survey programme was put into practice under the Second Five Year Plan reflected a basic confusion. The *Sixth Evaluation Report* issued by the Planning Commission in June 1959 is an eloquent testimony to the fact that the term "larger-sized" does not mean anything in particular. Says the Report :

> The Rural Credit Survey Report did not lay down precise criteria for classifying societies into large and small; it only stated certain broad

principles and left the States to fix the sizes for the two categories. But the States have not adopted a uniform practice. For example, in most States a membership of 500 is regarded as a norm for large societies. *But in U.P., the norm is set at 1,000 members while in Bombay a society which has a minimum membership of 100, to start with, may be classified as a large society. Again in some areas, a small society may cover more than three villages, while in others some large societies cover only two villages each. Further, some small societies in certain areas have a larger share capital than some large societies in other areas.* Finally, the small society is not always a one-village society; our study shows that it covers, on average, nearly two villages.[20]

Nor do the so-called "larger-sized" societies come out any better in terms of performance. The Evaluation Report gives the following interesting facts :

Large societies are also expected to help the small cultivator more than the small. The extent to which this objective had been attained up to the time of our enquiry is indicated by Table 7.4.

In both large and small societies, the small farmers — those with five acres and less land — are proportionately more than the medium or the large cultivators. But small cultivators constitute a higher proportion of the total membership of small societies than of the large, the respective percentages being 42.3 per cent and 35.6 per cent.

TABLE 7.4: Distribution of members in large and small societies

Size of holding group	Distribution of members		Distribution of members per 100 households in each group	
	Large societies	Small societies	Large Societies	Small societies
25 acres and above	4.9	7.2	34.2	44.0
10-25 acres	14.5	15.7	35.7	40.2
5-10 acres	17.8	18.3	29.2	31.2
2-5 acres	2.3	4.8	5.7	8.1
	} 35.6	} 42.3	} 20.1	} 18.6
2 acres and below	13.3	17.5	14.6	12.5
Landless	27.1	16.6	20.2	12.6

Both types of societies have attracted higher proportions of the large cultivator in the villages than the small, and they have amongst their members, more or less, the same proportion of the small cultivators — about 20 per cent — in the villages.

> The large society seems to have attracted the landless worker much more than the small.... But these data about the landless members should be interpreted with great caution. The category described as "landless" in the records of different societies does not necessarily include persons belonging to the same classes. *In some societies, members who are well-off and do not resort to borrowing have been classified as landless. In some others, small traders have been put into this group.* These discrepancies reduce the comparability of the data of different areas.
>
> The principles followed by cooperative societies in fixing the maximum credit limit (mcl) for their members vary widely from area to area. In a number of blocks the mcl is larger for members of large societies than of the small ones. In others, the same limits apply to both. Right in land still remains the more important consideration taken into account in settling the limits. Only in a few cases is the credit limit related to the crop produced. *The discrimination in favour of land-owners against tenants persists and there is not much difference between the large and the small societies in this respect.*
>
> During these two years the total loan given by the large society was, on the average, six to eight times as large as that by the small society. But the proportion of members who received loans was, more or less, the same in both types of society, while the amount of loan per member was somewhat higher in the large societies.

In terms of the management of cooperative societies, the *Evaluation Report* writes :

> . . . another fact that this section of our enquiry has brought out is the dominance of the headquarters village in the management of the large society. In as many as 13 out of the 23 multi-village large societies for which we could get information, *the majority of the members of executive committees were from the headquarters village*. In two large societies comprising two villages each, eight out of the nine executive members were from the headquarters village while in large

societies covering three villages or more, about 70 per cent of them belonged to this category.

In pure business terms, the large society has a much better chance of paying its way than the small, but the relatively stronger position of the large society may be due to any one or more of several reasons, e.g. government contribution, actual or prospective, to the share capital of the large society, which is likely to influence favourably the people's faith in the society — the selection of the better among the small societies for amalgamation or expansion into large society, their larger total funds, etc. Only a more intensive study can separate the importance of each of these factors.

The Fundamental Fallacy

Evidence piled up during half a century of cooperative endeavour in this country has clearly indicated that bureaucracy and orthodox banking have been the biggest hurdles in the way of the Movement coming into its own and delivering the benefits expected of it to the poor and underprivileged sections of our population. The Survey was fully aware of this evidence, which it cited copiously while analyzing the causes of the failure of Cooperation in India. Yet the Survey dismissed the whole of it in a most off-hand manner without making even a casual effort to understand it. And that is exactly where the Survey committed the fundamental fallacy which led to all its subsequent mistakes.

The fallacy has two, though related, aspects. The first aspect is a more or less morbidly depressing view of the objective situation in which Cooperatives have to operate. The second aspect is a more or less distorted view of the role of Cooperation itself. The two distortions stand and fall together. If the objective situation is really as depressing as the Survey has portrayed, then the obvious remedy is the type of "cooperation" which the Survey has suggested. And, vice versa, it may be added that if the objective situation is not already as depressing as the Survey would have us believe, it will become as depressing if the policies adopted by the Survey are implemented.

How does the Survey look at the objective situation in India? The *General Report* of the Survey contains the following graphic statement:

"One may consider an institution for the rehabilitation of *crippled children struck down by the malady of infantile paralysis.... No one has yet suggested that those children should depend on themselves as much as possible and form themselves into a mutual association for individual rehabilitation*".[21]

It is this view of the objective situation which persuaded the Survey to reject summarily what it termed as the "reputed causes" of the failure of Cooperation. And such a rejection is logically inescapable. Similarly, on this assumption, the short shrift given by the Survey to what it termed as the "deeper causes" is also justified and valid. There has to be a Cooperative Movement before it can make a "fundamental statement of cooperative and economic objectives, viz. 'better farming, better business and better living".

In this way, the basic contention of the Survey boils down to a simple and straight assertion, namely, that so far there has been no Cooperative Movement in India. The chances of such a Movement arising were very remote on account of the paralysis engendered by the "colonial economy" created by British imperialism. Nor will the chances improve so long as that "colonial economy" continues to obtain.

The Report of the Survey does not say all this very explicitly, but this is the implied argument which runs through all its readings and recommendations, e.g. when the Survey emphasizes "the total impracticability of any attempt to combine the very weak in competition with the very strong". It is this line of argument which emerges when the Survey says that "the problem is not so much one of re-organization of cooperative credit as of the creation of new conditions in which it can operate effectively for the benefit of the poor".

We have, therefore, first of all, to evaluate the Survey's description of the objective situation in India. On the face of it, the Survey's description of the objective situation breathes some sort of lofty humanism over-brimming with concern for those whom life or the social situation has not given a square deal. But, in effect, it declares that an overwhelming number of our cultivators, who constitute nearly 70 per cent of our population, are nothing better than "crippled children struck down by the malady of infantile paralysis".

(How) can such a State be a democracy in which the majority of the people decide the policies to be pursued by their Government? It has to become a paternalistic State, a sort of benevolent despotism in which a microscopic minority of "able-bodied" and "grown-up" people dictate the course of events.

But fortunately for India and unfortunately for the authors of the Survey, our cultivators are not a race of crippled children. No doubt, the cultivators are faced with big and difficult problems. No doubt, the cultivators are handicapped in respect of resources for tackling and overcoming those problems.

But it was these cultivators who rallied round and rescued the nation during the course of our struggle for independence. It is these cultivators who have sustained the fabric of our democracy ever since we have become free. And it is these cultivators who encourage our planners to plan for a rapid and all-round revolution in our rural scene.

The picture painted by the Survey does not reflect the plight of our rural population. It only reflects the plight into which the bureaucratic mind plunges whenever it faces a task involving the mobilization of masses of men. The bureaucrat has always tended to believe that he alone is the repository of initiative, intelligence and sense of responsibility and that the lot of the people who pay his salary can be improved only if they quietly surrender to his governance and guidance.

The view adopted by the Survey about the role of Cooperation is equally preposterous. Cooperation is treated as a set of impressive institutions that shall form the decorative facade of a completed social structure which has already been straightened, systematized and cleansed of its old debris by the all-round action of an almighty State. It does not occur to the authors of the Survey Report that at that distant stage the triumphant State may not need the cooperative facade at all.

Shorn of its linguistic trappings, the Survey stands for using the Cooperative Movement as a channel for extending the bureaucratic arm vertically and horizontally, till it embraces the whole of our rural population. The truth is, however, that if India has inherited a colonial economy, the task of Cooperation is to liquidate this colonial economy and replace it with a more equitable scheme of things and destroy the disadvantages cf the cultivator. Cooperation can mobilize the cultivators against all odds and set their face against the old order. And it can call upon the State to lend a helping hand.

But experience in many countries goes to suggest that a positive State has its own ambitions and vested interests and that once it invades a sphere of human life, it does not easily retire. Thus, Cooperation can never accept an existence by proxy. It can never trail behind the bulldozer of the State to settle down on a prepared soil like a precious plant. On the contrary, it has to be the bulldozer as well as the plant.

CONCLUSIONS

Cornerstones of Cooperation

In the last analysis, every policy for reorganization of cooperative institutions depends upon what we understand by Cooperation and what place we give to it amidst an array of ideologies trying to reshape our society.

But the Survey has nowhere in its voluminous Report tried to define the meaning and role of Cooperation, so that it is not clear whether the Survey had any positive conception to employ in its evaluation of the record of performance and to project in the formulation of recommendations for reorganization. We can deduce, however, that in the mind of the authors of the Survey, Cooperation is not an ideology in its own right, that it cherishes no values of its own and that, at best, it is a neutral sort of institutional device which can be moulded in any manner and integrated at will with any other sort of institutions.

But cooperation is a well-defined ideology in its own right. It is a self-sufficient system of values which lay a limit to all social institutions including the State. No doubt, the value system of Cooperation is endlessly plastic in its approaches and methods. But at the same time, we must recognize that the value system of Cooperation is fairly rigid and uncompromising when it comes to its fundamental principles.

The meaning and role of Cooperation can be understood better if we look back at the history of its origin and growth in Europe. The history must be taken as a whole because it is related to a concept which has maintained its ideological identity in the midst of all changes, even aberrations, in the development of practical details. What is most important in the development of this cooperative ideology is how it has, from time to time, defined its relation with the State.

Cooperation had its birth in an atmosphere which was more or less completely dominated by the categories of *laissez-faire* doctrines of State and society. These categories in their turn were derived from a materialist world view in which morals were a secondary cementing force, a hedonistic psychology and ethics according to which the natural as well as the ethically normal instinct of man was to pursue his own individual pleasure and power without let or hindrance, and a negative theory of the State in which the Government had no positive functions beyond the police duty of maintaining law and order and in which freedom was defined as "the absence of restraint". The social situation was, as a result, very conducive to a competitive capitalist economy which sanctified pursuit of private profit as the highest ideal and contemplated social good as an inevitable by-product of individual greed and combativeness.

The founding fathers of the Cooperative philosophy presented a cogent and calculated counterblast to all these dismal doctrines. They restored the primacy of morals above material prosperity. They systematized an alternative psychology and ethics according to which mutual aid rather than individual self-seeking was the natural as well as ethically normal instinct of all healthy human beings. They redefined liberty as an outcome of voluntarily accepted self-restraint. They denounced competition as an agency for generating social good and held up Cooperation as the only royal road to the "greatest good of the greatest number".

In this first phase, Cooperative philosophy was rather hostile to the institution of the State as such. And such an attitude was natural also in the circumstances then prevailing. Almost all European States, which had emerged out of their feudal cell, were, at the time, under the spell of *laissez-faire* doctrines and as such completely dominated by the rising capitalist class. The public policies of these States showed no concern for organic communities possessing collective consciousness but, on the contrary, assumed the individual as the only starting point, thus leading to such an atomization of the social whole as was conducive to an increasing concentration of coercive power in the hands of a centralized State.

Cooperation has all along kept intact its positive disapproval of competitive capitalism. But with regard to the State, its attitude has undergone changes with the changing character of the modern State. In so far as the State has shed away its unconcern for the underdog and assumed the role of an agency for broad social welfare, Cooperation has given up its hostility to the State and is prepared to play partner with it. But at the same time, Cooperation has emphasized and insisted that the weak be aided to create and build voluntarily and from below rather than be spoon-fed and shepherded by a bureaucratic hierarchy mechanically imposed from above. By implication, therefore, Cooperation has increasingly identified itself with a decentralized and structurally supple system of society in which a variety of autonomous communities act out of their collective consciousness and for the collective good.

An interesting opportunity for redefining its contours has been provided to Cooperation by the rise of the modern socialist State. To start with, Cooperation itself was counted as a school of socialism. In fact, the word "socialism" was used for the first time in a magazine devoted to the

Cooperative cause. But as socialism branched into many schools at war with each other, Cooperation asserted its own identity and defined the terms on which it could join hands with a socialist experiment in human welfare.

The attitude of Cooperation to socialism is fundamentally determined by its decentralist and communitarian approach. Cooperation has no use for those varieties of socialism which advocate that the State is the only or even the most important agency for undertaking the task of social reconstruction and that welfare can best be distributed by an administrative apparatus securing a stranglehold on all strategic spots of a social situation. On the other hand, Cooperation considers itself a natural ally of those schools of socialism which minimize the role of the State and which, instead, put their trust in a variety of voluntary organizations spontaneously created by people according to occasion and need and organically sustained by mutual faith and collective consciousness rather than by routine rules and ponderous procedures.

In such a scheme of things, self-help is, of course, the cornerstone as well as the canopy of all human endeavour. But self-help is not to be defined so narrowly as to exclude mutual help which is the other most important cornerstone of Cooperation. Help is to be given and accepted all along, but without any strings attached. Cooperation is a constant drama of free give-and-take. The State is welcome to enter on the stage of this drama as one of the actors. But if it tries to become the controller of the drama even from behind the scenes, Cooperation will not have it in the team and will better go it alone.

The Survey committed an error when it conceived of State help to cooperatives as State partnership in their share capital. The error became somewhat sinister when the State was advised to take care of its investments like an orthodox banker by participating in the management of cooperative societies. The Survey also committed a mistake in assuming that a State apparatus, built up for supervision, audit and training, will wind itself up after the Cooperative Movement has "come up". The apparatus will, on the contrary, tend to grow at the cost of the Movement. No administrative apparatus can be trusted to work for its own liquidation.

II. SEMINAR ON PLANNED PRODUCTION CREDIT (ICU, NEW DELHI AUGUST 1959)

In the Introduction to its report on this Seminar, the ICU refers to the perennial efforts of the Government of India, since Independence, to improve the means and thereby raise the production potential of small and marginal farmers. Most of the problem has eventually crystallized into the manner in which the small farmer without tangible means can be given credit. Since the small farmer can offer no security in accordance with orthodox banking norms, ideas have been put forward that credit should be linked with production and technical supervision. On May 16, 1959 the Government of India also formulated a scheme for the provision of supplementary credit to four hundred thousand farming families throughout the country based on the planned production of each family. The credit was to be channelled Statewise through cooperative banks.[22]

An impression, however, began gaining ground that the cooperative banks were reluctant to undertake this scheme because they felt that there are risks involved in lending money to small farmers. In this total situation and in consideration of the fact that the Indian Cooperative Union, which believes that the welfare of the small farmer is the primary concern of the cooperative movement and which has itself run a pilot project in supervised credit with some measure of success, decided that it would be useful if cooperative banks were brought together to exchange views.

The Indian Cooperative Union, therefore, sent out invitations to 20 cooperative banks throughout the country to join in a Seminar on Planned Production Credit. There was encouraging response to the invitation and the Seminar was held at Vigyan Bhavan in New Delhi on August 24- 25 1959.

The participants in the Seminar spent half of the first day in visiting the Supervised Credit Project of the Indian Cooperative Union in the Mehrauli belt near Delhi, where they met loanees and the field staff concerned with the project and also saw some of the operations. The rest of the period was devoted to a discussion on planned production credit. The final report of the seminar and other relevant papers are published in this document.

The Seminar began by clarifying exactly what issues within the broad framework of the problem before them should be dealt with. It decided that the main consideration should be devoted to the farmer without tangible means and how he could be assisted by the cooperative banks. In terms of credit, the Seminar also decided that more attention should be paid to short-term credit facilities, how banks would provide such credit to the landless tenants and how it would devise methods by which technical assistance would go with credit.

The participants, in turn, gave a picture of the situation in each of the States and what useful organization and power already existed which made Planned Production Credit feasible. They also outlined various examples where the banks had been able to do useful work in this matter and the various obstacles and pitfalls they had encountered.

Considerable discussion was devoted to the question of the risk which the banks would be taking in Planned Production Credit Programmes. The participants agreed that risks ought to be taken but certain losses were inevitable which did not reflect upon the character and integrity of the people but which might be due to genuine reasons of distress. How such losses should be met found place in the discussion.

The participants all agreed that the object of the entire programme should be to strengthen the small farmer and to create conditions for him to stand on his own legs rather than perennially look to the State or society to prop him by grants and subsidies. In accepting this view, Shri Annasaheb Sahasrabudhe, as a special invitee to the Seminar, outlined his experience in the Gramdan villages of Koraput, where, he said, he had worked on behalf of the Akhil Bharat Sarva Sewa Sangh. Shri Annasaheb said they had given short-term credit to about 7,000 families. All these villagers were below-sub-marginal Adivasis whose annual income did not come to more than Rs. 200. His experience, he said, had convinced him that one actually ought to go further than the Planned Production Credit programme. Credit activity must be followed up by planned developmental activity. He said the task of amelioration required that every farming family should be provided with employment for the off-season also, so that if each could find work for about 230 to 300 days a year, then alone would the credit activity have stability, security and significance.

He said he was glad to know that the banks were willing to share the risks with the Government in providing credit to the farmer without tangible means, but he was convinced that unless credit was linked not only with production but with an all-round development, pumping money into such programmes would be of no help. There would be hardly any risk if a planned developmental programme were tied in with the credit programme. The problem was to see how an employment programme at the service cooperative level could be introduced. Shri Annasaheb pointed out that what he called the agro-industry was not a year-round industry, but it could be made so by developmental programmes in agricultural farm industries or in allied village industries. Otherwise, one would expect the small farmers to subsist for 365 days on the work of 100 days in a year and also to increase production sufficiently to be able to repay whatever type of loans they got. In a situation like this, the rehabilitation programme would really become a permanent relief programme.

The participants felt that there was validity in the approach of Shri Annasaheb Sahasrabudhe, and they decided to keep his suggestions in view in formulating any conclusions.

Report of the Seminar

The Seminar on Planned Production Credit, sponsored by the Indian Cooperative Union, concerned itself primarily with the problems of the small farmers, especially the marginal and sub-marginal farmers. It believed that service cooperatives provided the most effective means of assisting them with various services including that of credit.

There were two approaches which emerged. One approach was that the marginal and sub-marginal farmers, estimated at about two crore families, have at present an income of about Rs. 14.5 per month, and find employment for about 100 days in the year. It was felt that if credit alone were provided to these farmers without the necessary guidance in planning, technical matters and in creating additional avenues of employment during the off seasons, the chances were that even the credit provided may not be effectively or properly used. Further, the expansion of employment opportunities to 300 days in the year would involve not only allied agricultural industries but also cottage and other industries. The programme of development should, therefore, be planned and integrated, and credit given should be a part of an employment and production plan. The provision of credit under such a scheme of development would have to be a long-term one ranging from 10 to 12 years.

Another view was that while additional avenues of employment would be necessary for the amelioration of this class of farmers, it was not likely that occupations other than allied agricultural industries could provide any significant employment. The reliance, therefore, would have to be predominantly on agriculture and allied industries. It should, therefore, be possible to meet the requirement of such farmers within the framework of short- and medium-term (five-year) loans. The contingency of long-term loans would be remote. It was also pointed out that if different businesses, such as agriculture and cottage industries, are mixed up though one cooperative, the problems of providing technical guidance would be too great. It would also mean an expansion of loan business, as all kinds of requirements would have to be covered. This would put extra burden upon the financing agencies as well as the service cooperatives. It was, therefore, felt that a programme developed for the rehabilitation of small farmers may, to start with, confine itself to the development of agriculture and allied industries, and the financial requirements of such a programme could be met by short- and medium-term loans.

The Seminar took note of both these points and felt that the two approaches had considerable force and validity. The size of the country being large and there being variations from State to State, perhaps both the approaches could be tried on an experimental basis in different areas to see the results.

The cooperative banks were not only generally interested in the problem of rehabilitation of the small farmers but were also willing to play their part in this programme of national importance. Owing to the nature of the problem and the difficulties now faced by the small farmers, it was obvious that with the best of will and organization, a programme of rehabilitation could not be made a fool-proof banking proposition. A certain amount of losses was bound to arise and any attempt to ignore this point would only postpone an early solution of the problem.

The Seminar was, however, of the view that the losses involved should be shared by the various participants in the programme. The primary cooperative society, the district central bank, the State cooperative bank and the Government should all share such losses. The proportion in which these should be shared between different agencies has primarily to be determined in terms of their capacity as well as their obligations. The programme of rehabilitation of small farmers was primarily the duty and responsibility of the State. The State would, therefore, have to take the major responsibility. Even if the cooperative banks were not in the picture, the Government had the responsibility to carry out this programme. Thus, normally, the Government would have to bear the entire burden of such a programme. But in this case the cooperative banks may also be interested to participate in this venture and play their part according to their capacity and thus share part of the Government burden.

Since it had also to be safeguarded that there was no laxity towards repayment, where it could responsibly be made, it was necessary that the primary cooperatives and the district central banks should also undertake a measure of the responsibility and share part of the losses.

The Seminar felt that once this was agreed to in principle, specific arrangements could be worked out from State to State, between the Government and the cooperatives. Some of the suggestions made may be mentioned here :

- The consensus of opinion was that for the loans advanced to such farmers a 15 per cent bad debt fund would have to be provided. It was, however, necessary to ensure that this fund was set up and operated in such a manner that the banks would have complete assurance of realizing their claims on this fund, where justified, without any loss of time.
- The Seminar emphasized that it was not a credit programme in the normal sense of the term. Here the operations would have to begin by effective planning, technical guidance and close supervision of the operations. Credit would have to be provided not so much in cash as by way of services in kind. The help required by the small farmers or by their service cooperative in this matter would have to be multiple. These services are normally not provided by any banking institution. The banks deal normally with creditworthy people who also have sufficient technical and managerial know-how. It was, therefore, imperative that adequate technical and supervisory staff would have to be made available to the service cooperatives and to the banks to carry out this programme satisfactorily. Such assistance may be needed for an initial period of at least five years.
- Since such a programme would also involve an effective coordination between the staff of different field organizations, such as the Community Development, National Extension, Agriculture, Revenue, Cooperation and Development Departments, it was desirable that these agencies must have clear working arrangements with the banks in the villages where such programmes are taken up.

The Seminar also discussed why the credit accommodation made available to them by the Reserve Bank was not fully utilized. The reasons for the non-utilization were primarily administrative, organizational and procedural, operating within the banks themselves, and between the banks, the State Governments and the Reserve Bank. It was necessary to simplify and smoothen out the procedure to eliminate delays.

The Seminar visualized that in the coming years the functions and business of the banks would expand considerably. Revitalizing and strengthening the banks, and training their personnel, were, therefore, imperative. The Seminar suggested that the Cooperative Banks should take initiative and organize a Standing Committee consisting of the Chairmen of the State Cooperative Apex Banks. This Committee could formulate policies, coordinate and sponsor training and other programmes of improvement in the methods of record-keeping, management, etc., in which considerable advance has been made in many parts of the world.

The Seminar was also of the view that the cooperative banks put together were a considerable force in their contribution to national development. It was necessary in discussing cooperative credit and related problems that representatives of the cooperative banks should also be actively associated and their views and experience should be taken.

The Seminar considered the scheme for planned production credit recently sponsored by the Government of India. It expressed its appreciation of the scheme and the purposes underlying it. The various measures outlined in this Report are the prerequisites of success of such a programme. The Seminar hoped that the committee appointed by the Government of India further to examine this scheme would also take into account these suggestions.

The present restrictions on making short- and medium-term loans would need to be removed and relaxed if such loans had to be provided to farmers who have no tangible assets to give by way of security. If the present rules laid down by the Reserve Bank in this matter were continued, the banks would not be in a position to provide these loans. For instance, it would be necessary that the medium-term loans made available to the banks were for a minimum period of five years. The present system of 75 per cent of the medium-term loans being for a period of three years and the remaining 25 per cent for a period of five years would have to be changed into a total period of five years. The present rules require that the first repayment of the medium-term loans fall due after the twelfth month of loaning. Taking into account the difficulties of the small farmers, a minimum initial period of 24 months would be required, during which no repayment could be expected. Even in the case of short-term loans, revisions may be necessary in the present policies. For instance, in the case of sugarcane producers, there are large numbers of small cultivators who would require financial assistance. The present practice is to give loans for a short-term for a period of 12 months whereas the loans can be repaid only in about 15 months because of the nature of business.

Another difficulty which would have to be removed is the system of fixing the maximum credit limit of the banks. As in the case of cooperative societies, so in the case of the banks, the credit limit is fixed in terms of a certain multiple of their share capital and owned funds. The multiple now permitted in the borrowing capacity needed revision and enhancement. The major security for loans advanced to such agriculturists would be in the form of personal security or mortgage of assets created out of the loans. For short-term loans the main security should be in the form of crop, and the main security in the case of medium-term loans would be in the form of produce created out of the land. The medium-term loans should be secured by mortgage of assets created out of the loan.

The Seminar recommended that the loans given should be in kind as far as possible.

The Seminar also recommended that the cooperative banks should develop greater personal contact with the clients. The general practice at present is to give such loans on the recommendations of the cooperative department. In certain areas the practice in vogue is to provide the loans to cooperatives on the recommendation of the officer of the cooperative department. The banks would do well to build up personal and direct contacts with the borrower and make their own assessment of the needs and requirements.

In short, the Seminar recommended that so far as the terms of loans made to farmers were concerned, these should be consistent with the period of time necessary to permit repayment by the borrower from his production.

The Seminar recognized that our agriculture was subject to the vagaries of weather; floods and droughts are not uncommon, and crops are destroyed year after year. Normally, this burden was passed on to the agriculturist himself. After Independence, the Rural Credit Survey had recommended that the National Relief and Guarantee Fund should be established in the country to provide some kind of crop insurance to act as a cushion against losses from such calamities. Unfortunately, this recommendation had not yet been wholly implemented in all the States. In undertaking a programme for the rehabilitation of the small farmers, this problem assumed even greater proportions. The small farmers were in no position to bear the risk of natural calamities such as floods, droughts, etc., which destroy crops completely. The Seminar, therefore, recommended that special provision would have to be made to guarantee losses which might accrue on account of natural calamities. This was a responsibility which neither the farmer nor the banks could be expected to undertake and must squarely rest upon the Government.

The Seminar considered the requirements of finances for such a programme. In the absence of any other estimates, the Seminar considered the estimates formulated by the Ministry of Community Development and Cooperation, which were discussed recently at the Mysore Conference of State Ministers of Cooperation. These estimates suggest that about Rs. 400 crores may be required at the end of the Second Plan and Rs. 1,000 crores by the end of the Third Plan. The Seminar also took note that a committee had recently been appointed by the Government of India to find resources of this order of credit.

The Seminar was of the view that all available national resources had already been tapped by the Planning Commission and had been taken into account in drafting the Second Plan and in considering the outlay for the Third Plan. The Seminar was convinced that the requirements of finances for the rehabilitation of the small farmers could come only from within the Plan resources and, therefore, recommended that these requirements should be given first priority from out of the national Plan resources.

III. FROM THE SEMINAR ON COOPERATION (ICU, NEW DELHI, AUGUST 1959)

The bulk of the Report of this Seminar is contained in Chapter 3 of this book. The Seminar, in its final session, after deliberating larger themes such as the philosophy, objectives, present status and future direction of cooperation in India, homed in on the more specific "tasks of cooperation" in the context of national development. The most important of these tasks was, of course, credit. As a large part of the discussion is repetitive of what has gone before in this chapter, we reproduce below only those paragraphs that make specific recommendations. These spell out the proposals of a representative section of the cooperative movement regarding agricultural credit.

Agricultural Credit: Suggested Remedies

It has to be recognized that credit by itself, even if it were available, cannot fully meet the requirements of the small farmers. The task of assisting the small farmer is essentially a measure of rehabilitation. This requires not only credit but also initial grants to place some minimum resources in the hands of the small farmers — individually or through their cooperatives. Such a rehabilitation task cannot be performed by banking institutions.

We have to contend with a complex situation, two aspects of which require special consideration. Firstly, the only type of financial aid available to a small farmer today is in the form of loans on strict commercial terms. No rehabilitation grants are provided. The channels of available aid are the Cooperative Banks and the Reserve Bank. It is obviously beyond the scope of banks to employ their funds for rehabilitation purposes. Secondly, the farmer is expected to become a member of a cooperative society before he can even get loans. With the best of will and organization it is inconceivable that in the near future all the small farmers would join cooperative membership — if cooperatives are to be promoted and organized on the sound lines recommended earlier in this report. If the farmers are pressed to join cooperatives because that is the only way for them to get credit facilities, then the present criticism that the people join cooperatives only to get government money will remain valid and the cooperatives so formed would be utterly lacking in cooperative content.

Yet the small farmer must be aided and rehabilitated at the earliest. The entire reliance on the banking structure (the Reserve Bank and the cooperative banks) on the one side and the restriction of credit facilities through cooperatives alone on the other does not permit of a fuller, immediate and countrywide help being provided to the millions of our small farmers.

The Seminar is thus led to the firm conclusion that the problem of agricultural rehabilitation and credit should be tackled by an agency which is wholly devoted to this problem. The Union Government should set up an Agricultural Rehabilitation and Credit Corporation (ARCC) which will take speedy and deliberate measures to rehabilitate the small cultivator. Even as the Government has subscribed capital for steel and such other plants, it should provide adequate capital to this Corporation from out of the national plan resources.

The Corporation should be free to give grants or loans. It should also be free to employ the cooperative or any other channel for providing aid to the small farmers. But its basic and long-term objective should be to foster a rapid growth of cooperatives which should ultimately take over all or most of its functions. It should, therefore, treat the cooperative banks as its first and intimate allies and provide them with finance and other assistance on a priority and preferential basis. This will ensure rapid development of cooperation because cooperatives will no more be forced to die or become dormant for lack of adequate working finances as at present. An increasingly larger number of cultivators will move into the cooperative fold which promises sympathetic and timely help.

But the Corporation should not restrict its operations to the cooperatives. In areas where cooperatives have either not yet come up or do not fully cover the agricultural population, the Corporation should evolve alternative transitional methods of supplying agricultural credit speedily and directly to the cultivator. The cultivators are thus enabled to augment their income through increased productivity will join the cooperative fold much more readily than cultivators who are starved of credit simply because they are not yet in a position to form a cooperative.

At the sane time, it should be ensured that the newly available supplies of credit go to the poorer cultivators in the first instance. A scale of priorities can be established so that the poorer cultivators be first taken care of. A real breakthrough in this direction needs a thorough revision of the prevailing criteria of creditworthiness. The Cooperative Movement should advocate and assert its own criteria of creditworthiness, i.e. *character and productive capacity of the cultivator.*

The development of cooperative banking institutions should be diversified according to the needs of particular populations and areas as well as in keeping with the range of functions to be performed. No uniform or rigid pattern should be enforced. The situation in the cooperative sector will, for a long time, continue to demand much more particularized and closer attention than is habitually practised by banking institutions. The cooperative banks should, therefore, avoid taking up too many and unrelated functions so that their operations do not become unwieldy. The banks should try to become specialized for doing fuller justice to the varied needs of cooperative credit. Several banks in the same area may take up the same type of operations if the range of those operations is, or becomes, too large for a single bank. Similarly, unrelated operations in the same area may also be undertaken by separate banks. This will lead to promptness and plasticity. The federal device of cooperation will always ensure a proper ccordination of their plans and policies at some level.

With a view to strengthening and coordinating the various Apex State Cooperative Banks, the Seminar considers it essential that a National Cooperative Bank of India (NCBI) be established at the earliest by all the State Apex Cooperative Banks joining together. The State Cooperative Banks should, through the NCBI, maintain a close liaison with the ARCC so that their requirements receive immediate and prior consideration.

This active association will prepare the ground for their taking over of most of the functions of the ARCC as soon as practicable.

The ARCC and the NCBI on their part should evolve some suitable institutional arrangement so that the two can work together as a confederation in order to coordinate better their policies and plans. This will also assure a speedier transfer of the function's of the ARCC, which is a transitional institution, to the NCBI, which is envisaged as the ultimate guardian of all cooperative credit. With the setting up of the ARCC, the Agricultural Credit Department of the Reserve Bank should be wound up. Its functions of providing credit to cooperative banks would be taken over by the ARCC, and its function of inspecting and supervising Apex Cooperative Banks will be taken over by the NCBI.

These steps will relieve the Reserve Bank from its exacting and mounting responsibility regarding agricultural credit. This, in itself, will be greatly advantageous from another important national point of view. In the present state of rapid national development, the Reserve Bank of India is being more and more called upon to direct its attention towards maintaining sound fiscal policies, supervising the ever-expanding operations of commercial banking, curbing inflation and securing the stability of the rupee. To those who fear inflation it should be pointed out that, firstly, the resources we want to requisition for the ARCC are not outside the total plan outlay. If our economy can soundly undertake an investment of, say, Rs. 10,000 crores, then the Seminar suggests that at least 10 per cent of this outlay should be earmarked for ARCC. There can, therefore, be no question or danger of inflation on account of credit supply to agricultural producers. Secondly, the seminar suggests that credit should be related to production plans.

At the same time, the Movement should devote serious thought to the problem of attracting private resources into the cooperative fold. The growth of institutional credit is likely to have two consequences. Firstly, the excesses committed by the private moneylenders will be considerably toned down. Secondly, quite a part of the resources operated at present by the private moneylenders will become idle. The Cooperative Movement should devise incentives to attract these idle resources to augment supplies of cooperative credit. The private moneylenders may be offered attractive rates of interest so that they feel encouraged to deposit their money in cooperative banking institutions and do not divert them to other fields.

IV. COOPERATIVE CREDIT – WHO BENEFITS?

(Published in the *Times of India* 6 December 1965)

One can hardly quarrel with the rich for trying to become richer. But what is one to do about a socialist apparatus which goes out of its way to aid the rich in their pursuit of increased prosperity? And this at the cost of those who richly deserve a dose of socialism for their very survival!

The cooperative movement is believed to be an instrument of the weak. Following the recommendations of the All India Rural Credit Survey 1954, there has also been active State participation in the capital and management of agricultural cooperative credit societies – the most important wing of the cooperative credit movement – to further safeguard the interests of the weaker cultivators. It is essential, therefore, to take a close look at the flow of agricultural cooperative credit to the rich and the poor rural households.

During the decade 1952-62, there had been a vast expansion of Government-sponsored cooperative credit to the rural population. While in the year 1952, cooperative credit was no more than three per cent of the total credit available to the cultivators, in 1962 it rose to 15 per cent. In money terms, the increase had been even more spectacular. From Rs. 25 crores, cooperative credit had risen to Rs. 254 crores annually. But the crucial question is: who benefited from this phenomenal increase?

According to the *Reserve Bank of India Bulletin,* only three per cent of the total cash loans advanced by cooperatives go to rural households with assets less than Rs. 1,000 each, which constitute nearly a third of the total rural households in the country. By contrast, a third of the total credit goes to not more than five per cent of the rural households in the uppermost bracket of prosperity, each with total assets of Rs. 20,000 or more.

This gloomy picture remains unchanged even if we vary the asset groups to analyse the Reserve Bank's statistics. Taking the households with total assets of less than Rs. 2,500 each, we find that half the rural population, composed of these households, gets a little over a tenth of the total loans, while more than half of the loans go to households with assets of Rs. 10,000 or above which are only 13 per cent of the total households. The rural households between these two asset groups form nearly a third of the total rural population; by an interesting coincidence, they get as much share in the total cooperative credit (Table A)

TABLE A

Asset Group (Rs.)	Distribution of rural households	Share of loans from cooperatives (per cent)
Less than Rs. 2,500	53.0	10.8
Rs. 2,500 to Rs.10,000	33.7	34.2
Rs. 10,000 and more	13.3	55.0
	100.0	100.0

It will be interesting here to see how closely the pattern of distribution of cooperative credit resembles the distribution of total assets amongst the rural households (*Reserve Bank of India Bulletin,* June 1965) (Table B)

TABLE B

Asset Group (Rs.)	Distribution of rural households	Share of loans from cooperatives (per cent)
Less than Rs. 2,500	53.0	9.6
Rs. 2,500 to Rs.10,000	33.7	32.4
Rs. 10,000 and more	13.3	58.4
	100.0	100.0

There is a common belief that the overwhelmingly large flow of credit to the richer rural households is due to "approach", "influence" and "political pressure". It is also believed to be the outcome of the fact that the bureaucrats administering the credit and the rich cultivators belong to the same social class. Furthermore, both these phenomena are considered beyond control or cure; an intolerable situation is thus accepted and endured, almost without protest.

The principal factor responsible for the diversion of cooperative credit to the rich, almost to the exclusion of the poor, is nothing but the officially approved credit policy. The essence of this policy is to relate cooperative loans to the assets possessed by the borrower. Inevitably, credit is beyond the reach of the many whose assets are scanty, and is readily available to the few who are men of means. Cooperative credit thus becomes an instrument of accentuating, rather than mitigating, economic disparities.

Are we discovering this situation for the first time? Certainly not. The state of affairs was no different 10 years ago. In 1954 after a detailed study of rural credit, specially the working of cooperatives, the All India Rural Credit Survey observed: "We have here the curious position of cooperatives departing from the cooperative principle where security is concerned by adopting ownership as the basis instead of personal character and repaying capacity ... the result is a bias of the cooperative credit system towards the big and large and away from the medium and the small."

The authors of the Rural Credit Survey were led to the conclusion that cooperatives had failed, but acting on the conviction that cooperatives can and must succeed they recommended a substantial expansion of cooperative credit. The survey clearly laid down that this expansion must be combined with firm measures to ensure that the interests of the weaker producers are fully safeguarded: "In the devising of the system, in prescribing who shall control it at different levels, and in providing for the personnel who are to run the system, it will, therefore, be of paramount importance to ensure that the interests of the weaker sections, adequate finance is made available to him on conditions not more onerous than to the bigger cultivator or the owner of larger land".

Despite these clear warnings about the "paramount" importance of providing safeguards at "every stage", the bulk of Rs. 230 crores pumped through cooperatives, on the advice of the Rural Credit Survey, has been delivered at the wrong doors. Do the authorities concerned in regulating and controlling cooperatives credit bear any responsibility for this situation? The Agricultural Credit Department of the Reserve Bank which controls the cooperative credit system and the Union Ministry of Cooperation must render an account to the public for their gross failure to safeguard the interests of the weaker producers. A glance at the mounting annual expenditure during this period on the establishment of the Agricultural Credit Department and Union Ministry of Cooperation only goes to compound their negligence.

The situation must cause concern in the highest quarters particularly to Parliament. The question has also become urgent in view of the reports that during the Fourth Plan cooperative credit supply is to be expanded further to Rs. 650 crores: an increase of more than 100 per cent. Cooperative credit must be expanded. But who are going to be its beneficiaries? This question cannot be ignored any longer.

NOTES

1. *All-India Cooperative Review,* August 1955, p. 297.
2. Syamanandan Sahaya, Quoted in All-India Cooperative Review, August 1955, pp. 249-50.
3. *Proceedings of the Reserve Bank of India,* pp. 23-24.
4. *All-India Cooperative Review,* August 1955, p. 256.
5. *Report of the Indian Cooperative Congress,* p. 134.
6. Quoted in the Report of the Agricultural Finance Sub-Committee, 1945, p. 32.
7. Quoted by E.M. Hough in the Cooperative movement in India, p. 74.
8. Report of the Agricultural Finance Sub-Committee, p. 82
9. Report of the Cooperative Planning Committee, p. 74.
10. Report of the Agricultural Credit Organisation Committee, p. 9.
11. Report of the Rural Banking Enquiry Committee, 1950, p. 48.
12. All-India Rural Credit Survey, General Report, p. 2.
13. The General Report, pp. 140-42.
14. Review of the Cooperative Movement in India, 1939-46. RBI, pp. 104-5.
15. Review of the Cooperative Movement in India, 1946-48, RBI, pp. 93-94.
16. Proceedings, RBI, 1956, pp. 7-8.
17. All-India Rural Credit Survey, General Report, p. 473.
18. Figures for Column A are taken from Census of India, 1951, Vol. I. Part I-A, p. 41

    Figures for Columns B and C are computed from Column A on the basis of the survey's estimate that 29% of the rural population is self-supporting and 80% of the villagers are self-supporting agriculturists.

19. All-India Rural Credit Survey, General Report, p. 23.
20. Sixth Evaluation Report, pp. 106-7.
21. All-India Rural Credit Survey, General Report, p. 279.
22. This has since been revised.

REFERENCES

All India Rural Credit Survey vis-a-vis the Cooperative Movement in India. (Sita Ram Goel) *Indian Cooperative Union,* 1961.

All India Cooperative Review, August, 1955 (quote credited to S. Sahaya, Chairman, Bihar State Cooperative Bank).

All India Rural Credit Survey, General Report, RBI, 1954

Census of India, 1951, Vol. I, Part I-A.

From the Seminar on Cooperation, August, 1959, ICU, New Delhi.

Hough, E.M., *The Cooperative Movement in India,* 3rd Edition, 1953.

Proceedings of the Reserve Bank's Standing Advisory Committee on Agricultural Credit,

1956.
Report of the Agricultural Credit Organisation Committee (Nanavati Committee), February, 1947.
Report of the Agricultural Finance Sub-Committee (Gadgil Committee), 1945.
Report of the Cooperative Planning Committee (Saraiya Committee), 1946.
Report of the Rural Banking Enquiry Committee, 1950.
Report of the Technical Meeting on Cooperatives in Asia and the Far East, 1949.
Report of the Third Indian Cooperative Congress, 1958
Reserve Bank of India Bulletin, June, 1965.
Review of the Cooperative Movement in India 1946-48, Reserve Bank of India.
Shyamanandan Sahaya, quoted in *All India Cooperative Review,* August, 1955.
Sixth Evaluation Report, Planning Commission, June 1959.
Venkatappiah, B., All India Rural Credit Survey, Reserve Bank of India.

8

COOPERATIVE ADMINISTRATION

This chapter contains two short essays that appeared in journals and newspapers at various points in the year 1967. Written several years after the era of the ICU's intense struggle and confrontation, out of which most of the earlier chapters of his book arose, these essays show that little had changed in the cooperative scene since the 1950's. The crux of the problem, manifested as a general debility and dependence of cooperatives on outside pillars of support, remains that of bureaucratic suffocation. Ostensibly intended to protect and promote cooperative institutions as instruments of development, this bureaucratic presence in reality arises from, and contributes to, a specific political shape of statism that alienates agents of civil society, whether commercial or social, from identifying with the institution.

I. DISSOLUTION OF THE COOPERATIVE DEPARTMENT – AN IMPERATIVE

IS the Cooperative Department inevitable? Before an answer is attempted to this question it is pertinent to examine the circumstances in which the Cooperative Department initially came to be established in India, the results expected of it, and its actual performance.

It is necessary to recall that cooperation as an idea and cooperatives as an institution were first introduced in India by the British rulers in 1904 on the recommendation of the Maclagan Committee. Distressed by the chronic poverty of the mass of small cultivators accentuated by occasional famines, the Committee suggested that the Government should introduce cooperatives in India particularly for providing credit and relief to the poor cultivators. The recommendation was accepted by the Government. There were, however, two ways open to authority for implementing this recommendation: one was to propagate the ideals of cooperation among the intelligentsia and leaders of the country who in turn could explain the objectives and advantages to the cultivators and help them organize, run and develop their own cooperatives; the other was to establish an official machinery to perform these tasks. The latter path was chosen and this is how the cooperative department came into existence. Several explanations are possible as to why the British Government preferred this course.

For one, it fitted into the general pattern and style of functioning of the Imperial Government in India – the creation of official departments. For another, it had little choice at that particular period in Indian history. For, just at the time the British decided to introduce Cooperation, the Indian National Congress had adopted "Non-Cooperation" as its basic weapon. Increasingly, the popular leaders stayed away from the administration and evinced little interest, let alone offer help, in supporting even such programmes as cooperation which in principle stood for the good of the people.

It may well be argued that the nationalist movement (which included the articulate sections of the intelligentsia) was really too preoccupied with political action to have concerned itself with ventures of this kind. But it is important to note that even when, under Gandhiji's leadership, the core of the nationalist workers was actively engaged in a variety of constructive programmes intended to protect and promote the economic interests of the weaker sections, the cooperatives figured nowhere in the programme. To make matters worse, cooperatives were further alienated from the national movement when the official machinery started providing them with aid. As was to be expected, pressures grew on the Cooperative Department to confer patronage only on those cooperatives that were supporting the British Raj or were at least not openly hostile to it. In the given set-up it was not possible even for the most enlightened Registrar of Cooperatives to toe a line radically different from the one followed in general by administration of the day.

Thus, in the eyes of the nationalist movement, cooperatives came to be identified mainly as a channel for distribution of official patronage. Commenting on the cooperative movement in the pre-independence days, one of the prominent nationalist leaders, Kamaladevi Chattopadhyaya, said :

> "Cooperation was then the hallmark of service to the British regime. For, in all the British colonies, cooperation was part of the Government and cooperatives were sponsored, administered and run by the Government as one of its departments. Cooperation was doled out to the people as one of the many 'benefits of British rule', and those non-officials who helped in this task were duly rewarded with titles by the British Raj.... For most of us who grew up in opposition to the British regime in India, cooperation had no special significance except as a means of winning of favour of the rulers".

There were of course exceptions and some patriotic leaders did take interest in cooperatives in their respective areas. But such cases were too few to make any noticeable difference to the character acquired by the cooperative movement under official sponsorship.

The net effect was that the cooperative department had the field all to itself without the pressures of public opinion. The power inherent in the distribution of patronage completely distorted its outlook, actions and integrity. The very purpose for which it was set up was debased, during the 40 years of cooperative development at the hands of this department under the British rule. It found that cooperatives were by and large dominated by well-to-do and influential persons who were using cheap cooperative credit to expand their private money-lending operations among the poor cultivators at exorbitant rates of interest. The advantageous position gained by these elements in village cooperatives was attributed in no small measure to the social affinity and collusion between them and the officials.

Surely, the Maclagan Committee could have expected events to take this turn and it would be fair to say that the Committee had all along in view the need for fostering a genuine popular cooperative movement. In fact this was the attitude and outlook of all the Committees and Commissions which subsequently examined the working of cooperatives during the British Raj. But they pinned their faith entirely on the proper selection of the Registrar who, according to them, had to be different in mould and mind from the general run of administrators. It was repeatedly stressed by these committees that the Registrar should be a friend, philosopher and guide, and they continued to lament the fact that this recommendation was not being heeded sufficiently. Naturally, the British rulers could ill-afford to let one of their limbs fraternize with the poorer sections of the society to the degree required for fostering popular cooperatives.

The crux of the matter is that cooperatives being fundamentally democratic in character could not grow in their fullness in a regime which was not only non-democratic but had to spend all its energies and administrative brilliance in thwarting the national struggle aimed at establishing a sovereign democratic republic. Besides being a people's movement, it was too much to expect an official department, notwithstanding the qualities of the Registrar, to bring it to life and infuse it with social purpose and vigour.

With the advent of freedom the fortunes of the cooperative movement were totally transformed. To quote Kamaladevi Chattopadhyay: "In no time in the history of this country was cooperation highlighted as it is today, pressed with a kind of feverish urgency, like a house-building programme."

Though the climate for the growth of the cooperative movement in India changed completely, it was accompanied by a total neglect of the means necessary for putting the opportunity to good use. The ruling party under Mr. Nehru's leadership paid no attention whatsoever to the machinery necessary for developing cooperatives. The cooperative department – the legacy of the British – was blindly adopted as the sole instrument of development. This was typical of the general attitude of the ruling party towards administration. It assumed that after Independence this and other departments would automatically shed their outlook, attitude and the manner of working acquired in the course of decades of foreign rule and adjust themselves to the new situation. Though on several occasions Mr. Nehru himself got a bitter taste when he came in direct contact with the cooperative departments, he did no more than fly into a rage at their bureaucratic and stifling character. Occasionally while addressing cooperative conferences he would narrate his personal experience and then express his conviction that the cooperative department was the most unsuitable agency to develop cooperatives. But nothing was done to remedy the situation and to create, support and encourage any other institutional agency to replace the cooperative department. On the contrary, cooperative law was so revised as to bestow more autocratic powers on the department. Its numbers increased a hundred-fold and vast sums were placed at its disposal. While thousands of advisory boards and committees have been set up by the Government in various fields, in the case of the Cooperative Department not even an advisory committee has been set up to keep a check on its working.

One can forgive the British rulers for relying entirely on their departmental machinery for developing cooperatives but one is at a loss to find a single satisfactory reason why this reliance has been continued and compounded by the democratic government during the last two decades – in fact of the evidence of almost total failure of the movement in the pre-Independence days and its continued failure in the 20 years following freedom to remedy the many weaknesses exposed by the Rural Credit Survey, particularly need to serve the most needy and deserving sections of the society. The late Mr. V.T. Krishnamachari who presided over the Planning Commission for over a decade remarked sorrowfully: "The more and more we have expanded the cooperative movement since independence, the less and less confidence it commands in the community."

This is the background in which we should consider the question posed: Is the Cooperative Department inevitable? According to the Chamber's dictionary "inevitable" means "certain to happen". In this sense one can easily say that given the inertia and unimaginativeness of our political leadership, there is no prospect of any significant or radical change in the conceivable future, and it is, therefore, certain that the cooperative department will continue to wield the powers that it has and, if anything, add to them.

If the word "inevitable" is used to mean necessary or essential, the answer is obviously no movement can be generated by a department howsoever worthy its officials might be and howsoever lovable the Minister presiding over it. Cooperation envisages the furtherance of initiative, autonomy and self-reliance on the part of the members themselves. As long as cooperatives continue to be manufactured, controlled and directed departmentally there can be no genuine cooperation.

Another dictionary meaning of the word "inevitable" is "unavoidable". It is impossible to grant that the department is an unavoidable evil or a necessity without which we can make no progress. In fact, its record clearly shows that it is the main obstacle in the way of solid and vigorous development of the movement. We cannot, however, wish it away. Cooperative leadership would have to work very hard at the political level to secure the support of various political parties to curtail the legal, administrative and financial overlordship of the department. And this by itself cannot, and will not, be enough. Simultaneously, an alternative institutional framework would have to be developed and supported to undertake the task of cooperative development. Here, one does not have to go far for an answer. The proper agency for development should be the cooperative unions and federations which by and large are in a moribund state today because all attention and resources have been concentrated by authority on the expansion of cooperative departments.

As a first step, a National Commission should be set up to lay down the broad lines for transfer of powers and functions from the departments to the apex cooperative institutions. The aid and assistance to be provided to such bodies may not amount to more than a quarter of what is now being spent on the maintenance of the departments. The Commission should watch the progress and report annually to the nation, indicating the improvements brought about through these measures in the substance of cooperative institutions at large.

One is not certain, however, that the cooperative leadership in the country is fully cognizant of the present state of affairs and is ready to work for such radical reforms. Some of the so-called leadership is in fact a creation of the departments and sustained by them and is naturally not interested in any such reform. The rest is easily pacified by such doles as "de-officialization" – a word which has been in fashion since Mr. Nehru lashed out against bureaucratic interference by departments. It is totally mistaken and misleading exercise to take out one or more official from the membership of the managing committee of a cooperative society so long as the department retains any power to interfere. In fact, nothing suits the bureaucracy better than to have power without any burden of responsibility. The movement has, therefore, to strike at the root of the problem if it wants a real change; and this implies actual transfer of powers and functions from the departments to the apex bodies so that initiative rests with the movement and its autonomy is preserved not only in form but also in substance.

It is necessary, for instance, that the movement must relieve the cooperative departments of the function of examining the economic and technical prospects of new cooperative ventures and the work connected with initial education of promoters. Both these tasks are now being performed by the department in an entirely artificial and amateurish way. Cooperatives are being organized today in diverse fields – agriculture, industry, transport, housing, distributive trades, etc. The type and quality of skill required to examine the economic and technical feasibility of a cooperative venture in any of these fields simply does not exist in the departments. The subsequent collapse of many cooperatives or their failure to meet the expectations of members is directly traceable to poor prospecting and promotional work.

Another important aspect of the work of these departments that must be taken over by the cooperative unions relates to supervision and inspection. Neither at the time of promotion nor subsequently, while providing aid, have the departments cared to exercise any vigilance to ensure the flow of benefits to those sections of society which are expected to be the main beneficiaries. This failure is primarily responsible for distorting the image of the cooperative movement and discrediting it in the public eye. The power of audit, however, should vest neither in the department nor in the unions. Audit should be independent and left primarily to the chartered accountants.

It is often argued that cooperatives will fail if the department were to shed its functions of inspection, supervision, audit, etc., and that in such a situation it cannot be "held responsible" for any failure. Well, there has been so much failure, on official admission alone, during the last 60 years that one can surely ask "in what way has the department been held responsible?" Has any of its officials been punished or penalized? This bogey of accountability of the department has been advanced for so long that it has ceased to deceive anyone any longer. It is in any case odd that the department is expected to assume greater accountability than the concerned institution itself. In these circumstances, can one ever expect the cooperatives to develop or assume responsibility for their shortcomings or failure or have an incentive to strive for success?

Another argument advanced is that the department is trying sincerely to promote strong, autonomous and successful cooperatives but is handicapped in this task by the lack of proper and strong cooperative unions at the State, district and block levels. Unions are nothing but federations of primary ineffective and unsound primary cooperatives and then expect them to produce some miracle at the apex or federal level.

Putting all these facts together, one is forced to conclude that in the interests of the cooperative movement, the department is not only not inevitable but must be cut drastically to size at the earliest, and a time limit fixed for its ultimate dissolution. Correspondingly, its functions must be entrusted to and taken over by the State unions and other apex bodies at the appropriate level. Today, however, the department is so well entrenched that it will take all the energy the movement can muster to dislodge it.

There is not much time at the disposal of the movement to secure these changes. In the changing political complexion, cooperatives cannot take political support for granted. For instance, the Chief Minister of Haryana is reported to have said recently that his Government would abolish cooperatives (and Panchayats). He is by no means alone in questioning the support hitherto extended to cooperatives by the Government. Before we realize it, in some State the political adversaries of this movement and the departmental machinery may join hands in a destructive partnership. Clearly, the immediate task before the cooperative leadership is to consolidate political support and make the dissolution of the department inevitable.

II. TWO WEAKNESSES OF THE COOPERATIVE MOVEMENT

Two weaknesses of the Indian cooperative movement are a matter of deep concern. These are lack of economic viability and absence of inner dynamism. While the weaknesses are commonly acknowledged, the underlying causes and possible remedies have received insufficient attention.

As for economic viability, the trouble starts at the very beginning. Apart from rare exceptions such as the excellent work done by the National Cooperative Development Corporation, generally no detailed feasibility study worth the name is conducted prior to the registration of a cooperative. Its economic aims and the precise expectation of its members are also not clearly formulated and related to available and potential resources.

Inspectors of State cooperative departments are expected to hold meetings of the promoter members to ascertain and assess facts. But the department officials are too busy to perform this and other functions assigned to them properly and efficiently. For one thing, each five-year plan has raised the target for new cooperatives. For another, the scope of cooperation has been extended to cover, besides agricultural credit and urban savings, marketing and processing, joint farming, small-scale village and cottage industries, consumer cooperative stores, housing, transport and construction. Of course, the departmental staff has been increased manifold in all States. But the quality of the staff remains a problem. In any case, salaries offered are too poor to attract suitable and experienced men.

Ordinarily, an economic venture involves the pooling of capital, management and labour. Since cooperatives are generally promoted to protect labour from exploitation, the first step usually is to isolate and eliminate the middlemen. In practice, this means the elimination of the principal source of capital and management. Labour is thus left to its own resources. It can raise only a small amount of capital and must depend on governmental agencies.

The Government is surprised when demands are made on it for capital, and advises cooperatives to be self-reliant. But it would be better if it assesses in advance what it would take by way of resources to replace the middleman, what are the chances of raising the required resources, at what cost and under what conditions, before new societies are registered.

Similarly, members who may be good at skilled work are unable to perform management functions such as the planning and supervision of production, supply and sales, raising of capital, maintenance of accounts, allotment of work and fixing of wage norms. They cannot afford to buy management skills in the open market and, therefore, run to the Government for "managerial subsidy" which finally doles out small and arbitrary amounts which can do anything except secure good management.

In the resulting situation several unfortunate things happen. Either a cooperative dies prematurely or it struggles with inadequate resources and further impoverishes its members or the middleman re-enters the scene under one garb or another and assumes control providing fuel for the charge that there are a number of "bogus" cooperatives.

Instead of rectifying the fundamental error and concentrating on a detailed and thorough initial prospecting and promotional work, the Government appears to think that the remedy lies in tightening "supervision" and "inspection". An army of inspectors is, therefore, employed at tremendous cost.

The lack of financial resources cannot be advanced as an excuse for the deficiencies in question. Apart from the heavy expenditure on cooperative departments, the Government is investing substantial funds each year by way of loans or grants to cooperatives. But not even a fraction of this sum is set aside for assessing the soundness of the ventures. What would it matter if, say, five per cent of the available amount is spent on laying a sound foundation?

The truth is that prospecting and promotional work is not regarded necessary by the authorities. They assume that since the official policy provides for promotion of cooperatives and funds are earmarked in the annual budgets, all that is needed by way of a passport to success is a certificate of registration.

The reasons for the absence of inner dynamism in cooperatives are also not far to seek. Mr. Gomulka made the classic statement that "human consciousness cannot be planned". Here in India, we are attempting to do so. Else the Government would not be setting targets for cooperative development. No wonder that towards the end of each year there is a great rush to find people to put their thumb impressions on the forms for enrolment with cooperatives.

The root cause of the trouble is the total dependence of the Government on the official machinery to promote cooperatives. This dates back to 1904 when cooperation was first introduced by the British rulers on the recommendation of the Maclagan Committee. During the years the British were spreading their cooperative idea in India, the nationalist forces were rising and preaching non-cooperation. There was no place for cooperatives in Gandhiji's constructive programme. There was thus hardly any link between the popular movement and the cooperative until the end of the thirties when popular ministries took over in the provinces.

It was only after independence that the cooperative movement received full popular support from Mr. Nehru, the Congress and the Planning Commission. But they never gave serious thought to the instruments which are required to foster and nurse a popular and socially significant movement. The cooperative department set up by the British out of the historic necessity was blindly adopted as the spearhead of the cooperative movement. It was expanded in numbers and armed with autocratic powers. But even an advisory committee was not set up to review its programmes, problems and progress.

This indifference has been carried to such an extreme that even the highest organization in the cooperative movement, the National Cooperative Union of India, is treated with scant respect and seldom associated with any important decisions. The position of the State cooperative unions, except perhaps for Maharashtra, with the respective State governments is even worse. Thus organizations which should have been supported and strengthened to shoulder responsibility for the promotion of cooperatives were pushed into the background.

The first drastic step required to remedy the situation is to build up and strengthen the National, State and District cooperative unions and to equip them to take up the entire promotional work from the departments.

The unions should set up qualified units to study and examine economic prospects and technical feasibility, help promoters to define the economic and social aims of proposed cooperatives, impart initial education to prospective members and to train personnel. Besides, they should have facilities to conduct case studies and periodic evaluations to identify reasons for failures and success; and to transmit this knowledge widely, especially to the prospecting units and policy-making organs in the country. They can also maintain a small unit for "social inspection" of cooperatives to ensure that they continue to adhere to the social purpose for which they were set up.

The vast structure for supervision and inspection maintained by the departments can then be dismantled over a period of time. During the transition, the department should be required to have prior consultations with the unions in exercising its powers and functions.

During the first 10 years, the Government should meet the entire cost which the unions incur for providing these services and thereafter scale it down to zero in a phased manner. The unions should by that time raise their own revenue by way of service charges and contributions from their members. Thus, in a 20-year period, at the most, we can create powerful organs within the cooperative movement for its promotion and regulation.

9

PROMOTING A NATIONAL PLATFORM FOR VOLUNTARY ORGANIZATIONS FOR RURAL DEVELOPMENT

BY THE mid-fifties, rural development in India began to be dominated by large government programmes, which, while termed "community development", were bureaucratic in their approach and tended to be somewhat disdainful of, if not actually hostile to, voluntary efforts. The ICU's commitment to enlarging civil and democratic spaces for action in the face of an encroaching development State moved beyond the cooperative domain to forge partnerships with other voluntary organizations working on rural development. In April 1956, it led an initiative to bring together a number of such organizations in a seminar on "The Role of Voluntary Organizations in Rural Development". One of the outcomes of this seminar was the resolution to establish a national platform, the Association of Voluntary Agencies in Rural Development (AVARD), to function as a co-ordinating body providing services such as research and evaluation, training of personnel and exchange of experiences, information-dissemination and advice in fund-raising, seminars, workshops and liaison with Government. AVARD was in place and functioning by the following year, with crucial assistance from the ICU in its formative years. The organization has survived until now. And in the nearly four decades of its existence AVARD's membership has risen to about 500 voluntary organisations engaged in rural development.

AVARD continues to play an active and significant role in influencing policy in support of voluntary action, social justice and decentralization. Since the enactment of the passing of the 73rd Amendment to the Constitution in 1993, AVARD is concentrating on strengthening Panchayats. Besides, it continues to facilitate cooperation among member voluntary organizations for sharing experiences and ideas.

AVARD has been a pioneer in block-level planning for socio-economic development. It has assisted a number of its member organizations as also State Governments in preparing local area development plans for a cluster of villages or blocks. For the implementation of these plans it has assisted member organizations with training, technical staff and in fund raising. AVARD was also the first among voluntary organizations to demonstrate (1) how food-for-work programmes could be used as an effective instrument for generation of rural employment and augmenting agricultural growth, (2) how minor irrigation projects could be planned to ensure that water reached the fields of the marginal and small farmers, (3) that voluntary organizations acted only as a catalyst, mobilize local initiative and build up local leadership and representative institutions and to shoulder continuing responsibility and (4) that development and struggle were not mutually exclusively, as is often believed, but are two sides of the same coin.

The discussions at that seminar, 40 years ago, mirror many of the issues that non-governmental development agencies face even today. Also, there are many parallels between them and the more recent advocacy on decentralization and autonomy related to the Panchayati Raj legislations of the 1990s. Among these is the acknowledgement that devolution of power to people would involve some wastage of funds, some discord, but that these must be seen as part of the praxis. The 1990s discussions have of course come some way in recognizing discord, or more explicitly, local power struggles, as integral to decentralized development, while earlier they were seen as a necessary evil. Voluntary agencies were perceived as crucial, then and now, in enabling the people's representatives to understand and more effectively assume their new powers. Part of the special historical perspective that this book offers, however, lies in the participants' romanticization of rural life and of notions such as "community", and in the paternalism implicit in the role-perception of voluntary organizations in that period.

This chapter presents extracts of the Seminar report reflecting these discussions. A substantial amount of preparatory work preceded the Seminar, among which was a detailed "Statement of Questions" covering the range of topics to be addressed by the Seminar, and intended to guide small-group discussions. The extracts presented here include the introductory and keynote addresses and the consolidated report of the four group discussions, all abridged and with minor alterations in language and format. Alist of the participating organizations is appended at the end of this chapter.

REPORT OF THE SEMINAR ON THE ROLE OF VOLUNTARY AGENCIES IN RURAL DEVELOPMENT

The Seminar was sponsored by the Delhi School of Social Work, Indian Cooperative Union, Indian Adult Education Association, Jamia Millia, American International Association, Cooperative League of USA, American Friends Service Committee and CARE.

Fifty-eight delegates representing twenty-eight organizations attended the seminar. (The participating organizations readily agreed to meet the travelling, board and lodging expenses of their delegates.)

Welcome Address By L.C. Jain, General Secretary, ICU

In welcoming the participants to the Seminar, he outlined some of the important issues before them. Last year, he had the opportunity of travelling round the country and meeting representatives of different organizations. Many of them seemed uncertain of their future role and were feeling somewhat lost. The reason for this was that during the First Five Year Plan, the Government had entered the field of rural development extensively. The impact of the expansion of Government programmes had told upon the work of these voluntary organizations and they did not know where they stood. Their sense of being lost was further accentuated by the fact that they were scattered and, in some cases, functioned in isolated areas, with no proper communication and cooperation with each other.

This experience was shared early this year with the representatives of a small voluntary group of agencies. There was a spontaneous response to the idea of bringing together voluntary agencies from different parts of the country to consider their future role. This Seminar was the outcome of that effort.

There were several important issues facing the country which were of vital importance to voluntary agencies. He referred to the great debate which was going on in India on the subject of centralization and decentralization and on the value of the rural community. The present structure was one where the majority of the people lived in small communities spread all over the country. If, in the process of bringing better amenities and economic opportunities to these people, we were going to destroy this present structure, we must very carefully examine whether there was anything of value in it that might be destroyed. Industrialization as it was understood brought people together in concentrated areas, provided them with factory employment and built up urban areas and slums where workers lived and toiled. If we followed this pattern in India, it would result in the displacement of millions of people and create serious social problems.

A suggested alternative to uprooting communities was to extend amenities and employment opportunities close to their present abodes. This required a new technology which could operate on a small scale and increase productivity. The West had produced appliances to suit their own needs, and if in India we were simply going to import these unthinkingly, we would bring into this country problems which might have serious social consequences. Technology, Shri Jain declared, did not preclude small-scale operations. But it had to be developed in favour of small-scale industries, since the major developments in this area had so far been in the interests of large-scale industry.

It was essential to evolve a system which would deal with our problems in the general context of our social, religious and economic background, and thereby preserve certain valuable features of our rural life. We should do everything within our power to preserve these small communities.

The Government through the Community Projects Administration and National Extension Service was playing the leading role in rural development work. Looking at the projects and activities run by private and voluntary agencies, it was evident that in purely quantitative terms the work of these agencies was very small, almost insignificant, considering the total needs of the country. On the other hand, we had also to realize that this problem of development was not merely an administrative and governmental one. It was a national problem which required total national effort. Since national resources were limited, we should try to pool them towards the common goal of raising the standard of living of the people. The situation demanded the maximum use of resources in the interests of the people.

Another problem was the coordination between the Government and voluntary agencies that would have to take place in order to solve the rural problem in an integrated way. Before independence we had a government that we could not turn to. People had to fall back on their own resources and during that period several private and voluntary agencies engaged in various forms of social work were established. After independence, the Government entered the fields of reconstruction and development. There was a popular expectation that the national government would solve all the problems. Many people did not believe that there was an alternative to governmental action in this matter. The new responsibilities assumed by the Government in this field were correspondingly leading to the extension of governmental machinery and power, and to the concentration of financial resources in the hands of the State. This, Shri Jain said, would lead to an extensive governmental control over various aspects of national life and might impair democracy in the long run. It was thus the responsibility of voluntary agencies to educate public opinion on this issue.

At this Seminar it might be useful for the voluntary agencies to look into their own weaknesses and shortcomings. In experience and in resources, voluntary agencies were limited. In such a situation the best service they could do themselves was to stand as close as possible and to share the resources and experiences to the maximum extent possible. It was hoped that the deliberations of the Seminar would enable the participants to discover a clear direction for future efforts.

Keynote Address by S.K. Dey, Administrator Community Projects, Government of India

Shri S.K. Dey began by describing the economic and social conditions that existed in India on the eve of Independence. It had been the British policy to systematically destroy village industries and to make people dependent on imported goods from England. The result was a one-way flow of men and materials from the villages to the towns, whereby the cities became increasingly more powerful as commercial and administrative centres and the villager and his problems became of secondary importance.

After independence, there followed a transitional period when British officers were replaced by their close counterparts and efforts were made to bring about an Indian orientation. But the *status quo* was maintained. Soon the Government realized that the root cause of India's problem lay in the villages. But a great deal of misunderstanding existed. Officials and political representatives saw villagers as incapable of organizing themselves for constructive work; the villagers did not trust the development officers or the political representatives.

The country had inherited a powerful machinery of government which had to coordinate with different agencies and formulate an integrated pattern of administration. Since the village formed the focal point, government programmes had to be well planned so as to extend services in a coordinated way in the fields of irrigation, cooperation, communication, health, marketing, etc. In order to fulfil this objective, it was felt that a few pilot areas would have to be established.

Numerous problems faced the government. First, the people had lost the capacity of getting together for a common purpose. Second, they had lost faith in themselves. And third, in general the political representatives had lost contact with the people. It was necessary to bring political representatives nearer to the people and also create an opportunity whereby they would be eager to produce and train leaders from the ranks. Effective leadership and participation, Shri Dey said, were the outcome of social, economic and political consciousness among the people and, therefore, it was most important that the government make it possible for this to grow. Under the previous regime district courts, hospitals, veterinary hospitals, cooperative offices, panchayats, agricultural research stations existed at the district level. However, their energies were used in entertaining visiting officers rather than building up firm contacts and confidence between the villagers and the government. Consequently, villagers were afraid and suspicious of these government institutions and did not avail of their benefits. In view of this situation, the government decided to bring its apparatus closer to the people by establishing a system of blocks each consisting of 100 villages with a population of 60,000 to 70,000. At each block headquarters, there would be a specialist in the following fields : agriculture, animal husbandry, cooperatives, panchayat, social education, rural engineering and public health. In order to coordinate the work of these specialists, a development officer was appointed. However, it became evident that this plan was not adequate as it was impossible for one man, however capable, to coordinate the needs of 60,000 to 70,000 people at the village level. It became necessary to place multi-purpose workers at the village level. This worker was called the village-level worker, and it was hoped that the name would be replaced by the expression "Gram Sevak". A Gram Sevak was usually a matriculate who had received a year's training in several fields. In addition to the Gram Sevak, a specialist for consultation was stationed at the block level.

With this extent of government participation at the village level, there was some fear about India going communist. In Shri Dey's opinion, if India went anywhere there was a danger she might go fascist. However, in view of the fact that there was increased government participation, it was important to establish and strengthen institutions through which villagers might participate. For civic affairs it was important to build panchayats and, for economic affairs, cooperative institutions grow in strength. Government agencies would function only as a channel through which technical and financial assistance would flow. In order to ensure growth of internal strength from within the panchayat, a block advisory committee had been established. This committee consisted of the block development officer other than the members of the staff on the government side, representatives of panchayats and cooperatives, representatives of the State legislatures and parliament and representatives of the district board from the area. They would constitute the non-official members of the committee. Their function would be to chalk out programmes of village improvement. These programmes would be analysed at the block headquarters and examined by the block advisory committee ; they would then be forwarded to the Development Commissioner at the State headquarters or the Chief Secretary of Government who was the head of departments at the State level. Coordination would be attained at the ministerial level through the cooperation of the State Development Committee with the Chief Minister of the State as the chairman, the Development Commissioner as the secretary and Ministers of the various development departments as members.

Clearly this programme and its accompanying pattern of administration visualized joint consultation and joint responsibilities between organizations of the people's representation and the government, from the village up to the State headquarters.

The Central Government had no jurisdiction over the States with regard to agricultural development, public health, education, village industries, cooperatives, etc. It could only give advice, guidance and finances. Central ministries could not administer State ministries directly. Following the pattern in the State headquarters, at the Central level, a Central Development Committee was established, which consisted of the members of the Planning Commission, the Agriculture Minister and also, by option, the Minister of Health and other ministers with the Prime Minister as the Chairman of the Committee. Under the Committee an organization called the Community Projects Administration functioned in close collaboration with the various ministries of the Centre. Advisers from every Ministry were nominated, and there were currently 15 to 20 advisers for every Ministry. Thus the entire Central Government was involved in the work. In addition, clear targets and procedures were laid down and responsibility was assigned to various agencies.

CPA was a messenger-boy organization for carrying the messages of the established Ministries of Government to the doors of the villagers

On October 2, 1952, the project was launched as a pilot project in 165 blocks in different parts of the country. At first, Shri Dey said, there was a feeling of pessimism. However, the government machinery went into action and the people cooperated by building thousands of miles of roads, sinking wells, etc. They began to use improved seed. After three years all the activities were reviewed and the outcome was that it was felt that a larger part of the country would have to be covered during the First Five Year Plan. The National Extension Service was introduced as younger brother of the CPA. There was no change in the technique of administration. The only changes were in the amount of finances and the nature of the staff. In the NES there were between Rs. 400,000 and Rs. 500,000 to be spent over a period of three years. In addition, in order to cooperate with the people's organizations in the work of national reconstruction the Government of India would give funds through the State Governments. Government contributions would, however, have to be equally matched by funds from the people's organizations.

The success of the CPA thus far was most encouraging. A large number of schools had been built. Cooperative societies and panchayats had been established, sizable quantities of fertilizers and good seeds had been distributed, and more than a million acres of land reclaimed and irrigated. The most encouraging fact about this development had been that the villagers had gradually increased their participation and shown their curiosity and interest for self-help. It would be a national defeat if the CPA was not able to bring the people's representatives nearer to the people and aid them to develop leadership in the work of reconstruction, especially at a time when there was an overwhelming sense of enthusiasm amongst the villagers. It was essential for the CPA to build up the people's institutions through which the people would control their economic and political activities.

(After Shri Dey had concluded his address, he invited questions. During this discussion, Shri Dey expressed his disappointment about the voluntary agencies which, he said, were city-based and did no work in the rural areas. Most of the workers in these organizations, he alleged, were not willing to get down to the jobs in the villages. Shri Dey was challenged on this point. In reply he made this offer : If there were any voluntary agency carrying out a rural development project, the CPA would give it the utmost assistance. It would not stand in the way or interfere but would help the agency in every manner.)

A Consolidated Report of the Four Group Discussions

Objectives

The concept of a Democratic Welfare State presumes not only the provision of the necessities of life and welfare services to all its citizens by the civil apparatus of government, but equally the participation of democratic bodies of the people themselves in securing these.

In India today, two conflicting trends are in interact. The Government is fast expanding its areas of direct operation not only into a wider field, but deep down into the lives of the people, touching almost all aspects of life. The government is also anxious to extend democratic participation through popular effort. But in fact, the activities of the Government are leading to the definite ascendency of governmental control over popular effort.

It is within this context that the physical and moral justification of voluntary agencies is sustained and it becomes important to strengthen them. Voluntary agencies can act as an effective brake on the concentration of power in the hands of the Government and can help distribute the focus of power more. At the same time, voluntary agencies can stimulate popular initiative and interest in self-reliance among the people. Thus, voluntary agencies are essential to preserve and promote freedom and develop democracy in the country. They are the surest guarantee against the danger which democracy may face if the State continues to extend its machinery and control in different aspects of national life.

The voluntary agencies gathered at the seminar are mainly those engaged in rural development. Rural society today is afflicted with serious problems of unemployment, underemployment, lack of education, social services and medical aid. The task of bringing employment opportunities and creating social services for the millions of inhabitants of rural India is tremendous and requires great effort and dedication. Voluntary agencies should devote themselves to this task with a sense of mission and urgency. In addition, voluntary agencies must concern themselves with the preservation of certain basic social values which obtain in the rural society today. These values may be defined as man's closeness to nature and to his neighbour, which permits more intimate personal relations with fellow human beings, man's unique relationship with his work which allows for greater self-expression, and man's relationship with himself where he is devoted to his religion and has more time and opportunity for reflection. It is very likely that if due care is not taken we may destroy these precious values in the process of enriching the rural society with greater economic opportunities.

The heavy industrialization envisaged in the coming years is bound to have a profound influence on the present structure of the rural society. It is a matter of vital importance that the programme of industrialization must avoid leaving in its wake social and psychological problems which, for example, the West has come up against. India today is in a privileged position to learn from the Western experience. We can avoid the mistakes made there. We can adopt and apply to our situation the highest accomplishments of the West such as atomic energy and technological ability. It is, however, essential for the fulfilment of India's national needs and aspirations that the technological ability of the West is employed to innovate and produce plants and tools which do not require immense capital resources that India does not possess, and which may not lead to concentration of wealth and power either in the hands of a few individuals or the State. In short, technology should be made to serve our needs by producing efficient and economic plants which can operate on a small scale and which will enable India to maintain a decentralized structure of society.

Normally, the growth of welfare services depends on the economic capacity of a community to pay for such services. The rate at which its economic capacity increases depends on what resources it can channel for economic development. The experience of the West has, however, shown that all these factors are interdependent. Further, the changed circumstances of the world demand that welfare programmes cannot be postponed until surplus economic capacity has been developed by a nation to meet the cost of welfare activities. The two must be undertaken simultaneously. In the present era of planning it should not be difficult to strike a balance between the two in assigning resources. In this context, the idea that every village community must function within the limitations of self-sufficiency needs to be reconsidered and redefined. For, if the concept is carried to its conclusion it would mean keeping down the level of development and ignoring the pressures of the present world. But inasmuch as the concept of self-sufficiency represents an effort on the part of each community to produce and provide itself the maximum out of its own labour and resources, it is highly commendable. Such a concept necessitates that each community harness its resources and partake of the fruits with due regard to the needs and resources of its immediate neighbouring communities as well as the country at large.

This will prevent the isolation of each community and also ensure the maximum and fairest use of local and national resources for the benefit of the people as a whole.

Thus the basic general objective of rural development emerges as an effort to promote a democratic society, to provide greater economic and social benefits, and to promote happier human relations. This is a dynamic approach which aims at elimination of want and hunger but does not fail to see the treasures hidden under dirt and poverty and to seek to preserve them. Further, it aims to restrict the administrative preponderance of the State and to build up the authority of the people and their local self-governing institutions so that in the process of securing more bread their lives are not darkened by the loss of democracy.

Voluntary Agencies vis-a-vis Government

The task before us in sheer physical terms is overwhelming. The available resources are too little. There is also the recognition that if the pressing problems of rural India are not effectively tackled within a short time, there is, potential danger that democracy itself may not survive. We, therefore, cannot afford any duplication of effort or waste of the limited resources at our command. We cannot function at cross-purposes. The overall objective of both the government and the voluntary agencies is to serve the people. It should then be no problem to bring about the coordination and cooperation between governmental and voluntary agencies as well as among the voluntary agencies themselves.

In the rural areas there are three types of agencies engaged in development: government, voluntary and private profit-making. The private profit-making agencies perform specialized services like tractor and tubewell engineering and may be eliminated from our present consideration. It is the government and voluntary agencies which conduct allied multipurpose activities.

A voluntary agency may be defined as a democratic body of the people, like the panchayat or a cooperative, or a non-governmental agency trying to help such democratic bodies of the people, but free from government control, free to determine its policy and not dependent on governmental assistance alone. It should be a non-profit and preferably non-political organization. Trusts should also be included as voluntary agencies.

In terms of size, the activities of the Government and the voluntary agencies bear no comparison. During the Second Five Year Plan there will be an even more extensive growth of governmental activities. But, nonetheless, there is a scope for voluntary agencies to play a role distinct from and yet complementary to that of the Government. For, despite its ambitious target of covering every single village in India through CPA and NES during the Second Plan period, government effort cannot make more than a dent on the total problem. So while we must be gratified with what we plan to do with our limited resources, we must not raise hopes too high. Extensive coverage is a significant step but the crux of the problem is the depth and content of this coverage, and the quality of performance.

Again, this type of development work essentially means working with people for whose benefit the development is planned. Developmental agencies have, therefore, to be very human, to have respect and consideration for human beings served by them. It is here that the voluntary agencies can find an appropriate and important role for themselves. They can meet a real need and the efforts and the Government can easily complement each other. In fields where human relations are important in determining success, voluntary agencies can make the most effective contribution.

Panchayats and cooperatives are the people's bodies. From the point of view of our objectives of strengthening democracy at the base, and for practical reasons of speedy and substantial development, it is essential to make these bodies living and effective institutions. The work involved is mostly with human material. In the context of the social and economic control exercised by a few individuals in most villages, it is extremely important that leadership capable of acting with impartiality and integrity is helped to emerge. Caste and other divisions in the village community make the task more difficult. Considerable patience, insight into human nature and perseverance is, therefore, required for this work. The Government's own experience has shown that despite their resources, panchayats and cooperatives have not made much progress. The Government should, therefore, recognize the urgent need for help in this field and welcome the assistance of voluntary agencies. Panchayats and cooperatives should be enabled to manage their own affairs without interference from outside and disruption from within. In selecting the areas for such intervention, voluntary agencies can act in consultation with the Government.

While voluntary agencies might concentrate on the human aspects of the problem in the coming years, the Government should entrust developmental activities to these local self-governing institutions and provide them with adequate resources. As an experimental measure, a few blocks should be selected for such a devolution of powers and resources. The services of technical and administrative staff should also be placed at their disposal to help them in planning and execution.

Such an experiment where a programme is planned and executed by a community with the Government's participation, rather than the converse as in the present case, would be a genuine community development programme. Admittedly, in the present state such an experiment might lead to some waste of funds and resources, more perhaps than occurs through centralized efforts. This, however, is a condition which will not last beyond the initial stages. Further, this is the only way to help democratic bodies gain experience and to enable them to function properly. The experience of the general elections and the few years of working of the Community Projects Administration has shown that the masses of our people, despite their illiteracy, ignorance and backwardness, possess a great sense of responsibility and good judgment. As for discord among members of such bodies, we must remember the fact that no city corporation, State Cabinet or even Central Cabinet is free from problems of this nature. Denying responsibility or powers to local bodies or being overcautious in trusting them with development work on this account will be injurious to national interests. On the other hand, the pressure of responsibility is bound to act as unifying influence and the constructive nature of developmental effort will at once lend direction and purpose to local bodies and minimize the chances of quarrels and conflicts.

In addition to this programme of strengthening local bodies there are many other fields of service for voluntary agencies. Historically, their role has been one of pioneers in rural development. The results of their efforts have been adopted and are being applied on a large scale by the Government today. Nevertheless, the need remains in practically all aspects of development work in rural areas for voluntary agencies to continue to act as pioneers. They should be one step ahead of the Government, constantly breaking new ground and seeking to raise the quality of performance in each field.

The number and resources of voluntary agencies are very small. They can, therefore, ill-afford to expand quantitatively or to perform repetitive services. Thus, their object should be to establish differences in quality where they are engaged in similar fields with the Government. Or they should boldly plunge into new experiments which have a greater likelihood of success under voluntary agencies by virtue of their flexibility and freedom of operation. In essence, voluntary agencies should act vertically whereas government is stretched horizontally.

Voluntary organizations can cooperate with the CPA and NES at the State and local levels, mainly at the stage of experimentation in methods and programmes, and in areas where the Government has not taken responsibility for providing welfare services. Voluntary organizations can also carry on work in small areas and implement developmental work with the help of government resources if necessary. The extent of the resources should, however, correspond to similar projects run directly by the Government. In the next Five Year Plan an experiment may be made where a few blocks would be operated by voluntary agencies alone and a few blocks jointly operated by voluntary agencies and the CPA on a mutually agreed basis. Experiences from such experimental efforts, along with experiences in areas where local self -governing institutions are responsible for development blocks, would be extremely useful in shaping future public policy in this field. The Governments can encourage and assist agencies specializing in particular fields. The methods, materials and experience gained by such agencies can be used by governmental and voluntary bodies for national development.

In all projects where voluntary agencies cooperate with the government agencies, it should be ensured that the flexibility and autonomy of the agencies are not compromised. It would, indeed, be useful to devise a more systematic liaison between the Government and voluntary agencies to facilitate adequate consultation, coordination and realistic contact with each other so that there is fuller appreciation of the problems on both sides, and the maximum sharing of experience.

Approach to Community Development

In working in the rural areas, a proper psychological approach is necessary if a project is to succeed. Whom shall a voluntary agency approach? With whom will it work? With what attitude will it enter the rural area? What particular features will it look out for and foster? The basic approach determines the physical targets, but here one has to consider the psychological aspect of the problem.

In the rural areas, life is more integrated and homogeneous and, therefore, the role of the voluntary organization has to be in harmony with the whole life of the community. Even when the agency is specialized in one field of service, it must integrate its activities with other organizations working in the community. A voluntary agency has to share with the community their skills and resources with the full approval of the people and with their active participation. The human and personal approach becomes extremely important in rural development. And this should not be sacrificed in the anxiety to achieve physical targets.

Another distinguishing feature of the voluntary agency should be its ability and willingness to adapt rapidly to changing conditions. It is not suggested that an agency should not follow any principle but only that it should not become self-righteous or too rigid and orthodox.

In order to promote democratic functioning a voluntary agency has to involve people at every stage and help facilitate the emergence of local leadership. In the initial stages voluntary work is likely to be paternalistic, but the ultimate goal should be to help the people develop the ability to meet their own needs, with the goal that the voluntary organization can ultimately withdraw from the scene of influence. They should work with the people rather than work for the people. All democratic action requires preparation for participation in social action. The role of a voluntary organization is thus to help the community to prepare for social action.

The promise of material improvement is the most appealing force which can determine action in rural development. But material improvement is tied up with the development of attitudes and modes of thought within the community. It is, however, impossible to determine which should come first. The two are interrelated. One starting point is to work around felt the needs. But in order to advance further, it is necessary to harmonize the concept of felt needs with a new concept of "induced" needs. Voluntary organizations, by responding to the felt needs of the community, can secure their confidence and obtain their cooperation. Meanwhile new needs should be "induced" and transformed into "felt" needs by the process of education. But on no account should these induced needs reflect the bias of the organization or its workers, or tend to be utopian or emotionally disruptive. The dissemination of new values will not conflict with the democratic functioning if the people are helped to internalize these values through a process of persuasion and education.

Various agencies will necessarily have diverse approaches and different areas of intervention. Nevertheless, it is possible to have a basic agreement on the demarcation of areas and coordination of efforts. In a sense, diversity in itself is a contribution, inasmuch as it avoids uniformity. The basic consideration to be kept in mind is that no two agencies should work for the same purpose in the same area especially where there is no scope for two agencies.

In the course of their work, voluntary agencies are likely to come into contact with other organizations aligned with political parties. Voluntary organizations have to work with the whole community and in view of the fact that the community has various political interests it is desirable that voluntary agencies should not have any political interests. It is desirable that voluntary agencies should not have any political bias or identify themselves with any political party. However, they may cooperate with other democratic organizations having a political bias, only at the level of developing welfare programmes in a given area. This policy should also hold true for working with religious organizations. As long as religious organizations are not interested in proselytisation, voluntary agencies may cooperate with them in the development of welfare programmes.

Programme

In terms of the long-term objectives, a voluntary agency should emphasize the educational process in a broad context. Capital and material development should proceed hand in hand with the development of social welfare. As stated earlier, the contribution which a voluntary organization can make is through its emphasis on the quality, rather than on the quantitative aspects of the programme. Some of the major fields in which voluntary agencies can contribute work are in the training personnel, in setting up rural industries, in establishing cooperatives and helping in family planning.

The cumulative experience, zeal and missionary spirit of workers in voluntary organizations qualify them to undertake the training of personnel, and it would be useful to prepare a directory of non-governmental agencies engaged in training. The directory should cover the agencies engaged in giving training in the field of rural services, social education, rural industries, rural health, agricultural extension cooperation and so on. The directory should also include information regarding training facilities provided by the Government.

In organizing cooperatives, agencies can attempt to provide for (1) education of the entire community on the principles of cooperation, (2) education of members and prospective members of cooperative societies. (3) advocacy for modification of laws regarding cooperative societies, (4) evaluation of existing societies , (5) research, and production of materials on cooperatives, (6) technical assistance to cooperative societies in matters of agricultural techniques, record-keeping and accounting. An immediate positive step should be the organization of non-governmental cooperative development associations in districts and States to foster cooperative societies.

With regard to rural industries, voluntary agencies can help in developing new designs, organizing marketing facilities and providing technical assistance and training. However at present voluntary agencies may not be able to do much for rural industries as these need tremendous resources. They could use their resources more effectively in the organization of cooperatives. A separate seminar on small-scale industries might examine this problem more thoroughly.

With regard to family planning, voluntary agencies can mobilize public opinion and provide facilities for the education of the people. They can also organize family planning centres wherever possible.

From time to time, it may be necessary for voluntary organizations to respond to emergency needs. But when relief work is undertaken, it should be as constructive as possible in terms of the broader objectives. The primary objective should be to work for long-term programmes which should obviate the necessity for chronic relief measures and lessen the danger of emergency relief situations.

Finance

The experience of voluntary organizations in most Western countries in fund-raising is not applicable to India. The sources of voluntary contributions are severely limited in this country as the financial resources available for national development are being increasingly concentrated in the hands of the Government. Heavy taxation has further circumscribed the scope of voluntary organizations for raising funds from the public. Nevertheless there have been generous voluntary contribution from individuals as is evidenced by the Bhoodan Movement. This source of funds should be developed to the greatest extent possible. However, since the Government has appropriated large financial resources it would be just to seek its assistance for voluntary effort. The mere acceptance of funds from the Government need not jeopardize the spirit of voluntary service of these agencies. The Government is itself accepting aid from foreign countries without in any way compromising national independence and freedom. It should be possible, similarly, for voluntary organizations in the country to accept the Government's aid without sacrificing their flexibility and autonomy. Government assistance to voluntary effort must become a conscious and deliberate part of public policy, with no suggestion of patronage or charity. Government supervision is permissible to the extent of ensuring that proper accounts are maintained and that funds provided are used for the intended purposes. By and large, a voluntary agency should try to raise its operating expenses from non-governmental sources.

As regards aid from foreign organizations, it must be welcomed provided that the motives of both the donor and the recipient organizations are candidly examined, and no strings are attached. Technical assistance and training of technical personnel are also useful forms of foreign aid.

Where foreign organizations are working in India with foreign funds, it is better for them not to undertake direct operational responsibility for programmes. Rather, their approach should be to select counterpart Indian voluntary agencies and work through them.

Voluntary agencies in India need special advice on fund-raising techniques. An attempt may be made to persuade religious and other trusts to support constructive development activities of voluntary agencies. Voluntary agencies might also try to raise funds through community chests. The capacity of panchayats and local bodies to raise funds should be explored further. The Education Fund and the Common Good Fund accruing from the net profits of the cooperative societies may also be considered as additional sources of income for voluntary agencies.

Coordination, Evaluation and Information

Voluntary agencies are autonomous bodies scattered all over the country. Few have knowledge of the work of other agencies. They lack channels of communication or of exploring areas of cooperation among themselves. There is hardly an agency which possesses surplus resources to share with others, yet all of them are rich with experience which, when shared with others, will add to their strength. Their greatest asset is in their workers. These workers, however, lack facilities for travelling to visit the activities of other agencies. In the present situation where voluntary agencies are at the crossroads, where sources of support are diminishing and governmental support cannot be taken for granted, it is sensible for them to work more closely together and to bring strength to each other.

A council of voluntary organizations will, therefore, be an appropriate and extremely useful body to explore areas of mutual cooperation, strengthen existing agencies, foster development of new agencies where ecessary and act as a spokesman on behalf of its members in placing ıeir programmes and problems before the country and the government.

There are seven fruitful and important areas where such a Council can ender much-needed service:

1. *Research and Evaluation* : Every agency needs evaluation of its efforts and systematic and objective investigation into problems facing its special field of activity. Few agencies have facilities for carrying out such studies. Here the Planning Commission has done well in establishing the Programme Evaluation Organization to evaluate the working of the CPA and NES. Voluntary agencies too should make suitable arrangements for evaluation of their activities.
2. *Training of Personnel and Exchange of Experience* : Very little sharing of facilities and experience among the agencies has taken place so far. The Council will act as a channel for such a flow of experience as well as the facilities for training of agency workers.
3. *Information* : The activities of the agencies are neither known to each other nor to the larger public due to the inability of each agency to publicize its work on a national scale. The people have no means of knowing the size and significance of the efforts of voluntary agencies. The extensive publicity of governmental activities on the other hand leaves the public with an impression that the Government alone is acting in this field. Apart from anything else, this limits public support for voluntary effort. An information service will, therefore, enable the people to know more about the work of voluntary agencies, and the agencies themselves to learn more intimately of each other's activities. Further, the Information Service will help the agencies to keep in close and constant touch with the plans and projects of the Government in different parts of the country.
4. *Advisory Service for Fund Raising* : Difficulties in fund-raising experienced by practically all agencies have been discussed, and it is obvious that all of them need to pool their ideas and influence on this subject, take the advice of experts, if necessary, and strengthen the sources of financial and material support for their activities.
5. *Exchange of Publications and Literature* : The Council will also act as a post office for the exchange of materials among the

agencies and also help to popularize and introduce them for use by governmental and other national and international bodies.

6. *Seminars and Conferences* : The Council can periodically convene seminars and conferences to promote the objectives mentioned above to facilitate the review and examination of the objectives and activities of the voluntary agencies. Such seminars can create enlightened public opinion on matters of policy and the significance of the voluntary efforts.
7. *Liaison between Agencies and Government* : Voluntary agencies need more effective liaison with the Government and Council will help in performing this function.

A Council of Voluntary Agencies would be an appropriate body to undertake these functions. As a start to giving shape to the idea, a small preparatory committee from among the participants of the present seminar should be set up.

The preparatory committee appointed by the Seminar for this purpo met before the Seminar concluded and has decided to set up an organization named Association of Voluntary Agencies for Rural Developme (AVARD). AVARD will perform the following functions for the bene of voluntary agencies :

1. Research and Evaluation.
2. Training of personnel and exchange of experience.
3. Exchange of information.
4. Advisory service for fund-raising.
5. Exchange of publications and literature.
6. Seminars and conferences.
7. Liaison between agencies and government.

LIST OF PARTICIPATING ORGANIZATIONS

The following organizations participated in the seminar :

1. Indian Adult Education Association, Delhi.
2. Indian Village Service, Etah.
3. Indian Cooperative Union, New Delhi.
4. American Friends Service Committee, Delhi.
5. American Friends Service Committee, Madhya Pradesh
6. American Friends Service Committee, Orissa.
7. Ingraham Institute, Ghaziabad.
8. Delhi School of Social Work.
9. Research, Training & Production Centre. Jamia Nagar, Delhi.
10. YMCA Rural Demonstration Centre , Martandam, Travancore-Cochin.
11. Jamia Millia Islamia, Delhi.
12. Allahabad Agricultural Institute.
13. All India Mass Education Society.
14. Tata Institute of Social Sciences.
15. Dorabji Tata Trust Rural Welfare Board.
16. Literacy House, Allahabad.
17. CARE (Cooperative for American Remittances to Everywhere).
18. American International Association and Cooperative League of the USA.
19. The National Christian Council of India.
20. Bharat Sewak Samaj.
21. M.S. University of Baroda, School of Social Work.
22. Ford Foundation.
23. Service Civil International.
24. All India Women's Conference.
25. World Neighbours.
26. Community Projects Administration.
27. All India Khadi and Village Industries Board.
28. United States Technical Cooperation Mission.

Two organizations, the All India Sarva Sewa Sangh and the Servants of India Society, who had accepted the invitations, could not send their representatives due to pressing last-minute engagements.

ACTION

Action was the ICU's forte. It was in the field from the day go. Its field work covered a wide range: farming, rehabilitation, handicrafts and handlooms development, consumer protection, welfare and research.

A brief account of some of the ICU's major endeavours on the action front are presented in this section, excluding its work at Faridabad in rehabilitation of NWFP refugees, which, as explained in our introduction, is so substantial as to require a book of its own.

This part of the book starts with an account of its rural development work through multipurpose cooperatives for landless agricultural workers; community development effort and agricultural extension. Next is its help to handicraft artisans in finding a secure place in the post-independence economic milieu, particularly through the instrument of the Central Cottage Industries Emporium, followed by its role in consumers protection and promotion of their interests through consumer co-operatives especially through the instrument of "Super Bazars".

Then an account of the help to Tibetan refugees in their rehabilitation, organization of social welfare services for rural and urban communities and finally research and publication in aid of its efforts at both advocacy and action – its major research outputs have been reproduced in the preceding section on Advocacy.

10

RURAL DEVELOPMENT

The ICU undertook a most innovative pilot project under non-official auspices to show how a community development programme can be conducted as an effective instrument of productivity and an active ally of the weaker sections of the village community – two attributes which official projects strived for but failed to acquire. A radical innovation of the project was the extension of credit to the farmers without the deadly practice of security insisted by all credit agencies – which invariably deprived the marginal and small farmers from access to development credit. The project replaced security with technical guidance and supervision. The credit needs and repayment plans were determined on the basis of individual farm plans developed in consultation with each farmer. There was transparency, making public all the details of borrowings. Repayments were record-breaking and by the borrowers on their own initiative. The ICU's pilot project did succeed in its aims – and was later wound up. A report prepared on the project is reproduced here. The circumstances that led to its closure are also recalled.

I. COMMUNITY DEVELOPMENT – MEHRAULI

Introduction

Since 1956 the Indian Cooperative Union has been experimenting with a programme in rural development and credit in 15 villages in Mehrauli near the Qutab Minar. This report explains why this project came into being, what progress has been achieved in these few years and what relevance it has in the broad context of the many programmes to increase agricultural production and to improve the conditions of the small farmers in the country.

Genesis of the Project

In 1952, the Government launched the Community Development Programme on a national basis. The objective was to aid, assist and counsel the millions of our farmers in building a new life, by helping them to raise farm production and family income and to make the village communities active participants in the economic and social endeavours of an independent India.

The Community Development Programme has extended rapidly, since its modest beginning in 1952, and by the end of the Third Plan it is expected to cover all the villages in the country. As was inevitable, a programme of this pioneering character and purpose, and of such vast dimensions has had both achievements and shortcomings to its credit. Its successes and achievements are well known and have even provided inspiration and stimulus for similar programmes in other developing countries.

For India itself, the success of this programme being of vital importance, appreciation of its achievements and criticism of its shortcomings have often featured together in Press, Parliament, State legislatures and particularly in the reports of the Programme Evaluation Organization of the Planning Commission.

In 1955-56, public opinion appeared to be concerned more with the shortcomings rather that with the achievements of the programme. That was the period of general stocktaking in the country as the lessons of the First Plans and the tasks for the Second Plan were being considered. There was also a growing feeling that publicity about the achievements of the programme had somewhat outpaced its performance; that it was more popular with the outsiders than with the village "community" for whom it was intended, and that its contribution to "development" specially in raising food production was below expectations.

A number of non-official organizations including the Indian Cooperative Union, engaged in rural development work, which met in a Seminar in Delhi in April 1956, also expressed concern about the gap between achievements and expectations. They were, however, unanimous that whatever be its weaknesses the aims of the programme were laudable and that it must succeed. Its weaknesses were attributed mainly to the fact that the programme was rather young, its resources inadequate and its hands and feet bound in out-moded policies and unworkable procedures.

The Seminar concluded that the non-official organizations interested in the ultimate success of the programme could not stop at criticism. They should go further and offer constructive solutions and demonstrate the efficacy of their approach.. They also decided that the Government having entered the field of rural development in a big way, the non-official organisations should concentrate on programmes of experimental and intensive nature, the results of which might help to improve the qualitative aspects of the general CD Programme and provide training facilities.

The Seminar set the Indian Cooperative Union thinking. The ICU first turned its thoughts to pin pointing the major shortcomings of the CD Programme primarily based on the programme evaluation; important shortcomings requiring an effective solution were identified.

The "benefits" are absorbed by well-to-do landowners

(i) The benefits are too often absorbed by more prosperous and influential land-owners and the programme has suffered from the weakness of not reaching out to small farmers or tenants.

Technical and other services are very inadequate

(ii) The technical and other staff provided is so little in terms of the actual requirements that there is no provision for proper planning, assessment or guidance. Too few specialists and organizers are called upon to handle the problems of too large an area and too large a number of people The services, therefore, prove to be inadequate and self-defeating. They are also not available in time. On the other hand, the requirements of agricultural operations are so dependent on weather that unless the service agency is swift and sufficient in strength and resources, it does not meet the need of the situation.

Credit policies not designed to suit the circumstances of the small farmers

(iii) The policies of different credit agencies are not based to suit the conditions and needs of the small farmers. For instance, credit is provided in terms of the share capital and not in terms of actual needs for conducting the business property; credit is provided not on the security of trust and confidence or on the basis of productive and repaying capacity but either on production of guarantors or pledgable assets.

Wrong manner in which new cooperatives are promoted

(iv) Small farmers are asked to form and join cooperative societies before they are entitled to receive credit facilities. This inevitably results in individuals joining the cooperatives primarily to obtain monetary and other benefits and not so much from out of understanding and appreciation of cooperation.

Lack of timely and sufficient assistance

(v) Where individuals do become members of the cooperative societies, their hopes are frustrated when they are not able to get either urgent attention or full assistance.

ICU's New Programme

ICU decide to set up a small scale community development project[1] to find out how these shortcomings could be removed, what was required in technical, financial and organizational resources to achieve the kind of results generally expected of the CD programme. It would also devise policies and procedures which, if adapted to the CD organization would allow such a programme to become a more effective instrument of productivity and an active ally of the weaker sections in the rural community.

Within the framework of these general aims, the project also undertook to work on certain specific objectives:

(1) Demonstration of improved agricultural methods in an effort to increase yield of basic crops
(2) A small scale demonstration of short term supervised credit as a means of obtaining basic production data and developing credit procedure applicable to the area
(3) Conducting a pilot operation in one area (along the lines recommended in the Delhi State Plan and All India Rural Credit Survey[2] for development of cooperative credit and marketing societies in order to develop organisational, educational and managerial techniques and procedures applicable to general use in the area
(4) Analysis and evaluation of techniques and procedures employed in carrying out the above objectives with publication of results applicable to extension of similar development in other areas.

The programme started in October 1956, just before the Rabi sowing, now covers fifteen villages in the Mehrauli area in Delhi.

Funds for the Project

The funds required for the project since its inception have been donated to ICU by the Cooperative League of USA and the American International Association for Economic and Social Development. These have been in the forms of (a) A Revolving Loan Fund, (b) Cost of Project Staff, equipment, cost of demonstrations etc., (c) Services of a consultants.

Main Features of the Programme

The main features of the programme launched by ICU may be summarised as follows :

(i) It is designed to serve the small farmers. The assistance is restricted to farmers, tenants or owners whose holding is below 15 acres (unirrigated). This ensures that "benefits" are not sucked away by big landlords.

(ii) A period of 10-12 days has been fixed for the field staff within which the applications for loans and grants received from the farmers should be considered and funds disbursed where the applications are approved

(iii) The requests for assistance from the farmer is jointly examined by the Village Level Worker and Agricultural technician. Their recommendation is based on an assessment of the land, man, capital resources of the applicant, actual requirements in terms of potentialities, prospects of repayment from the increased income or production etc.

(iv) Security for the loans advanced is that of the individual himself

(v) For short-term loans for seeds, the field staff makes estimates of seed requirements of the area well in advance and seed is procured and distributed in time for the sowing season.

(vi) Where loans are given for purchases of livestock or equipment, the borrower is free to make the purchase. The Centre, however, provides guidance and through field staff keeps up-to-date information regarding utilization of the loans.

(vii) Demonstration plots are established to propagate improved agricultural practices.

(viii) The development of a cooperative is sought to be achieved in stages, over a period in which it is proposed to have an advisory committee to begin with, then a village development association, then discussion of cooperative principles and practices, training of a few willing selected persons in the village as office-bearers of cooperative institution and then finally the formation of a cooperative institution and then finally the formation of a cooperative if the prospective members have been helped to arrive at a decision to do so through the aforesaid process.

(ix) Where the Centre is unable to meet a particular need of the area or the individual, it tries to find out governmental or other sources which might be able to do so. The Centre then helps the applicant to approach them and pursue his request.

Subsequently additions were made to include programmes of home science, education, village industries, etc.

Definition of Small Farmers

At first the project had to adopt a definition of small farmers. It was felt that a person owning or cultivating an area upto 5 acres of irrigated or 15 acres of unirrigated land could be considered as a small farmer. Those above this limit could be considered as better-off farmers. The Mehrauli area being largely a dry-farming area the limit of 15 acres was adopted by the ICU project.

Restriction of Aid to Small Farmers

It was felt that this restriction should be applied in a manner that the village community was not divided into two hostile camps: small farmers versus better-off farmers.

It was decided that technical advice in improved agricultural practices should be provided to all farmers in the village, small or big.

Supply of seeds, fertilizers, insecticides, livestock, wells, etc., on a *loan or grant basis* should be restricted to small farmers. The other farmers could get these supplies and services on a *cash-payment basis.* In exceptional cases, however, credit could be extended to the better-off farmers.

Preference for Progressive Farmers

Within the above framework, assistance was to be provided to those satisfying the following qualifications :

(a) Willingness to accept advice regarding improved methods of cultivation.

(b) Self-cultivating farmer.

The project has so far provided credit facilities to 1,234 families of cultivators composed as follows:

(a)	*Small farmers*		
	Landless	78	6.32
	Below 1 acre	51	4.13
	1 to 5 acres	405	32.82
	5 to 15 acres	685	55.51
			98.78
(b)	*Better-off farmers,* i.e. having an area more than 15 acres	15	1.22
		1,234	100.00

In addition, seeds, fertilizers and insecticides etc. were provided on *cash-payment* basis to more than 500 cultivators mainly from villages adjoining the ICU project area. These also included some of the better-off farmers from the project area.

What is the extent of coverage?

In the 15 villages in the project area there are 1,421 families of cultivators (based on surveys conducted by the Block Development Organization).

Out of these, credit facilities were extended to 1,234 or to 81 per cent of the families. If services provided on cash-payment basis are also included the coverage of the project is even higher than 81 per cent.

How are needs assessed?

The village-level worker and the agricultural technician discuss with each farmer how he can increase his output or income. The farmer is almost always ready with the answers. He describes his present position, the hurdles in his way, and what he is sure he can achieve if these hurdles or limitations are removed.

These are noted down in a record sheet (Pass Book, which served as a farm plan, given as annexure at the end of this chapter) for each individual farmer. Through a process of discussion – a final plan emerges

– which is essentially the farmer's own plan, no doubt suggestions about improved agricultural practices are made by the project staff. The members and the project staff have learned to place themselves in the position of the applicant farmer.

Material, cash and labour resources required are then estimated. The farmer indicates how much he can put in on his own – and the gap that the project might fill. Once they are satisfied, the village level worker and the agricultural technician, have then the responsibility to secure the necessary resources and to ensure prompt delivery to the applicant farmer.

The actual results are recorded in the individual record-sheet of the farmer concerned. All future plans and progress are recorded in the same sheet.

This builds up the necessary basic material first for individual and then for village farm planning, assessment of results and also that of the judgment of the project technicians and staff.

Streamlined and Comprehensive Service

Ordinarily, a farmer is unable to get all his production requirements from one source. Irrigation and Agricultural departments provide taccavi loans for certain purposes. The Community Development Project under its schematic budget provides loans and grants for certain purposes. The credit cooperatives meet part of the needs of the agriculturists. Invariably, the aid given by these agencies is not enough for the purpose for which the farmer borrows. For instance, a bullock may cost Rs. 200. If the farmer is given only Rs. 100 from these agencies, he cannot be expected to buy half a bullock. Such absurdities are not uncommon, This uneconomic loan is very often not used for productive purposes; or the farmer has to secure the balance from the money-lender.

Once the money-lender is also brought into the picture, he manages to see that the farmer first repays his capital and interest (which is exorbitant). Thus the loans received from cooperatives or government agencies remain in arrears and overdues increase. But for this situation it is not the money-lender but these agencies themselves that are to blame.

Furthermore, this process involves enormous costs to the farmer in terms of waiting (often without eventual success) upon these departments and their officials. These costs are of course nowhere recorded. But they can be easily imagined.

The project decided to remedy this situation drastically.

In the ICU project, any amount needed by a farmer for any productive purposes, over and above his own resources, is met in full by the project.

The amount of aid is determined entirely by actual costs involved in obtaining a particular item or service. No *a priori* limit was set on the amount that can be loaned to an individual.

The project also provides composite services which a multipurpose cooperative is ordinarily expected to provide. The project undertook to provide seeds, fertilizers, insecticides, agricultural tools and implements, aid for milch cattle, bullocks, other draft animals, construction or repair of wells, pumping sets, levelling of land, building, bullock-carts, etc. A farmer included in the project does not have to run to three or four agencies and offices to meet his different needs, thus saving his "costs" of obtaining aid.

To ensure that aid is used for the purpose it is sought for, it is given in kind, wherever possible, rather than in cash.

Swift Delivery of Aid

One of the worst features of the Government and cooperative agencies providing credit to the farmers is that aid is seldom given in time. The farmer's life is completely tied to seasons and weather. In all his major operations and requirements time is the essence of the matter. Seed has to be sown at a particular time or not at all.

It is in this aspect that the money-lender scores heavily over the government and cooperative even though the latter provide much cheaper credit.

This project laid down that the aid must be provided within 10-12 days from the date on which a farmer made the first request. Whether the answer was yes or no, it had to be given within this time limit.

This is one of the important aspects, in which the project has been a success. The farmers in the area have acquired the confidence that they can get aid from the project without delay.

How to be Different from the Money-lender

In the beginning, the project staff was required to deliver the aid to the farmer at his hut or farm, just to make him feel the difference between the money-lender's classic treatment and that of a social project.

Furthermore, each farmer was given a pass-book. Every time he borrowed or repaid he got an entry made in his presence. The pass-book is kept by the farmer in his own possession. Where illiterate, he can have it read out to him by someone else. The pass-book (in Hindi and English) also explains the objectives of the project and the terms and conditions of loans.

Type of Loans and Period of Repayment

Generally loans for seeds, fertilizers, insecticides are given as *short-term loans* for a period of 15 months.

Loans for bullocks, milch cattle, agricultural tools, wells, etc. are usually given as *medium-term loans* for a period of three to five years.

Loans for irrigational tanks or other land improvement measures are treated as *long-term loans* for a period of 10 to 20 years. If the irrigational tanks for some reason prove to be failures, the entire loan is to be treated as an outright grant.

The period of repayment can be extended by the Project Director, if due to bad crop or natural calamities or sickness the repayment will cause hardship to the farmer, specially if he is not likely to be left with enough for subsistence till the next crop.

In short, the period of repayment of loans is assessed on the basis of the purpose and the potentialities.

Security of Loans

It is a well-known fact that the terms and conditions of Government and Cooperative Agencies, in the matter of security, are such that no poor farmer can really get any benefit of the "socialist" pattern of development assistance. Only those with tangible assets and property to mortgage or with rich relations and friends can take advantage of taccavi loans, irrigation loans, cooperative credit and loans from the schematic budget of the Community Development Project[3].

Recently, a relaxation has been made that cooperative credit can be given on the security of the crops. This is, however, restricted to short-term needs for seeds and fertilizers only.

The main justification given for such strict terms of security is that the small farmers are not considered credit-worthy. With aid denied they will perhaps never become credit-worthy.

The ICU believes that the small farmer is *aid-worthy,* and it is the duty of the government and other agencies to help him sufficiently and effectively to become credit-worthy.

The other justification given is that there is risk involved in giving loans without security. In terms of poverty and lack of employment opportunities, the country is like a vast prison. Where will a borrower in a village run away to? This should be enough security for those who are unaccustomed to think in any other terms.

The Indian Cooperative Union decided to seek only one type of security : the goodwill and productive capacity of the borrowing farmer: It relied only on one axiom : trust begets trust.

For getting a loan from the ICU project a farmer is required to sign only a simple bond. His application is recommended by a member of the "Village Loan Committee" organised by the project. The recommending person has, however, no personal obligation to repay in the event of default.

Rate of Interest

Interest (simple) at the rate of 6-1/4 per cent is charged on all types of loans.

Loans Extended

A total number of 3,492 loans were made up to Rabbi 1960-61. The total amount loaned up to 31st March, 1961 is Rs. 5.07 lakhs.

	Rs. in lakhs
Medium term	2.86
Short term	1.00
Long term	0.97
Marketing and artisans	0.24
Total	5.07

What has been Recovered

The recovery as on 15th May, 1961 on amounts due against the loans advanced has been satisfactory as the following table shows:

	Percentage of recovery to net amount due
Medium term	80
Short term	90
Long term	100
Marketing and artisans	93

With the current harvest repayment now in progress, nearly full amount is expected to be recovered.

In the majority of cases no reminders were necessary and farmers repaid the instalments on their own.

In the case of a wilful defaulter, the pressure of the community is first brought upon him and legal processes are resorted to only when this has failed. In four years of the operation only in 10 cases has there been resort to legal processes for recovery.

Technical Assistance

As stated above, the first and foremost technical assistance provided is in the formulation of a production plan.

Constant advice is then made available for implementing the plan, after resources have been found and made available.

The project staff keeps in close touch with the farmer on the one hand and with the technical and research agencies of the Government on the other, to act as a channel for the latest improvement on developments in agricultural practices.

At the same time the project has become a centre where all these specialized Government agencies have extended in the field the results of their research.

For introducing new practices or improved seeds, demonstration plots have been used. Farmers who agree to set up demonstration plots are guaranteed a minimum return on the basis of their previous crops. Invariably the successful demonstration plots are guaranteed a minimum return on the basis of their previous crops. Invariably the successful demonstration plots extended the idea to other farmers in the subsequent period.

The project received full cooperation and technical guidance from the Farm Advisory Wing, Indian Council of Agricultural Research, Pusa Institute, and the Council of Scientific and Industrial Research.

Combination of Credit and Technical Assistance

The village credit cooperative society ordinarily provides credit to a farmer without reference to his agricultural plan or practices. Seldom does the cooperative advise the borrower member on improved practices. Such advice is supposed to be the business of the Agriculture Departments or Community Development Project.

On the other hand these departments provide technical advice, suggest new seeds, fertilizers or improved agricultural practices. They assume that it is the business of the farmer to obtain necessary funds for implementing these new ideas. In some cases they advance the funds themselves from their departmental budgets.

By and large, there is no coordination between credit agencies and technical assistance departments. Only recently, a combination of these two is being attempted in the Package Programme sponsored by the Food and Agriculture Ministry and the Ford Foundation.

The ICU project recognised from the very beginning that the small farmers need not only credit, but also an urgent improvement in agricultural practices. Both credit and technical hands being scarce, the two can be used effectively and economically only when combined.

While much thought has been given to the linking of credit with marketing, as in the Rural Credit Survey Report, little thought has been given to the importance of linking technical advice and credit.

The linking of credit and marketing is sought mainly as a form of security. It has no relation to productivity which is the major attribute of linking credit with technical advice. When credit and technical advice are delivered separately and in an uncoordinated manner, both are unhelpful and wasteful, and do not result in increased production.

It is interesting to note that the linking of credit and marketing as envisaged by the Reserve Bank of India has not solved even the problem of overdues. In fact the overdues are on the increase.

The ICU closely watched this happening in the villages in its own project area. To fulfil the prescribed targets – some large-sized cooperatives were rushed into existence. The large-sized cooperatives brought large-sized loans. These were distributed hastily. There was no relationship of these loans with the production plans or needs of the farmers. Perhaps little was produced to be marketed. Apart from misuse and embezzlement that followed, the overdues of these societies have brought their activities to a standstill. Whom does this sort of development benefit?

In the ICU project, the combination of technical advice and credit was made more effective, by making the agricultural technician responsible for securing the necessary credit and services for the farmer, once the production plan is approved.

To enable the technician and the project staff to fulfil the obligation, it was found necessary to delegate powers commensurate with responsibilities.

Delegation of Powers to Project Staff

For guiding this project the ICU set up a policy committee which concerns itself with: broad principles and policies; approval of the annual budget; and review of progress.

The Director of the project is a member of the policy committee. Within these broad principles and the annual budget, the Director is entitled to make any decision. He can sanction loans, procure and distribute supplies, determine the period of repayment and other terms.

The principle followed is the same as in giving aid to the farmers: trust in the sincerity and integrity of the employees. The employees furnish a simple guarantee through fidelity insurance. There has been no single instance of misuse or lapse on the part of the employees.

The Project Director submits progress reports once a month. He may provide aid, where satisfied, even beyond laid down policies, but at the end of the month he must report. If he has made a mistake, it can be rectified for the future. He must also report where policy decisions need to be amended to suit the local conditions.

He cannot deny aid – such cases he must report to the policy committee.

He can delegate any of his powers to his staff. The project staff is thus conscious of the confidence placed in it; its initiative is not thwarted. It not only implements policy but also plays a part in revising it and shaping it to make it more suitable and of greater service.

This avoids their (the field workers) looking helpless and ridiculous in the eyes of the village community.

Impact on Production and Income

An intensive study was made of the effects of loans and technical assistance rendered on a random sample of 69 cultivators participating in the programme up to Kharif 1959. The results of this study showed that:

(a) A large proportion of the cultivators altered their cropping patterns during the period, changing from single grain crops to mixed crops and cash crops.
(b) Per acre yields were progressively higher than the averages for the area.
(c) There was a substantial increase in the marketable surplus of the majority of the cultivators.
(d) There was an increase in the gross farm income and off-farm income of a great majority of the cultivators and who participated in the marketing programme earned Rs. 2 per maund more than cultivators who sold at the time of harvest.

Better Irrigation Required for Better Results

As will be seen production and income have definitely gone up but these are modest increases. Since the Mehrauli Block is primarily a dry farming area, no real impact on production could be made until irrigation facilities were improved and long-term development measures initiated. A start was made with the sinking of an experimental tank in Sultanpur village through the efforts of the Ministry of Food and Agriculture and the untiring zeal and guidance of Shri M.A.T. lyenger, ICS, who suggested and supervised the construction of this tank. The Union extended full cooperation as well as assistance in the construction of the tank, and the channels. The joint endeavours of the villagers which were required in the digging operations provided stimulus for group work and much needed employment to the unemployed and the underemployed.

The large volume of water available from the new well caught the imagination of the entire village as well as the inhabitants of the neighbouring villages.

Thereupon, the Farm Advisory Wing of the Ministry of Food and Agriculture, the ICU and the Village Development Committee unanimously agreed that the work should not stop merely with the construction of the well and the following additional objectives were adopted :

(a) urgent and maximum use of water available;
(b) *fair distribution* of water to ensure its benefits extend to as many farmers in the village as possible;
(c) proper planning of production for the immediate crop (Rabi 1960-61);
(d) provision of adequate and timely technical and financial aid to the cultivators concerned to accomplish these objectives.

By the end of December 1960 all these jobs were completed. It has been possible through these efforts to provide irrigational facilities for an area of 82 acres. The following table gives the summary of the crops sown during the last crop season (Rabi 1960-61) with the approximate value of crops yield achieved:

Crop grown	Area (acres)	Yield (per acre)	Total Yield	Value (approx.) Rs.
Wheat	43.4	30 mds.	1,305 mds.	26,100
Gram	12.0	13 mds	180 mds.	2,520
Potato	1.0	150 mds	150 mds.	1,350
Pea	1.5	Sold green pea		1,200
Vegetable	8.5	Sold in market		9,500
Summer Vegetables	12.0	Standing in the field		
Green fodder	0.9	Used as fodder		600
Nursery & Orchard	2.6	Being developed		
Total	82.0		Total	41,270

This statement gives only the value of 67.4 acres as the 12 acres were sown later with summer vegetables and its yield is not yet known. Also the orchard and nursery (2.6 acres) are still being developed. On the basis of the experience of our demonstrations the income from it should be at least Rs. 1,000 per acre. From 68 acres a total gross income of Rs. 41,270 was achieved in one crop season whereas in the best years the farmers could not have got more than Rs. 13,065 as the crop previously consisted of gram and barley only. Thus a net increase of over Rs. 28,000 was obtained.

After observing the successful operation of the Sultanpur well the people of many neighbouring villages are eager to construct similar wells in their villages.

The unanimous demand of all the panchayats and cultivators of the areas is for priority to be given to irrigation in the coming years, now that the success of the Sultanpur tank has shown the way.

At the start, there was strong social inhibition against poultry keeping in the project area. But the ICU introduced the latest technology with high output and profits and there was widespread adoption of poultry and its practice on a professional basis, overcoming conventional inhibitions.

Social Services

Medical Aid

The Union set up a medical aid centre with a health van and a medical officer to serve 14 villages in the area. Since then a Janata Health Cooperative Society with a membership of 478 persons has been organized which now manages the medical centre with organizational and financial assistance from the ICU and the Unitarian Service Committee of Canada.

Education and Home Science

The project started schools in the villages not covered by the Education Department – and gradually handed them over to the department.

Assistance was provided to village development committees in construction of drinking water wells at the middle and high schools in the area. Sets of books were gifted to primary and other schools in the area.

Literacy classes were organized for adults, as well as leadership training programmes, which included visits to agricultural research stations, cattle shows, fairs, etc.

Programmes for women included craft classes, advice on infant and child care, home improvements and sanitation.

These are described briefly, for there is nothing unusual about these services, and they were identical to those provided in other CD Projects– if anything, they were perhaps less intensive than those in CD Projects.

Aid to Village Artisans

Due to paucity of resources, a small project was initiated to assist the leather workers who make largely shoes for the local village market.

They are able to sell their products mainly at the harvest time. But due to limitation of funds they cannot stock enough shoes during the slack period for sale at harvest time. The project, therefore, provided over Rs. 14,000 as loan to 58 artisan families. They were thus able to buy raw material in quantity, stock sufficient quantity of finished products for the harvest time and within a year improved their annual earning from 50 to 100 per cent.

They have now formed an industrial cooperative society which has been recently registered. If the cooperative is able to get a loan from the Cooperative Bank or the Government the members will repay the Union's loan, which will then be employed to help another group of artisans in the area.

Marketing

To begin with no marketing programme could be developed as the programme started in a dry-farming area and concentrated on small farmers who did not have much of a marketing surplus. The proximity of the Mehrauli mandi further encouraged the farmers to sell their produce individually. In the second year, a small marketing programme (with only 10 mds. of wheat) was developed which did not make much headway due to a bad crop in 1959-60. A record crop this year promises more resolution (expected to handle 1,200 mds.) in the programme. The following policies govern this programme :

(1) Storage facilities are provided on payment of storing and handling charges.
(2) Market value of the grain is assessed on the day on which it is put in storage. Against this cash advance of 75 per cent is given to the farmer.
(3) The market price at the time of storage is guaranteed as the minimum price by the project. The farmer has the option of finding a customer within three months. If a higher rate is secured, 75 per cent of the excess above the minimum guaranteed price goes to the farmer and 25 per cent to the project.

As the primary cooperatives are formed in the villages they will be federated into a marketing society to take over this work.

COOPERATIVES, ADVISORY COMMITTEE AND PANCHAYATS

When the project was first conceived it was planned to begin work through the cooperatives existing in the project area. It was found, however, that these cooperatives did not have a good reputation. Not only were their membership, outlook and loaning policies restricted but they were also controlled by a few strong people in the village. It was abundantly clear that the primary objective of the programme *to deliver aid to the small farmers* along policies suited to their needs could not possibly be served through these cooperatives. The idea of working through them had to be given up.

The small farmers were then approached to form their own cooperatives, but the reputation of the existing cooperatives was a great deterrent and the small farmers were reluctant at that stage to venture into forming a cooperative.

Since it was the aim of the ICU project to put no precondition of jointing a cooperative before being entitled to aid, the small farmers were not pressed to set up a cooperative. The programme thus began with individual farmers, but side by side a motivation in programme through cooperative education and information in improved agricultural practices was carried on. An Advisory Committee of the participating farmers was set up and subsequently as panchayats were set up in the area, the project sought advice from these bodies in all principal matters.

As the project gained ground and its benefits were understood and appreciated, and as the knowledge of cooperative principles and practices spread through the educational programme, a climate in favour of cooperatives was born. But the actual formation of cooperatives was retarded because of the initial antagonism of the cooperative department towards the project. Registration of three cooperatives formed remained in abeyance for 4 to 8 months. Now, these companies are being registered. This will pave the way for other villages in the project forming cooperatives more rapidly.

The task of construction of tanks and channels and the distribution of water and its effective use based on a new cropping pattern have provided a strong stimulus in bringing the individual cultivators together in a cooperative venture. Similarly, individual farm planning has extended to village production plans, as in the case of Sultanpur village.

Panchayats Facilitate Co-ordination

One of the most beneficial results of the establishment of the panchayats in the area has been that they are exercising influence on the official and non-official agencies to co-ordinate their programmes.

Ever since the ICU started the project it made several efforts to secure coordination with official agencies in the area. The ICU was "advised" to take away its project to some other area!

The situation has happily improved with the emergence of the panchayats, and more sympathetic administration. A co-ordinated plan for development of the area has now been agreed upon in a joint meeting of the panchayats, ICU, Development, Cooperative and Panchayat departments of the Delhi Administration. Efforts are being made to secure the cooperation of the Delhi Corporation also, which has a concurrent jurisdiction with the local panchayats in the area.

Lessons from the Project

1. This experimental Project of the Union has shown that it is possible to devise institutional measures by which most of the benefits of the village development programmes can be delivered to small farmers. By the suitable adoption of policies and practices evolved in this project, the Community Development Programme can benefit small farmers and negate persistent complaints that its benefits are absorbed only by well-to-do farmers.
2. Another lesson is that for effective results and economic use of the resources credit must be related to technical advice. The small farmers need both technical advice and credit facilities (to put the advice in practice). Where the two are un-related to each other, the chances are that both will be unhelpful and wasteful.

This means that the agricultural extension agencies, the Community Development Programme and the cooperative development agencies cannot function independently, if scarce technical and credit resources are not to be wasted and definite gain in production is sought. Besides wastes to the Government, the wasteful costs to the farmer, in trying to chase different agencies is too enormous and unforgivable. The ICU project shows that a combination of technical advice and credit is both feasible and fruitful. It also shows that establishment of panchayats does help to "force" such coordination from below.

3. The next most vital reform needed is in credit policies of taccavi loans, schematic budgets of the CD Programmes, cooperative financing agencies, irrigation departments, etc., providing loans to agriculturists.

   (a) The project has demonstrated that in the great majority of case, no other securities than trust and potential for increasing agricultural production (based on farm planning), are required to ensure repayment of loans.

On the other hand, cooperatives and other Government agencies which give loans only to "credit-worthy" persons, and with due safeguards of security show a very poor repayment record, and heavy overdues. It will be of interest to investigate as to why they have such heavy overdues despite cautious selection of loanees and tangible security.

(b) Risk is further reduced if credit is given in kind and not in cash, this also ensures timely availability of proper seeds and fertilisers.

(c) The amount of credit extended to a person must be equal to his *need* and not his *status*. Uneconomic loans are self-defeating.

(d) Repayment period must be related to the production plan and potentiality. In natural calamities concession must be shown so as not to inflict greater suffering on the farmers.

(e) Wilful defaulters must be sternly dealt with.

(f) Each participant individually or as a member of a cooperative should be enabled to maintain his own account in the form of a pass-book. Thus honest accountancy and dealings are ensured to him.

4 The next lesson is that if an extensive-intensive coverage is to be achieved the resources now provided under the various development programmes will have to be increased and pooled. From the funds provided in the ICU project for 15 villages (dry farmed area and small farmers) a measure can be had of the short- medium- and long-term requirement of the small farmers. (Average per cultivator Rs. 80 for short term and Rs.400 for medium term). This excludes long-term loans. Even in these villages the needs will further increase with irrigation facilities planned. If adequate resources are not provided for the village development programmes no real change in the economy of farmers or in the income of individual families can be expected. But provision of additional resources should be made only after other reforms suggested above are implemented to ensure efficient and economic use of the current resources or else the additional funds will also go to wrong hands and be wasted.

A propos of this we must understand what credit means to a small farmer. It is not sufficiently realized that a small farmer dependent on a village money-lender for credit needs is working on the most expensive capital. He pays an interest at the rate of 25 to 40 per cent. On the other hand joint-stock companies running big business and industry run their business on the cheapest capital, i.e. the shareholder money. Shareholders are not paid any interest. They are paid only a dividend if and when the company makes a profit. It will be a miracle if any one of our most brilliant industrialists, traders, bankers and administrators could run a business on such an expensive capital as does a small farmer in the village.

In paying a heavy rate of interest the small farmer is "saving" more than anyone in the country. But his savings are appropriated by someone else – and he is forced into perpetual impoverishment and a state of non–credit worthiness as far as government and cooperative credit agencies are concerned.

The indebtedness of the farmer to the money-lender not only reduces the farmer to an eternally condemned economic state but also to a state of social indignity and personal humiliation.

Before independence, one could blame the money-lender. But today it is futile for he still continues to supply the bulk of the credit to the cultivators in a more flexible and prompt manner whatever we may hold against his exploitation. Today, we have the power and the resources to release the small farmer from his crushing burdens and bondage. What is needed is a combination of boldness and practical wisdom and a massive attack on this centuries-old disease in our system.

5. One of the lessons of the project is that a rigid approach requiring all future development to be done through existing cooperatives will negate the very objective of assisting weaker sections. As long as the control of existing cooperatives remains in the hands of persons unsympathetic to the idea of helping the weaker sections, and as long as the past overdues and financial irregularities of such cooperatives are not set right, there is little hope that the small farmers will join such cooperatives.

   There should, therefore, be preparedness to set up new cooperatives consisting predominantly of small farmers, where the existing ones will not serve the purposes of bringing them benefits. While through a cautious approach a period of two to three years may be required before a cooperative is formed, very often cooperatives formed in haste die or disappear in this very same period. Ultimately, therefore the seemingly slow method ensures a longer lifespan.

6. As the farmer gains experience in improved practices from the first contact for a loan and technical assistance, he requires less attention in subsequent crop seasons thereby freeing the technician and village-level workers to take on a large area. The progressive farmers are very effective in convincing others of the efficacy of improved practices. Thus the overhead costs of the project in relation to the same persons or area can decrease after a few crops and the same staff can be revolved over a larger area.

A CD Block ordinarily has 80 to 1,000 villages. For the first two years it could concentrate on 15-20 villages on intensive development. The experience of its staff, the results obtained in these villages as well as progressive farmers in these villages could then help in radiation of results in groups of 20-25 villages in each subsequent year. Thus in about five years it could provide more intensive-extensive coverage than what obtains today. It could spend another two to three years for a recheck of the entire area, before the project staff is withdrawn substantially.

If the ICU project had not been confined to 15 villages (by virtue of its having limited resources) within this period, it could have covered at least three times the number of villages with the same staff costs, and even a larger number of villages if it were to do a new job with the experience now gained.

Training of Project Staff

There was no facility or possibility of the Project staff being provided training prior to their starting work on the project.

"Learn as you work" was the motto adopted. The village-level workers who had to face most of the problems were too preoccupied in their own area and there was little contact even among the different VLWs. Each VLW was thus struggling by himself.

To remedy this situation Saturdays were devoted to thinking, review and discussions among members of the project staff, in the earlier stages of the programme. The Research and Evaluation staff of the Union also joined in these Saturday reviews. In course of time, the weekly reviews became fortnightly and then monthly and sometimes even less frequently specially during sowing and harvesting times.

There were only minor changes in staff. Most of them have stayed in the project since they were employed.

Training of Others

As the project made progress it was recognized that while the training of the project staff had to be ad hoc and informal the project should also develop a formal training syllabus for assisting other non-official organizations.

A trial training programme was conducted to develop the syllabus and training technique. Two batches of trainees from voluntary organizations were provided training the first course took four months and the second three months. This has since been further condensed to two months. Seventyfive per cent of the time is reserved for field training, and the rest for lectures, study and discussions.

Apart from offering training facilities – the project staff has participated and assisted in training programmes run by other organizations.

Evaluation

Since 1956 the Union has published three evaluation reports on the project. The last of these: "Rural Development and Credit Project in Delhi – An Evaluation Report" covering Rabbi 1957-58 to Kharif 1959 was published in 1960.

This year the Union has requested the Programme Evaluation Organization of the Planning Commission to do the evaluation.

It was understood that no single solution could have universal application to all areas in the country, but that a solution once found in one place would pave the way for further experimentation and adaptation.

The project was not intended as a basis for a prototype to be duplicated in its entirety in other areas. Rather it was intended to develop methods and procedures for extending credit and technical assistance to cultivators with relatively small land holdings, by utilizing improved farm plans, proper supervision and technical guidance. It was felt that these would provide useful answers to the problems of agricultural extension, regardless of the institutional and organizational framework in which they may be employed.

It was hoped to devise policies and procedures which, if adapted to the Community Development Programme of the Government would allow such a programme to get rid of the shortcomings noticed in its operations. The ICU, however, failed to enthuse the CD Ministry to have a look at this project.

But the ICU is happy to record that of all the various agencies of Government concerned with this type of programme the Ministry of Food and Agriculture has been the most sympathetic and helpful. The Farm Advisory wing, the Pusa Institute, the Indian Council of Food and Agriculture provided maximum technical advice and guidance. The ministers, senior officials and technical officers of the Ministry paid personal visits – and on several occasions – to the project area. The Ministry of Food and Agriculture also studied the Evaluation Report of the project, and considered it useful to circulate it to the State Governments. Several of the State Governments also found the information useful.

Voluntary Organizations

The Association of Voluntary Agencies for Rural Development has through several reports in its Newsletter disseminated information about the project among voluntary organizations. Some of the voluntary organizations such as the Rural Welfare Board Dorabji Tata Trust and the Rural Development Department of the ACC, have studied the Project.

Conclusion

In presenting this report, the Indian Cooperative Union seeks no credit for any idea or achievement that may appeal to the reader or the authorities. It would, however, welcome any criticism or comment which would help to clarify or improve upon the ideas, policies and procedures suggested here.

The only object of presenting this report is to share this experience with individuals, authorities and organizations in the country who are interested in strengthening the Community Development programme, cooperatives, agricultural production programmes, and even more so in ensuring a speedy and substantial improvement in the condition of the weaker sections in the village community.

The Union will consider its labour and costs amply rewarded if any of the lessons of this project are able to advance, even to the slightest degree, the economic well-being and welfare of the small farmers, in any corner of the country.

II. EXTENSION

Though as explained in chapter 14, the CD Ministry turned its back towards the Mehrauli project, the ICU's labours were partly rewarded by the extensive use of the Project's experience by Ministry of Agriculture.

One of the groups which visited the ICU's Mehrauli project was the Ford Foundation team of 1959-60 whose report, "India's Food Crisis and Steps to Meet It", laid the bases for the Intensive Agricultural Districts Programme (IADP) or "Package Programme" as it was later called since it attempted to provide farmers all inputs needed to achieve rapid increases in food production in one package. Beginning initially in selected districts, the Package Programme later became the major national scheme for increasing agricultural production.

The Extensive Directorate of the Government of India, as well as the Ford Foundation specialists, working on the Package Programme studied the Mehrauli project. Mehrauli influenced the IADP patterns of staffing, individual farm planning and training of village-level workers. The Package Programme made use of the project's experience in general, but also that of selected ICU personnel, especially its Project Director, B.L. Dhar, and its Consultant, Dr. A. C. Felder.

A detailed report on the project was included in the First Central Training Course for key personnel of the Package Programme held in December 1960. Dhar and Felder served on various technical groups set up by the Package Programme authorities; gave lectures in the initial training programmes for agricultural extension officers, co-operative personnel and village level workers working in the Package Programme districts in Bihar, Rajasthan and other States. During the first two years of the Package Programme, ICU personnel helped to train IADP personnel for 5,000 villages in seven districts in farm planning, identification of the poorest households and establishing plans, project monitoring and methods of consultation with communities.

Gramdan Cooperatives

The ICU also extended its help to the Bhoodan movement which wanted to form cooperatives for Gramdan villages that is, where most of the land of the village had been pooled together. On the request of Jayaprakash Narayan, the ICU assisted in the planning and organization of Gramdan movement in Bihar and U.P. The ICU studied the structure of Gramdan Movement in these States and also held several meetings with the workers of the movement. After the study tour and subsequent meetings and discussions, draft by-laws of the Gramdan cooperatives at various levels were prepared in consultation with the workers and agencies connected with the Gramdan movements as well as the officials of the Cooperative Department.

NOTES

1. The project was called Rural Development and Credit Project to avoid confusion with the Community Development Programme of the Government.
2. This had to be modified due to reasons discussed elsewhere in this Report.
3. The following rules govern the grant of taccavi loans, as adopted by the U.P. Government: (Subject to minor differences similar rules obtain in other States. Rules governing taccavi loans are generally followed by other Government Agencies like Irrigation Departments, Community Development Projects, etc.)
   The amount which can be made available under the taccavi loans shall not exceed in case of:

   (a) Bhoomidars, 60 times the land revenue.
   (b) Sirdars, 10 times the rent.
   (c) Adivasis, 2 times the rent.
   (d) Asamis, an amount equal to the rent.

   As regards security, the following conditions are imposed by the U.P. Government:

   "If personal security is offered the applicant must produce at least two well-known and substantial sureties".

   These rules throw more light than anything else on the process which is making the rich richer, and the poor poorer. The disparities range from sixty to one. Since the rent paid by an Asami is bound to be very small the actual amount he will receive under these rules will be very small and possibly never enable the Asami either to construct a well or to acquire a pumping set or livestock or anything else that is productive, and possible under the taccavi loan. His economic capacity and condition will thus remain static, if not lead to steady impoverishment.

   At the same time, the Bhoomidar who gets as much as 60 times the land revenue should have no difficulty in sinking a well, and acquiring the equipment or livestock, or anything else that will further add to his income and thus enable him to acquire control over more land. He will thus pay more land revenue and next time receive more taccavi loan and so on and so forth.

REFERENCES

Possibilities of Cooperative Organisation, *International Labour Review,* December 1950.
Report on the Efficient Conduct of State Enterprises, by A.D. Gorwala.
Report of the Reserve Bank Committee on Finance for the Private Sector.
Rural Development and Credit Project in Delhi - An Evaluation Report, 1960.
Ten Eventful Years, ICU, 1958.

ANNEXURE

PASS-BOOK

COOPERATIVE DEVELOPMENT & RESEARCH CENTRE

INDIAN COOPERATIVE UNION
(1956-57)

DEVELOPMENT CREDIT PROGRAMME

Name:

Father's Name:

Village:

Loan Account No.:

COOPERATIVE DEVELOPMENT & RESEARCH CENTRE

Sunanda, South Delhi

Rules Regarding Short and Medium-Term Loans Under Development Credit Programme

1. *Area:* These loans may be advanced only in such villages as are selected by the Indian Cooperative Union from time to time.
2. *Purpose:* Short-term loans may be granted to help farmers to meet their crop expenses and increase their production. So these loans are ordinarily to be granted for the purchase of improved seed, fertilizers, insecticides, etc. They are repayable at the end of the harvest.

   Medium-term loans may be granted :

   – for the purchase of live-stock, including milch cattle;
   – for the purchase of agricultural equipment;
   – for the undertaking of minor irrigation projects; and
   – for the undertaking of minor land improvement projects.

3. *Period of Loans:* Short and Medium-term loans are to be granted for maximum periods of six months and three years respectively.
4. *Rate of Interest:* The rate of interest will be 6-1/4 per cent per annum (simple interest) on actual amounts outstanding for both types of loans.
5. *Selection of Loanees:* Applications for these loans should be accepted only from the farmer who fulfils the following conditions:

   (a) his land-holding should not exceed 15 acres but exceptions may be considered where due to extraordinary circumstances a farmer holding more than 15 acres deserves help;
   (b) he is a self-cultivating farmer;
   (c) he is willing to accept advice regarding improved methods of cultivation; and
   (d) he is found to have a fair debt record and is willing to repay loans under stipulated arrangements.

6. *Quantum of Loans:* The maximum amount of loan to be advanced will be determined on the basis of the following factors:

(a) the need of the farmer, and
(b) the repayment capacity of the farmer.

The need of the farmer will be determined by a technical analysis of his farm operations by the agricultural technician appointed by the Centre. His opinion in this matter will be final. The repaying capacity will be determined on the basis of the net saleable surpluses from the crops raised during the last one or two years and the expected surpluses from the crops sown during the current year.

While considering the loan applications the indebtedness of the farmer to other agencies (government, cooperative and private) will also be taken into consideration.

No loan will be granted to any applicant who fails to give correct information regarding his assets and liabilities and farming operations.

7. *Mode of Payment:* All the short-term loans will be granted in kind except in special circumstances. Medium-term loans may be granted either in kind or in cash but where they are granted in cash the borrowers will be obliged to secure the assets and services required by them from reliable sources, at reasonable prices and in accordance with their genuine technical needs as determined by the staff of the CDRC.
8. *Supervision:* Village organizers and agricultural technicians will be responsible for supervising the utilization of loans and the borrowers should be willing to accept their advice. Any loan not utilized for the specific purposes for which it has been taken will be recovered immediately even if the repayment be not due at that time.
9. *Mode of Recovery:* Loans may be repaid in cash or kind as may be convenient to the borrower at the due date. The price of agricultural produce on the basis of which amounts to be paid in kind will be determined shall be fixed by the CDRC taking into account the current market rates prevailing at the time of repayment.
10. Short-term loans will be recovered at the end of the harvest in full while medium-term loans may be repaid either in half-yearly or monthly instalments.
11. Village organizers and agricultural technicians are authorized to recover loans from the borrowers, to whom they will issue official receipts and make entries of recoveries in passbooks which will be issued to the borrowers.

INDIVIDUAL CREDIT STATUS INFORMATION

Date ....

I. FAMILY INFORMATION

1. Operator's Name .... Village ....

2 Adults (ages): Men ...., Women ....
Number of Labourers ....

3. Boys in household (ages): ....

4. Girls in household (ages): ....

II. INVENTORY

Item	Number	Value
1. Land owned	xx	xx
a. Irrigated		
b. Dry		
c. Total		
2. Land rented	xx	xx
a. Irrigated		
b. Dry		
c. Total		
3. Buildings	xx	xx
a. Home		
b. Others		
c. Total		
4. Wells		
5. Home Eqpt.	xx	xx

6.	Clothing, etc.	xx	xx
7	Others		
8.	Livestock	xx	xx
	a. Animal Power		
	b. Cattle		
	c. Milch Animal		
	d. Total		
9.	Farm Equipment	xx	xx
	a. B. Carts		
	b. Ploughs		
	c H. Tools		
	d Total		
10.	Cash	xx	
11.	Cash Due	xx	
12.	Total Assets	xx	xx
13.	Debts	xx	
14.	Net Worth	xx	xx

III. FINANCIAL STATUS NOW COMPARED TO 12 MONTHS AGO:

1. Last year I had cash Rs. .... but now I have Rs. ....

2. Last year I owed debts Rs. .... but now I owe Rs. ....
3. Last year I sold or lost capital goods valued at Rs. .... but I acquired capital goods valued at Rs. ....

IV. LAST YEAR (FULL 12 MONTHS) CULTIVATION RECORD

Nature of Crop		Cash expenses during last 12 months					Total Yield	Home use	Marketed	
Crop	Acres	Labour	Seed	Tax	Manure	Other				

V. LAST YEAR OTHER INCOME EARNED

I earned a total of Rs. .... from ....
and Rs. .... from ....

VI. MONTHLY CASH EXPENSES Rs. ....

VII. MONTHLY GRAIN CONSUMPTION Mds........... Srs...........

VIII. I PLAN TO DO THE FOLLOWING TO INCREASE MY INCOME:

1. .... Cost Rs.
2. .... Cost Rs.
3. .... Cost Rs.
4. .... Cost Rs.

IX. I WOULD LIKE DEMONSTRATION/INFORMATION ON THE FOLLOWING :

1. .... month
2. .... month
3. .... month
4. .... month

Agricultural Technician Farmer

LOAN ACCOUNT

Term	Date	Particulars			Dr. (Advances)		Cr. (Repayments)		Balance		Signature
		Article	Quantity	Rate	Rs.	nP.	Rs.	n.P	Rs.	n.P.	
Medium		Particulars									

MEMORANDUM

Date	Name of the person visiting	Remarks and impressions

11

DEVELOPMENT OF HANDICRAFTS AND HANDLOOMS

Beginning with 1951, three significant developments brought the Indian Cooperative Union to the field of handicrafts development. The Government of India handed over the management of a shop in New Delhi called "Refugee Handicrafts" to the ICU. The ICU organized an All India Exhibition of Handicrafts and products of Cottage Industries produced through Cooperatives. The Union also set up a department for the export of handicrafts. The chief aim of these moves was to restore confidence in the future of handicrafts and cottage industries, about which there was general pessimism and which at the time seemed to face extinction before the rising machine industry.

Thereafter its involvement with this sector expanded in geometrical progression with a nationwide survey of handicrafts and taking over the management of the Central Cottage Industries Emporium. An account of these two principal developments is summarized here. The full survey report is, however, too big to be reproduced here. Only the policy chapter is reproduced.

I. SURVEY OF HANDICRAFTS

Introduction

Following up the recommendation of the First Handicrafts Marketing Conference held at Trivandrum in February 1953, the All India Handicrafts Board invited the Indian Cooperative Union to undertake a Survey of the Marketing of Indian Handicrafts. The Indian Cooperative Union accepting the assignment appointed a Survey Team headed by Dr. Rajkrishna.

The Indian Cooperative Union, in a note on the objectives and methods of the Survey submitted to the All India Handicrafts Board and accepted by it, said:

> The problem of the marketing of handicrafts has two different aspects.
>
> Firstly, goods that are being produced in satisfactory quality and competitive costs at present need to be marketed more intensively and extensively. This requires more enterprise and a bigger network of selling organizations.

But the number of handicraft products that satisfy the necessary quality and cost conditions is comparatively small. Therefore the provision of a bigger network of selling organizations and greater enterprise, although much needed, does not constitute the crucial aspect of the problem of marketing. The crucial aspect of the marketing problem is inseparable from a transformation of production.

The problem is to improve production in every respect: material-utilization, machinery and methods employed, designing, finishing, packing etc., so that newer, better and cheaper goods are produced. Such a *radical improvement of production is a precondition of any substantial expansion of sales.*

Therefore, though the aim is to expand sales, it cannot be achieved without a prior reform of production so as to improve quality and reduce costs. The Survey Team should collect data from this point of view. The task of the Survey should be to collect data about the quantity and composition, costs and methods of production, employment, and the financing and marketing procedures of handicrafts at present, with a view to facilitating the drafting of concrete improvement schemes. The Survey Team should visit handicrafts centres in various States and study the present position of handicrafts fully from the economic, technical and commercial points of view and assess the scope for the development of cooperatives.

Thus the scope of the Survey was extended. The Survey Team had to study not only the marketing, but also various aspects of the production of each handicraft. But, on the other hand, the Survey Team thought it was more practicable to restrict its study to a few, major localized handicrafts in view of the limited time and resources at its disposal. It felt it would be more helpful to the Board and the State Governments concerned to have concrete data and suggestions about the measures required for development in selected handicrafts in specific areas.

The Survey Team began its work in October 1953. During the first two months it studied all the available preliminary data, drew up its questionnaires and tour programmes, and surveyed the ivory industry in Delhi. Thereafter, the Team visited important handicraft centres in Andhara, Hyderabad, Madras, Mysore, Travancore-Cochin, Assam, West Bengal, Bihar, Orissa, Uttar Pradesh, Rajasthan, Madhya Bharat, Bombay, Saurashtra, Kashmir and Manipur.

From the outset, the Team faced the almost complete absence of elementary aggregate statistics about handicrafts, such as the number of production units, output and employment. Until a complete census of small establishments is held, only approximate aggregate statistics could be compiled on the basis of data supplied by the Industries Departments of the States concerned, cross-checked with information directly collected by the Team from local traders' and workers' organizations, where they existed, or experienced merchants and master craftsmen.

Apart from collecting the available figures the Team tried its best to make a qualitative study and assessment of the situation in each craft. In every important handicraft industry in each area selected for the Survey, the Team visited a few small, a few medium sized and a few big units of production, including private, cooperative and government units. It interrogated the managers and proprietors of these units on different aspects of production and marketing. Besides, it studied the marketing structure in the markets themselves. It held long discussions with the Government officers concerned in the Industries and Cooperative Departments of the States visited, representatives of traders' and workers' organizations, where they existed; office-bearers and prominent members of artisans' cooperatives; and, last but not least, a good number of individual workers working in their humble cottages who contributed considerably to the understanding of their problems.

The data collected by the Team and its recommendations on important individual crafts are being submitted to the All India Handicrafts Board in the form of a monograph.

This Report contains the overall analysis and recommendations of the Survey Team on the problem of handicraft marketing.

Chapter 1 : Policy

"Mixed Economy" is a fact as well as a policy: As a fact it means the chaotic mixture of different forms of economic organizations which medieval feudalism and modern *laissez-faire* have left behind. As a policy, it means not an uncritical acceptance of this inherited medley, but the conscious "rationalization" of it by the Welfare State.

In the field of handicraft marketing, as in other sectors of economic activities, we start with the facts of a "mixture". There are at least four types of marketing agencies functioning side by side : 1. complicated chains of profit-seeking middlemen, 2. government agencies, 3. cooperative agencies and 4. nonprofit-making agencies other than cooperatives.

A basic question of policy immediately presents itself. How is the mixture to be rationalized by the Welfare State wedded to a policy of mixed economy?

Under the mixed economy policy, no single form of economic organization is accepted or rejected *a priori*. All kinds of enterprize may exist side by side. But their relative importance, the proportion of the total output handled by each, keeps changing. It would change even if the State did nothing. But when the State has ceased to be a mere onlooker and become the initiator and active promoter of change, it must have a definite policy as to the manner in which the proportions are to change; and take appropriate measures to see that they do change in the intended manner. It must decide, sector by sector, whether it eventually wants private enterprise or direct governmental enterprise or (assisted) cooperative enterprise to predominate. A mixed economy policy is not only not inconsistent with, but requires, a definite and declared preference for different kinds of organizations working in each field. A mere endorsement of the existing mixture or the eulogization, in turn, of its several elements is not enough.

A mixed economy policy requires, in fact, a more thorough planning than a plain economic nomism would. For, the State has not only to determine the proper sphere of each type of organization; it has also to see that the different types do not work at cross purposes; that they not only "coexist" but cooperate for the public good. It has to create conditions in each type which may make its maximum contribution without frustrating others.

What type of enterprise do we want to dominate the handicraft marketing sector as a matter of long-term policy?

This involves a fundamental policy decision on which all subsidiary decisions should be based. We should clearly visualize the organizational pattern we want to bring into being in the long run. And every specific measure of State intervention, regulation and promotion should be related to it. An odd assortment of unprincipled and uncoordinated schemes might only damage the working harmony, such as it is, of the existing framework without either reforming it or replacing it.

In order to fix the role of different types of agencies in the handicraft marketing field we should: 1. examine the present situation, for that would indicate the limits of what could be done, and 2. discuss the inherent competence of each to " deliver the goods" to those we want to benefit on terms which we consider fair.

It is a pity that an accurate, or even reasonably correct, quantitative estimate of the relative share of private, State and cooperative enterprise in the handicraft trade cannot be given. The relevant statistics are simply not available. Nevertheless, we have made an attempt to arrive at some rough estimates from the meagre data available and from our own field investigations in selected areas.

The total value of handicraft output may be indirectly estimated as follows:

	Rs. in crores	*Source*
Production of "small enterprises"	910	Final Report of the National Income Committee.
Less : Production of "small industries" akin to or allied with large industries	303.3	Report of the Reserve Bank Committee on Finance for the Private Sector
Less: Production of handloom cloth	185	Handloom Weaving Industry 1952-53 Annual.
Less: Production of khadi and industries	172.2	Planning for Full Employment Report of the All India Khadi & Village Industries Board.
Production of small enterprises in industries other than handloom, village and small industries	249.5	

Making allowance for other non-handicraft industries, we may estimate the total value of handicraft production to be at least Rs. 100 crores. The total value of handicraft production in the areas visited by the Team has been estimated by us at Rs. 31.1 crores.[1] On this basis too, total handicraft output should be at least Rs. 100 crores. Assuming handicraft production to be at least Rs. 1,000 crores, cooperative and public marketing do not seem to be handling more than 3 per cent of it. For, the total sales of industrial societies other than weavers' societies was Rs. 2.36 crores on 30.6.1952.[2] And the total sales of public emporia during the last five years have averaged only Rs. 82.0 lakhs. Since the sales of industrial cooperatives include numerous articles other than handicrafts and the sales of public emporia include handloom fabrics, the sales of handicrafts proper should be much less than Rs. 3.18 (2.36 plus 0.82) crores.

Thus over 97 per cent of handicraft production is handled by private agencies, not more than 2 percent by cooperative agencies and not more than 1 per cent by public marketing agencies.

Quantitatively, the role of private enterprise in the field of handicraft marketing has been and still is today so overwhelmingly important that there is little prospect in the near future of supplanting it or even reducing it to an insignificantly small size. The entry of public and cooperative enterprises in this field is a recent development and so far neither has captured a sizable sector of the market. Moreover, owing to the peculiar drawbacks of public and cooperative enterprise it is likely that in spite of all criticism, in spite of unfair competition from them, private enterprise will continue to hold its own and handle the bulk of handicraft output for a long time to come.

We draw attention to the preponderance of private enterprise not with a view to recommending it in principle. On the contrary, we have concluded from our field studies all over the country, without any *a priori* prejudice against it, that whatever be its intrinsic merit, whatever the service it may have rendered in the past, at present it has degenerated into a purely parasitic phenomenon. It exists mainly on the sweat and suffering of the working artisans. It has not shown any concern for their continued employment or minimum well-being nor any foresight and sense of responsibility for the future of handicrafts. It has failed to meet the challenge of competition through a radical adaptation of production to changing conditions; instead it has responded to it by intensifying the exploitation of the workers through wage reductions, sharp practices and unfair deductions. It has played the self-stultifying game of making quick, speculative profits by deliberately lowering quality standards, using bad and adulterated materials, cutting sizes and dimensions, and supplying goods of shoddy quality inferior to the approved samples. Thus it has damaged the reputation of Indian handicrafts abroad and impaired their long-term prospects. It has failed even to bear the normal risks and responsibilities of marketing. The burden of financing the movement of goods has been passed on by it to the artisans through the increasing use of the system of consignment purchase and late payments. And such finance as it has had, has been used for usury at the expense of the craftsmen. There are a few exceptional dealers in every craft, but their existence only throws the shady activities of the ruling majority into bold relief.

We thus confront a difficult situation. We have to face the fact that neither the fate of the artisans nor the future of handicrafts can safely be left in the keeping of middlemen and yet the quantitative supremacy of private enterprise will compel us to accept its continuance for a long time.

Extremism of any kind obviously cannot meet the situation. In spite of its serious failings the continued existence of private enterprise has to be accepted. But its working must be reformed partly through legislation, partly through persuasion and voluntary discipline by recognised dealers' associations. The Government has to provide certain facilities to help the dealers to improve their production and extend their markets. These should include an inspection service, a publicity service, a technical extension service, a design service and a market intelligence service. A combination of these measures should enable the private sector to overcome its deficiencies and continue to play its due part in handicraft marketing. These measures are discussed in greater detail in subsequent chapters.

Reaction against the weaknesses of private enterprise should not, however, produce an unthinking enthusiasm for State enterprise. For, in the first place, the marketing of consumer goods, specially consumer goods which are not articles of necessity for the masses, is normally considered to be a legitimate field for private enterprise even in socialist thought. The total field of retail trade is so vast that it would be nearly impossible for any government to set up a centralized apparatus to manage it. In large countries it is vaster still. By its very nature retail trade has to be dispersed and decentralized. And the kind of service which retailers are supposed to render to consumers is not one which government administrations are equipped to render. In view of this, the entry of Government in the handicraft trade, as in retail trade in general, has to be specially justified. It is clear that in principle, and in the long run, there is no justification for it. This should be borne in mind by all those who would seem to think that the substitution of State enterprise for private enterprise is in itself desirable in every field; and that, therefore, for the improvement of handicraft marketing all that is required is that government agencies take the place of private middlemen.

Secondly, State enterprise has its own inherent weaknesses. It is quite possible that the substitution of State enterprise for private enterprise may not improve the situation at all. The same deficiencies may continue to exist, may even be aggravated. The authorities may conceal or explain away the same old bad practices with the help of a new terminology.

As the Report on the Efficient Conduct of State Enterprises by Mr. A.D. Gorwala points out:

A public enterprise from its very nature is subject to certain important handicaps which need not arise in private business.
Since the public enterprise is to be financed by government, the importance of accurate estimates and prompt action is often not sufficiently appreciated. Again, for the same reason of lack of personal risk, important matters are likely to be treated as routine and dealt with in a dilatory fashion. The direction and management in private enterprise is generally more personal and has a great deal at stake in the success of the concern. It will also often be experienced and continuous. As against this, the management and direction of a public enterprise will generally be impersonal, and occasionally even detached. Since most public enterprises are new, often it will be inexperienced. If, moreover, the enterprise is run as a government department or permanent government servants are employed in it, the likelihood of changes in personnel due to transfer, promotion, etc., is also bound to be great. Again the authority running a public enterprise is not likely to be able to use his own discretion to the same extent as the director in charge of a private concern; while the latter is autonomous, the former is generally controlled. Rules and regulations in the matter of appointment, promotion, reduction, dismissal are bound to be more rigid in a government-owned and managed enterprise than in a private concern, built up on the bases of "hiring and firing". A further disadvantage from the business point of view that a public enterprise has to bear is the insistence on the Government being a model employer.

In the government emporia established so far for the marketing of cottage industries products, the full impact of all these handicaps can be felt.

They are incurring inordinately heavy expenses on establishment and overheads on the strength of government grants. The prices of similar goods are not only not lower but even higher than in the market. Nor are the margins lower. They often buy and sell through the very same middlemen whom they are supposed to replace. Their losses are explained away and debited to the exchequer. Design and process monopolies are created and preserved with public money. The treatment of artisans is no better in respect of wages, general behaviour and promptitude of payment than in the past. The system of consignment purchase is preserved and extended. Purchase procedures provide many opportunities for undesirable discrimination.

Thus government enterprise would need no less reformation than private enterprise in order to prove its positive enterprise. So far the case for it is merely negative : it rests on the failure of private enterprise. It should first prove in practice that it can render a more efficient and cheaper marketing service before any attempt is made by it to replace private enterprise. In other words it should offer a "quality competition" rather than a "volume competition" to private business. Expansion in the volume of business will follow inevitably (provided funds are available), if there is improvement in the efficiency of the marketing service. There is no reason why consumers and artisans would not be eager to avail of the service of government agencies rather than private middlemen if it is better. But a mere increase in the number of government marketing agencies, without a proved superiority in actual functioning, may only create the illusion of progress without doing much real good.

Thus the role indicated for government enterprise is transitional and twofold. First, it should set new standards of marketing service and influence the private trade by a quality competition, to reform itself. Then it should pave the way for cooperative enterprise which, in our opinion, should dominate handicraft production and marketing in the long run.

Almost universally, cooperation is now accepted as the best form of organization for handicraft marketing and production. It is, therefore, unnecessary to dwell upon its merits in detail. We may only cite the following passage, from an ILO study,[3] in which the case for the cooperative marketing of handicrafts is succinctly set out.

> In addition to facilitating the solution of problems of production, cooperative organization provides a well-established and proved instrument in all questions concerning the search for remunerative and stable markets. Efficient marketing requires capital, knowledge of the market, the capacity to wait, the establishment of standards of quality, the ability to keep in touch with technical progress and readiness to change products to suit changes in consumers' tastes. In the sale of most products this is a specialized and full-time occupation, and the inability of the individual craftsmen to give sufficient attention to this aspect of economic activity has generally been the cause of his economic subservience to the trader and the entrepreneur. The problems associated with marketing, though relatively simple when production is for the immediate needs of the village, increase immensely in complexity as soon as the boundaries of trade are

enlarged, and become especially intricate where production is for export. Through cooperative organization in marketing, the small producer and artisan are enabled to give full attention to their normal work while drawing the benefits of efficient and large-scale trade, supervised by trained and paid employees specializing in this branch. Cooperative marketing of the products manufactured by individual artisans or in the small factory is essential to the process of cooperative production.

The promotion of cooperative enterprise is, however, beset with numerous difficulties of its own. But there can be no doubt that a cooperative structure should be the ultimate aim of policy in this field for sociological as well as practical reasons.

On the whole the policy indicated is: (1) that the working of private enterprise has to be accepted for a long time, and has to be reformed, (2) that government enterprise has to be extended to cover the transition, because of the centralization of initiative and financial capacity in the hands of the State that has already taken place and (3) that ultimately there is little to choose between these two either from the point of view of the welfare of craftsmen or the future of handicrafts and, therefore, the objective should be to have in due course a network of production and marketing cooperatives at all levels to take the place of the merchants and take over the management of government depots and emporia. It is in the light of this basic preference that all our specific recommendations have been made.

II. CENTRAL COTTAGE INDUSTRIES EMPORIUM

"One of the biggest operations of the ICU has been in the field of handicrafts. The domestic marketing outlet for handicrafts managed by the ICU is the Central Cottage Industries Emporium in New Delhi. This is the only shop of its kind in India where handicraft goods and handloom fabrics from every corner of the country are displayed and sold." (from *Ten Eventful Years - ICU*)

Historical Background

The independence of India in 1947 opened a new chapter in the life of the traditional crafts and craftsmen who under the foreign rule had suffered from gross neglect. The national Government initiated a countrywide programme for the encouragement and development of crafts. The twin objectives of this programme were to preserve the traditional craftsmanship and excellence of skill as a part of national heritage, and to help the crafts to find a secure place in the developing national economy. Several measures were adopted by the Government to advance these objectives. One of the important and urgent needs of almost all the crafts in the country was in the field of marketing of their products. It was in this background that in 1948 the Government established the Central Cottage Industries Emporium with the object of developing a market for cottage industries products

During the first four years, 1948-52, the Emporium was run and managed departmentally by the Union Ministry of Commerce and Industry. By 1952, the Emporium was able to achieve an annual sales of only Rs. 2.50 lakhs, and was running at a loss. Departmental management was considered to be one of the principal factors for this poor performance. In the interest of rapid development and expansion of handicrafts the Government decided to entrust the management to an experienced non-official organization interested in the welfare of the craftsmen and in the development of handicrafts. The ICU was chosen. The Government called upon it to take over the management of the Emporium.

Enters ICU

ICU took over the management of the Emporium in November 1952 and immediately initiated a series of steps to push up the sales and to eliminate operating losses. The ICU managed the Emporium for about 12 years from 1952 to 1964. During this period the sales rose by over 30 times from Rs. 2.50 lakhs to Rs. 80.17 lakhs. The Emporium also became self-supporting, meeting not only its operating costs but also development expenses. From a tiny sales depot in 1952 the Emporium soon developed into the largest single emporium in the country with an extensive international reputation. Today the Emporium additionally serves as a show-window for foreign tourists and importers visiting the country. In recent years exporters and importers have increasingly used the Emporium as a ready reference for the best in existing handicrafts and an indicator of future possibilities. Indeed many importers have established direct business relationships with the Emporium.

What were some of the main factors behind this impressive growth? The first step taken by the ICU was to provide the Emporium with a dynamic set-up alive to the need for providing to the craftspersons an assured and exporting market. Apart from its own resources of experienced workers to guide and run the Emporium (including Kitty Shiva Rao, Tejivir Singh, Prem Bery, Krishna Kapur, N.N. Datta, Bharat Sahay, R. Kalyansundaram, the ICU invited distinguished persons from trade, industry and public life (including Bharat Ram (DCM), K.A.D. Naoroji (Tatas), G.D. Mehra (Burmah Shell) M.A. Sreedhar (Dastur & Co.), Fori Nehru, Pupul Jayakar, Shrimati Indira Gandhi and representatives of handloom/ handicrafts industrial cooperatives) to serve on the Managing Committee. The Committee was vested with the power of laying down broad policies, setting targets, approving the annual programme and budgets, and reviewing the working results from month to month. Powers relating to purchases, production, pricing, selling, appointment of staff were vested fully with the principal executives. The administrative, financial and other operating procedures were subjected to a constant review, with the help of national and international experts, and brought in line with the most advanced department stores in the world. The Emporium was enrolled as a member of the National Retail Merchants' Association of the USA to enable it to have access to the operating results of about 200 topmost retail stores in the USA, on a continuous basis. The Marketing Research Corporation of India's services were used for periodic marketing research, and those of IBCON-Management consultants for organizational and pay structure.

Second, the efforts to provide the Emporium with good management were combined with a ceaseless drive to select, procure, design, develop and produce the best merchandise for sale at the Emporium. A group of buyers backed by designers were trained for this purpose. Their job was to visit producers in different parts of the country at frequent intervals and to select quality merchandise, and to advise and assist the producers in designing and making modified and new products to suit the market. To gain insight into the problems of production and to absorb the initial risks of promoting products based on new designs the Emporium started a Production Centre of its own, backed by a designers group which included Riten Mazumdar, Prithvish Neogy, Shona Ray, Seena Kaul, Suman Benegal, Una Kathpalia, Maya Seth, Malvika Nakra. Periodic exhibitions were held to popularize new designs and to create consumer interest in the new merchandise.

Third, simultaneous attention was paid to assist the producers in the far corners of the country with market information. The knowledge of the market which they have through direct contact was furnished to them periodically and first hand by the buyers of the Emporium. The buyers themselves were kept regularly informed of the market trends through a system of detailed analysis of sales of various products, sales during various seasons, and sales response of domestic and foreign customers to different products.

Fourth, the terms of trade were substantially altered to benefit the producers. Until 1952 the Emporium used to procure all merchandise on consignment basis which meant that the producers had not only to finance the marketing organization (through goods) but also to bear the risk of unsold goods. The ICU found that in many cases this was due primarily to insufficient time given by the purchasing agencies to the producers which often led to cancellation of orders, loss of business and criticism of craftsmen. The ICU remedied this situation by formulating a sales budget in advance for the coming year and allowing sufficient time for the producers. The sales budget also enabled the Emporium to carry adequate stocks in anticipation of sales and thus ensuring the fulfilment of its sales target besides helping the producers.

Fifth, there was emphasis on attracting consumers. The showroom itself was renovated frequently. Special display artists were appointed for presentation of the merchandise. Fixtures were so designed as to enable the customers to handle the merchandise directly and with ease. The Emporium was the first retail outlet to introduce price marking of all merchandise giving a sense of security to the customers, something unknown particularly in the field of handicrafts. The selling terms and practices were brought in line with the best of department stores in the world. Special customer services were provided which included overseas shipment, gift wrapping, gift coupons, custom-made articles. Other conveniences provided sought to enlarge the Emporium as not merely a shopping centre but also a social civic centre by adding a cafeteria, flower shop, art gallery, selected books and phonograph records and assisting cultural organizations/theatre groups with sales of their tickets. A sustained and vigorous programme of publicity and exhibitions kept the Emporium itself and its special merchandise always in the public consciousness. The Emporium is identified in the public mind with its mascot, the Bankura horse from Bengal.

Expansion of sales area, sales and service staff and other essential facilities were carried out swiftly at different stages to take advantage of the sales potential and targets. Initially, the Government provided help in the expansion, subsidies towards rent and interest charges and developmental grants towards publicity, designing, market research and training. By 1961, the ICU had succeeded in making the Emporium financially self-supporting and subsidies and grants were discontinued.

Over the years, therefore, the Emporium has developed a successful management team and an attractive and efficient enterprise where both products and marketing have a tremendous variety and are capable of change. The Emporium has emerged as a market leader. It is a model for all other such enterprises, and many emporia in the country have drawn on the experience and training facilities of the Emporium.

ICU Steps Out

In 1963, the ICU concluded that it was time for it to withdraw from the management of the Emporium. The reasons for the decision outlined in a memorandum to the Government of India in August 1963 were :

> On 31st October, 1963, it would be exactly 12 years since the Government entrusted the management of the Central Cottage Industries Emporium to the ICU under a special Agreement.

During these 12 years the Emporium has registered a phenomenal growth both in terms of volume of sales which have risen from Rs. 2.5 lakhs a year to Rs. 70 lakhs a year, as well as in the extension of its services of designing, production, market research besides retail sales. From a small sales depot it has now become the leading handicrafts emporium in India. It has also earned a good standing and reputation both within the country and abroad. There are other aspects of it which have grown correspondingly with its sales and service. From an initial working capital of Rs. 2 lakhs it now has a working capital of nearly Rs. 18 lakhs. the number of its employees has risen from about 20 to about 350. its business contacts and contracts have multiplied manifold.

In the initial period when the management of the Emporium was entrusted by the Government to the ICU the Emporium's inability to pay its own way was recognized by the Government. Accordingly stipulations were made for losses being written off by the Government during the first-three years (although this did not become necessary) and the Government providing (a) rent-free accommodation and (b) interest free working capital loans in the initial years. The Government also provided development grants for promotional work, expansion and improvements.

During the last two years, however, the Emporium has become a fully self-supporting institution. Interest free loans and rent-free accommodation have been given up and the Emporium is now paying rent at the economic rate and interest at 4.75 per cent to the Government. Development activities are now being financed from the revenues of the Emporium itself and grants for these have been discontinued.

Furthermore the emporium has reached a stage where it has a promise of great expansion in the coming years. Consequently, its responsibility as provider of regular and continuous employment to the thousands of craftsmen in the country will increase in the coming years. Correspondingly, its responsibilities in terms of capital, contracts with suppliers, employees, etc., will further increase. It is, therefore, time that there was an overall review of the position of the Emporium and the future role of the ICU in relation to the Emporium.

Twelve years ago, the Emporium was at a very nascent stage. The Government had then sought the services of the ICU to develop the Emporium and to expand it into a vigorous marketing centre. As will be seen from the review of the growth in the last 12 years outlines above the task assigned to the ICU has been well achieved and foundations have been laid for its continued expansion. The Government must, therefore, consider whether the services of the ICU are at all required any further. The ICU on its own part would like that the Government should now take over the Emporium and run it under its own auspices or convert it into a legal entity of its own in such form as the Government may determine.

In suggesting this, the ICU is also guided by the fact that it is a voluntary service organization, the aim of which is to assist in the development of such projects as serve the need of deserving communities like farmers, craftsmen, slum-dwellers, etc. Without any financial interest in the profits of the Emporium and purely acting on the service motive the ICU has put in 12 years of sustained work to raise the Emporium to its present level. Under the present arrangement the Government is the owner of the Emporium but the responsibility for contracting loans, etc. and meeting losses is that of the ICU. One of the conditions of the Emporium loans is that all the assets of the entire ICU remain mortgaged to the Government. The loans required for the Emporium are to be met out of the authorized maximum credit limit of the ICU. In the beginning when the Emporium was taken over by the ICU, everything was on such a small scale that these points did not matter. But these are now acting to restrict the scope of expansion of other important activities of the ICU in the field of rural development, research, social welfare, etc. Moreover, the relationship between the Government and the ICU in the matter of management of the Emporium is determined by three months' notice clause by either side. Considering the large responsibility and stakes involved in an institution of this size and importance, such a provision is not at all conducive to stability. A sense of insecurity persists amongst the producers, suppliers and staff which must be removed in the interest of its secure and sustained growth.

The Government accepted the ICU's recommendations and a new body, the Central Cottage Industries Association, exclusively devoted to the management and development of the Emporium was created which took over the management of the Emporium from the ICU in July 1964. The ICU repaid the entire loan of Rs. 18.16 lakhs as well as transferred to the new Association the excess of Rs. 66,821.35 of assets over liabilities.

The ICU also handed over to the Association its Export Section, the tourist shops at Santa Cruz Airport, Bombay, Palam Airport, New Delhi and the Ashok Hotel, as well as auxiliary services attached to the Emporium, Mallika Flower Shop, Bankura Cafe, Rachana Records and Book Shop and the Kunika Art Centre.

Postscript

The Emporium's sales in 1994-95 had exceeded Rs. 33 crore and it has set up large branch emporia in Bombay, Calcutta, Madras, Bangalore and Hyderabad (Secunderabad). In New Delhi, 1995, it moved out of the old army barracks to its own new spacious premises in Janpath.

NOTES

1. See appendix at the end of the chapter.
2. Report of the Reserve Bank Committee on Finance for the Private Sector, p.162
3. Possibilities of Cooperative Organization, International Labour Review, December, 1950

APPENDIX

SUMMARY STATEMENT SHOWING ESTIMATED PRODUCTION AND EMPLOYMENT IN SELECTED HANDICRAFT CENTRES

Name of the Craft	Estimated Production (Rs. in lakhs)	Estimated
1. Dyeing and Printing	690.71	35,235
2. Floor Covering	535.10	38,260
3. Brocades	617.00	60,610
4. Ivory Carving	10.30	892
5. Potteries	3.80	740
6. Papier Mache	2.40	310
7. Horn Articles	0.90	250
8. Toys	7.19	1,195
9. Wood Carving and Inlay	11.95	1,516
10. Metal Ware	892.18	209,325
11. Mats and Matting (fine only)	5.63	1,910
12. Silver Filigree	2.62	310
13. Leather Art Goods	25.35	1,195
14. Shell Work	9.00	1,400
15. Chikan Work	10.00	2,000
16. Embroidery and Zari Embroidery	290.21	10,000
Total	3,114.34	365,148

12

CONSUMER COOPERATIVES
(A Chain of Super Bazaars)

DEMON OF HIGH PRICES FINDS ITS MATCH

> The first salvo in the people's fight against high prices was fired with the opening of Super Bazaar in New Delhi on Friday. Thousands of people, bubbling with enthusiasm, flocked towards the multi-storey building to see the first big cooperative department store in the capital.
> It was a grand show by all standards. For the first time in recent months people had the thrill of buying goods at prices cheaper than they had got used to. The time-consuming ritual of inauguration was dispensed with. The people themselves were the VIPs. Mercifully there were no speeches, no tape to cut. The National Anthem was played and rose petals – 10 maunds in all – were showered on the jostling jubilant crowd.
>
> *The Statesman, 15th July, 1996*

FOR a long time the ICU had planned to promote a chain of consumer cooperative stores to help the people to have some control over prices and quality. It conducted a survey of retail trade in Delhi in the early 60s. Its findings were accepted by the Government. At the time the ICU had also submitted a scheme for a consumer owned chain of super markets to make a dent on the monopoly of the private trade in consumer goods. This scheme lay with the Government till the devaluation of the rupee in 1966.

In 1966, the Indian Cooperative Union took a big hand to place the consumers cooperative movement on a completely new and dynamic footing through the establishment of the largest ever consumer department store in the country, namely Super Bazaar at Delhi.[1] It liberated the cooperative consumer stores from the practice of being mere retailers of rationed goods. Indeed, it decided to sell only non-rationed items and thus made an emphatic entry in the market which was hitherto the monopoly of the private trade. It decided also to challenge many anti-consumer practices of the private trade such as retail price maintenance, unreasonably high margins, often no fixed prices and uncertain quality. To sustain the impetus, Super Bazaar developed means for systematic, widespread and updated information on prices for the consumers. It decided also not merely to compete with private retail trade but also to become a market leader on the strength of innovations in every aspect of its operations.

One immediate indication of its impact was the swift multiplier effect – many large department stores sprung up across the country within the first year and private business also approached Super Bazaar for counselling. A number of market associations in Delhi approached it for "recognition" in terms of approved quality and prices. At the policy level, the Fifth Plan became the first plan to recognize the crucial importance of large department stores in influencing the trade in consumer goods and called for the setting up of "50 large department stores".

The circumstances and manner in which the pioneer consumer cooperative store, Super Bazaar, came to be set up by the ICU and the various "firsts" it scored in innovations make a fascinating story which is recounted here, also for the added reason that it is of great instructive value to those concerned with the development and direction of the public distribution system.

The devaluation of the rupee in June 1966 led to an excruciating spurt in the prices which caused serious concern to Prime Minister Smt. Indira Gandhi who had in any case been widely criticized including within the Congress Party for allegedly yielding to the World Bank/IMF pressure for devaluation.

The ICU was approached to take some practical and urgent steps to combat rising prices. It was like "summons" from the Prime Minister, said Inder Gujral and Romesh Thapar – the PM's two emissaries to the ICU General Secretary L. C. Jain. The latter expressed reluctance on account of the ICU's past sad experience in helping the Government. "Forget the past", said Gujral, "this government means business". Later, N.K. Seshan, Special Assistant to the PM, phoned to reiterate the Prime Minister's serious concern and commitment to back up the ICU's efforts. It was followed by a meeting with C. Subramaniam, then Agriculture Minister. He approved, across the table, the ICU's strategy to set up a large Consumer Cooperative Store (named Super Bazaar – Apna Bazaar), in Delhi, to start with, to be followed rapidly by a network in major towns. These stores were to serve as an alternative for the consumer and as a social brake on the unbridled trade.

But the Minister wanted to know: how soon? The ICU said it could do it all within two weeks – 15 days to be exact – provided the required government support was "delivered" to the ICU within two days and at its doorstep – rather than the ICU having to go round the corridors of the Government as an applicant; and provided there was no interference by Government in either business matters or in appointments. "Go ahead" said the Minister. He designated a senior official, S. Venkitaramanan, (who later became Reserve Bank Governor) on behalf of the Government to assist the ICU in the prosecution of the project. It was a unique experience for the ICU – the Minister and Venkitaramanan were true to their word – and delivered to the ICU some of the toughest facilities with an electric speed.

The most important was finding a suitable building ready for use. The New Delhi Municipal Committee (NDMC) backed by the Home Ministry resolutely refused to part with the building where Super Bazaar in New Delhi is located (next to the Shankar Market). Within 24 hours the possession of the building with about 100,000 sq. ft. covered area was made over to the ICU after Subramaniam called an inter-ministerial meeting late at night at his residence. S.C. Chabbra, the then NDMC President, was bitter but later when the Super Bazaar opened on the appointed day, he was the first to exult with joy and extend full support.

The second was finding adequate capital. The cooperative store needed cash credit limit of Rs. 1 crore to procure and stock. The sum was too big for the cooperative bank and no other bank (including State Bank of India) was willing to provide this facility. Two days were already lost in chasing these banks. Their plea was: they had no experience of such a business. But, nor did anyone else in the country. Someone had to dare. Desperate, the ICU apprised Subramaniam, who promptly spoke to T.A. Pai, Chairman, Syndicate Bank, and the latter agreed to fly overnight with his officials from Manipal to Delhi – as that Bank did not have a branch in Delhi or in North India as a whole at the time except a tiny office in Asaf Ali Road. On arrival the next day the first thing K.K. Pai, General Manager of the Bank, did was to hand over a cheque book to N.N. Datta, ICU Secretary incharge of setting up the Super Bazaar and told him he could issue cheques upto Rs. one crore from that moment. "What about the formalities for opening the account", asked Datta. "All that can be done later in the evening", Pai said.

The Bank's Branch Manager, P.S.V. Malliah (who later rose to be the Chairman of the Syndicate Bank) was installed next to the office of the Super Bazaar General Manager. The relationship was cemented further as Super Bazaar provided 4,000 sq. ft. rent-free accommodation to the Bank (and later faced adverse audit comments on that !) which extended timely and adequate credit (including advances to producers supplying to the Super Bazaar) making it the smoothest experience ever. The bank staff used to sit up past midnight to collect the daily sales proceeds running into lakhs of rupees and in thousands of small coins. It set new precedents for a banker-borrower relationship.

Meanwhile, within 48 hours, Venkitramanan had delivered GOI's cheque for Rs. 16 lakhs towards the share capital grant/loan.

Fourth was protection from government interference. What he did even more remarkably and resolutely was to shield the Cooperative Store from pressures from Ministers, MPs, Civil servants for appointment of their nominees on the staff of the Super Bazaar. About 1,500 persons were initially recruited within the first 10 days.

Fifth, backing the Cooprative Store in its struggles with monopoly houses. Because of this solid backing by Subramanian and Shri Venkitaramanan it became possible also to withstand pressures from powerful suppliers and on their behalf from various ministries. Example: Super Bazaar had decided not to accept any supplies from any source which insisted on Retail Price Maintenance (RPM), i.e. the manufacturer fixing the minimum rather than the maximum retail price. Hindustan Lever (HL) was one of the giants which insisted on RPM clause but Super Bazaar stuck to its policy and declined to retail its product Dalda though it was a popular brand of vegetable oil. HL walked out of Datta's office in a huff, but another vegetable oil producer, DCM agreed to supply Rath on Super Bazaar terms. Within a week Rath sales skyrocketed. HL complained to the Commissioner, Consumer Supplies, in the Commerce Ministry, who, believe it or not, took the side of the giants (who wanted to fix the minimum rather than the maximum retail price!), summoned Super Bazaar, General Manager, Datta, and asked that Super Bazaar should abide by RPM in the interest of the consumers ! Datta said sorry, "Super Bazaar's view in this matter was the very opposite, it wants to break RPM". When the Commissioner persisted and pressed harder, Super Bazaar sought Venkitaramanan's help. That put an end to the Commissioner's zeal. Soon Hindustan Lever were knocking at the Super Bazaar's door for an entry on the latter's terms.

Sixth, then there was a politically delicate matter which if not sorted out would have robbed the Super Bazaar of a thrilling start. Subramaniam was proud that as promised the Super Bazaar's opening ceremony will be on dot, on 15 July, 1966. He had asked Indira Gandhi to inaugurate it – and she had agreed. The ICU General Secretary, L. C. Jain, Chairman of the Super Bazaar suggested to the Minister that it would be better to have the inauguration by "the first customer" who entered the Super

Bazaar at 5 p.m., the scheduled time, rather than by the Prime Minister. Subramaniam saw the force of the idea. We do not know what he did but he did change the commitment he had made to the Prime Minister. An hour before the store was to open there were milling uncontrollable crowds of consumers. The police chief said he had no other alternative but to *lathi-charge* them. *Lathi Charge!* We were aghast. How could the store open with a lathi-charge. We said, No. We had a better alternative. We advanced the opening by an hour. When the store opened it became difficult to identify who the first customer was who took the Prime Minister's place, for, there was a stampede. Hundreds made a bid to be the first! Smashing dozens of show windows and counters! The stampede, however, put a stamp on the fact that the cooperative store was *of* the consumers and not only *for* them.

Now a look at the major steps and innovations by the Super Bazar Management. Within a week, the ICU was organized and registered, the Delhi Consumer Cooperative Society, to start the consumer department store.

The initial planning, organization and leadership was provided by the ICU which had gained considerable experience of retail marketing during the period it managed and developed the Central Cottage Industries Emporium. The ICU constituted a core management team drawn from the ICU and Emporium to set up and manage the Super Bazaar, comprising of its most experienced organizers and marketing experts, including, N.N. Datta, B.L. Dhar, Teji Vir Singh, Gulshan Nanda, Kamala Rana, V.P. Gulati, G.R. Sehgal and Pritam Lal. This team was reinforced by a new entrant, Margaret Alva.

To assist this management team, a Work Study Team was set up to analyse and remedy the operational problems on a *daily* basis, comprising Col. Brij Mohan (on loan from Defence Ministry), D.N. Chabbra (Chartered Accountant on loan from Burmah Shell), Prof. D.D. Joshi (Operational Research, Agra University), C.H.S. Jhabwala – architect who designed the layout of the store and B.L. Dhar from the management.

Being the first of its kind was not a matter of all glory. There were problems galore for lack of past experience to fall back upon. The most baffling of these problems the management team faced was to hazard a guess about the volume of sales in the first year. For, on that estimate depended the build-up of stocks, the size of staff to be recruited, capital to be raised and other facilities. After agonising debates, the team settled on a sales target of Rs. 5 crores for the first year. It was principally arrived at by postulating estimated monthly purchases of major groups of items:

groceries, vegetables and fruits, textiles, drugs, household goods by a lower middle class family. Certain assumptions were made about the number of such families who may shop at the Super Bazaar. The actual sales at the end of the first year were Rs. 4.8 crores against the target of Rs. 5 crores.

The most formidable challenge before the Super Bazaar management was setting its selling price right – since its aim was to subdue any unwarranted price rise. It decided that without any compromise with quality, its selling prices for all items must be not only lower than the prevailing market prices but must also be seen to be so by the consumers. It had also to figure out what items to stock and how many needs of the consumers to meet. It hit upon a strategy of "comparative shopping". Certain retail markets were identified (such as Paharganj, Karol Bagh, etc.) which were regarded by the consumers as being relatively cheaper. Some days before the Super Bazaar was to open, its staff from the purchase department (called "buyers") were given a budget of Rs.15,000 to purchase common consumer items against cash memos from these selected markets. The cash memos were analysed for price levels and price trends, itemwise.

The quality of the items was also considered. The cash memos were locked away as proof of prevailing prices – in case the Super Bazaar prices were to be challenged by private trade.

This exercise also imparted first-hand knowledge to the newly recruited staff of the purchase department called "buyers", as to the type and range of the goods the consumers required, besides the first-hand knowledge of quality available in the market.

The "buyers" then had their challenge defined for them in terms of what to stock and at what prices to buy which would enable them to fix the selling prices below the prevailing market level; and what would be the margin available between their purchase cost and selling price. Thus, they acquired the price phobia which was to prove to be the ultimate key to success.

Since the number and range of items dealt by the "buyers" ran into thousands, it was recognized that the controls could not be manual. ICT which was engaged to computerise accounts and inventories were asked also to provide critical computerized information to the management and to the "buyers" in particular on a *daily* basis itemwise. The information was to include : stock in hand of a particular item, what proportion of it was in the store-room, what proportion at the sales counter, how much quantity sold the previous day and the balance at the sales counter at the start of business the next day. Adequate stocking of the right goods at the sales counter was the name of the game.

Initially, the Super Bazaar found it very difficult to enter the drug retail business without specialized knowledge and infinite precautions and vigilance. It sought and was able to obtain advice and assistance from a reputed chemists firm (Nath Bros). Once started, the Super Bazaar drug store became the largest retail outlet in Delhi. It was also the first to open 24 hours; and soon the first to set up branches at the premier government hospitals.

Same pattern was followed to enter text-book retailing. It decided to seek advice from a reputed firm (Ramakrishna Book Sellers) to set up the largest outlet for school text-books and notebooks for students at reasonable prices.

Retailing vegetables and fruits was a tougher nut to crack because wholesale trade in these perishable commodities is in the hands of a few large operators who work as a cartel and no new entrants can walk in. To start with, the ICU used its own contacts with neighbouring villages where it had been working with farmers and vegetable growers and through their help developed an alternative supply source. This was backed up by taking on lease 200 acres of DDA Park area for growing quality vegetables to have a captive source of supply. Once its retail sales picked up, its supply sources broadened. The accurate weighing, washing and packaging of vegetables made it consumer easy.

Another tough nut to crack was the wholesale market in groceries specially pulses and spices which are very vulnerable to adulteration. Here the Super Bazaar decided to place the control of procurement and purchase in the hands of some of the most trusted public workers of Delhi (Roop Narain and Memobai of unimpeachable integrity) supported by professional managers. Women's voluntary groups and cooperatives came forward with organizing processing and packaging of spices. And, all these were again tested by the independent lab, sponsored by the Super Bazaar.

Textile wholesale trade is equally closed to new entrants. Super Bazaar had decided to have three large sales/showrooms one each for mill cloth, handlooms and khadi. Supplies of khadi and handlooms presented no difficulties. But given its trading channels and practices, mill cloth was a tricky business. Again, Super Bazaar, had to use a contact in the trade to assist it to fathom the intricacies. The department was placed under Viswa Nath, an ICU Board Member representing consumer cooperatives and who had some familiarity with the textile trade practices.

Industries Corporation whose function was to assist Small Scale Producers to avail of the Super Bazaar's marketing facilities.

ITC were engaged to computerize the entire inventory and daily sales to maintain full control over what is stocked, how much and to monitor stock/sales ratios for an effective cost reduction on account of inventory. It was the first organization in India to install computers for sale and inventory control.

To maintain up-to-date accounts, the accounting department's supervision was entrusted to a firm of Chartered Accountants, other than the auditors.

While on the ICU's suggestion, the Government acquired from the New Delhi Municipal Committee the five-storey building adjacent to the Shanker Market for the department store, it was an expensive location and the rental burden was expected be high. To ease the rent burden, the Super Bazaar worked out a formula : fixed rent of Rs.5 lakhs a year plus one per cent commission on sales to be paid to NDMC. NDMC agreed to the terms. Soon after, the Super Bazaar licensed the frontage of the building to advertising agencies for display, which brought an income of Rs.5 lakhs annually thus earning an amount equal to the fixed rent!

The moral is that to keep the prices down, the cost of operations, cost of credit, cost of inventory were all kept down and concentration on goods other than rationed goods vastly broadened the consumer base yielding high volume and fast turnover.

Postscript

A view of the present status of the Super Bazaar is provided by the Annual Report, Ministry of Civil Supplies, Consumer Affairs and Public Distribution, 1994-95)

The Cooperative Stores Ltd., New Delhi, popularly known as the "Super Bazaar" registered in 1966 to serve as a model retail outlet offering a wide range of essential consumer goods of daily use under a single roof with modern retail facilities, today is the largest chain of consumer cooperative outlets in the country. It is running six department stores in Connaught Place, INA market, Patel Nagar, Trilok Puri, Palam and Noida. In addition, it has 155 branches (upto 1994) including 18 drug stores in different parts of the city of which six outlets provide round-the-clock service. The 24 hrs. drug service is of great help to public. It is also operating 37 mobile vans which are exclusively covering villages in different blocks of Delhi. As on 31.3.94 the membership of Super Bazaar was 33,196. The total sales turnover was Rs. 117 crores in the year 1993-94.

The Super Bazaar, has been running in profit since 1972-73, after wiping off its accumulated losses amounting to Rs. 1 crore till 1971-72. The Super Bazaar has been consistently declaring dividend of 6 per cent over the last several years; so far the Government of India has received a total dividend of Rs. 52 lakhs.

Super Bazaar has been making efforts to introduce modern techniques for improving its operations. It has introduced computerization of its sales operations and has installed 28 alpha numerical machines in the sales area of Connaught Place and selected three of its branches. It has plans to cover all its branches likewise.

The quality testing laboratory of the Super Bazaar is rendering a signal service in the field of consumer protection. All consumer goods, particularly edible items sold in the Super Bazaar, are tested for their quality before these are sent to the sales counter.

As a model Consumer Cooperative Store in the Capital, the Super Bazaar has been fixing prices of consumer goods generally at rates lower than those in the open market and has consistently been supplying quality goods. A price list of various items of daily needs is published in the leading newspapers and in monthly bulletins indicating the comparative prices of a large number of consumer articles in Delhi. The Super Bazaar procures manufactured goods as far as possible directly from the manufacturers. It gives preferential treatment to apex cooperatives, State Federations and State Government Corporations for purchases of goods.

The Super Bazaar is playing a leading role in serving the consumers of Delhi by providing them quality goods. It pioneered self-service system in the country which has become very popular and has been adopted by other leading consumer stores in most of the big cities. The Super Bazaar has proved to be an effective instrument in maintaining the supply-line and price-line. With a view to checking the rising prices of fruits and vegetables in the Capital, the Super Bazaar has made adequate arrangements for an extensive sale of these commodities through mobile-van shops, especially to the inhabitants of resettlement colonies and in the rural areas.

NOTE

1. The name Super Bazaar was given by Som Benegal, ICU Secretary.

13

WELFARE

I. RESETTLEMENT OF TIBETAN REFUGEES

IT was in the year 1959 when the first Relief Camp for the Tibetan Refugees was organized at Misamari, the foothill of Assam. Thousands of Tibetan refugees entered India through the hills of Assam along with their God King, His Holiness the Dalai Lama.

The ICU deputed its Director for Rural Development, Gopi Krishna, to help in organizing the camp at Misamari. A small tented city was born overnight. But unfortunately, some of the horses and cattle which they had brought along with them from Tibet died on the way for want of adequate food. The first terrible experience was to see some of the refugees die after taking large quantities of food as they were very hungry and had not taken anything for a number of days while on the run. The ICU was only one of several voluntary organizations which came to Misamari to assist these refugees. The over-all arrangeme'nts including shelter, food and medical assistance were provided by the highly experienced Army units.

After a study made by the ICU along with a representative of the Central Relief Committee a report was submitted to the Government in which it was suggested that the Tibetan refugees should be shifted to some cooler places as they could not bear the heat.

Shifting of Refugees

The authorities decided to shift them to Dalhousie, Chamba, Dharamshala, Simla, Kulu Manali, Palampur, Darjeeling, Kalimpong, Mysore. The ICU decided to help the refugees in shifting from Misamari to other places. The first batch of the Tibetan Refugees was shifted by train from Assam to Pathankot. From Pathankot they were sent to Dalhousie by bus. A number of cottages were requisitioned in Dalhousie through the local

Deputy Commissioner on the instructions of Sardar Partap Singh Kairon, the then Chief Minister of Punjab, and through the dynamic efforts of Acharya J.B. Kirpalani and Sucheta Kirpalani, both MPs and Chairman and Vice-Chairman of the Central Relief Committee.

Organization of Tibetan Handicrafts Training-cum-Production Centre at Dalhousie

As in the case of West Punjab refugees, the ICU moved swiftly from relief work to rehabilitation supported by the Minister of External Affairs.

It was a very tough task to start a Work Centre for training the Tibetan refugees in various skills. Language was a very big problem. The refugees could not understand any Indian language nor could the ICU Director speak the Tibetan language. The communication started with signs, gestures and by some practical visual demonstration. The mysteries of nature unfolded when some of the refugees got hold of a few papers and files, lying in the hands of the ICU Director, and expressed by different ways and signs that they could make handmade paper! Some of the refugees went out and collected green leaves strewn around and started crushing them between two stones making pulp of the collected green leaves. It was how the manufacturing of handmade paper by Tibetan refugees at Dalhousie was initiated.

Of course only making handmade paper could not solve the rehabilitation problem. Gopi Krishna went round the entire campus visiting the refugees in different cottages located on different hills. He found that they had brought with them small articles like blankets, carpets, a few clothes, clay models of Lord Buddha, etc. This proved to be the key to the future. They were beautiful articles. They could be trained to produce them. He arranged a number of meetings with the refugees at different levels to discuss the possibility of giving them proper training in various Tibetan arts and crafts. Fortunately, there were a few elderly Lamas who could help in making carpets, blankets, woollen clothes, etc., provided proper equipment was arranged. So. instructors were also available from within their own ranks. One industrial organizer was deputed by the ICU at Delhi. Soon the Dalhousie Tibetan Refugees Training-cum-Production Centre was humming with activity. The trainees were imparted not only technical skill but also made familiar with the equipment and raw material market. By turn they accompanied the Industrial Organizer to the markets at Amritsar and Ludhiana for equipment including looms, yarn, spinning wheels, vegetable dyes, etc. Both men and women were anxious to learn the new skills. Eventually, crafts, articles such as woollen carpets, cushions, aprons, table mats, handmade paper were developed and produced on a large-scale.

Thus the future prospects which looked bleak when they had arrived at Dalhousie started brightening up.

Educational Activities

As language was a barrier, the Project organized an educational institution known as the Tibetan School. This school started with 25 children and in two months time the number rose to 700. Children were taught Tibetan language, arithmetic, Hindi, English and speaking and writing. It was amazing to find that the Tibetan refugees in ages between 15 years, 30 years, 45 years and 60 years and small kids and children all came to learn together at this school. This was perhaps the first Tibetan school among all other refugee camps which were simultaneously started. Other schools in various parts of India were started after the Dalhousie experiment was found to be successful. Besides giving education to the children and young boys, they were also given training in various sports and mass drill.

Cultural Activities

Cultural resources of the Tibetans are rich. Most of them knew how to dance and sing. The ICU organized a Cultural Unit of the Tibetans and encouraged them to perform various types of dances, drama and plays. It was certainly a new experience to see them dancing and singing in their multi-coloured costumes on every Sunday in the open maidan.

The Dalhousie centre also brought cheer to His Holiness the Dalai Lama when he spent a week there.

The ICU conducted multi-purpose programme for the rehabilitation of the Tibetan refugees in Dalhousie for about three years with the cooperation of the Ministry of External Affairs, Punjab Government and Central Relief Committee. The ICU then wanted to prepare the Tibetans to discuss with the manager their own affairs. His Holiness the Dalai Lama was requested to depute some of His officers to take up the responsibility. Within a few months they were ready to take over the management themselves and soon the Project was handed over to the Tibetans. It was a happy and wonderful day when the Director of the

Project along with his team of workers left the Dalhousie Campus for Delhi in a Jeep, seen off by thousands of Tibetans including men, women and children from Dalhousie Hall Cottage for Pathankot. The entire route from Dalhousie Cottage Campus (top hill) to the bus-stand chowk was lined up on both sides by the Tibetan friends with red flowers and garlands and prayer wheels in their hands to bid good-bye.

SOCIAL WELFARE

In its work in the rural areas the ICU soon became convinced that development work could not proceed piecemeal or in compartments, that development has to be attacked in an integrated way. This led in the early stages to the formation of community centres, to fulfil some of the basic urgent needs of the farm families. But the ICU realized that it could only act as a catalytic agent or initiate the required services in the interim and withdraw as soon as others could step in.

Rural Health

In 1955 the ICU began a Rural Health Service, radiating around Chattarpur in the Qutab Minar area, to serve some 50 square miles where its member cooperative farming societies were located. creation of social services. The rural health service after three years was transformed into one of the few rural health cooperatives in the country. It was named the Janta Rural Health and Welfare Cooperative Society, Chattarpur, with a membership of 700 and an elected managing committee of 15 members. The ICU continued to assist the society.

By 1966-67, the total number of patients treated at the Chattarpur dispensary of the Society including from the surrounding villages was 43,847, records the ICU annual report of the year.

In April 1967, the ICU opted out and made over its responsibilities to the Lok Kalyan Samiti. The Samiti is primarily engaged in medical work in Delhi and had intimate realations with the ICU.

Slum Areas

The ICU also extended social welfare work to certain urban areas of Delhi. Centres were set up in a stone-crushers' colony at Jhandewala and in an integrated community of 600 displaced families from Pakistan settled at Nabikarim in Delhi. At these centres ICU workers organized literacy programmes, nursery schools, family planning education, recreation and sanitation drives. Dispensaries were also opened, and the services of a doctor provided. The ICU also joined hands with the Central Social Welfare Board and the Delhi authorities in a slum clearance project in the Idgah area, and took on the social welfare aspects of the project.

Jhandewalan (1964)

The programme and activities included :

1. Nursery School
2. Medical Aid
3. Craft Programme for Women and Girls
4. Evening Literacy
5. Recreation
6. Reading Room and Library
7. Creche for Working Mothers

ICU reports of the period give a working glimpse :

> Children from the nursery are being regularly transferred to the local Municipal Schools. The medical officer has by now established a good referal service with all the local hospitals and the patients find it possible to get hospitalized, if necessary. Nearly 80 per cent of the women in the basti have been trained in knitting, sewing and embroidery. The library, reading room and recreational services are now being completely handled by the local Gandhi Club, which was started during the year. It has a membership of 60. It has offered to take over the nursery and craft programme by the end of the year. The Gandhi Club has also been entrusted with the total responsibility of sanitation of the basti. Its members go to the Corporation offices quite often, instead of depending on the workers of the Community Centre. Since most of our services are now concentrated in the basti below the temple, and the people in the upper area are now economically better off, it was decided that work be continued only at the lower centre.

Najafgarh J.J. Colony

At the request of the community in Idgah, from where more than 3,000 families were shifted to the new colony on Najafgarh Road as a result of slum clearance, it was decided to extend some of our services in the new area till such time as the Municipal Corporation stepped in to take over all welfare services. The ICU, therefore, started a nursery school in two shifts with an attendance of 90 children in April 1964.

Malkaganj Project

Malkaganj Project has the best participation from the community in the following programmes and activities :

Nursery in two shifts : 100 children
Craft for women and girls : 125 women
Evening Recreation, Literacy Reading Room, etc : 150 people
The Advisory Committee is very active and interested.

During the year 1964 stress was laid on the community sharing more and more responsibilities of running their own welfare services. Each project was, therefore, directed towards this goal. This was the only way in which the ICU could gradually withdraw from the slums effectively. And it did. In 1966, the centre was handed over by the ICU to the Lok Kalyan Samiti.

Bihar Relief (1966)

In response to an appeal from Jayaprakash Narayan, Chairman of the Bihar Relief Committee, the ICU raised Rs.11,000 through 14 collection points for the drought affected areas of Bihar. Besides cash, woollen garments worth Rs.13,000 were donated through the Central Cottage Industries Emporium. In addition foodgrains, blankets, sarees, chaddars, clothes, shoes, vitamins were sent to the Bihar Relief Committee at Patna. The agencies that gave their support and cooperation in this drought relief work were the Delhi School of Social Work, Miranda House, St. Stephens College, Delhi University Women's Association, AVARD, Delhi State Social Welfare Advisory Board and all the handloom depots of the ICU. The material collected was sent to Patna through the Central Relief Committee. The Ministry of Defence donated 18 jeeps to the Bihar Relief Committee for relief work operation in Bihar. On the request of Jayaprakash Narayan the ICU arranged to collect these jeeps and to deliver them at Patna.

14

ENCOUNTERS WITH BUREAUCRACY

NO book on the ICU would be complete without a narration of some of its encounters with the Government right from its inception.

To start with, the Registrar of Cooperatives would not issue registration certificate. Ultimately, it was with the intervention of Prime Minister Nehru (who was one of the earliest contributors through the PM's relief fund to the ICU and supported its aims and objectives) that the ICU was registered finally in November 1948. The reasons for the reluctance of the Registrar were quite interesting. Till then the Department of Cooperatives had not come across a society like the ICU which proposed to act like a mother cooperative to foster other cooperatives. He thought that fostering cooperatives was the preserve of his department, and he could not allow a cooperative society to encroach upon the functions of the department. The next argument was that the ICU intended to cover a wide range of activities which was unheard of and, therefore, not permissible. For example, the ICU wanted to extend its work to agriculture, industry, housing, consumer cooperatives, in the economic sphere. The department found it odd and therefore unacceptable that the ICU also wanted to undertake such functions as training, research, extension and education which in its view could not be combined with economic activity of the kind envisaged by the ICU.

However with that exposure in dealing with the bureaucracy, the ICU felt that it was a little better prepared to face the real world. But it soon discovered that the cooperative department was merely a small arm – rather inconsequential arm – of the vast government bureaucracy. The very first endeavour the ICU plunged into was to resettle landless agricultural labourers and small cultivators who had been given shelter temporarily in the refugee relief camp at Kingsway. They were itching to get out of the relief camp and to work on land and start cultivation. But they had not found any land. The ICU helped form them their teams and included some of its own volunteers. The teams started to scout for land which had been vacated by Muslim migrants who had evacuated to

Pakistan. Where was that land? What was happening to it? These teams discovered that in and around Delhi there were about 6,000 acres of such land which could have been available for the purpose of resettlement of the refugee cultivators but this land had been allotted to three or four powerful individuals who were themselves refugees and were big landlords before partition. The most powerful among them was the distinguished civil servant, M. S. Randhawa, who was then Deputy Commissioner of Delhi. He had about 1,200 acres allotted to him. Then there was Datar Singh, Adviser to the Ministry of Agriculture, who had been allotted about 3,000 acres and so forth. After mutual consultations the ICU and the cultivators in the Kingsway Camp decided that the best thing was for the latter to occupy these lands by moving out of the camp with their families, lock, stock and barrel. One early morning they moved to the villages around Delhi principally in the Mehrauli Block and occupied those lands. The ICU had meanwhile raised some resources and inputs for them to bring the land under the plough which had hardened as it had been lying fallow for about a year.

When the landlords came to know what had happened they began to mobilize the administrative machinery to evict the cultivator families. The ICU too moved with lightening speed and organized a meeting of all the political parties and raised the question whether after independence India was going to recreate landlords or give ownership to the small cultivators and landless workers who were going to work on it with their own hands. The ICU gave a call for "land to the tiller". There was widespread support from the representatives of the political parties to giving the land to the tiller. The ICU took up the resolution to the authorities concerned and also to Prime Minister Nehru. It invited Nehru to visit Chatarpur, a village in Mehrauli where the cultivators had started the ploughing operations and with the help of the ICU formed a multipurpose cooperative society to carry on joint farming. During his visit, the cultivators apprised him of the whole issue of land allotment in favour of the big landlords. And this is the official minute[1] Nehru recorded after his visit:

Land to Government Servants

> During my visit to Chatarpur[2] yesterday, I was told that a large area of land including mango groves has been given by the Custodian of Evacuee Property to Mr. Randhawa who was till lately the Deputy Commissioner of Delhi. Presumably this was given because

Mr. Randhawa had lost some property in Pakistan. I do not know what the facts are and I should like you to inquire. *Prima facie* it is odd that a Deputy Commissioner should be given land in this way in the very area under his jurisdiction. Are there any other cases of this kind in regard to Government servants? Please find out from the Ministry of Relief and Rehabilitation and the Custodian of Evacuee Property as well as from any other source that you may consider necessary.

To Vallabhbhai Patel[3]

New Delhi
28 September, 1948

My dear Vallabhbhai,

Two days ago, I went to Chatarpur, some 10 miles from Delhi, to visit a cooperative farm, which has been started by refugees. I was told there that adjoining this farm was a large area of several hundred acres which had been given, presumably by the Custodian of Evacuee Property, to Randhawa, who was till lately the Deputy Commissioner here. I was further informed that another several hundred acres had been given in the same way to Datar Singh.[4]

I was greatly surprised to learn of this for a variety of reasons. For Government officials here to be given evacuee land seemed to me improper, for the Deputy Commissioner, Delhi, to be given land in Delhi Province also did not seem right, and for these very large areas to be given to a single individual also appears to me to be wrong in principle.

Someone told me that this was done by some kind of exchange for land in Pakistan. That does not seem to be a sufficient justification. When land is so scarce and so many unfortunate people need it, it seems to me very unfair for large slices of it to be given to our officials. I do not know if you have heard about this. I shall be grateful if you could kindly inquire.[5]

Yours sincerely,
Jawaharlal Nehru

Meanwhile, an interesting development took place. Adwina Mountbatten visited the villages where the ICU was working. On return, she reported to Nehru that the ICU's village cooperative was doing good work, and it was a successful example of rehabilitation. Nehru in turn sent the report to the Chief Commissioner of Delhi who sent it to the then Deputy Commissioner (Rameshwar Dayal). The Deputy Commissioner in turn deputed his Tehsildar for a report. They reported that no one knew of the ICU in the Mehrauli villages and that no refugees had been settled there, and that the ICU must have managed to get some false publicity. This report travelled back to Nehru. Meanwhile, he had himself visited the place. He laughed and sent the report to ICU President Kamaladevi Chattopadhyaya saying - see how the administration functions! She decided it was not a laughing matter. She wanted the Deputy Commissioner to explain the basis of his report to the Prime Minister. The end of the story is that the Deputy Commissioner had to apologize. The explanation given by him was however, hilarious. He said he had been given the report orally by the Tehsildar on the phone and therefore there might have been some mistake in taking down the facts correctly!

After a prolonged campaign the Government agreed to withdraw the land allotment in favour of the landlords and to allot it to the cultivators. Just when we thought that we had got over the obstacle we found that the authorities refused to allot the land in the name of the cooperative societies formed by the landless agricultural workers. The Government insisted that the allotment will be made only in the name of each individual member and not to the cooperative society. The ICU saw danger in it – that it would destabilize the cooperatives. It would SOW the seeds of tension among the members who may differ with each other on other grounds. And lastly, if the land was in the name of individuals some of them could be pressurized to resell it which would lead to the breaking up of the whole endeavour. Much as the ICU tried, the bureaucracy would not budge. Meanwhile the government officials began a campaign among the cultivators that while the authorities were willing to give the land to each individual family, the ICU was obstructing the process and insisting that the allotment should be in the name of the cooperative. To start with, the cultivator members explained that was their own idea and not that of the ICU. It is they who had moved the application for joint allotment in the name of the cooperative. They were not in favour of individual allotment. But gradually, some individual members were weaned away from this position by the inspectors and thus brick by brick the wall of unity of the members collapsed. The land was eventually allotted in the name of individuals.

As the ICU had apprehended, over a period of time the elite in Delhi began to set up farm houses in the villages around Delhi. Individual allottees were offered attractive prices and they began to resell the land.

Some of them then engaged themselves as landless wage labourers on the big farms whereas in their cooperatives they were owners themselves. Others collected the cash and moved out of the Delhi villages to remote areas of Rajasthan. It certainly threatened the existence of the multi-purpose cooperatives.

Still a large number of members held on and it seemed that the multi-purpose cooperatives would survive. But that was only a short-lived hope. Something else was happening in the system to destroy them. It was the recommendations of the Rural Credit Survey report sponsored by the Reserve Bank. Based on this report it was decided to abolish village-level multi-purpose cooperatives and merge them into larger-sized cooperatives ostensibly to make them viable. One cooperative for a "cluster of villages" rather than confined to an individual village. The members were no longer a homogeneous group basic to a cooperative. With the enlargement of the geographical area (cluster of villages) members also lost the day-to-day control over the management. More than that the new large-sized cooperatives were to confine to credit and to give up "multi purpose" character. The Registrar set about liquidating village level cooperatives and giving birth to large societies. The rationale was that large societies will have a large capital base of Rs 1 lakh each on the basis of which they could borrow larger sums from the cooperative banks for their economic activities. But to raise the capital base of Rs. 1 lakh required that the members themselves contribute one-fifth or Rs. 20,000 to the share capital to which under the new policy the Government would contribute Rs 80,000 as its share in the capital of the cooperative. But the members of course did not have Rs. 20,000 to contribute. The cooperative inspectors showed them how to manipulate the account books in which their contribution would be shown to have been received on paper against which the Government would disburse Rs 80,000 as its contribution. All this had to be done in a great hurry as the end of the financial year March 31 was on hand, and the inspectors had a target fixed for them for registering or bringing to life a given number of cooperatives and to distribute the budgeted sum by way of share capital. On the same day on which they received the Government money the books of the cooperatives showed that loans worth Rs 1 lakh had been extended to the members, though the amount actually received by the members was only Rs. 80,000. A certain percentage of Rs. 80,000 was paid as commission to the inspectors. The ICU was aghast. The cooperatives it had helped to build disappeared. By this time Professor V. K. R. V. Rao had become a member of the Planning

Commission looking after co-operation as one of the subjects. The ICU took the story to him. At first he wouldn't believe it. But when he called in his advisers they confirmed that what the ICU had reported was not unique to the villages of Delhi, it was happening all over the country. Madhav Das who was the principal adviser was a very knowledgeable and experienced person and his voice carried weight with Professor Rao.

What Rao tried to do later to apply correctives we do not know. But we do know that the result was zero. The process continued unabated and today the wholesale corruption one notices in the cooperatives owes its beginning to that period when cooperatives of the old (village multi purpose) were buried and were born new large cooperatives under the most corrupt conditions imaginable. That, however, was not the end of the travails. In the meantime, the Government had also launched the community development projects. For this purpose, the country was divided into 5,000 blocks; each block headed by a Block Development Officer (BDO). One BDO also came to the Mehrauli block with his paraphernalia, set programme and projects. They were at unease with the ICU's presence there. Their attitude was : we are incharge of development officially; the ICU was an encroacher and should leave the area. It tried to offer them cooperation – argued with them that, the ICU had been in this area from 1948, five years before the CD Programme was even conceived and that its knowledge of the area, contacts with the people and experience could be of some use to them. But that was not to be.

The ICU did not have to wait for long to find out what its role should be in the new circumstances. The media and Parliament were growing critical of the deficiencies and distortions in the official community development programme all over the country. The ICU thought the most constructive thing to do would be to list all these deficiencies and to see whether practical ways could not be found to overcome them. It launched an experimental project in the Mehrauli block. The design of the project, strategy, approach and results obtained were incorporated in a special ICU publication, *Community Development,* extracts from which appear elsewhere in this book.

Here, we would like to record that efforts made to get the leading lights of the CD Ministry (its head, S.K. Dey) or the local BDO to take a look at what the ICU had done did not succeed. They were simply not interested and their attitude in fact became more hostile to the ICU. However, a number of individual MPs, various committees (Public Accounts Committee, Estimates Committee) visited the project, so also the Deputy Governor of the Reserve Bank B. Venkatasubbiah, and

Morarji Desai, then Union Finance Minister. After his visit, Shri Morarji commented that if the entire CD Programme could be run the way the ICU ran its Mehrauli project it would be a miraculous achievement for India. He sanctioned a loan of Rs 2 lakhs for the ICU's revolving fund for the project. However, the loan had to be routed through one of the administrative ministries and that happened to be the Ministry of Community Development. Under the rules of business, the Finance Ministry could not make the loan directly. The Ministry of Community Development (CD), however, would not agree to the loan. The ICU never received that loan. It then took its report on *Community Development* to V.T. Krishnamachari (V.T.K.), Deputy Chairman of the Planning Commission, who was the father figure of the Community Development Programme in India.

V.T.K. found what the ICU had done was inspiring and useful. It shared with him the problems it was having with the Ministry of Community Development and the BDO at the ground level as also its earlier experience of how the multi-purpose cooperatives organized by the ICU soon after independence had all been dissolved to make room for large societies. He was also told how the CD Ministry had thwarted the release of the loan of Rs 2 lakhs to the ICU's revolving fund. Aware of S.K Dey's political clout with Nehru at the time, VTK suggested that the best thing in the circumstances would be to have the ICU project in Mehrauli evaluated by the PEO – Programme Evaluation Organization of the Planning Commission, which was set up to evaluate the working of the official CD Programme. The ICU welcomed the suggestion wholeheartedly. The director of PEO at the time, Jyoti Bhattacharjee, visited the project, collected all the relevant details, and designed the programme for evaluation to which the ICU consented. PEO then included evaluation of the ICU's project in its programme schedule for that particular year. The programme schedule was sent by PEO also to the Ministry of Community Development in the normal course. Believe it or not, that Ministry resolutely opposed the inclusion of the ICU project for evaluation by PEO! The grounds were that PEO was meant to evaluate only the official Community Development Programme and it should not undertake evaluation of any non-official programmes. In view of the opposition of that ministry even VTK threw up his hands and said there was nothing he could do about it. The ICU however did not give up. It decided to approach S.K. Dey. It pleaded with him that since the Ministry believed that the ICU project was not worthwhile, PEO evaluation will expose the ICU if its claims were false. The Minister was not persuaded. But when the ICU persisted, it received a communication from the Minister, to the effect that "no further correspondence on this subject will be entertained by the CD Ministry from the ICU". Thereafter, the ICU decided to wind up the project, but continued to serve the villages as best as it could.

In the matter of agriculture and rural credit the ICU was convinced that the cooperative credit will have to be liberated from the strangulating control of the agriculture department (ACD) of the Reserve Bank of India (RBI). It felt that ACD's choking control over cooperatives was facilitated by the lack of a national cooperative bank which could be a buffer between ACD and individual apex cooperative banks, i.e. State level cooperative banks. The ICU decided to convene a meeting of the apex banks to discuss the possibility of forming a national bank to boost cooperative credit as well as to resist any ACD policy which in its view was not in the best interest of the cooperatives or was not positive in terms of raising the productivity of small farmers or artisans. The ICU sounded some of the apex banks which warmly welcomed the idea and wanted it to take the initiative. The ICU sent formal invitations for the meeting to all the cooperative banks and received very good response. ACD came to know about the meeting and was incensed. It set about pressurizing the apex banks not to attend the meeting and in any case not to support the proposition of setting up a national bank. ACD also applied informal threat since for their funds the apex banks relied mainly on ACD. When the meeting took place in Bangalore on the appointed day, except for representatives of two cooperative banks, no other bank came to attend. Thus the idea of forming a national cooperative bank mooted in the late 1950s died a premature death (though efforts were being made even in 1995 by the National Cooperative Union of India to revive the idea).

And now over to Faridabad, the rehabilitation project where the ICU was working simultaneously. It organized a number of industrial cooperatives as different from the farming cooperatives in the Mehrauli block. There is a separate book on Faridabad on the anvil, which tells the story at length how the people through self-help built the town and built for India an inspiring example of carrying the impetus of the freedom movement into the second phase of a social revolution in India. Faridabad was part of Punjab (now Haryana. The ICU's experience of the Cooperative Department of Punjab was worse than that with the cooperative department in Delhi. Here again the department would not register the Faridabad cooperatives.

The ICU had formed industrial and service cooperatives for making bricks, carpentry, blacksmithy, weaving, making of buttons, cardboard boxes and cooking stoves for domestic use, hosiery products, a network of consumer cooperatives and transport cooperatives which towed the materials from source to site. The Government acting through its own special agency, the Faridabad Development Board (which was headed by Dr Rajendra Prasad and had Sudhir Ghosh as its member-secretary) advanced a loan of Rs. 24 lakhs to the ICU specifically to provide capital to these cooperatives of refugees who were resourceless, to build the factories and workplaces and acquire equipment and machinery. These industrial cooperatives, inspired by the example of INDUSCOS in China formed under the leadership of Sun Yat-sen, made a promising beginning. They imparted new skills and provided employment, output and services.

ICU cooperative organizers (especially, S.D. Kshirsagar on deputation with the ICU from the Bombay Industrial Cooperative Association) ran training classes for an hour each day to orient each member to grasp the cooperative principles and practices, and help them sort out the working problems. There was no Cooperative Inspector around the place to assist them. But the Cooperative Department would not even register them, nor respond to any entreaties made to it. As the book on Faridabad tells the detailed story of the relationship of the ICU with the Faridabad Development Board, under its new administrator, S.G. Brave, ICS, who replaced Sudhir Ghosh and the Rehabilitation Minister at the Centre, Ajit Prasad Jain deteriorated sharply to the point that the ICU had to inform the Minister that it could not function in Faridabad any more and that the Faridabad Board or the Ministry should itself take over the activities including the loans given to the cooperatives.

Suddenly, the Cooperative Department of Punjab became active. Its inspectors descended on Faridabad, and went around telling the office-bearers of cooperatives that they had no liability to return the loan of Rs. 24 lakhs which they had taken from the ICU, since they were not a registered body! The inspectors instigated the office-bearers to file formal arbitration proceedings against the ICU repudiating the loans. The Assistant Registrar appointed as arbitrator promptly gave awards all against the ICU. A long battle followed. The union resorted legal action and simultaneously took the issue to the community at large at Faridabad in whose resettlement it had played not an inconsiderable role. It also approached the general body of members of the cooperatives and explained to them that their office-bearers had been misguided by the cooperative inspectors. As a result of these efforts over one year, the members pressed their office-bearers to convene their respective general body meetings and place the matter before them, where they repudiated the action of the office bearers in launching arbitration proceedings against the ICU. Further, they confirmed the loans which they had received from the ICU and reiterated that as persons of honour they would repay their debts. And they did. The Rehabilitation Ministry then declined to entrust the factories to the industrial cooperatives and auctioned them all to private parties.

The Rehabilitation Minister also decided to have the ICU liquidated. His Ministry called the Registrar of Cooperatives, Delhi, and ordered him to liquidate the ICU. By then a new Registrar had taken over. He protested that he could not liquidate a society without sufficient grounds which had not been communicated to him by the Government of India. Moreover he had to first issue a show-cause notice to the ICU. He was overruled and asked to obey the orders of the Government of India.

It so happened that at that time Delhi had just got its first elected government. Chaudhary Brahm Perkash was the Chief Minister. The Registrar of Cooperatives, Delhi, was under him. The Registrar reported to the Chief Minister what had transpired at the meeting in the Rehabilitation Ministry. Chaudhry Brahm Perkash was livid. He could not accept the Government of India calling his subordinate officials and giving them direct orders. They had to communicate through him.

He was also aware of the ICU's work in the villages and among the refugees. He also knew its office-bearers intimately. He tried to contact the ICU President Kamaladevi Chattopadhyay, or the Vice-President

Srinivas Malliah, and the General Secretary L.C. Jain, who were all away at that time at Trivandrum attending the first conference on development of handicrafts. Chaudhary Brahm Perkash suspected that probably the GOI move to liquidate the ICU had been timed during the absence of its principal office-bearers. He forbade the Registrar from carrying out the GOI orders and conveyed this also to the Minister of Rehabilitation. He asked that if the Rehabilitation Ministry had any complaints against the ICU, they should be forwarded to the Delhi Government with all the facts. Only then any action would be taken against ICU, if warranted.

Meanwhile, the Rehabilitation Ministry had gone ahead and appointed a liquidator – one of the senior officials – who was trying to enter ICU premises and take over its offices. But he was asked by the ICU to produce a letter of authority from the Registrar which the latter declined to give until the matter had been formally referred to the Delhi Government by the Government of India. The end of the story is that the Government of India did not write anything to the Delhi Government on the subject and eventually cancelled the appointment of the liquidator.

The ICU thought the ordeal had ended there. But no, it discovered that meanwhile the Union Ministry of Rehabilitation in their proceedings before the Public Accounts Committee (PAC) of Parliament (1959-60, twenty-fifth report, Second Lok Sabha, March 1960) had indicted the ICU and informed PAC that the loans that were given by it to the ICU could not be recovered. The ICU was not invited to these proceedings. But when they were concluded they were given wide publicity. The ICU was dumbstruck. It then addressed a memorandum to PAC stating that the ICU's accounts had been audited regularly each year by a firm of chartered accountants approved by the Registrar of Cooperatives. These audited accounts had in fact been submitted also to the Rehabilitation Ministry and that ICU had urged the Ministry to settle the loan of Rs 24 lakhs and that it was prepared to account for every paisa.

The ICU's auditors were also upset at the misleading publicity and wrote independently to the Minister for Rehabilitation stating the factual position and pointing out that the statement made by the Minister in Parliament that the ICU had not maintained accounts or there were irregularities in its accounts were baseless. The ICU appended the auditors' comments to its memorandum to PAC, and urged it that the matter be reopened and that the ICU be given an opportunity to present its side of the case.

The PAC Chairman was sympathetic but was inhibited because, he said, there was no such precedence of a hearing by PAC after its report had been laid on the table of the House. The ICU persisted with its appeal to PAC that gross injustice had been done to it, that it was a public body, it was running various other programmes on behalf of the Government and therefore any allegations made against it had to be adjudged fairly. As luck would have it, PAC decided to set a new precedence. It held a special session, invited the ICU and the officials of the Ministry of Rehabilitation to be cross-examined. The result was a supplementary report by PAC (1960-61, Thirty Seventh Report, Second Lok Sabha, April 1961) which exonerated the ICU and, if anything passed strictures against the Ministry of Rehabilitation. It left no alibi for the Ministry then to delay holding negotiations and the entire loan of Rs 24 lakhs was then accounted to the satisfaction of the Rehabilitation Ministry.

On another front, the Union Secretary (Kashmir Affairs) Vishnu Sahay, wanted the ICU to send a team overnight to Kashmir for helping with the marketing of handicrafts which had been disrupted due to political developments following the arrest of Sheikh Abdullah. (This was because the ICU was running the Central Cottage Industries Emporium on behalf of the Ministry of Commerce and Industry). The Kashmir Government received the team of five persons mainly women sent by the ICU but directed that they stay at the Nedous Hotel because of security problems. The team spent two weeks in Kashmir, accomplished the tasks assigned to it to the satisfaction of craftspersons and the authorities and came back. Nothing was heard about this matter until much later in an entirely different context, to which we shall return. The context was that the Commerce and Industry Ministry was asked by Nehru to organize an exhibition and sale of Indian handicrafts in London on the occasion of the coronation of Queen Elizabeth. In turn the Ministry asked the Cottage Industries Emporium run by the ICU to organize the exhibition and sales. It gave a temporary loan of Rs. 4 lakhs for the purpose. The exhibition in London was a great success. The goods taken there were all sold.

The ICU wrote to the Commerce and Industry Ministry that it was in a position to return the loan from the sales proceeds which had accumulated in London. The Ministry took the view that ICU could not adjust the loan against sales proceeds which it wanted to be credited to the government first and then only the repayment issue could be considered. The ICU pointed out that this was a linked transaction – loan and sales. It had no separate funds to settle the loan account once the sale proceeds had been credited to the Government. It should be settled at one go. It led to an internecine war between the ICU and the Commerce and Industry Ministry which then appointed a cost audit team to look into the ICU accounts. The audit team could not find anything to object. The only allegation it came up with related to the visit to Kashmir of the ICU team from the Cottage Industries Emporium – that the team had stayed in a luxury hotel (Nedous Hotel to which reference had been made earlier!) ignoring the ICU's explanation that it was done as per the directions of the State Government.

Citing this as an example of complete extravagance in the functioning of the ICU's management, the report recommended that Government should not adjust the London exhibition loan against the sales proceeds. Some rules were also quoted to say that such an adjustment would not be permitted by the Comptroller and Auditor General (CAG). The ICU petitioned CAG and pointed out that it had no option except to adjust the loan against the sales proceeds which it was ready to repatriate if adjustment was approved. Finally CAG gave his "informal" nod and closed the matter.

This account will not be complete and fair without recalling also the heart-warming encounters with some of the most dynamic and constructive administrators.

First, G. Mathias, who later rose to be the Chief Secretary of Karnataka, was a rare experience. He was the Financial Adviser to the Ministry of Food and Agriculture (MFA) in the late 40s, when the ICU started its village development activities. ICU had been pressing the Ground Water Exploration Organization (GWO) of MFA to prospect the Mehrauli villages for groundwater availability, as it was starved for water. It was a rocky area and open wells used to go dry so very often. The only hope the villagers saw was in deep bore-wells. At first, GWO said their drills were not working. Then they argued that the ICU would have to bear the costs even if the drilling failed to find water. It would have to make an advance deposit. GWO would also not make a commitment as to when it will be able to start the work. "What was its precise role?" The ICU inquired of GWO. Could the poor villages ever be helped on these terms? "None of your business" was the attitude of GWO. Desperate the ICU knocked several doors in MFA without success. Finally, it contacted Mathias. He was aghast. He called GWO and told them if that was their idea of serving the villages, then they had better wind up and save the Government some precious resources. Result: the drilling rigs were out in Mehrauli the next morning to the delight of the villagers. The mission was not successful as the soil proved too rocky for the rigs. However, GWO still raised bills against the ICU but promptly withdrew when the ICU said that it would refer them to Mathias.

The problem of irrigation in Mehrauli, however, persisted for nearly eight years until, one day by chance, a senior member of the Indian Civil Service (ICS), M.A.T. Iyengar, walked into the ICU's rural development office at Mehrauli. He wanted to enlist himself as a voluntary worker. Surprise of surprises! How come? we inquired. We learnt that he had been shunted out by the West Bengal Government for some unorthodox methods to combat acute drought relief in Purulia district. He was waiting for a posting. How did he hear about the ICU? From Sudhir Ghosh, Administrator of Faridabad. Ghosh told the ICU that the people of Purulia worshipped Iyengar, but he was victim of a witch-hunt because the Bengal bureaucracy could not stomach his popularity. Iyengar brought his own sandwiches for lunch and would not accept anything other than water – all through the year he came to Mehrauli each day.

He had long talks with farmers and proposed that like Bengal, large tanks be built in each village in Mehrauli to store rainwater as also tap whatever subsoil water was available. The idea worked to everyone's delight. Distribution channels were so constructed as to cover the maximum number of small holdings. However, open tanks were vulnerable to high evaporation losses. Just then, the Chairman of Central Water and Power Commission (CWPC), C.L. Handa, visited Mehrauli. He approved of the tanks. "Larger the wound, more the blood", he said was the principle on which they were based. He was wanting to experiment with methods of lowering evaporation losses in large irrigation reservoirs. He found the ICU's Mehrauli area most hospitable. So, one of his technical assistants was attached to the ICU for experiment: to spread a thin film of oil through a floating drum on the surface of water and then to measure the impact on evaporation losses.

With water available, vegetable crops were introduced. The agricultural scientists at the Pusa Institute were looking for opportunities for field application of their researches and new variety of seeds. They approached the ICU for collaboration. They were a different lot than the extension staff of the Block Development Organization. Led by Dr. J.V.A. Nehemia, the Pusa agricultural scientists adopted the villages where Iyengar had introduced tanks. What the farmers reaped were no ordinary vegetable crops – they were dripping with cash. The scientists were revered by the village folk.

When launching its cottage industries development programme, the ICU had a unique and thrilling response from one who was at that time popularly described as "bureaucrat of all bureaucrats": Shri S.A. Venkataraman, ICS Secretary, Ministry of Industry and Commerce (I&C). the ICU had formulated a scheme for starting a marketing service for different cottage industries products made by artisans cooperatives across the country. It was proposed to make a modest beginning. For this, the ICU sought a "loan" of Rs. one lakh from the I&C Ministry. ICU President, Kamaladevi took the proposal to Venkataraman. He was very cordial and read the proposal right there. But as he came to the end be became suddenly rude: "No, I cannot give you any loan". She was stunned. "Why?", she asked. He said, "As Secretary of the Ministry, I do not give loans. I only give grants". Besides, he said, "Kamaladevi, this scheme of helping Cottage Industries will hardly be able to repay the loan. What it needs is a grant". Greatly relieved she said that she would send him a revised proposal. "Do you have that much time to waste?", he asked with a twinkle in his eyes. He called his private secretary, dictated a letter from Kamaladevi to the Secretary of the Ministry, had it typed and got her to sign it right there. "You can go now", he said, "the cheque will follow". And, before 5 p.m. that very day, a messenger delivered the sanction letter and the cheque. Apparently, after Kamaladevi left, he had called one of his Under Secretaries (S.A. Tekchandani) and instructed him to go to the AGCR (Accountant General Central Revenue) and have the cheque issued and delivered before the end of the day. That was like sunrise in the ICU's working experience with bureaucracy. In terms of prompt and constructive response always devising ways to help the ICU had similar heart-warming experiences at the hands of several other distinguished civil servants including Dharam Vira, S.Y. Krishnaswamy, S. Ranganathan and K.B. Lall, and in particular the dynamic Industry Minister, Manubhai Shah. They could always find a solution out of a difficult situation.

Even in the most difficult Cooperative Department, there were happy encounters. The Chief Commissioner of Delhi had agreed to provide to the ICU on deputation for three years two inspectors from the Cooperative Department. Not many were interested, but two persons volunteered: Ratan Singh and Moti Ram. They were gems. In promoting new cooperatives, they were most educative and constructive, and altogether very cordial. At one stage, a retired army officer, Capt. Hukum Singh Lather, became the Registrar of Cooperatives, Delhi. He too was not an ordinary person – precise, tough but helpful. His stewardship of the Cooperative Department brought in a breath of fresh air – after prolonged adversrial tensions between the department and the ICU. The ICU had similar cordial relations with Punjab Registrars of Cooperatives: N. Sehgal, ICS and Mian Fateh Singh.

NOTES

1. Note to the Principal Private Secretary, 27 September, 1948, *J.N. Collection*
2. A village near Mehrauli in South Delhi where 35 refugee families were resettled. The Indian Cooperative Union arranged a 400-acre land for cooperative farming by refugees.
3. *Sardar Patel's Correspondence 1945-50,* Vol 6, pp. 505-506.
4. Datar Singh (1987-1973); associated with various agricultural and cattle utilization programmes, pioneer in scientific breeding and dairy farming in India; Vice-President, CAR, 1947-1952; Development Adviser for Kashmir, Govt. of India, 1955-59.
5. Vallabhbhai Patel replied on 29 September that he was not aware of the land transactions and would let Nehru know about them after making enquiries. (Source: Selected Works of Jawaharlal Nehru)

15

TRANSFORMED ROLE AFTER 1968

IN the first flush of freedom for 20 years (1948 to 1968), the ICU was like a flame setting fire to and lighting almost all the nooks and corners of our socio-economic landscape. Its activities by their very nature were mostly visible - like the Faridabad township, Cottage Industries Emporium, Super Bazar. The ICU was all over the place where people were in the lead striving for a new life – be it refugees, landless workers, farmers, artisans, weavers or consumers at large. Often, the ICU was there ahead of the Government. Its main business was to put people into business, and withdraw. It was all there while building the facilities – farms, Faridabad, Cottage Industries Emporium or Super Bazaar, but with the task over, it always opted out taking nothing for itself. Indeed, at the end of all these major endeavours the ICU was penniless and is without one square inch of property, but is rich in experience and no less as a motivational and moral force.

By 1968, it emptied its hands of all "doing" roles for a variety of reasons. In conformity with Gandhiji's blessings the ICU was bound not to become dependent on government. Nor did it want to depend on foreign contributions. In any case, the ICU was not willing to submit itself to a new procedure clamped in the mid sixties by S.K.Dey's Ministry requiring cooperatives to seek that Ministry's prior permission for any foreign contributions. This was nearly a decade earlier than the Foreign Contributions Regulation Act (FCRA), 1976. It was an administrative fiat without a legal basis; and was clearly directed at the ICU as part of the continuing conflict between that Ministry and the ICU. There was no question, of course, of its sponging on the projects, properties, businesses it had helped to create for the refugees, artisans, consumers.

Further, the stream of volunteer forces that came to the ICU surging in the early decades of freedom had begun to abate – one reason being that over time many more voluntary groups had begun to emerge.

Taking all these reasons into account the ICU decided it should stay away from direct organization/management of any programme or project.

It had done enough of that in its first 20 years. It came to the conclusion that henceforth it should concentrate on providing consultation to other voluntary agencies or government as per their need. It was a turning point for the ICU from the texture or tempest of the previous eventful 20 years – a new phase as it were. To those who were used to its hectic pace, it looked as if the organisation had gone into hibernation or disappeared from the scene. True, in this phase beginning 1968, the ICU became faceless and invisible. But as the following brief account would show it was there all along doing its bit, but as an actor behind the scene.

For example, its representatives continued to serve for several years on the governing body of the Cottage Industries Emporium at the instance of the Government, even after handing over the management of the Emporium to the new Association. The ICU's Secretary, R. Kalyansundaram, served also on the Expert Committee set up by the All India Handicrafts Board for Rural Marketing Centres for village industries. The ICU continued to serve AVARD and its individual member voluntary organizations for rural development as also Gandhian organizations for Gramdan villages, on specific aspects. It was associated with AVARD in the preparation of Block Development Plans in U.P., and on a similar exercise in Rajasthan for the Industrial Development Services. It served also on the advisory committee of the Rural Manpower Programme (Food for Work) of the Government of Uttar Pradesh and on the Board of the Dr. Rajendra Prasad Memorial Trust for Rural Development in Bihar.

In rehabilitation it continued to assist the Tibetans even after it had formally withdrawn from the resettlement project at Dalhousie; and it served also on the governing body of the Sri Lanka Repatriates Rehabilitation Cooperative Bank at Madras.

Between 1977 and 1980, its General Secretary served as non-official Chairman of the All India Handicrafts Board and the Northeast Handlooms and Handicrafts Development Corporation.

A strong and sustained effort was to carry its experiences of development in the planning system especially on decentralization and people-led development. Its General Secretary served on various State Level planning bodies, particularly U.P. State Planning Commission in the seventies and Karnataka's Economic and Planning Council in the eighties; and on various working groups of the Planning Commission, and the Administrative Reforms Commission, especially on cooperatives.

In 1979, the Reserve Bank of India (RBI) set up a Committee to Review Arrangements for Agricultural and Rural Credit - (CRAFICARD), which included L.C. Jain as a member, who acted as a conduit for conveying the ICU's in depth experience with cooperatives and rural credit, particularly the ICU's long-held view that agricultural credit must be liberated from being a department of RBI and entrusted to a specialized bank. This input was of some help to the Committee in deciding on the establishment of the National Bank of Agriculture and Rural Development (NABARD) and merging in it the Reserve Bank's Agriculture Credit Department (ACD). The ICU followed promptly with a paper outlining "The Challenges and Tasks before NABARD".

Its research division having been handed over to the Institute of Social Studies later converted as Trust and popularly known as (ISST), the stream of the ICU's own independent studies and publications also came to a halt. However, since the seventies and eighties, its advocacy continued mainly through lectures by Kamaladevi to groups across the country – the tireless traveller that she was, and through publications in leading journals of analytical papers and articles on issues which were of deep concern to the ICU throughout particularly on crafts, rural credit, rural poverty, on the plight of handloom weavers or of disadvantaged groups such as the Scheduled Castes and the Scheduled Tribes, backward regions, and the crying need for decentralization to vest power with the people – through panchayats and cooperatives.

The ICU also participated actively in the cooperative education and training programmes of the National Cooperative Union of India. Meanwhile, Samakhya (Cooperative Development Foundation) based at Hyderabad emerged on the scene and found that the ICU's publications and reports provided a rich armoury in continuing the battle to make the cooperatives a force for the nineties and beyond. This book owes a lot for its birth to Samakhya for its support by way of funds, fire and fellowship. Ramakrishna Hegde's entry as Deputy Chairman into Yojana Bhawan along with L.C.Jain as Member of the Planning Commission in 1989-90 provided a fortuitous opportunity to launch a studied assault on the draconian co-operative law. Just as he had given a new deal to the Panchayats in Karnataka as Chief Minister in the eighties, Hegde was equally keen on a new deal for cooperatives and ending the bureaucratic regime. This led to the setting up of the Brahm Prakash Committee by the Planning Commission to formulate a model Cooperative Law – which in the nineties has become a forceful weapon in the hands of cooperators to press for democratic legislation for cooperatives. They have already tasted success in Andhra and hopefully similar enactments will soon adorn the cooperatives everywhere.

Together then Panchayats and Cooperatives could provide the much needed representative institutional underpinning to economic and social development, fortified by entry of a large number of women in the panchayats, who could provide the much needed social force for transformation, and generate as powerful an impetus for equity based and people-led development as witnessed at the dawn of freedom of which the ICU was only a small child.

REFERENCE

Reports of the Public Accounts Committee Relating to the Rehabilitation Ministry, Second Lok Sabha, Parliament, (1959-60 and 1960-61)

ACRONYMS

(FOR THE BIBLIOGRAPHY)

AICU	All India Cooperative Union
COPAC	Committee for the Promotion of Aid to Cooperatives
FAO	Food and Agriculture Organization
ICU	Indian Cooperative Union
INC	Indian National Congress
IIM	Indian Institute of Management
IRMA	Institute of Rural Management, Anand
ICA/ROAP	International Cooperative Alliance, Regional Office for Asia and Pacific
ILO	International Labour Organization
KVIC	Khadi and Village Industries Commission
MCDC	Ministry of Community Development and Cooperation
NABARD	National Bank for Agriculture and Rural Development
NCCF	National Cooperative Consumers' Federation
NCUI	National Cooperative Union of India (formerly AICU)
NDDB	National Dairy Development Board
NAFSCOB	National Federation of State Cooperative Banks
NPC	National Planning Committee

SELECT BIBLIOGRAPHY

General

Argyle, Michael, *Cooperation : The Basis of Sociability.* London, Routledge, 1991

Atwood, D. W. and B. S. Baviskar, *Who Shares? Cooperatives and Rural Development.* Delhi, OUP, 1988

Bagchi, A. European and Indian entrepreneurship in India 1900-1930. In *Elites in South Asia,* edited by E.R. Leach and S.N. Mukherjee, Cambridge, Cambridge University Press, 1970

Banerjee, Joydeb, *Cooperative Movement in India.* Calcutta, Navana Printing Works, 1961

Barve, S. G., *With Malice Toward None : A Critique of New India's Plans and Aspirations.* Bombay, APH, 1962.

Baviskar, B.S., Cooperatives and Caste in Maharashtra. In *Two Blades of Grass–Rural cooperatives in Agricultural Modernisation,* edited by Peter Worsley Manchester, Manchester University Press, 1971.

Bayley, J. E. and Edgar Parnell, *The World of Cooperative Enterprise.* Oxford, Plunkett Foundation, 1994.

Bedi, R. D., *Theory, History and Practice of Cooperation.* Meerut, Loyal Book Depot, 1981

Behl, K. C., *The Romance of Cooperation.* Amritsar, Inland and Foreign Trading Co., 1936.

Bhatnagar, K. P., *Cooperation in India and Abroad.* Kanpur, Kishore Publishing House, 1960.

Bowen, E. R., *The Cooperative Road to Abundance–The Alternative to Monopolism and Communism.* New York, Schuman, 1953.

Bowner, A., *Economic Planning and the Cooperative Movement – Design for Study.* Manchester, Cooperative Union Ltd., 1950.

Casselman, P. H., *The Cooperative Movement and Some of its Problems.* New York, Philosophical Library, 1952.

Chakrabarti, P. K., *Problem of Cooperative Development in India.* New Delhi, Sultan Chand & Co., 1983.

Chatterjee, B.B. (ed), *Micro Studies in Community Development, Panchayati Raj and Cooperation.* Delhi, Sterling, 1969.

Chaudhuri, Pramit, *The Indian Economy–Poverty and Development.* New Delhi, Vikas, 1978.

Chaudhury, P. K. *et al., Cooperatives as Institutions for Development of the Rural Poor.* Comilla, BARD, 1987.

Cohen, B. J., *Question of Imperialism–the Political Economy of Dominance and Dependence.* London, Macmillan Publications, 1979.

Dayal, Rajeshwar, *Community Development Programme in India.* Allahabad, Kitab Mahal, 1966.

Desai, A. R., *Rural India in Transition.* (2nd ed), Bombay, Popular, 1979.

Dharia, Mohan and Morarji Desai, *Democracy and Cooperative Development.* Delhi, ICA, 1978.

Doctor, Adi H., *Sarvodaya : A Political and Economic Study.* Bombay, APH, 1967.

Dooren, Pierre, *Cooperatives for Developing Countries : Objectives, Policies and Practices.* Oxford, Plunkett Publications, 1982.

Dubhashi, P. R., *Principles and Philosophy of Cooperation.* Pune, VMNICM, 1970.

Dubhashi, Weeraman *et al., State and Cooperative Development.* Calcutta, Allied, 1971.

Dulfer, Eberhard and Walter Hamm, *Cooperatives–Clash between Member Participation,* Organisational Development and Bureaucratic Tendencies. London, Quiller, 1985.

Dutta, S. K., *Cooperative Societies and Rural Development* – A Politico-Economic Study. New Delhi, Mittal, 1991.

Dwivedi, R. C., *Democracy in Cooperative Movement–An Indian Profile.* New Delhi, NCUI, 1982.

— (ed) Role of Government in Promoting Cooperative Development in Asia Regional Consultation. (Papers presented by C. Srinivasa Sastry, Rai Singh and K. Sundararajulu), New Delhi, ICA, 1988.

Fauquest, G., *Cooperative Sector.* Translated from French by L. Purcell Weaver, Manchester, Coop. Union, 1951.

Flanagan, Desmond, *Centenary Story of the Cooperative Union (1869-1969).* Manchester, Cooperative Union, 1969.

Gadgil, D. R., *District Development Planning.* (RR Kale Memorial Lecture, 1966), Bombay, APH, 1967.

— *Towards a Cooperative Commonwealth.* (Prof. Brij Narayan Memo-

rial Lecture,1960), Chandigarh, Punjab University Publications Bureau, 1961.

Garoyan, Paul Mohn, *Equity vs Equality Within Cooperatives.* Cork, University College,1984.

Gopalakrishnan P. K., *Development of Economic Ideas in India: 1880-1950.* New Delhi, PPH,1959.

Gray, Hugh, The Landed Gentry of the Telangana, Andhra Pradesh. In *Elites in South Asia,* edited by Edmund Leach and S. N. Mukherjee, Cambridge, Cambridge University Press,1970.

Gupta, K. K., *Impact of Cooperative Advances on Weaker Sections.* Bombay, NAFSCOB,1986.

Haleja, T. N., *Principles, Problems and Practice of Cooperation.* Agra, Shivlal Agarwala, 1973.

Hanson, A. H., *The Process of Planning–A Study of India's Five Year Plans 1950-64.* London, OUP 1966.

Hayek, F. A. von (ed), *Collectivist Economic Planning.* London, Routledge and Kegan Paul Ltd., 1956.

Hill, M. Dilys, *Democratic Theory and Local Government.* London, George Allen and Unwin Ltd., 1974.

Hough, E. M., *The Cooperative Movement in India.* 4th ed. Revised by K. Madhava Das, London, OUP, 1959.

Infield, Henrik F., *The Sociology of Cooperation.* New Jersey, Gleun Gardue,1955.

—— *Utopia and Experiment-Essays in the Sociology of Cooperation.* New York, Frederich A. Praeger, 1956.

International Labour Organisation, The Development of the Cooperative Movement in Asia. Geneva, ILO, 1954.

Jain, Sugan Chand, *Community Development and Panchayati Raj in India.* Calcutta, Allied, 1967.

Kavoori, J. C. *et al., History of Rural Development in Modern India.* Volume I, Delhi, Impex India, Gandhian Institute of Studies & AVARD, 1967.

Keilhan, Wilhelm, *Principles of Private and Public Planning– A Study in Economic Sociology.* London, George Allen and Unwin Ltd., 1951.

Kennedy, Liam (ed) *Economic Theory of Cooperative Enterprises.* London, Plunkett Publications, 1983.

Krishnaswami, O. R., *Cooperative Democracy in Action.* New Delhi, Somaiya Publication Pvt. Ltd., 1976.

—— *Fundamentals of Cooperation.* New Delhi, S Chand & Co. Ltd., 1978.

Lal, Chaman, *Miracle of Cooperation.* Punjab, Dharmashala Cantt.,the author,1957.

Lewis, W. Arthur, *The Principles of Economic Planning.* London, George Allen and Unwin Ltd., 1954.

Madan, G.R., *Cooperative Movement in India–A Critical Appraisal.* New Delhi, Mittal, 1994.

Madane, M. V., "Cooperative Growth in Indian Economy–a critical assessment". In Ashok V. Bhuleshkar (ed) *Growth of Indian Economy in Socialism,* New Delhi, Oxford IBH, 1986.

Mahajan, V. S., *Planning Development and Economic Policies in India.* Delhi, Kalyani Publishers, 1974.

Malambo, J. M., *Study of the Indian Cooperative Movement.* Kabwe (Zambia), President's Citizenship College, 1978.

Malaviya, H. D., *Village Panchayats in India.* New Delhi, All India Congress Committee, 1956.

Maslennikob, V., *Cooperative Movement in Asia and Africa–Problems of Developing Countries.* Moscow, Progress, 1983.

Mathur, B. S., *Cooperation in India.* Delhi, Sahitya Bhawan ,1982.

Mathur, M. P., *Cooperative Movement in India and Abroad,* Part I & II. Allahabad, Indian Press Publications Ltd., 1953 & 1954.

Mehta, V. L., *Cooperative Movement in New India.* Bombay, Bombay Cooperative Union, 1958.

Melnyk, George, *Search for Community–From Utopia to a Cooperative Society.* Buffalo, Black Rose Books, 1985.

Miller, Raymond W., *Conservative Looks at Cooperatives,* Athens, Ohio University Press, 1964.

Mongia, J. N., *Cooperatives in India.* New Delhi, Neer Enterprises, 1982.

Mukherjee, Nirmal, *Decentralisation Below the State Level–Need for a New System of Government.* New Delhi, Centre for Policy Research, 1989.

Mukherji, P., *Cooperative Movement in India : A Study of Cooperative Principle and its Diverse Applications in India and Abroad.* Calcutta, Thacker Spink and Company, 1923.

Myrdal, Gunnar, *Asian Drama : An Inquiry into the Poverty of Nations.* Volume I, London, Allen Lane, The Penguin Press, 1968.

Narayan, J. P., *Towards Total Revolution.* Ed. by Brahmanand, Bombay, Popular Prakashan, 1978.

NCUI, Anthology of Cooperative Thought, 3 Vols., Delhi, 1975, 1976, 1977.

Pai, M. R. (ed), *A Decade of Planning-A Commentary*. Bombay, Popular Prakashan 1969.

Prakash, Daman, Our Civil Society and Cooperatives : Cooperative Institutions as True Contributors to the Enrichment of our Civil Society. New Delhi, ICA, 1994.

— Social Objectives and Cooperatives–Cooperatives in Social Reference to Poverty Alleviation, Social Integration and Employment Generation, New Delhi, ICA, 1994.

Prasad, N. and B. N. Juyal, Impediments to Development in Developing Countries. (Report of a seminar held at Varanasi) in 1965, Varanasi, Gandhian Institute, 1966. (No. 11).

Puri, S. S., *Ends and Means of Cooperative Development*. Delhi, NCUI, 1979.

Rajaguru, R. B, and S.S. Puri, *Cooperative Development in the Eighties*. Delhi, ICA, 1981.

Randall, Rosemary and J. Southgate, *Cooperatives and Community Dynamics*. London, Barefoot Books 1980.

Ranga, N. G., *Panchayat Landlordism vs Peasant Economy*. New Delhi, Ministry of Food and Agriculture, 1958.

Samiuddin and M. Rahman, *Cooperative Sector in India*. New Delhi, S. Chand & Co. 1983.

Saxena, S. K., *Cooperatives in India and Pakistan : Some Aspects*, New Delhi, ICA Domus Trust, 1992.

— *International Cooperative Movement : Traditions and Change*, New Delhi, ICA, 1983

Shah, Tushaar, *Fertile Grounds : Why do Cooperatives Thrive in Surat?* Field notes from Olpad Taluka, Anand, IRMA, 1992.

Shojakhani, Mohsen, *Cooperative Movement in India*, Delhi, Renaissance Publishing House, 1994

Shukla, G. P., *Cooperative Rural Development in India : A Plan*, The Mall, Lucknow Universal Publishers , 1949

Singh, Mohinder, *Cooperatives in Asia* . New York, Praeger Publishers,1970.

Singh, S. N., *Should Indian Cooperatives Not Gain from the Japanese Experience?* Anand, NDDB, 1992.

Singh, S. N. and B.A.Shah, *Cooperative Societies Act and Accoutability of Registrars*. Anand, NDDB, n.d.

Sinha, B. K., *Mahatma Gandhi and the Cooperative Movement*. New Delhi, NCUI,1970.

Srivastava, G. P., *Traditional forms of Cooperation in India.* New Delhi, ICU and Ocean Publishers, 1962.

Subrahmanyam, B., *Need for Strong, Viable and Self-reliant Cooperatives : Some Suggestions,* Bombay, NAFSCOB, 1993.

Taylor, Carl C., A Critical Analysis of India's Community Development Programme, New Delhi, Government of India, 1956.

Vidwans, M.D., *Principles of Jurisprudence in a Cooperative Commonwealth,* Poona, University of Poona ,1966.

Voorchis, Jerry, *Cooperative Enterprise: The Little People's Chance in a World of Bigness,* Delhi, Interstate,1975.

Weerman, P. E., *Concept and Functioning of Cooperative Democracy,* Delhi, ICA, Delhi 1971.

— *Cooperative Principles,* New Delhi, ICA, 1975.

— *Need of Planning for a Cooperative Set-up,* Delhi ICA 1972.

Wilson, M. L., Comments on Community Development Programme in India - Report of a Survey, CPA, Government of India 1956.

Winfred, A. John and V. Kulandaiswamy, *History of Cooperative Thought,* Coimbatore, Rainbow Publications 1980.

Agriculture Cooperatives

Beteille, Andre, *Studies in Agrarian Social Structure.* Delhi, OUP, 1974.

Bremen, Jan, *Patronage and Exploitation: Changing Agrarian Relations in South Gujarat,* India. London, University of California Press, 1974.

Democratic Research Service : Cooperative Farming: The great debate between Jawaharlal Nehru, C. Rajagopalachari and others. Bombay, DRS, 1959.

Deshpande, S. H., *Some Problems of Cooperative Farming.* Bombay, Himalaya, 1977.

Digby, Margaret, *Cooperatives and Land Use. Rome,* FAO, 1957.

Dulfer, Eberhard, Imperatives for the Operational Efficiency of Agricultural Cooperatives in Developing Countries : A paper prepared for FAO of UN, Rome, FAO, 1971.

Gill, Manohar Singh, *Agricultural Cooperatives.* New Delhi, Vikas, 1983.

— *An Indian Success Story : Agriculture and Cooperatives,* Bombay, Somaya. 1993.

Infield, Henrik F. (ed) *Cooperative Group Living : An International Symposium on Group Farming and the Sociology of Cooperation.* New York, Henry Koosis and Company, 1950.

Khusro, A. M., *The Economics of Land Reform and Farm Size in India.* New Delhi, Macmillan India, 1973.

Khusro, A. M. and A. N. Aggarwal, *Problems of Cooperative Farming in India.* Bombay, APH, 1961.

Malaviya, H.D., *Land Reforms in India.* 2nd ed, New Delhi, All India Congress Committee, 1955.

Mamoria, C. B., *Agricultural Cooperative Structure in India.* Allahabad, Kitab Mahal, 1983.

— *Agricultural Problems in India.* 3rd ed, Allahabad, Kitab Mahal, 1960.

Masani, Minoo R., "The Dangers of Joint Cooperative Farming". In *A Decade of Planning* edited by M.R. Pai, Bombay, Popular Prakashan, 1969.

Mehta, J.B., *Cooperative Farming and Agrarian Development in India.* Delhi, S. Chand and Co., 1961.

Mehta, Vaikunth L., *Cooperative Farming.* Bombay, The Bombay State Cooperative Union, 1958.

Misra, B. R., *Vinoba - The Economics of the Bhoodan Movement.* Bombay, Orient Longman, 1956.

Nanekar, K. R. and S.V. Khandewale, *Bhoodan and the Landless.* Bombay, Popular Prakashan, 1973.

Patil, R. K., *Land Reform and Cooperative Farming in India.* Bombay, The S.V. Khandewale Bombay State Cooperative Union, 1957.

Raj Krishna, L. C. Jain and Gopi Krishna, *Cooperative Farming : Some Critical Reflections.* New Delhi, ICU, 1956.

Ranga, N. G. and Paruchuri, *The Plan and the Peasant : An Appraisal of the Second Five Year Plan.* Nidubrolu, Indian Peasant Institute, 1956.

Rao, C. H. Hanumantha, *Technological Change and Distribution of Gains in Indian Agriculture.* Delhi, Macmillan, 1975.

Reddy, D. Obul, *Cooperative Agricultural Development Banks : A Case Study of Andhra Pradesh.* Delhi, B.R. Publishing Corporation, 1986.

Schiller, Otto, *Cooperative Farming and Individual Farming on Cooperative Lines.* New Delhi, All India Cooperative Union, 1957.

Srivastava, S. K. *et al.*, *Agricultural Economics and Cooperation : A Study in Agricultural Economy and Cooperative Development with special reference to India.* New Delhi, S. Chand & Co.. 1970.

Tewari, R. N., *Agricultural Planning and Cooperatives,* Delhi, S. Chand & Co., 1970.

Thorner, Daniel, Agricultural Cooperatives in India : A field report. Bombay, APH, 1964.

— *The Agrarian Prospect in India.* Delhi, OUP, 1956.

Cooperative Credit

Aeschliman, Chet *et al.*, : *An Assessment of the Thrift Cooperative System in Southern India.* USA, World Council of Credit Unions, 1994.

Catanach, I. J., *Rural Credit in the Western India : 1875-1930 : Rural Credit and the Cooperative Movement in the Bombay Presidency.* Berkeley, University of California Press, 1970.

Choubey, B. N., *Principles and Practice of Cooperative Banking in India.* Bombay, APH, 1968.

Ghosal, S. N., *Agricultural Financing in India with Special Reference to Land Mortgage Banks,* Bombay, APH.

Goel, Sita Ram, *All India Rural Credit Survey vis-a-vis The Cooperative Movement,* New Delhi, ICU, 1961.

Kalyani, N. A., Problems of Long Term Credit for Agriculture through Land Development Banks. Bombay, Bombay State Cooperative Land Mortgage Bank Ltd., 1970.

Krishnan, V., *Indigenous Banking in South India.* Bombay, Provincial Coop. Ltd., 1954.

Laud, G. M., *Cooperative Banking in India.* Bombay, Cooperative Book Depot, 1956.

Naidu, V. Tirupati, *Farm Credit and Cooperatives in India.* Bombay, Vora and Co., 1968.

Rangnekar, D. K., *Agricultural Finance in India with Special Reference to Cooperative Movement.* Bombay, Cooperators Book Depot, 1952.

Reddy, Obul, *Working of the Cooperative Development Banks in Andhra Pradesh.* Hyderabad, Osmania University, 1983.

Singh, Prabhu N., *Role of Development Banks in a Planned Economy.* Delhi, Vikas, 1974.

Subrahmanyam, B., *Deposit Mobilization : A Study of Kheda District Central Cooperative Bank.* Bombay, NAFSCOB, 1985.

— *Need for Strengthening of Cooperative Credit Institutions : Some Remedial Measures,* NAFSCOB, 1993.

Webster, F. H., *Cooperative Thrift, Credit Marketing and Supply in Developing Countries.* London, Plunkett, 1978.

Rural Development/Poverty Alleviation/Social Welfare

Dwivedi, R. C., *Role of Government in Promoting Cooperative Development in Asia.* Delhi, ICA 1989.

Franco, F. and P.G. V. S. Chand, *Operation Flood and the Voluntary Sector : A Study of Tribal Dairy Cooperatives in South Gujarat.* New Delhi,Indian Social Institute, 1991.

George, Shanti, *A Matter of People : Cooperative Dairying in India and Zimbabwe.* Delhi, OUP, 1994.

Knopnick G. V. (ed), *Cooperation as an Instrument for Rural Development,* Belgium, ICA,1978.

Kurien, V., Managing Socio-economic Change : The Role of Professionals (Sarabhai Memorial Lecture), Anand NDDB,1978.

— *Role of the Elite in Modernization of a Predominantly Rural Society,* Anand, NDDB, 1978.

Nanavati, Manilal B., Agencies of Rural Reconstruction : (1) Village administration (2) Cooperative Movement. Reprint from the *Indian Journal of Agricultural Economics,* Vol. VII, No.2, August, Bombay, Akhil Bharat Press,1952.

Ramakrishnayya, M., *Managing Rural Change : The Cooperative Method.* Hyderabad, Samakhya,1984.

Sriram, M. S., *A Study of the Indicators of Sickness in Rural Cooperatives.* Bangalore IIM, 1991.

Singh, Kartar and Mukunda Das, *Impact of Operation Flood at the Village Level.* Anand, IRMA, 1982.

Verhagen, Koenraad, *Cooperatives and Rural Poverty : Eight Questions Answered.* London, The Plunkett Foundation ,1980.

Cooperative Law/Legislation

Arora and Kalra, *All India Cooperative Law Digest : 1912-1986.* Chandigarh, Punjab Law Agency, 1986.

International Cooperative Alliance, *Cooperative Legislation in Asia - A Study,* Part One New Delhi, 1991.

Mukherjee, B. B (ed): *The Law and Principles of Cooperation,* 5th ed., Calcutta, Thacker Spink and Co.1959.

Patel, G. D., *The Indian Land Problem and Legislation.* Bombay NM Tripathi Ltd., Law Publishers Princes Street, 1954.

Rajagopalan, Shashi and Rama Reddy, *Cooperative Perspective on*

Indian Policy and Legislation, Hyderabad, Cooperative Development Foundation, 1992.

Sharma, B. D. and Anita Manchanda, *Supreme Court on Cooperative Law : 1961-87,* New Delhi, NUCI,1988.

Singh, V. P., Facilitation of Effective Cooperative Legislation in Selected Countries of Asia : A Study Report, ICA 1990.

Tyagi, R. B., *Recent Trends in the Cooperative Movement in India,* Bombay, APH, 1968.

Venkatramiya, R. *et al., Row's Encyclopaedia of Cooperative Societies Law in India.* Allahabad Law Publishers, 1966.

Vij, B. Dass, *Law and Principles of Cooperatives,* Jullunder, Punjab Coop. Union, 1965.

Weerman, P. E., *Role of Law in Cooperative Development.* Delhi, ICA, 1971.

Weerman, P.E., Dwivedi and P. Seshadri, *Indian Cooperative Laws vis-a-vis Cooperative Principles,* RC, New Delhi, ICA,1986.

Yeo, Peter, *Cooperative Law in Practice : A Handbook of Legislation for Coop. Development.* London, Plunkett & Holyake Books, 1989.

Consumer Cooperatives

Dwivedi, R. C., *Consumer Cooperatives : Glimpses of Cooperative through Press.* New Delhi, Cooperative Times, 1988.

Goyal, S. K., *Consumer's Cooperative Movement in India.* Meerut, Meenakshi Prakashan, 1972.

Herath W. U., *An Overview of Consumer Cooperation in Asia.* New Delhi, ICA, 1989.

Government of India (Publications)

Various Committees and Working Groups

– Agricultural Finance Sub-committee (Gadgil Committee), 1944.

– All India Rural Credit Survey Committee (Gorwala Committee), Report, August 1951 – December 1954.

– Committee on Consumer's Cooperative, February 1961 – May 1961.

– Committee on Cooperative Law (ST Raja Committee), June 1956 – May 1957.

– Committee on Cooperative Processing, August 1960 – April 1961.

– Congress Agrarian Reforms Committee, 1949.

– Cooperative Planning Committee (Saraiya Committee) Recommendations 1946.

– Evaluation of the Cooperative Movement by Sir Malcolm Darling, 1957.

– India, Advisory Planning Board : Report (Chairman – K.C. Neogy) 1947.

– India, Reconstruction Committee : Two reports on the progress of reconstruction planning, 1994.

– Recommendations of Mehta Committee on Cooperative Credit, May 1960.

– Report of the Committee on Cooperative Administration (Mehta Committee) April 1963 – October 1963.

– Report of the Committee on Integration of Cooperative Credit Institutions, 1976.

– Report of the Special Working on Cooperation for Backward Class (Bhargava Committee) June 1961 – September 1962.

– Report of the Study Team on Cooperative Training, April 1961.

– Report of the Sub-committee on Crops – Planning and Production (edited by K.T. Shah) Chairman T. Vijayaraghavacharya, 1948.

– Report of the Sub-committee on Rural and Cottage Industries (edited by K.T. Shah), Chairman, S C Dasgupta, 1948.

– Report of the Sub-committee on Rural Marketing and Finance (edited by K.T. Shah) Chairman, Raindas Pantulu, 1947.

– Report of the Team for the Study of Community Projects and National Extension Service. 3 V., November 1957.

– Report of the Working Group on Non-agricultural Cooperatives (Varde Committee), 1963.

– Report of the Working Group on Panchayats and Cooperatives, July-October 1961.

– Resolution of the National Development Council, November 1958.

– Village and Small Scale Industries Committee (Karve Committee), October 1955.

– Working Group on Cooperative Farming (Nijalingappa Committee), December 1959.

– Working Group on Cooperative Policy (Damle Committee) Report, 1959.

– Working Group on Industrial Cooperatives (Ryan Committee), July 1958.

– Working Group on Industrial Cooperatives (Second), September 1962 – May 1963.

Reserve Bank of India, Bombay

– All India Rural Credit Survey - The General Report 1955.
– Review of the Cooperative Movement in India 1939-40.
– Report of the Committee on Cooperation in India, 1951.

Planning Commission

Darling, Sir Malcolm, Report on Certain Aspects of Cooperative Movement in India, 1957.

Saraiya, R. G., The Place of Cooperation in the First Five Year Plan of the Planning Commission, 1951.

Ministry of Community Development and Cooperation (MCDC)

Krishnamachari V.T., Address by V.T. Krishnamachari at the Sixth Development Commissioner's Conference, Mussoorie, 1957.

— Community Development in India 1958.
Report of the Study Team on Pachayati Raj Finances, Part I, 1961,
Report of the Committee on Cooperative Credit (Sri V. L. Mehta Committee) May 1960.

Indian Cooperative Union

– All India Rural Credit Survey, vis-a-vis The Cooperative Movement, 1961.
– Community Development Programme, 1961.
– *Cooperative Farming : Some Critical Reflections,* (Raj Krishna, L.C. Jain, Gopikrishna), 1956
– Cooperative Law in India - A disquisition, 1964
– Cooperative Law : Proposed new features, 1960
– Report on Cooperative Development and Rural Credit in Philippines, 1959.
– Report on the Marketing of Handicrafts, 1955.
– Rural Development and Credit Project : An Evaluation Report covering Rabi 1956-57 to Kharif 1957, 1958.
– Rural Development and Credit Project, 1960.

National Cooperative Union of India

– Cooperatives and Consumer Protection : Paper presented at the Fourth Indian Cooperative Congress, 1963.

- Cooperative Developments in India 1956-62 : A Report, 1963.
- Cooperation in Independent India, 1963.
- Cooperative Movement in India, 1963.
- Employer-Employee relationship in Cooperative Sector : Report of the National Workshop, 10th and 11th February,1977.
- People's Leadership in Cooperation, 1963.
- Platinum Jubilee of Indian Cooperative Movement : Cooperation and Community, 1980.
- Round Table Discussion on Professionalisation of Cooperative Management, 1974.

Vaikunth Mehta National Institute of Cooperative Management, Pune

- Cooperative Development and Leadership : Seminar Paper, edited by C. Dinesh and G. Ojha, Seminar Papers, 1989.
- Management of Handloom Cooperatives, edited by S.B. Rao, Pune, 1978.
- Papers and Proceedings on Workshop on Cooperatives and Technology -2001 AD, 1982.

Gokhale Institute of Politics and Economics, Pune

- Role of RBI in the Development of Credit Unions, by B. Venkatappiah, 1960.
- Writings and Speeches of Prof. D.R. Gadgil on Cooperation, New Delhi, Orient Longman, 1975.

Institute for Rural Management, Anand

Working Papers

- Determinants of Enduring Cooperative Performance : by KV Raju, 1995.
- Factors affecting performance of Village Level Organisations, by Sankar Datta, 1995.
- *Harnessing People's Power : Reflections on the Experiences of Sahayog in Rajasthan*, by P. Thomas and V. Ballabh, 1995.
- *Re-engineering India's Cooperatives : A Framework for Action*, by Tushaar Shah, 1995.

INDEX